Oksana Sarkisova is Research Fellow at the Vera and Donald Blinken Open Society Archives of the Central European University, Hungary, where she received her PhD in History. She is also Director of the Verzio International Human Rights Documentary Film Festival, Hungary.

Kino Series

Joint General Editors: Birgit Beumers & Richard Taylor

Editorial Board: Birgit Beumers, Julian Graffy, Richard Taylor & Denise J. Youngblood

Marina L. Levitina, *'Russian Americans' in Soviet Film: Cinematic Dialogues between the US and the USSR* (2015)

Rachel Morley, *Performing Femininity: Woman as Performer in Early Russian Cinema* (2017)

Oksana Sarkisova, *Screening Soviet Nationalities: Kulturfilms from the Far North to Central Asia* (2017)

Forthcoming:

Jamie Miller, *Propaganda and Popular Entertainment in the USSR: The Mezhrabpom Studio* (2018)

Julian Graffy, *Through a Russian Lens: Representing Foreigners in a Century of Russian Film* (2018)

Birgit Beumers, *The Cinema of the New Russia* (2019)

To my parents

OKSANA SARKISOVA

SCREENING
SOVIET
NATIONALITIES

Kulturfilms from the Far North to Central Asia

SERIES EDITOR RICHARD TAYLOR

BLOOMSBURY ACADEMIC
LONDON · NEW YORK · OXFORD · NEW DELHI · SYDNEY

BLOOMSBURY ACADEMIC
Bloomsbury Publishing Plc
50 Bedford Square, London, WC1B 3DP, UK
1385 Broadway, New York, NY 10018, USA
29 Earlsfort Terrace, Dublin 2, Ireland

BLOOMSBURY, BLOOMSBURY ACADEMIC and the Diana logo
are trademarks of Bloomsbury Publishing Plc

First published in Great Britain 2017 by I.B.Tauris & Co. Ltd
Paperback edition first published by Bloomsbury Academic 2021

ISBN: HB: 978-1-7845-3573-5
PB: 978-1-3502-4245-6
ePDF: 978-1-7867-3040-4
eBook: 978-1-7867-2040-5

To find out more about our authors and books visit
www.bloomsbury.com and sign up for our newsletters.

Contents

Contents

List of Illustrations

Film stills are courtesy of Russian State Documentary Film and Photo Archive (RGAKFD).

General Editors' Preface

Cinema has been the predominant art form of the first half of the twentieth century, at least in Europe and North America. Nowhere was this more apparent than in the former Soviet Union, where Lenin's remark that 'of all the arts, cinema is the most important' became a cliché and where cinema attendances were until recently still among the highest in the world. In the age of mass politics, Soviet cinema developed from a fragile but effective tool to gain support among the overwhelmingly illiterate peasant masses in the civil war that followed the October 1917 Revolution, through a welter of experimentation, into a mass weapon of propaganda through the entertainment that shaped the public image of the Soviet Union – both at home and abroad for both elite and mass audiences – and latterly into an instrument to expose the weaknesses of the past and present in the twin process of glasnost and perestroika. Now the national cinemas of the successor republics to the old USSR are encountering the same bewildering array of problems, from the trivial to the terminal, as are all the other ex-Soviet institutions, while Russia itself is now the world's sixth largest area for distribution.

Cinema's central position in Russian and Soviet cultural history and its unique combination of mass medium, art form and entertainment industry, have made it a continuing battlefield for conflicts of broader ideological and artistic significance, not only for Russia and the Soviet Union, but also for the world outside. The debates that raged in the 1920s about the relative merits of documentary as opposed to fiction film, of cinema as opposed to theatre or painting, or of the proper role of cinema in the forging of post-Revolutionary Soviet culture and the shaping of the new Soviet man, have their echoes in current discussions about the role of cinema *vis-à-vis* other art forms in effecting the cultural and psychological revolution in human consciousness necessitated by the processes of economic and political transformation of the former Soviet Union into modern democratic and industrial societies and states governed by the rule of law.

Cinema's central position has also made it a vital instrument for scrutinising the blank pages of Russian and Soviet history and enabling the present generation to come to terms with its own past.

This series of books intends to examine Russian, Soviet and ex-Soviet films in the context of Russian, Soviet and ex-Soviet cinemas, and Russian, Soviet and ex-Soviet cinemas in the context of the political history of Russia, the Soviet Union, the post-Soviet 'space' and the world at large. Within that framework the series, drawing its authors from both East and West, aims to cover a wide variety of topics and to employ a broad range of methodological approaches and presentational formats. Inevitably this will involve ploughing once again over old ground in order to re-examine received opinions but it principally means increasing the breadth and depth of our knowledge, finding new answers to old questions and, above all, raising new questions for further enquiry and new areas for further research.

The continuing aim of this series is to situate Russian, Soviet and ex-Soviet cinema in its proper historical and aesthetic context, both as a major cultural force and as a crucible for experimentation that is of central significance to the development of world cinema culture. Books in the series strive to combine the best of scholarship, past, present and future, with a style of writing that is accessible to a broad readership, whether that readership's primary interest lies in cinema or in political history.

Richard Taylor & Birgit Beumers
Wales, October 2015

Acknowledgements

Every book is a journey, and this was a long and exciting one. A cherished friendship with Neia Zorkaia inspired me to pursue it. Over the years, during which my research and writing was taking shape, I benefitted from the advice of many colleagues and friends who shared their expertise and comments and offered generous support: Peter Kenez, Mária M. Kovács, John MacKay, Barbara Wurm, Petr Bagrov, Denise Youngblood, Thomas Tode, Olga Shevchenko, Christopher Marcisz, Anna Geréb, Nina Dymshits, Sergei Kapterev, Vladimir Zabrodin, Jeremy Hicks, Adelheid Heftberger, Jeanpaul Goergen, Alexander Semyonov, Sergei Glebov and Ivan Golovnev. I am especially thankful to Alexander Deriabin and Evgenii Margolit for their long-term friendship and the countless occasions on which they open-heartedly shared their immense knowledge on Soviet cinema. I am very grateful to Birgit Beumers and Richard Taylor for their encouragement and timely advice.

The roads of our past define those we take in the future. I would like to express my deep appreciation for the dedicated work of the Moscow Film Museum staff of the 1990s who, under the leadership of Naum Kleiman, curated thoughtful film programmes recharting established cinematic canons and stimulating new ideas without imposing conclusions. After my first visit to the RGAKFD in Krasnogorsk, my interest in cinema took on a new dimension as I became fascinated by films that, for the most part, remained unacknowledged in the annals of film history. I further learned to cherish the minute details of film history by following the dedicated and inspiring work of Naum Kleiman, Yuri Tsivian, Emma Widdis, Nikolai Izvolov, Nancy Condee, and the late Alexander Troshin and Rashit Yangirov.

I am very thankful to István Rév and my colleagues at the Central European University and the Open Society Archives for supporting me throughout my doctoral research, and the subsequent expansion and reframing of its main themes, without losing trust that the venture will bear fruit.

Acknowledgements

Especially warm thanks to the devoted staff of the Russian State Documentary Film and Photo Archive (RGAKFD), Russian State Archive of Literature and Art (RGALI), Russian State Archive of Socio-Political History (RGASPI), State Archive of the Russian Federation (GARF), Muzei Kino Archive and Gosfilmofond, and personally to Natalia Kalantarova, Natalia Akulina, Elena Kolikova and Anna Bulgakova who always provided a helpful hand in the archival labyrinths.

Over several years, I have benefitted from the editorial help and advice of Christopher Ryan, Meyko Boyton, Tom Schertz, and, last but not least, from Lisa Nóvé's impeccable sense of style and measure. Naturally, all the mistakes and idiosyncrasies of language remain mine.

My special gratitude to Balázs Trencsényi who shared my journey and to Márk Trencsényi who taught me new ways of seeing the world.

Earlier versions of parts of this book appeared as the following publications: 'Across One Sixth of the World: Dziga Vertov, Travel Cinema, and Soviet Patriotism' in *October* 121 (2007), pp. 19–40. 'Arctic Travelogues: Conquering the Soviet North', in Scott MacKenzie and Anna Stenport (eds), *Films on Ice: Cinemas of the Arctic* (2015), pp. 222–234. 'Taming the Frontier: Alexander Litvinov's Expedition Films and Representations of Indigenous Minorities in the Far East', in *Studies in Russian and Soviet Cinema* 9.1 (2015), pp. 2–23. 'The Adventures of the *Kulturfilm* in Soviet Russia', in Birgit Beumers (ed.), *A Companion to Russian Cinema* (2016). They have been expanded and reworked for this publication.

Note on Transliteration

Transliteration from the Cyrillic to the Latin alphabet is a perennial problem for writers on Russian subjects. We have opted for a dual system: in the text we use a simplified Library of Congress system (without diacritics), but we have departed from this system (a) when a Russian name has a clear English version (e.g. Maria instead of Mariia, Alexander instead of Aleksandr); (b) when a Russian name has an accepted English spelling, or when Russian names are of Germanic origin (e.g. Yeltsin instead of Eltsin; Chaliapin instead of Shaliapin; Eisenstein instead of Eizenshtein). In the scholarly apparatus we adhere to the Library of Congress system with diacritics for the specialist.

Glossary

ARK – Assotsiatsiia revoliutsionnoi kinematografii (Association of Revolutionary Cinematography), since 1928 – ARRK, Assotsiatsiia rabotnikov revoliutsionnoi kinematografii (Association of Revolutionary Workers of Cinematography) – professional organization of Soviet filmmakers and film industry professionals in 1924–35, included Lev Kuleshov, Sergei Eisenstein, Nikolai Lebedev, Vladimir Erofeev, Vsevolod Pudovkin, and others. Organized regular film screenings and professional discussions, published *Kinozhurnal ARK* (1925–26) and *Kinofront* (1926–28).

Glavrepertkom (GRK) – Main Repertory Committee, created in 1923 and charged with reviewing all public performances, including cinematographic repertoire. In 1934, it was separated from the main state censorship institution Glavlit and came directly under the auspices of Narkompros. In 1936, it was transferred to the Committee of the Arts under the SNK SSSR. Glavrepertkom controlled also the repertoire of all the Republics and Oblasts in the USSR.

GUKF/GUK – Glavnoe upravlenie kinofotopromyshlennosti (Main Administration of Film and Photo Industry, or GUKF) existed between 1933–35; it was replaced by Glavnoe upravlenie kinematografii (Main Administration of Cinematography, or GUK) that functioned in 1936–38, when it was replaced by Komitet po delam kinematografii (Committee for Cinema Affairs) under SNK USSR and in 1946 by the Ministry of Cinematography of the USSR.

LEF – The journal of the Left Front of Art: an informal association of avant-garde writers, photographers, critics and designers in the Soviet Union. The journal *LEF* was published in 1923–25, later from 1927–29 as *Novyi LEF*.

Narkompros – Narodnyi komissariat prosveshcheniia (People's Commissariat of Enlightenment), state organ supervising cultural activities in the Russian Soviet Federative Socialist Republic (RSFSR), including cinema.

NEP – Novaia ekonomicheskaia politika (New Economic Policy) was introduced to foster the economy of the country at the 10th Congress of the All-Russian Communist Party in 1921. NEP followed the period of Civil War and War Communism; it abolished forced grain requisition, introduced a monetary reform and attracted foreign capital. It was abandoned in 1928 with the introduction of the first Five-Year Plan and the policies of industrialization and collectivization.

ODSK – Obshchestvo druzei sovetskogo kino (Society of the Friends of Soviet Cinema), a network of local cells established in 1925 with the task of enhancing the efficiency of cinema's agitation and propaganda impact on the audience; its first chairman was Feliks Dzerzhinskii, the head of Soviet secret police. ODSK established a network of amateurs interested in film and photography and published the newspaper *Kino*. In 1929 it was renamed Obshchestvo druzei sovetskoi kinematografii i fotografii (Society of the Friends of Soviet Cinema and Photography, ODSKF). By 1930, the organization had 110,000 members. Dissolved in 1934.

OGPU – Ob"edinennoe gosudarstvennoe politicheskoe upravlenie (All-Union State Political Administration), the secret police of the Soviet Union in 1923–34. In 1934 reformed as NKVD, Narodnyi komissariat vnutrennikh del (People's Commissariat for Internal Affairs).

Proletarskoe kino – *Proletarian Cinema*, monthly film periodical, first published in 1931 as a result of unifying the film magazines *Kino i zhizn'* (*Cinema and Life*) and *Kino i kul'tura* (*Cinema and Culture*); in 1933–36 known as *Sovetskoe kino* (*Soviet Cinema*), and since 1936 as *Iskusstvo kino* (*Art of Cinema*).

Proletkult – a wide network of cultural-educational organizations for proletarian amateur arts under the auspices of Narkompros from 1917 to 1932.

SNK – Sovet narodnykh komissarov (Council of People's Commissars), the highest government authority of executive power in the Russian Soviet Federative Socialist Republic (RSFSR) and since 1922, in the Soviet Union. In 1946, it was transformed into the Council of Ministers.

Soiuzkino – the central film organization in the Soviet Union, in charge of studios and distribution. In 1933 Soiuzkino was reorganized into GUKF and directly subordinated to the Council of People's Commissars (SNK). It was established after Sovkino ceased to exist in 1930, taking over most of its functions.

Sovetskii ekran – *Soviet Screen*, film periodical which was published with varying frequency between 1925 and 1929, and between 1929 and 1930 under the title *Kino i zhizn'* (*Cinema and Life*).

Sovkino – Soviet film and photo state company established in June 1924 with a monopoly on import/export and distribution, which later started its own production activities. Sovkino was liquidated in February 1930 and was reorganized into Soiuzkino.

Introduction: Projects of a New Vision

*The fundamental event of the modern age
is the conquest of the world as picture.*

Martin Heidegger[1]

In 1924, film critic Valentin Turkin made an urgent call that outlined an ambitious programme to ensure that Soviet film-makers maintained an upper hand against some 'shrewd German or American cinematographer who would offer to organize a geographic expedition across the USSR and would make a film that we would watch with stunned interest':[2]

> It is time for the Moscow film workers to take a train, get aboard a ship or a plane and to go up hill and down dale, to discover new Americas, to enter life, to visit the peoples of the USSR, nature, Donbass, the salt mines and fisheries, the Ural, the Volga, the shacks, nomad tents and factories. Only then will the audiences see the full variety of life, its vast diversity, its joy, only then will new life enter cinema and the cinema will fulfil its task.[3]

Echoing his call two years later, the journal *Sovetskoe kino* continued promoting cinema as a means to explore the new state, reminding its readers of the legacy of 'prehistoric' [*pervobytnye*] Pathé travelogues, which trained

1

cameramen in a new way of seeing.[4] The film industry proved ready to appropriate and overtake 'bourgeois' filming methods, yet the contours of the new image they were to promote did not appear all that clear. Among the many urgent questions that emerged with the creation of the Soviet Union, the question of representation was particularly pressing. How to make the audience perceive this new political entity as different from its imperial predecessor? How to show and to see in a Soviet way? Through which visual metaphors could the Soviet state be imagined, and of which ethnic and social types was it comprised?

The lack of immediate answers to these questions spurred a discussion regarding the 'cinematographic atlas', envisioned as a series of films showing the various, particularly little known, regions of the Soviet Union.[5] Appeals to use cinema's extensive reach and potent illusion of the real for developing a new, Soviet way of seeing fell on receptive ears. Nationalized film studios strove to gain the state's support by investing in 'edifying' films. Aspiring film-makers were eager to explore the country, and the audience was attracted to cinema halls with the promise of exotic scenery. The people deserved to have, as critic Konstantin Feldman put it, the 'possibility to see on the screen all the Soviet lands'.[6] Between roughly 1926 and 1940, a large corpus of films showing the territories and nationalities of the Soviet Union was created and distributed through both commercial and non-profit distribution networks across the country. Filmed in expeditions to various parts of the Soviet Union, these films helped configure a set of visual formulae, and taught audiences about the remote and exotic places that were to command their loyalties and affections as parts of a new 'motherland'.[7]

These expedition films were described as 'non-fiction' (literally 'unplayed' [*neigrovoi*]) and relied on the presumed 'truth' of the visual material. An editorial in *Sovetskoe kino* euphorically pronounced how 'real faces [that] live and move, real fields, real houses, real factories and plants with all their machines in motion [...] will be deeply etched in memory, will enter into the depth of one's heart'.[8] The modes of combining factual and emotional rhetoric sat at the core of the film debates of the 1920s, which stretched beyond cinema to 'literature of fact' and 'life-construction' in the visual and performing arts, generating a new form of documentary aesthetics.[9]

2

In these debates, the emphasis on grasping life 'as it is' coexisted with reflections on the constructed nature of the filmed material and its 'created geography'.[10] What Martin Heidegger, quoted at the beginning of this chapter, called 'the conquest of the world as picture', was earlier advocated by one of the first and most consistent defenders of non-fiction, Dziga Vertov. Vertov argued for the transformation of 'reality' by cinematographic means which he described as '*kinochestvo*', or 'the art of organizing the necessary movements of objects in space as a rhythmical artistic whole, in harmony with the properties of the material and the internal rhythm of each object'.[11] He saw the camera as the most powerful instrument for shaping the perceptual capacities of the viewers. Arguing for the camera's radically novel reflecting and structuring capacity, Vertov developed the 'cine-race' [*kino-probeg*], an assemblage of discrete recorded spaces united into a single entity through editing, which emerged as a new film form to master space.[12] The new generation of film-makers shared a fascination with transforming conventional perceptive habits that powered their drive to explore the Soviet space.[13] The audience, in turn, favoured films about remote parts of the world and, with the increasing reduction of imported films, of the Soviet Union. Seen as a substitute for travel in the context of limited recreational mobility, travel films contributed to shaping the Soviet spatial imagination and taught citizens to view the Soviet Union as a multinational resource-rich universe.

Before the notion of documentary became a conventional moniker for films shot without props and professional actors, sub-types of this cinematographic production were referred to as educational, scientific, popular-scientific or ethnographic and scenic films. In the 1920s, all of these terms, and more, fell under the umbrella term *kulturfilm*, which implied an element of 'ideological intentionality'.[14] This notion, originally coined by the German film industry, arrived in the Soviet context in the mid-1920s, where it remained under debate and in use until the early 1930s.[15] Understood as didactic films implying the status of objective truth, *kulturfilms* were made with the primary aim of supplying new knowledge and ordering the audience's ideas about the world.[16] Yet the concept itself remained controversial and had its supporters and critics. In the 1920s and early 1930s, *kulturfilms* featured in the production plans of every film studio in the Soviet Union and were the subject of a vibrant debate on the role and principles of non-fiction.

3

Contemporary historiography submerges these developments as part of the history of documentary cinema. Such an approach rests on what Timothy Boon refers to as a 'platonic notion of documentary', which accepts the existence of various forms of approximation to this ideal type, but fails to grasp the historical contingency of the concepts and the need for a historical approach to their cinematic embodiments.[17] Soviet film history requires recontextualization, focusing on the active polemic which developed around the concepts 'kulturfilm' and 'non-fiction'. Identifying the corpus of kulturfilms within the analysis of Soviet non-fiction allows us to see new dimensions of the Soviet cultural production of space, and to refashion the established 'canon' of Soviet documentary cinema; it also offers new directions for comparative and transnational analysis of the works. Expanding the field of view to incorporate both previously overlooked films and intellectual traditions allows us to move beyond the documentary/fiction and state/artist dichotomies towards reconstructing multiple agencies of film-makers, cinematographers, administrators, state and party functionaries of various levels, and a global crew of distributors, journalists, and film critics.

Reconstructing the history of kulturfilm in Russia poses numerous challenges, which only partially have to do with the scarcity and dispersal of primary sources. Kulturfilms downplayed the notion of individual authorship, often carried no credits, used unattributed found footage, were overshadowed by high-budget fiction productions and eschewed clear-cut definitions. Distributed primarily through a network of workers' clubs or as supplements to feature films, kulturfilms were rarely documented. Furthermore, kulturfilms spurred few reviews that could extend our understanding of reception patterns. And yet, this short-lived precursor to the documentary contributed some of the most lasting visual formulae with regard to the way the Soviet space is framed and remembered.

To understand the shaping of the Soviet visual legacy, my inquiry is driven by the following questions: What visual attributes did kulturfilms ascribe to the 'Soviet' landscape? How did film-makers present ethnicities and nationalities, and inscribe culturally heterogeneous communities within the homogenizing project of Soviet modernization? What were the reasons behind the disappearance of both the concept of kulturfilm and the genre of expedition films in the second half of the 1930s? And finally, how

4

can the history of Soviet *kulturfilm* be inscribed within the broader debates on colonial imagery and the Russian imperial legacy?

Constructing Soviet Nationalities

The history of *kulturfilm*, especially the representation of Soviet nationalities, cannot be fully understood outside the context of Soviet nationality policy.[18] The indigenization [*korenizatsiia*] policy of the mid-1920s aimed at 'fixing the wrongs' of the Russian Empire and gaining the loyalty of its nationalities. The policy implied differentiated approaches to ethnic groups, 'a pyramid of National Soviets [...] merging seamlessly with the individual's personal nationality',[19] and initiated the preparation of administrative cadres from the representatives of titular nationalities in each administrative unit. Terry Martin has argued that '[i]t was not the Soviet Union's formal written constitution of December 1922 that established the Soviet Union as a national entity, but rather the nationalities policy articulated in 1923'.[20] In more than one way, the Soviet Union inherited the logic of 'nationalizing empires' of the nineteenth century, but its official rhetoric aimed at breaking away from the 'prison of nations'.[21] The logic of indigenization required the *visible* presence of each institutionalized minority on the Soviet political stage. With the help of cinema, the abstract categories of 'nationality' and 'motherland' [*rodina*] acquired visual embodiments, and could be *imagined* and thus perceived as central categories for self-identification as well as the identification of 'others'. The 'localizing' of nations and ethnic groups on the screen enhanced a conceptual link between space and its inhabitants.

In the early Soviet years, the Bolsheviks exercised a double take on national identity by promoting minority nationalities deemed oppressed in the imperial 'prison of nations' and discouraging the 'Great Power chauvinism'.[22] At the same time, attribution of territory was a *sine qua non* element of identity for each official nationality in the Soviet Union. The films on Soviet nationalities surveyed the landscape as a primarily 'national' space, complying with Stalin's definition of the nation as 'a historically formed stable community of people which comes into existence on the basis of a common language, common territory, a common economy and a psychological character which manifests itself in a common culture'.[23] Non-titular

5

and diaspora nationalities rarely became central subjects in films, which supported the presumption that Soviet nationalities naturally possessed territory. At the same time, the marked absence of a depicted 'Russian' nationality in the collective portrait facilitated a tacit identification between 'imperial Russian' and 'Soviet' identity and space.

The Soviet Union was established as a multinational federation. The Soviet nationality policy, defined by Francine Hirsch as 'state-sponsored evolutionism', grounded the Soviet 'civilizing mission' in the Marxist concept of development through historical stages.[24] The elaboration of the Soviet nationality policy took place in close cooperation with authorities and ethnographers, who defined the categories of ethnicity, nationality and tribe applied by state policies.[25] Ethnographers in the Soviet Union used the notions *narodnost* (translated as ethnicity) and *natsionalnost* (translated primarily as nationality, but frequently used interchangeably with ethnicity). The difference between the two concepts, as the ethnographers attempted to clarify, was in distinguishing between peoples with 'national particularities' [*narodnost*] and peoples with national consciousness [*natsionalnost*], which presumed a transition from external classificatory ascription of visible features to subjective and internalized identification.[26]

While a definitive list of nationalities changed from over 200 registered and 172 codified nationalities in the 1926 census, to a 'consolidated' 57 in 1939, the concept of nationality remained entangled with 'ethnicity' and 'people' (*narod*), a carry-on of the nineteenth-century Populist legacy.[27] Applying a teleological developmental model from 'backwardness to civilization' to the mapping and classifying of lands and peoples, ethnographic theories envisioned *narodnost* developing to *natsionalnost*, and finally, *natsiia* (nation), which referred to civic and political consciousness.[28] The discussion on Soviet nations came to a climax in the late 1920s and early 1930s when the combination of the imposed class struggle paradigm and the unfolding attack against 'old school' ethnographers and Mikhail Pokrovskii's stadial history of social formations caused a profound transformation, which Yuri Slezkine described as the 'fall' of Soviet ethnography.[29] Beyond academic discussions, nationality, understood as ethnic descent, had a direct impact on the lives of Soviet citizens, determining their social and spatial mobility.[30]

The output from travel films and ethnography were seen as mutually complementary fields. With its broad outreach, cinema was the medium that could most convincingly answer 'the fundamental question of the state-building process [...] what is a multinational socialist federation supposed to *look like*?'[31] Ethnographers considered cinema the most adequate instrument to collect and preserve 'disappearing' cultural traces:

> We have to send cameramen to all the corners of our USSR, and their footage will be of enormous importance. Many of the poorly studied peoples are dying out. And, perhaps, already in a few years not a trace will be left of them. It is all the more important to preserve them on film.[32]

The ethnographic perspective turned films into a 'useful' entertainment. The didactic potential of bringing together ethnography and cinema was explored by Anatolii Terskoi in his book *Ethnographic Cinema* (1930), which exemplified the shift from the salvage rhetoric, concerned primarily with recording for preservation, to the 'fully Soviet' ethnography, which was expected to organize the viewers' opinions in line with the 'historical-materialistic character' of Soviet ethnography.[33] In the hands of the film-maker, Terskoi argued, 'ethnographic material stops being a simple recording of facts. It becomes a torrent of water for the mill of materialistic understanding of the history of human culture.'[34] Soviet ethnographer and linguist Nikolai Iakovlev backed Terskoi's argument and suggested that every ethnographic film depicted 'the dependence of the social life of a people on the stage of development of its productive forces'.[35] Terskoi declared the film-maker's role as 'forcing the whole mass of the viewers to become Marxists, to see what he [i.e. the film-maker, sic] wants and the way he wants'.[36] To this end, *kulturfilms* featuring ethnically-defined communities were considered the best source material. The non-fiction status of the footage, combined with the scientific authority of ethnography, naturalized the image of reality seen through ethnographic lenses. Along with Terskoi, many Soviet film critics and film-makers insisted on incorporating an ideological interpretation into each film in order to shape the image of the world or, in Vertov's words, 'decipher the visual with the help of the camera'.[37]

Films on minorities visualized distinct ethnic groups, demonstrating their transformation into 'socialist nations' via 'developmental' stages,[38] yet

7

the conceptual distinctions between these stages remained controversial. While the Soviet Union's imagined geography included the territories inhabited by 'the 'Buryats', the 'Chuvash' or the 'Tatars', the 'Russians', the 'Poles' or the 'Jews' had no sustainable ethnographic portrait. The nationality policy promoted so-called 'titular nations' in Soviet republics and allotted limited cultural resources to 'non-titular' nationalities.

David Brandenberger has described a 'weak Russian national identity' defined 'in opposition to the non-Russian peoples' and enhanced by the classificatory scheme that posited Russians as state-bearing people. Proclaiming the abolition of national oppression in the Soviet Union in the second half of the 1930s, Soviet policies gradually turned towards promoting 'the transition from the Great Russian past to the Soviet Russian present'.[39] Exempting 'Russians' from the ethnographic gaze, Soviet *kulturfilms* opposed 'backwardness' to a default modern identity which tied 'Russian' and 'Soviet' into a tight knot. At the same time, 'Soviet' encompassed more than a refashioned 'Russian' identity. It developed, with cinema's help, powerful supranational signifiers soliciting emotional responses. The projection of a multinational 'boundless' [*beskrainee*] space offered a lasting reference point for many Soviet subjects.

Virtual Travelling: Maps, Itineraries, and Politics of Vision

The desire to visually conquer the world gained new technical and conceptual capabilities in the twentieth century. Along with museums, dioramas, international fairs and exhibitions, cinema became one of the new 'heterotopic spaces' of modernity.[40] The proliferation and accessibility of mechanically reproduced images, such as postcards, photographs and films, altered the perception of the world, which appeared both increasingly diverse and easily accessible.[41] By the 1910s, films featuring remote lands and peoples had become a standard element of the composite programmes produced and distributed by major film companies.[42] These films combined the languages of contemporary ethnographic research and popular culture, successfully selling images of 'others' as both fascinating and frightening. The illusion of realism generated in the process of the social production of space was enhanced by the means of mechanical reproduction.[43] The indexical, photographic character of the recording and the reality effect achieved by cinema naturalized the meaning of cinematic landscapes for the audiences.

However, landscapes are not only a product of human interpretation, but are also the result of communication or, as W. J. T. Mitchell put it, a 'social hieroglyph that conceals the actual basis of its value'.[44] The ambitious mapping aims of travel films reveal a complex web of relations between cinema and cartography. Reflecting cinematic endeavours and appearing on screen as part of the scientific toolkit, maps claim full spatial control and represent one of the technologies of governance.[45] Both films and maps structure space by setting borders and establishing relations. Furthermore, as Matthew Edney has emphasized, a map 'elicits an emotional response: pride, gratification, belonging, affection, and pleasure, but also perhaps fear and anxiety'.[46] *Kulturfilms* actively used maps, drawing on cartographic authority to promote objective and impartial viewing. Tom Conley, pointing out the relations of both tension and homology between maps and films, wrote that 'symbolic and political effectiveness is a function of its [cinema's] identity as a cartographic diagram'.[47] Maps ensured visual control in travel films, and offered an authoritative commentary with particular lenses that facilitated the administration of power over a territory. At the same time, cinema itself was 'a map and a compass', which allowed audiences to make discoveries and see the world and its inhabitants in a new way.[48]

Perhaps the most ambitious photographic and cinematic exploration of the world was undertaken by Albert Kahn's *Archives de la Planète* (1908–1931).[49] Kahn's global project sent amateur and professional photographers and cameramen all over the world to record and create, in the words of the archive's director, Jean Brunhes, 'a storehouse of knowledge that might act as a sort of true picture of life in our age'.[50] *Archives* offered a quintessential example of the power of cinema to structure and assemble, to define and store not only activities and rituals, but entire communities on film. Driven by an archival desire and stirred by the phantom of salvage anthropology, this undertaking was constantly on the run to capture 'disappearing' peoples and cultures.

Cinema not only provided the best way to create records of continuously transforming sites, venues, and activities, but served as an active agent of change as well.[51] The controversial intention of 'preserving' and 'civilizing' cultures perceived as archaic and authentic on film was best exemplified in colonial cinema. David Henry Slavin, studying French colonial cinema of the interwar period, identified the implicit racial hierarchies which 'reinforced the machinery of cultural hegemony, non-coercive social control, and the underlying politics of privilege' as facilitating the viewers' identification with the 'bearers of civilization'.[52] French colonial cinema emphasized racial boundaries by focusing on dramatic examples of trespassing on imposed social roles. In Britain, state investments in non-fiction promotional films encouraged social hierarchies as well as communication and trade networks, and contributed to the imperial governmentality.[53] In the United States, film studios capitalized on the selling exoticism of ethnic difference.[54] At the same time, philanthropic agencies financed films which legitimized power imbalance as an educational tool for and about colonial subjects.[55] In Germany, the weakness of colonial discourse did not exclude the use of an ethnographic perspective combined with the notion of civilizational superiority, as exemplified in the *kulturfilms* welcomed by the German 'film reform movement' to promote the civilizing mission of (German, European, Christian) 'culture'.[56]

Travel films were also seen as an edifying pastime; 'film reformers' looked upon cinema as a means to instil ideas about 'civilization' and 'progress'.[57] Hans Schomburgk, Sven Hedin and Colin Ross authored films and published travelogues which enjoyed such great popularity that their names became travellers' trademarks.[58] The impact of their travels across Africa, the Americas, Russia, Central Asia and China extended beyond national borders, and certainly into the Soviet Union.[59] The idea of mapping, which travel films exemplified, helped to construct and justify the boundaries between 'cultured us' and 'backward others'.

The new spatiotemporal experience and the desire to know and master, which cinema offered, were part and parcel of a colonial relationship.[60] Early colonial travelogues established a range of visual cues, which enhanced their credibility in the eyes of the viewers and endowed the colonial world with a particular kind of affect.[61] Such visual cues included handheld cameras, natural lighting, nonprofessional actors, and indigenous languages.[62] The audience learned to identify ethnographic films through a number of visual conventions used to display 'authenticity'. Alison Griffiths suggests approaching the relationship of travel films and ethnography as 'the looking relations between the initiator of the gaze and the recipient'.[63] The ethnographic perspective increasingly portrayed the film subjects' lifestyles as naturalized.

Kulturfilms combined objective scientific authority with an emotional, affective relationship towards the filmed subjects. The ethnographic form of non-fiction cinema was defined most powerfully by Robert Flaherty's *Nanook of the North* (1922), which explored cinema's potential to provide an illusion of unobstructed access to the 'life of others'.[64] Focusing on the daily life of an Inuit family, Flaherty developed a narrative structure in which a 'primitive' subject received a name and identity and began to command the viewers' emotions.[65] Flaherty's success sparked further dramatized representations of indigenous peoples, and had a strong impact on Soviet film-makers. Soviet *kulturfilms* shared with their Western counterparts the surplus pleasure from the sights of 'exotic' cultural others, and struggled to reconcile picturesque and ideological within one narrative.[66]

Cinematic travelogues extended the rich tradition of literary travel accounts and augmented literary topoi with lasting visual imagery.[67] Throughout the 1920s and 1930s, the Soviet film industry actively engaged in developing a particular 'optical regime' that refashioned the interpretative formulae for seeing the state as a complex composite.[68] This ambitious Soviet 'visual literacy' was shaped by multiple influences and rooted in a complex politics of vision. *Kulturfilms* experimented with the visual vocabulary of the categories of familiar and alien, self and other, centre and periphery that gradually became codified as normative in Soviet popular culture. These films also shaped and widely circulated the concept of Soviet 'culturedness', which outlasted Soviet *kulturfilms*.[69]

Local Sights, Global Visions: Russian and Soviet Travel Films

Systematic production of travel films in Russia began with the series *Travel through Russia* [*Puteshestvie po Rossii*, 1907], by the Pathé regional office.[70] These travelogues took viewers to the Caucasus, northern Russia and Siberia, and introduced Russia as an empire that commanded the loyalty of its subjects. Organizations as well as film companies produced films for 'useful entertainment' that explored the imperial space in films like *Caucasian Vistas. Customs of Indigenous Population* [*Vidy Kavkaza. Nravy i obychai tuzemtsev*, 1909]; *The Don Cossacks* [*Donskie Kazaki*, 1908]; *Russian Types* [*Rossiiskie tipy*, 1908].[71] Along with commercial film studios, the Department of Hygiene, Upbringing, and Education of the Society for Preserving National Health advertised new resorts in *Batumi and the Caucasian Seashore* [*Batum i Kavkazskoe poberezh'e*, 1911] and *Over the White Sea* [*Po Belomu moriu*, 1913]. The Museum of Anthropology and Ethnography of the Russian Academy of Sciences surveyed natural resources and the lifestyles of the indigenous population in *Travel across Kamchatka* [*Puteshestvie po Kamchatke*, 1911], and the Agricultural Museum of the Ministry of Agriculture and State Property sponsored a film demonstrating the success of Stolypin's agrarian reforms, *The Peasant Riches of South Russia* [*Krest'ianskie bogatstva iuga Rossii*, 1912].[72] These and many more films put forth the image of the Empire as a diverse, prosperous and stable political and cultural entity. In 1911, Moisei Aleinikov listed close to 1,500 films for 'cultural enlightenment' screened in the Russian Empire.[73]

During World War I, the mission of cinema in belligerent countries was defined as encouragement of patriotism and mobilization of popular support for the war.[74] Cameramen travelled to and shot on the front lines and battlefields, and used landscapes to visualize the concepts of identity and belonging.[75] As in other countries involved in the war, Russian film-makers depicted the war as a patriotic mission. This depiction carried a consoling message of Russian imperial civilizational dominance, often represented metaphorically, like a *tableau vivant* personifying Russia as a noble woman with peasants and soldiers at her feet in *The Storming and Capture of Erzurum* [*Shturm i vziatie Erzeruma*, 1916].[76] War reporting also stimulated the experiments of combining action footage with staged scenes.

After the Revolution, imperial patriotism was replaced by the ideology of class solidarity. The Soviet film industry was assigned the complex task of translating the new ideology into popular and convincing images.[77] Following the nationalization of film stock, dozens of travel films were found in the storehouses of Alexander Khanzhonkov, Alexander Drankov and the Skobelev Committee.[78] Yet the list of films marked as acceptable

for workers' clubs in 1925 did not pay special attention to ethnic plurality of Soviet subjects except for *Valley of Tears* [*Dolina slez*, 1924], filmed
in the Altai region, which was declared 'interesting only for accompanying ethnographic lectures'.[79] A revival of interest in films exploring Soviet
national space(s) coincided with the consolidation of Soviet power in the
mid-1920s; the first Soviet feature-length expedition film, *The Great Flight*
[*Velikii perelet*, 1925], an account of a Moscow–Beijing journey, enjoyed
broad popularity.[80] The film's surveying aerial perspective, featuring a
flight across the Soviet Union to Mongolia and China, set an example
for Soviet film-makers by visualizing a centrifugal expansion of Soviet
ideology.

Kulturfilms gave a tangible form and shape to imaginative concepts
such as civilization and backwardness, and highlighted the entanglement
of colonizing and modernizing attitudes in the Soviet context. Apart from
the self-proclaimed, anti-colonial stance of political leaders, in what sense
can the Soviet era be considered 'post-colonial' as suggested by Alexander
Etkind?[81] The films discussed in this book demonstrate that, considering
the ongoing use of imperial frames of reference, post-colonial categories
require thorough contextualization in the Soviet period.[82] Such contextualization brings to the fore the Soviet film industry's engagement with and
transformative impact on the imperial representations of exoticism and
ethnic 'backwardness'.[83]

The cinematic landscapes of Soviet non-fiction relied on a didactic
fusion of vision and ideology. Soviet film-makers, while frequently distancing themselves from colonial rhetoric, actively used the concepts of
imaginary geography, such as 'the East' [*Vostok*] and 'the North' [*Sever*],
and perpetuated the civilizing mission discourses established in imperial Russia. To tease out the legacies of imperial rhetoric in Soviet travel
cinema requires an investigation of the processes of accommodation and
continuity between the imperial Russian and Soviet engagement with colonialism and orientalism, which offers a necessary refinement of Edward
Said's opposition of 'West' and 'East' as symbolic constructions exemplify-
ing categories of epistemic domination/subordination.[84] A combination of
colonial and anti-colonial discourses and practices posits the Soviet challenge to the 'Orientalist' paradigm.[85] Close contextual analysis of Soviet
kulturfilms allows us to discuss the visual strategies designed to challenge

the inherited colonial paradigm while making the elements used in crafting 'orientalist' portraits of Soviet ethnic minorities visible.

Soviet *kulturfilms* replaced actual travel for their audiences and introduced the territory of the 'new motherland', which was to command loyalty across distances and cultural variance.[86] This book does not aim at an exhaustive overview of Soviet *kulturfilms*, but offers a survey of emerging visual conventions of filming Soviet diversity and unity. Starting with Vertov and his powerful vision of the Soviet space as a unified multinational mosaic, I show how Vladimir Erofeev, Vladimir Shneiderov, Alexander Litvinov, Mikhail Slutskii, Viktor Turin, Amo Bek-Nazarov, Mikhail Kalatozov, Roman Karmen and other 'film workers' created their vision of Soviet diversity and unity. Equally important roles were played by the cameramen, who created lasting visual topoi emotionally affecting audiences. Mikhail Kaufman, Pavel Mershin, Ivan Beliakov, Vasilii Beliaev, Iakov Tolchan and Mikhail Glider are equal co-creators whose role in film-making remains insufficiently acknowledged.[87] Even less studied is the role of film administrators (Anatolii Skachko, Ilia Trainin, Turar Ryskulov and Berd Kotiev), scriptwriters and consultants (Sergei Tretiakov, Boris Lapin, Vladimir Arsenev, Mikhail Prishvin and Viktor Shklovskii), who were important agents in the multi-layered fabric of the film industry. The films that emerged from their cooperation underscored the Soviet landscape as a diversified structure that evokes, in a different context, Tony Ballantyne's description of an empire as a web constituting 'a complex fabrication fashioned out of a great number of disparate parts that were brought together into a new relationship'.[88] While the governance of the USSR was increasingly centralized, the Soviet space was continually portrayed as a culturally heterogeneous unity.

Circulating these images across the Soviet Union, cinema generated a 'global literacy' and instilled the Soviet world with distinctions. This new form of visual literacy should be viewed in the context of the changing epistemic conditions of knowledge enhanced by the proliferation of images depicting ethnicity through maps, engravings, illustrated albums, posters, photographs and other visual means.[89] The 'archaeological' impulse of my research is driven by interest in the epistemic foundations of the imposed categories of identity.[90] Through case studies of individual films and filmmakers, this book addresses the issues of power and representation in competing 'ocular fields' and emphasizes the plurality of the ethnographic scopic regimes, where the Soviet project both nourished and was nourished by Western colonial cinemas. It was in the process of dynamic transformation and discursive competition that the images of Soviet 'us' and ethnic 'others' were recorded and screened.

Across the Soviet Travelogues: The Roadmap

The structure of this book reflects the notion of mapping the dynamic transformations of spatial and ethnic units on film. My primary sources comprise a corpus of films preserved at the Russian State Documentary Film and Photo Archive (RGAKFD) as well as a selection of films on national minorities in the Gosfilmofond State Film Archive. In analysing the representation of nationalities on film, I focus on the work of the central studios in Moscow, for the most part leaving out the rich and equally important developments at studios in Ukraine, Georgia, and other Soviet Republics.[91] My narrative begins and ends with two paradigmatic travelogues encompassing the whole of the Soviet Union: *A Sixth Part of the World* [*Shestaia chast' mira*, 1926] and *A Day of the New World* [*Den' novogo mira*, 1940]. The years between these landmark films embody a period of active experimentation with new forms of solidarity and identity, as well as a search for the mechanisms to shape the viewers' image of the Soviet space. Individual chapters concentrate on films representing various regions of the Soviet Union including: the Far North, the Far East, the Volga Region, Siberia, the Northern Caucasus and Central Asia. By adopting a spatial principle rather than a chronological one, I emphasize the long-term legacies of visualizing particular regions and trace diachronic transformations which do not fit a single course of development.

The plurality of visual conventions cannot be ascribed solely to stylistic idiosyncrasies. Understanding the conceptual and visual polyphony of Soviet *kulturfilms* requires a comparative analysis of films as well as a diachronic analysis of film-makers' itineraries and the evolution of studio policies. To provide the required context, chapter one maps the controversial reception of *kulturfilms* as a concept, followed by its replacement with the concept of 'documentary'. It surveys the Soviet studio landscape and debates about audiences' needs in regard to *kulturfilms*. It further spotlights the history of Vostokfilm, the studio created for the purpose of representing national minorities in the Soviet Union.

Chapter 2 relates the history of the production and reception of Vertov's *A Sixth Part of the World*. It discusses 'cine-race' as a new film form, and elaborates on how it constructed the unity of the Soviet multi-ethnic space. It further looks at the film's critical reception and outlines the underlying conventions for representing both space and nationalities. The following chapters chart the changing imagery of different regions and areas defined by administrative borders – Buryat-Mongolia, Bashkiria, Dagestan and Chechnya, as well as those perceived as spatial units with loose boundaries, such as 'the North,' or 'the East', adding new perspectives to the discussion of the Soviet form of 'orientalism'.

Chapter 3 examines the concept of the Soviet Far North as elaborated by Vladimir Erofeev and Vera Popova in the montage film *Beyond the Arctic Circle* [*Za poliarnym krugom*, 1927]. The film is introduced in conceptual opposition to Vertov's approach of representing cultural diversity. The chapter further provides an analysis of frontier imagery in the media campaigns surrounding Arctic explorations in the 1930s. The films of Vladimir Shneiderov and Iakov Poselskii are studied as examples of an emerging hybrid genre of dramatized documentary where location shooting follows a prepared script.

Chapter 4 looks at the transformations of the cinematic Far East. Presented in early expedition films from an 'ethnographic' perspective, the region came to be portrayed as an imaginary frontier of 'civilization'. Alexander Litvinov's early travelogues are compared with the films of Amo Bek-Nazarov and Mikhail Slutskii on the Nanai and Chinese minorities. The comparison points out the blurred representational conventions applied in fiction and non-fiction. Furthermore, Slutskii's films set in the Birobidzhan Autonomous Oblast and the model Soviet town, Komsomolsk, highlight the changing role of re-enactment in films identified as documentaries.

Chapter 5 places *kulturfilms* on health and illness in the context of nationality politics. It considers the entanglement of ethnographic classifications with medical universalism by introducing *kulturfilms* representing ethnic groups through 'endemic' illnesses. In the 1920s, syphilis, tuberculosis and trachoma were the most 'cinematic' illnesses used to promote the Soviet hygienic discourse and to characterize ethnic communities. This chapter focuses on the cinematographic account of the Soviet-German medical expedition to Buryat-Mongolia, as well as the imagery of diseases in films on the Mari, the Chuvash and the Bashkir minorities. It outlines a gradual fading of the 'medicalizing' discourse supplanted by that of mass tourism, which promoted new set of attitudes towards the body practices and translated a uniformed prescribed outlook of a model Soviet citizen.

While present as a running thread throughout the book, the issue of imperial legacies most prominently comes to the fore in Chapter 6. Here I introduce travelogues to the Caucasus and look at the strategies of visual legitimization for the inclusion of such diverse territories as Dagestan, Chechnya and Svanetia in the Soviet Union. Further elements of colonial discourse are addressed in Chapter 7, which presents a variety of discourses on Central Asia, generated by film-makers arriving to the region from Moscow with the intention of recording life in the 'unembellished East'. This chapter includes an analysis of two expeditions to the Pamir Mountains, accounts for the Soviet national modernization discourse in Viktor Turin's *Turksib* and closes with Vertov's *Three Songs of Lenin* [*Tri pesni o Lenine*, 1934], which details the mechanics of technological production of an imagined Soviet community unified by a shared affective experience. I conclude with *A Day of the New World*, which constitutes a rhetorical and visual compendium of formulae for representing the Soviet Union.

The breakup of the Soviet Union spurred the search for new languages of self-representation, but left behind the visual metaphors that continue to command the emotional attachments and political loyalties of its former subjects.[92] Today, in the face of growing nationalist rhetoric, national plurality continues to be treated as a conceptual alternative to the nation-state. While the Soviet Union failed as a political project, its visual legacy continues to inform the spatial imagination of the twenty-first century.

1

They Must Be Represented: Kulturfilm and the National Niche in Soviet Cinema

Hundreds of thousands, millions of citizens of the RSFSR
who are illiterate or simply hiding from the rumbling 'Today'
should train their perception in front of the illuminated screen
of Cinema.

Dziga Vertov[1]

In 1925, a journalist writing for the paper *Kino* referred to two Yakuts discussing 'a few geniuses […] smarter than a policeman or a spy. They are like spirits sneaking all over the wide world with a camera. […] They are making films, discovering all sorts of fascinating stories'.[2] While ironically pointing out the 'naïveté' of this perception, the journalist emphasized the omnipresent cinematic powers of the new state, and exposed the broader underlying anxiety over and fascination with the new medium as a form of surveillance capable of uncovering new, hidden relations.[3] Hailed for its mechanical perfection and capacity to leave no detail unnoticed, cinema was perceived as the ideal form to survey the entire country, making its inhabitants familiar with the diversity of the lands and the transformations they undergo. In 1925, supported by the Academy of Sciences, the Museum of Anthropology and Ethnography, the Russian Geographic Society, and the Committee for Assistance to the Small-Numbered Peoples of the North, Kultkino studio approached the

18

Presidium of the Central Executive Committee with a plan to produce a countrywide series of ethnographic films.[4]

Kultkino's plans for a cine-atlas gave cinema the key role in shaping citizens' ideas about the Soviet space and its peoples as progressive and 'cultured'. Found among Vertov's papers, the unsigned concept of cine-atlas aimed at promoting the Soviet nationality policy as having 'more reason, healthy imagination, and fairness [*spravedlivost*] than those who pride themselves on thousands of years of culture and civilization'.[5] While formulated in opposition to colonial undertakings, it remained rooted in the imperial quest of making the space 'manageable and thus more rational'.[6] The project exemplified a hierarchical understanding of relations between the 'cultured' centre and 'backward' peripheries, populated by 'disappearing' cultures.

The grandiose scope of the Kultkino cine-atlas remained on paper, but attempts to design an all-encompassing structure that would centralize the undertaking did not cease. In 1928, cameraman Mark Naletnyi used his experience of filming in Bukhara and Siberia to convince the Society for the Study of the Urals, Siberia and the Far East to launch another cine-atlas project to inform viewers about the regions of the Soviet Union and identify 'the way along which this territory will develop'.[7] Naletnyi intended to make the signs of modernity – visualized through the growth of literacy, rational use of natural resources and sites of industrial construction – the crux of his project. Following the popularity of Soviet composite films made from archival footage, such as Esfir Shub's *Great Road* [*Velikii put'*, 1927] and *The Fall of the Romanov Dynasty* [*Padenie dinastii Romanovykh*, 1927], he proposed incorporating the existing footage on various territories and ethnic groups into composite works for the cine-atlas. The project was enthusiastically discussed as 'the strongest lever of cultural-enlightenment, which will have a global impact'.[8]

While Naletnyi's ambitious project never came to full fruition, the tension between 'original' and 'reappropriated' footage would become one of the constitutive features of the field, propelling individual film-makers to search for ingenious solutions to create their versions of a multinational Soviet Union.[9] The discussion of a Soviet cine-atlas continued onto a new level in 1931, as the Soiuzkino studio planned to produce 140 *kulturfilms* and 65 fiction films within the cine-atlas framework. The studio, however, lacked the resources necessary to realize this ambitious project, and it remained incomplete until the television era.[10]

Coming out of the cine-atlas discussions was a shared consensus that films making up a composite portrait of the new state should be made on expeditions to various parts of the Union to produce 'authentic' footage presented in a 'cultured' form. The number of individual films produced with the purpose of exploring the country's various regions grew throughout the second half of the 1920s. The ultimate criteria for just how 'authentic' these portraits were remained under dispute. Furthermore, the lack of a definitive understanding of 'ethnicity' and 'nationality' evoked debates on both the subjects of film and their viewing constituencies. Finally, the studios were wary of the financial losses caused by *kulturfilm* production, considered by many studio administrators as an ideological tax to be paid, but not encouraged. These multiple controversies made up the landscape in which film-makers worked. This chapter outlines these discussions on *kulturfilm* and the Soviet debates on their intended audiences, which exemplify the implied cultural hierarchies of the Soviet viewership. Finally, the chapter introduces Vostokfilm and positions its mission of catering to 'Eastern' minorities within the Soviet film studio landscape of the 1920–30s.

Cultural, Ethnographic, Documentary: The Elusive Film Classification

On 9 June 1926, the journalist, film administrator and aspiring film-maker Nikolai Lebedev signed a contract with the Kinopechat publishing house to write the monograph *Kulturfilma*.[11] Submitted in October 1926, the manuscript and its disaffected author received a biting review from Viacheslav Uspenskii, the director of the publishing house. Uspenskii frowned not only upon the author's stylistic flaws, but first and foremost on his ambiguous take on *kulturfilm*. Most writers on the subject, including those who, like Lebedev, argued for an increase in *kulturfilm* production, also expressed frustration with the ambiguity of the term.[12]

Lebedev strove to follow the German example in advocating *kulturfilm* production in the Soviet Union.[13] At the same time, he defined *kulturfilm* by everything that it was not: not fiction, not newsreel and not

20

advertisement. Challenged by his editor's expectation of a clear-cut definition in his manuscript, Lebedev identified it as 'any film which aims at organizing our thoughts, irrespective of the methods it uses – scientific, pedagogical, popularizing, or many others'.[14] He thus highlighted the variety of styles and genres implied by the term. Lebedev's colleague Vladimir Erofeev, a journalist and film critic, expressed similar views and attempted to adapt the German *Kulturfilm* for the Soviet context, arguing that the mix of education and entertainment was the key to success.[15] Emphasizing the international popularity of *kulturfilms*, Lebedev wrote of the special value of 'picturesque ethnographic films, showing the inhabitants of European cities an unknown, exotic everyday life'.[16]

The importance of the cinematic 'thought-organizer' was acknowledged by a broad circle of film professionals, from film-makers to administrators. The Soviet professional film guild, the Association of Revolutionary Cinematographers (ARK, since 1928 ARRK), created a 'Sector of Scientific and Cultural Cinema' and attempted to purify the definition of *kulturfilms* as films 'of a politically-enlightening, scientifically-educational, or newsreel character, without fictional plots, aimed at introducing viewers to the various branches of science and knowledge, as well as the social, political, and cultural life and working conditions.'[17]

Following the ARK Sector of Scientific and Cultural Cinema's 1926 definition of *kulturfilms*, critics advocated the active use of 'montage thinking' in creating *kulturfilms*:

> Real life should not be just secretly peeped at, but *filmed after having been understood in a certain way*. Those moments of real life should be selected, which from various sides demonstrate different social phenomena, everyday life, or facts, which we want to record and show in a certain way. At some point, a certain phenomenon should be *brought to life*, a real event organized and tacitly directed. In a word, one should organize the editing of the filmed material, approach all aspects of filming in an organized way, one should *edit and not simply report on life*.[18]

From the start, the desire to shape recorded reality according to a predetermined plan was a formative feature of *kulturfilms*. But, as demonstrated by the following discussions, this understanding was never completely uniform.

21

The campaign to promote *kulturfilms* peaked in the second half of the 1920s and was encouraged by the film and party administrators' attention to this form of cinema.[19] Kirill Shutko, supervisor of cinematic affairs in the Central Committee of the Communist Party, outlining the history of this phenomenon, somewhat anachronistically dated the launch of *kulturfilm* in the Soviet Union to 1922. He further pointed to the importance of 'the introduction of the audience to the boundless [*neob"iatnoi*] Soviet country' through *kulturfilms*.[20] Discussing the prospects for Soviet cinema in foreign markets, Soviet officials deemed the potential of Soviet *kulturfilm* on ethnographic and geographic themes as a welcome subject of export.[21]

Despite state support, the concept *kulturfilm* remained under fire. A number of film-makers, critics, and film officials sought to replace it with a more straightforward ideological notion. An alternative to *kulturfilm* influenced by the discussion on 'life-construction' in literature and the arts[22] was formulated by film-makers united around Dziga Vertov. Vertov organized the group 'Kinoks' [cine-eyes], including Mikhail Kaufman and Ivan Beliakov, and later Elizaveta Svilova, Ilia Kopalin, Alexander Lemberg and others, who pronounced the principles of technological superiority of the camera over human vision and the primacy of non-fiction over fiction cinema.[23] The Kinoks introduced the 'Kino-Eye' [*kinoglaz*] as a new filming method; they renounced 'literary skeletons with cine-illustrations' and offered instead a novel way of grasping and structuring visible life with the help of the camera.[24] For Vertov, the construction of space was central to his new way of filming. His manifesto emphasized the Kino-Eye proficiency for 'investigating the chaos of visible phenomena, *resembling space*',[25] exploring new ways of seeing and filming reality. Vertov's film *Kino-Eye: Life Caught Unawares* [*Kinoglaz: zhizn' vrasplokh*, Goskino, 1924], originally envisioned as a six-part film series, became his visual manifesto, advancing new principles of film construction.[26]

Discussing the work of cameramen for newsreels and non-fiction, critic Vladimir Fefer praised the Kinoks as the pioneers of new ways of filming in constant search of new ways of seeing. Fefer listed the occasions on which these cameramen endangered their lives to offer novel perspectives: climbing and hanging off roofs, riding a suspended cable railway, filming an advancing icebreaker from the ice, riding on the roof of a train, approaching a bear's den armed solely with a tripod and even hanging above a grave

ПРОБЕГ „КИНО-ГЛАЗА"
СКВОЗЬ СТРОЙ ГОСТОРГОВСКОГО АППАРАТА

КИНОК-ОПЕРАТОР КАУФМАН, С'ЕМКА НА ХОДУ С ПОЕЗДА.

Figure 1.1 Mikhail Kaufman on a cine-race. Back cover of *Sovetskii ekran* 21 (1925).

to get a good shot of a funeral.[27] By classifying the spontaneous, unprepared, and dangerous as 'authentic', Fefer's article emphasizes the role of a 'man with a movie camera', all too often unjustly seen as an apprentice or craftsmen, as a co-author of the film.

Vertov and the Kinoks rejected the idea of fiction film-making, but emphasized the constructed nature of cinema. In 1926, Vertov advocated the creation of a 'factory of facts' that would ensure the fast, efficient construction of 'film-things' [*kino-veshchi*]. 'Using bricks,' he argued, 'one can make an oven, the Kremlin wall, and many other things. From filmed material, one can construct various films. Just as one needs good bricks to make a solid house, so one needs good film material to organize a good film'.[28] This position resonated with the movement of 'literature of fact' (also rendered in English as factography) initiated by the writers and artists affiliated with the *LEF* journal, including Sergei Tretiakov, Osip Brik, Nikolai Chuzhak and Viktor Pertsov, who put forward the idea of 'art of life-construction'.[29] Albeit not rejecting the concept of *kulturfilms*, *LEF* writers, artists and critics emphasized that literature of fact and 'film-things' were made 'not simply to depict life, but to create it anew in the process'.[30]

The discussion on *kulturfilms* pivoted on the fiction/non-fiction divide, but also included those who called for crossing it.[31] Some, like the critic Ippolit Sokolov, advocated a flexible approach as long as the audience was introduced to 'the realm of reality', preferably represented with the help of 'advantageous' material. As an example, he referred to the popular US docu-dramas:

> It is much easier to make an interesting *kulturfilm* on a 'concrete' geographic and ethnographic topic with exotic material than on an 'abstract' social issue with everyday and uninspiring [*nevyigryshnyi*] material. *Chang*, *Nanook*, or *Moana* are easier to make than a technical or political film. [...] The editing of *kulturfilm* should create a united and coherent structure – unity, clarity and intention of thought.[32]

Despite different understandings of *kulturfilm*, all parties believed that it was one of the primary means of shaping an audiences' knowledge of the country. Tretiakov argued that Soviet cinema should 'turn the screen of random chronicle into a wide window through which we can observe with the eye of the master [*khoziaiskim glazom*] our country under construction'.[33] The audience would no longer see 'random' images, but would become transformed by the very act of viewing.

Although not a single cine-atlas was realized as a comprehensive project before World War II, the intention to survey, systematize and classify the whole country on film was consistently pursued. Sovkino Board member Ilia Trainin announced plans to film 'the whole of the Soviet Union in the coming three years'.[34] For Trainin, as for the majority in the film industry in the mid-1920s, *kulturfilm* provided a convenient, albeit loose, form for packing knowledge into an easily consumable visual form, which 'could be done not only in non-fiction mode, but also as fiction'.[35] The tension between commercially profitable and ideologically relevant topics remained another point of discussion.[36] Erofeev argued that the modest profits brought in by *kulturfilms* did not reflect 'uninteresting' film subjects, but rather suggested structural deficiencies in the production and distribution systems.[37] Many others sided with Osip Brik, who rejected the importance of financial gains altogether, stating that film-makers should not occupy themselves with financial matters: 'We shall say: your money problems are of no concern to us. We insist on the cultural line.'[38]

The *kulturfilm* debate peaked in March 1928 at the All-Union Party Conference on Cinema Affairs. Most film professionals shared the conviction of ARRK member Vladimir Sillov, lamenting 'the situation when, as soon as our viewer realizes that he [sic] is being agitated, the shutters automatically grow on his ears'.[39] Under the supervision of the top Party politicians, conference participants stressed the need to find new ways to produce political propaganda. The Plenum of the Governmental Film Committee, convened on 8 May 1929 and headed by the Party functionary Ian Rudzutak [Jānis Rudzutaks], authorized the creation of a working group on *kulturfilms*. This diverse mix of film-makers (Vsevolod Pudovkin, Sergei Eisenstein) and administrators (Pavel Bliakhin, Konstantin Shvedchikov and Kirill Shutko) were tasked with studying the audience and themes for new films and cadres.[40] The subsequent conference on 'Workers' Audience and Cinema', organized in Moscow on 5–6 July 1929, was attended by over 200 participants who requested further promotion for *kulturfilms*.[41]

At the same time, the long-running attempts to define *kulturfilm* turned towards finding meaningful replacements for the term.[42] A theorist of scientific cinema, Lazar Sukharebskii, fragmented the notion of *kulturfilm* into sub-types (scientific film, pedagogical film, propaganda film, chronicle and art-history [*iskusstvovedcheskie*] films) and argued for the establishment of separate film studios for each film type.[43] Shutko's edited volume, *Kulturfilma*, marked the beginning of the end of the concept by gradually but consistently replacing the notion of *kulturfilm* with political-enlightenment film [*politprosvetfilm*]. In the early 1930s, the notion of *kulturfilm* was used interchangeably with the latter. On 3–5 February 1930, the largest Soviet film studio Sovkino (at the time undergoing reorganization into Soiuzkino) organized the first meeting of film workers involved in the production and distribution of *politprosvet* and *kulturfilms* with representatives of other state institutions. The studio's leadership emphasized political content, which resulted in demands for an ideological message to be incorporated into the very structure of each *kulturfilm* beyond the level of textual commentary. But by the following year, the first Moscow conference of agitation-propaganda, scientific-educational, instructional films and newsreels, convened by ARRK and Soiuzkino on 18–22 April 1931, abandoned all references to *kulturfilm*, instead stressing the importance of 'political enlightenment'. In his programmatic speech, Vladimir Sutyrin, the General Secretary of the All-Union Association of Proletarian Writers and an active commentator on cinema affairs, called on film-makers to replace the 'shy' [*stydlivye*] *kulturfilms* with 'shameless' [*besstyzhie*] political-enlightenment films.[44]

Film-makers who preferred the concept of non-fiction to that of *kulturfilm* sided with this opinion. '*Kulturfilm* does not exist,' argued Esfir' Shub already in 1929, inviting her fellow film-makers to make sense of [*osmyslit'*] the facts and 'clearly communicate to the viewer the attitude of the author'.[45] Erofeev, who had actively supported *kulturfilm* in the mid-1920s, sided with Shub, claiming that the opposition of fictional cinema and *kulturfilm* is 'ungrounded' and 'ideologically false'.[46] The discussion on the role of newsreel initiated by the Department of Agitation and Mass Campaigns of the Central Committee of the Communist Party and Soiuzkino, further contributed to the marginalization of the notion of *kulturfilm* and returned to the idea of newsreel 'elevating the tastes' of the audience.[47]

With abandoning the notion of *kulturfilm*, the polarized 'fiction' and 'non-fiction' supporters fuelled a discussion on so-called 'documentarism', questioning the notions of 'document' and 'fact'. The pages of *Proletarskoe kino* (*Proletarian Cinema*) and other Soviet film journals, as well as the minutes of professional meetings, demonstrate that following the withdrawal of *kulturfilm* as a concept, a dramatic change in the use of the concepts of 'non-fiction', 'reality' and 'document' occurred. While political functionaries and film administrators sought to contain and control the interpretation of 'reality', film-makers actively reframed the notions of 'non-fiction' and 'newsreel', and searched for conceptual alternatives to the notion of *kulturfilm* as well as for institutional support of their work. In Shub's words:

> The so-called 'documentarists' also conduct newsreel work, but we are referred to as a movement outside newsreel. This is wrong. There could not be a documentary film – there is documentary or chronicle footage. That is why non-fiction film grew out of newsreel and is organically connected to it. But now we have it this way: there is a newsreel studio, which produces only the Sovkino-journal and separate editions of agitation-propagandist value for this or that campaign. And there are non-fiction film-makers, outside of the newsreel studio, who [...] exist outside the normal conditions of production.[48]

In the early 1930s, the most active film-makers in non-fiction production argued for the use of a new term, 'documentary cinema'. Preparing for the ARRK conference of 1931, Erofeev wrote an article, 'Technological Innovation of Documentary Cinema', where he argued for a new conceptualization of 'documentary cinema': 'technical innovation in film production [...] allowed us to replace the re-enactment of life events, as performed in fiction film [...] with the recording of authentic reality [*podlinnoi deistvitel'nosti*]'.[49] While emphasizing the imperfections of the proposed classification, he insisted on distinguishing between documentary cinema, fiction, and newsreel. At the same time, he asserted that the concept of documentary does not imply 'objective' or 'unbiased' film:

> Any film (including documentary) is a tendentious film, since there could be no objective art and objective science. Moreover, every frame which records a separate fact, is also tendentious, since already in the choice of this (and not another) fact for recording, and in the perspective of the camera, there is an attitude of the cameraman (and director-organizer) towards this fact. Does this, however, reduce the technical innovation of documentary film, which allows us to record life events without their artificial reconstruction? Not in the least.[50]

Siding with Shub and Erofeev, Vertov stated: 'Non-fiction film is not a direction in cinema, but a branch of the film industry. Documentary non-fiction film is confused with factualism [*faktitsizm*], documentarism, and so on. And yet, documentarism and the production of documentary films are not the same thing.'[51]

The 1931 ARRK conference provided a turning point in debates on the documentary. Presenters pointed out the existence of 'documents, which distorted reality and the fictional works that documented it'. They pejoratively labelled all those promoting non-fiction cinema as 'documentarists', who were treated as a single 'movement' and accused of 'fetishizing "reality"'.[52] Furthermore, 'documentarists' were blamed for 'only looking' at the world instead of attempting to change it:

> The time when newsreel was involved in the 'honest' recording of facts [...] has gradually receded to the realm of the distant past. The complicated task of actively being involved in our socialist construction stands before newsreels; [...] the task of the informer becomes the task of the organizer.[53]

The final judgment on what to consider 'reality' was transferred to the authorities:

> The main problem of documentary film-makers [...] is the fetishism of the document as such. They cannot comprehend that the point is not in the artistic approach to reality, but what comes out of it. [...] as a rule, re-enactments represent reality much better than material which is not staged; [...] the fact that one films a documentary and not fiction does not safeguard one from making a wrong film.[54]

The debate essentially aimed to safeguard a monopoly over the correct interpretation of material. The vague and changing guidelines allowed for criticism and censure of any artist deemed 'improper'. At the same time, the Central Committee of the Party announced that in terms of film production, fiction cinema rose to the top of the list of priorities, while *kulturfilm*, documentary cinema, and newsreels no longer yielded precedence.[55] To make acceptable films, the director relied on situational interpretations of reality and fact. 'Socialist realism', argued the former Head of Narkompros, Anatolii Lunacharskii, 'is rather unthinkable without a certain degree of romanticism. That is what makes it different from indifferently registering the events. It is realism plus enthusiasm, realism plus a vigorous spirit'.[56] The non-fiction status of footage no longer guaranteed the acceptance of the film. Any work could become suspect of political deviation and everyone was exposed to attack.

Erofeev and Vertov became the central targets of the attack on 'documentarists'. The campaign unfolded both in the press and at various discussion forums, such as the 'Evening of Documentary Cinema' on 24 February 1932. This discussion highlights the scope of criticism and main arguments used against 'documentarists', as well as the emerging generational ruptures. In the minutes of the discussion, film students of the State Institute of Cinematography held their teachers accountable for 'faulty methods'. One recent graduate, Olga Podgoretskaia, accused Erofeev of 'superficial enumeration' in his films and called for a clarification of his filming methods. She criticized Erofeev's approach to filmed footage and claimed that 'by material we mean a certain attitude towards it'.[57] Vertov, in turn, came under attack for 'abstracting events' and using metaphoric montage sequences.[58] In response, Erofeev accused his critics of confusing ideological and technical arguments. Nevertheless, both sides asserted the importance of the ideological function of newsreel and documentary footage.

In 1931, Soiuzkino was reorganized, its *kulturfilm* department closed, and the All-Union Film Newsreel Trust, Soiuzkinokhronika, was created, taking over film newsreel departments of Ukrainfilm, Belgoskino, Azerkino, Goskinprom Gruzii as departments of the Soiuzkinokhronika studio.[59] In the course of the year, use of the term *kulturfilm* in official debates and production plans was abandoned. Lack of a clear conceptual definition and also – albeit indirectly – *kulturfilm*'s foreign roots, sealed its fate. Along with *politprosvet* films, chronicle, educational, and scientific films became a new set of notions that allowed for further specialization and a higher degree of ideological control than *kulturfilm*. Ironically, with the waning of the 'anti-documentarist' campaign, the concept of documentary replaced the notion of 'political enlightenment' and emerged as an institutionally autonomous production and distribution network.

Giving the camera the power to shape and direct its audience led to increasing attempts to retroactively update film records with the most recent interpretation of the past and present. With the unfolding wave of terror in the second half of the 1930s, newsreels with 'incorrect' analyses or persecuted protagonists to be erased from the official historical narrative came under increasing scrutiny.[60] To this end, Soiuzintorgkino, the

Soviet monopoly responsible for the export of Soviet films, systematically reviewed previous exports to edit out those who, after the completion of the film, were identified as 'enemies of the people'. The painstaking desire to keep pace with political changes resulted in increased censorship and physical destruction of material, as witnessed by a representative of the Main Administration of Cinematography (Glavnoe upravlenie kinematografii, GUK) responsible for Soviet film policy in the US:

> The most serious work was on the newsreels, since it was impossible to review a huge archive with the old newsreels (all my employees are Americans and I, of course, could not tell them about the matter). I have informed Moscow in a telegram that I have decided to destroy all old newsreels up to 1 January 1937. Since I have received no answer to this telegram, I took this silence for an approval, and destroyed all old newsreels.[61]

Films distributed in the Soviet Union underwent similar adjustments. The decisions made about production and withdrawal from distribution were grounded in a certain perception of the audience. The characteristics and preferences of the envisaged audiences generated an extensive debate and shaped the production of films portraying Soviet spatial and national diversity. A discussion of the audience's needs demonstrates how the imagined audience shapes production plans and predetermines the reception of the film.

Think With Us, Think Like Us! Shaping the Audience through Film

> – *They are jeering at us –*
> *the Uzbeks and the Tajiks will say.*
> *– This is disrespect for us.*
> *The director will try to justify himself:*
> *– We made this film not for the East.*
> *We are showing it in central Russia.*
> *– This is no better for us. –*
> *We will answer him.*[62]

In 1926, *Pravda* published an article with the provocative title, 'We Have to Get Civilized'. In it, Nadezhda Krupskaia, Lenin's widow and an active promoter of adult education, argued for the importance of 'show' over 'tell' in reaching the broad masses of workers and peasants:

> Nowadays, peasants want to know everything in detail – how people live in our [Soviet] Union in villages and towns, how people live in other countries, what they strive for, how and what can they achieve. [...] We poorly calculate the potential of centralizing propaganda and agitation through cinema and radio, we don't factor in all the colossal influence they can have on the broadest masses. [...] We have to sharpen our radio and cine-weapon.[63]

Defining the needs and desires of the countrywide audience was a characteristic rhetorical figure in the polemics of the 1920s.[64] The implied separation between the 'civilizers' and 'civilizing subjects' highlights the power relations described by Alexander Etkind as 'internal colonization', and at the same time brings to the fore the concept of Soviet culturedness [*kulturnost*].[65] This argument was at the root of the Kultkino studio mandate to edify and 'enlighten' the audience through *kulturfilm*. However, the double bind between the audience's preferences and financial profits had a direct impact on production and distribution policies.[66] This paradox was exemplified by Viktor Shklovskii, who called on film producers to 'study the new audience, like people study arithmetic,'[67] but at the same time insisted on the 'struggle with the viewer, who is pressuring us [*napiraet*] through the box-office.'[68] The early Soviet film industry oscillated between the desire to shape, exploit, and control film-goers. Film policies were advanced on behalf of the imagined community of viewers, and accompanied by the first attempts to study audiences.[69] Several, albeit not systematic, studies of public 'taste' were undertaken by the network of the Society of the Friends of Soviet Cinema (Obshchestvo druzei sovetskogo kino, ODSK), created under the supervision of the head of the Soviet secret police, Felix Dzerzhinskii. Yet these attempts, intended as an aid in controlling film reception, did not develop a comprehensive understanding of the regional diversity of the Soviet audience.[70]

The limited number of proper screening venues was another repeatedly discussed issue. Sovkino targeted the broad masses, but *kulturfilms* were often shown in poorly equipped workers' clubs, which lowered audience turnout.[71] For a brief period of time, Sovkino ran a specialized *kulturfilm* movie theatre, Artes, in Moscow.[72] Although some of its screenings attracted full houses, the theatre ultimately proved unprofitable and closed.[73] The proponents of *kulturfilms* insisted that, while they lost out to fiction films in terms of audience numbers and revenues, the crux of the matter lay not in the disinterested audience but in the lack of sufficient campaigns drawing on interest in 'historical, socio-hygienic, ethnographic and geographical topics'.[74]

But what exactly constituted the needs and interests of Soviet audiences remained contested. Film periodicals published enthusiastic accounts of first-time screenings in remote villages and settlements. They boastfully reported on the Caucasian peasants' enthusiasm over newsreels on agricultural mechanization and on Turkmen nomads watching Lenin's funeral.[75] In the Far East, open-air screenings allegedly competed with the Easter procession of the Cross and lured away the youth.[76] Rich and poor alike were described as 'falling under the spell of cinema.'[77] 'Life gets closer', claimed one reviewer asserting the growing impact of educational films and newsreels.[78] Seeing the Soviet audience as a composite concept allowed policy-makers to advance the idea of special needs among the titular national minorities.[79] Perceived as more demanding and more naïve than audiences in urban centres, audiences with 'special needs' were located primarily in the countryside and the Soviet 'East'.

In 1925, *Sovetskoe kino* published a series of articles advocating the creation of special films for 'eastern' audience. Although, as Daniel Brower and Edward Lazzerini pointed out, 'no simple line on the map separated Western and Eastern peoples within the empire',[80] the discursive construction of geographic categories was grounded in assumptions about their fundamental differences.[81] Anatolii Skachko, a Dagestani representative on the Vostokkino board, argued:

> People of the East [*vostochnye liudi*] need very different films, made especially for them. [...] These films should take into consideration the psychology of the eastern peasant and his conception of the world from the perspective of communist criticism. [...] Until now, the mass viewers took what they saw on the screen to be real life. They *believe* the screen. This faith

should not be destroyed, but used for disseminating useful ideas. [...] the eastern films are needed not so much for the western audience, but rather for the eastern peasantry; and for them, a deep knowledge of eastern life and strict consideration of the psychology of the eastern viewer is required.[82]

To support his argument, Skachko quoted Nariman Narimanov, the first head of the Soviet Azerbaijan Government: 'In the East, where people are used to thinking not with logical inferences but with images, cinema is the only possible means of propaganda which does not require preliminary and gradual training of the masses'.[83] Arguing for the creation of a special 'eastern' film studio, Narimanov, who dabbled in scriptwriting, referred to a popular 'eastern' belief in 'people with cameras [who] are walking around unnoticed and quietly filming everything that happens in life.'[84] In order not to betray this belief, he further argued that these films should be as close and familiar to local audiences as possible.

The slogan 'Don't forget the East!' was a refrain for Soviet nationality and film policy alike.[85] For Skachko, 'eastern' audiences were not homogeneous but could be classified on a 'civilization' scale:

So enormous is the distance between cultured Tatarstan, greatly influenced by capitalist-industrial development and by Russian-European culture, and the remote corners of Kazakhstan, living until now in patriarchal clan relations and nomadic shepherd culture, that it is hardly possible to offer the same film to these two lands. [...] the perception of a Constantinople Turk, who is used to cinema, is very different from the perception of a Persian or an Afghani, who might encounter cinema for the first time.[86]

The approval of local audiences was considered a guarantee of authentic and truthful representation. Proletkino film-maker Dmitrii Bassalygo described the response of 'eastern' audiences as crucial for his fiction film *A Muslim Woman* [*Musul'manka*, 1925]:

I am little interested in praise and criticism of *A Muslim Woman* by Europeans. The most decisive moment for me as director and scriptwriter will be the moment when the film is judged by the inhabitants of Bukhara.[87]

The imaginary local viewer became a yardstick for measuring the success of the film.[88] The first films praised by critics as 'good oriental films' were dramatized fictions made with the participation of non-professional actors, such as *Alim*, set among the Crimean Tatars, applauded for its 'tactful exoticism'.[89]

Kulturfilms were expected to further part with clichés and show the 'unembellished East' along with the new regime's achievements in emancipation and industrialization.[90] The first Moscow film expeditions were criticized for their lack of organization and poor knowledge of local cultures and languages. Shklovskii ironically demanded maps and itineraries for these 'new Columbuses' and hoped that their 'authentic', 'unembellished' footage would not be discarded in favour of dramatic narratives.[91]

In contrast to the intense debates of the mid-1920s, the discussion on the needs of rural and 'national' audiences, plans for differentiated distribution and active audience research diminished through the 1930s. Ultimately, Soviet culturedness advanced a uniform model of 'high culture' for audiences.[92] Despite a prescribed ideological framework, Soviet film studios differed in implementing state policies regarding the production of films for and about national minorities, and thus, the dynamic studio landscape presented coexisting strategies of filming Soviet nationalities.

Vostokfilm: The Studio for the Soviet 'Other'

In the 1920s and early 1930s, Soviet film studios constituted a diversified landscape wherein state ownership coexisted with both private and foreign investment, and market competition mechanisms functioned in the context of state-imposed limitations on distribution. This complex configuration of centralization, regional autonomy, market rationality and ideological control defined the cultural production of the early Soviet period.[93] The desire to regulate was combined with dependence on the market, while reliance on competition coexisted with the tightening of state control. The Soviet film industry faced increasing political control and gradual, but consistent centralization. The All-Russian Photo and Film Department (Vserossiiskii fotokinootdel, VFKO) was established in January 1919 to replace the State Film Committee, and in 1922, VFKO was reorganized into the Goskino State Film-Photo Organization, which gained a distribution monopoly over most territory of the Russian Federation.[94]

In 1923, Goskino underwent an inspection that identified multiple failings including an overgrown staff, uncatalogued collections, poor storage conditions, faulty accounting, corruption, and censored films in distribution.[95] Official documentation on the available film stock was not found and a great deal of it was declared missing. 'By chance,' wrote an inspector, 'I went to the place where the negatives were stored and there, again by chance, I found a list of negatives, sorted by Iurii Zheliabuzhskii [film director, at the time Head of the Newsreel Department at Goskino]. This is the only document that remains from the Newsreel Department'.[96] Yet even this list was only of relative value since, according to Zheliabuzhskii's former assistant Svilova (later a member of the Kinoks and the wife of Vertov), the length of the films was only approximately measured and, in many cases, deliberately exaggerated as workers were paid according to the amount of material they processed. In the course of a little over a year, the newsreel department passed through the hands of a host of administrators until Vertov took charge in May 1922 and reorganized it into the Bureau of Photo and Film, where he started producing a new newsreel, *Kino-Pravda* (Film-Truth).[97]

Prior to the 1923 revision, Goskino created a Cultural Department, which later became an autonomous studio, Kultkino.[98] During its short lifespan, Kultkino laid the foundation for Soviet *kulturfilm* production. While imported blockbusters remained the primary source of income for the film industry, a campaign for tighter control over distribution ran parallel with a campaign to increase the number of *kulturfilms* in the repertoires of cinemas and workers' clubs.[99] All other Soviet film studios, irrespective of their specialization, also produced *kulturfilms*. Proletkino, an ambitious new company, positioned itself as *the* proletarian organization and invested in non-fiction production in an attempt to gain a monopoly over workers' clubs and non-commercial distribution networks.[100] In 1925, Proletkino produced the first Soviet expedition film, *The Great Flight*. Another active studio was Sevzapkino, founded in Leningrad on 9 May 1922, which acquired a monopoly on distribution in North-Western Russia along with the rights to produce films, run theatres and purchase and sell raw film materials.[101] Although its main source of income came from distributing imported films, the company also engaged in chronicle and *kulturfilm* production and strove to extend its reach all the way to Central Asia, opening an office in Bukhara.[102]

From 1923, Mezhrabpom-Rus (after 1928, Mezhrabpomfilm) also became an important agency in the early Soviet studio landscape. Mezhrabpom-Rus, created by unifying assets of the private studio Rus with the investments of the International Workers' Aid (Mezhrabpom) headed by Willi Münzenberg, aimed to mediate between the Western (especially German) film market and local studios, and to promote Soviet films on the international market. It came closest to adopting the German concept of *Kulturfilm* by actively investing in the production of scientific, educational and expedition films.[103] Its *kulturfilm* releases include Vsevolod Pudovkin's *Mechanics of the Brain* [*Mekhanika golovnogo mozga*, 1926] and Vladimir Shneiderov's explorations of the Pamir, as well as a number of films about life in the USSR which specifically targeted foreign markets.[104] Mobilizing funds and supporters worldwide, Mezhrabpomfilm survived a series of restructurings but did not fully submit to the Soviet centralizing policy until its dissolution in 1936.[105]

The press repeatedly described the existing competition among studios throughout the 1920s as 'squabbling', which became the pretext for centralizing the industry, and thereby 'harmonizing' production and distribution entities. To this end, in June 1924, Goskino and Sevzapkino merged to create Sovkino, a central distribution company.[106] The new organization received a distribution monopoly throughout the Russian Soviet Federation (RSFSR). While not initially established for film production, but rather for distribution that treated all studios equally in order 'to help the toilers of the borderlands to catch up with the toilers of the centre',[107] Sovkino announced its own production aims of making '100 per cent ideological and 100 per cent commercial' films in 1925.[108]

Sovkino's ambitious studio plans reached out through a growing network of film theatres and workers' clubs to the most remote parts of the country, as well as markets abroad where 'the toiling masses of China, Persia, Turkey' were allegedly 'looking at the Soviet Union with special inspiration.'[109] Out of the 746 educational films listed in Sovkino's 1927 catalogue of 'scientific cinema', 187 were described as geographical films.[110]

While part of their stock included pre-Revolutionary imports, Sovkino declared the production of Soviet geographic films its priority. By entering the field of production, Sovkino became one of the main targets of criticism for profiteering. To balance these accusations, the studio management listed *kulturfilm* production among its primary activities and commissioned some of the most extensive expeditions. It thus emerged as one of the largest producers of *kulturfilms* in the second half of the 1920s. Sovkino financed many of the films analysed in the following chapters, but remained a target of regular attacks for paying insufficient attention to the 'enlightening' mission of cinema.[111]

The Soviet press discussed the idea of a studio devoted exclusively to the representation of national minorities within the Russian Federation from the mid-1920s onwards. Some organizations with similar functions, such as the Eastern department within Goskino, the film department of the Scientific Association for Oriental Studies, and the short-lived Ethno-World studio (Etno-mir) created to 'serve' national minorities, attempted to fill this niche.[112] While these organizations did not have a significant impact on film production, a more visible change was instituted by a share company called Vostochnoe Kino (literally translated as Eastern Cinema), formed in March 1926.[113] The studio aimed to produce 'truly Eastern' fiction, non-fiction and ethnographic films; to promote cinematographic culture and movie-theatre networks in the national republics, and to develop local film production and distribution. It became fully operational by 1928 under the name Vostokkino.[114]

The studio's shareholders and management started off by denouncing imperial colonial practices and 'the profit-oriented perpetuation of exoticized and eroticized oriental imagery' and claimed a monopoly in representing the 'true life of the Soviet East'.[115] The studio leadership attempted to gain a monopoly over the production and distribution of films in the borderland territories by claiming the position of sole representatives of the indigenous communities who should have the exclusive right to 'illustrate Soviet life in these national territories'.[116] Some shareholders saw the commercial potential of the studio, and suggested 'pump[ing] money out of the population' in order to secure Vostokkino's growth and development.[117] The tension between ideology and commerce was formative for Vostokkino. Knowing the audience's desire for images of the 'exotic East', how could the studio balance commercial productions which would secure income to keep the studio in existence with low-cost, but low-profit, ideological *kulturfilms* which showed the 'East as it is' to secure state benevolence and justify the Vostokkino mission? Vostokkino tried to ride both horses at once. The elusive notion of 'the East' formed the core of the tension – they had to simultaneously challenge long traditions of exoticism in literary and visual representation, and follow the ideological guidelines moving from indigenization to cultural assimilation.

Vostokkino intended to use the medium of film to unify diverse nationalities in the 'Soviet outskirts' through a shared political and cultural programme devised in line with the developmental connotations of the Soviet nationality policy. Yet the geographic ascription of the studio was already challenged at the founding meeting. A Yakut representative disagreed with a presupposed 'division of culture into the progressive West and the backward East that exists in bourgeois states and societies' and proposed instead the 'neutral' title, National Cinema (Natskino).[118] Indeed, the studio included representatives of the most diverse national entities, from Karelia to Yakutia, which made any geographic reference problematic. At the same time, its assumed 'enlightening' mission rested on a presumed teleological development 'from backwardness towards civilization' where modernity, knowledge, and progress arrived from the centre. Vostokkino implicitly expanded elements of orientalizing rhetoric to the entire non-Russian population of the Russian Federation, which industrially and culturally did not match the urban centres of the Federation.

Throughout its existence, Vostokkino grew steadily, attracting a number of established writers, directors, and cameramen, including Shklovskii, Alexander Rzheshevskii, Osip Brik, Isaak Babel, Konstantin Paustovskii, Georgii Grebner, Viktor Turin, Alexander Razumnyi and other film and literature luminaries.[119] The studio filmed political meetings and festivities in Autonomous Republics and Oblasts, re-enacted historical liberation struggles and victories over prejudice and reported on socialist construction sites across the Soviet Union. Despite abundant access to 'exotic' material, the studio's commitment to non-profit production meant that it struggled to make ends meet.[120] Vostokkino's regional network continuously fell short of credit, work space, equipment and sometimes even 'warm shoes for the cameramen'.[121]

Unpredictable political twists and turns in nationality politics posed further challenges, as did the growing momentum towards centralization in Soviet cinematography.[122] Over the course of the 1920s, hagiographic portraits of the leaders of 'national uprisings' gradually replaced the representation of the revolutionary masses and abstract forces of modernity.[123] Restoration of the Russian historical myth led to yet another wave of re-filming history, which ultimately undermined the *raison d'être* of Vostokkino. In early 1930, Soiuzkino replaced Sovkino, further centralizing the industry. The new head of the studio,[124] Boris Shumiatskii, made the production of films 'intelligible to the millions' the studio's priority.[125] On 11 February 1933, Soiuzkino became, in a step cementing the centralization of the film industry, the Main Administration of Film and Photo Industry (Glavnoe upravlenie kino-fotopromyshlennosti, GUKF), directly subordinated to the Council of People's Commissars (Sovet narodnykh komissarov, SNK).[126]

The creation of GUKF subordinated the republican studios to the central authority. After 1933, not a single theme could be sent for production without the prior approval of the Central Committee.[127] Vostokfilm and Mezhrabpomfilm were the last studios to maintain their relative independence; the former dissolved on 10 August 1935, and its management, accused of overspending and mismanagement, was put on trial.[128] Full control over the film industry came hand in hand with control over the conventions representing Soviet space.[129] To introduce the milestones of this complex itinerary, the next chapter begins by looking at the first Soviet cinematic representation of the Soviet Union as a composite national entity, which left a lasting impact on the Soviet cinematic spatial imagination.

2

Absolute Kinography: Vertov's Cine-Race Across the Soviet Universe

'I am kino-eye. I am a builder. I have placed you,
whom I've created today, in an extraordinary room,
which did not exist until just now when I also created it.'

Dziga Vertov[1]

In 1925, two state corporations, Gostorg, the state foreign trade monopoly, and Mossovet, the Moscow City Council, commissioned promotional films to popularize their 'successes' during the New Economic Policy (NEP) years.[2] Vertov, known for his special penchant for grasping reality in a novel way, was invited to direct both films. The Mossovet commission resulted in *Stride, Soviet!* [*Shagai, Sovet!*, 1926], which critics nicknamed '2,000 Metres in the Land of the Bolsheviks' (allegedly, a title for export). Its brief survey of Soviet history from poverty and the destruction of war to stabilization and functional water closets ascribed the role of the agent of motion to the Moscow Council.[3] While the leadership in the capital was shown as having a transformative effect on the whole country, it was the Gostorg commission and its generous budget that allowed the crew to film beyond Moscow and to produce an ambitious all-Soviet cine-race.

The director, the studio, and Gostorg all sought to make the most of this partnership. Reviving his earlier plans for a network of Kinoks to survey the Soviet Union's transformation, Vertov intended to use Gostorg's

40

money to establish a new way of filming Soviet space. Gostorg wanted the best resources to promote its image and sought to gain credibility from Vertov's concept of capturing 'life as it is' on film. Initially, Gostorg wanted Mezhrabpom-Rus, at the time the best equipped studio in the Soviet Union, to produce the film, but Vertov found the choice of a studio with a 'commercial' reputation distressing and he successfully lobbied to transfer the production to the newly established Kultkino.[4] In turn, Kultkino saw the commission as a chance to boost its portfolio and improve its financial standing.

The Gostorg commission resulted in Vertov's spatially most ambitious film, *A Sixth Part of the World* (1926).[5] Far from being a run-of-the-mill, promotional film, it became a race to film the entire Soviet universe stretching eastward, northward, and southward, creating a highly ambiguous image of a 'union of borderlands'. The film earned Vertov both high praise as an 'epic cine-poet' and vilification as an 'exoticism-hunter'.[6] Introducing *A Sixth Part of the World* from concept to reception, this chapter focuses on the new conceptual and visual modes it implemented to represent the national minorities within the Soviet landscape, and argues that, despite the film's circumvented distribution, it launched a powerful new visual protocol for portraying the Soviet Union.

Dziga Vertov's fascination with travel and movement can be seen in his earliest works. His personal travelogue began when he moved from his native Białystok, in the former Pale of Settlement, to Petrograd and Moscow.[7] Having embarked on a career in film, he visited numerous sites of the Civil War, exhibiting newsreels and films using an improvised distribution network of cine-trains and travelling projectors [*peredvizhki*].[8] Following a period of producing and editing *Kino-Nedelia* newsreels and extensive travel across the country with cine-trains, Vertov launched a new film journal, *Kino-Pravda*, which became a testing ground for his evolving ideas on the structure and function of newsreels.[9] Developing a new prototype by using Constructivist editing principles, Vertov experimented with the spatial representation of the newly established political entity, the Soviet Union.

Following several earlier attempts, the film journal *Kino-Pravda 19* (1924), with the subtitle 'Black Sea – Arctic – Ocean Moscow. A movie camera race Moscow–Arctic Ocean', presented 'cine-race' as a new film form

uniting space via movement. The journal opened with a dynamic tracking shot, merging the movement of the train and the camera into a single
space-traversing action. Subsequent scenes with elements of found footage
included uncredited fragments from Flaherty's *Nanook of the North*. The
parallel editing of the Inuit (from *Nanook*) in the US with the Samoeds
(present-day Nenets) and the Voguls (present-day Mansi) in the Soviet
Union focused on 'borderland' populations with traditional lifestyles, presenting a generic North defined by remoteness, but connected to a greater
spatial whole. Creating a unified Soviet screen space permeated by the idea
of unity amid diversity, Vertov made the audience both an element of his
films and a part of the film network distributing 'film-things'.

Advertising the Soviet Universe

Both Kultkino studio and Vertov hoped to use the money from the Gostorg
commission to make not one, but several films. Originally, Vertov planned
a host of releases for 1926, including, under working titles, *Mostorg*,
Radio-Pravda, *Mossovet*, *Gostorg*, *The USSR*, and *Lenin*.[10] As Gostorg's
patronage created the conditions for an unprecedented scope of expeditions across the Soviet Union, Vertov intended to record footage for a travelogue across the USSR parallel with Gostorg's promotional film. Initially
envisaged under the title, *Man with a Movie Camera* [*Chelovek s kinoapparatom*], the cross-country film was described in his diary as a survey of
attitudes towards cinema and filming. One scene mentioned in his 1925
plans utilized a mobile film projector to show recordings of Lenin in the
Far North.[11] Vertov's notebooks contain ambitious plans to develop the
journey across the Soviet Union into a series of 'film-things' under the
general title, 'The USSR.'[12]

Making use of Gostorg's initial benevolence, Vertov also planned to
expand the geographic scope of the film east and west beyond the Soviet
borders. Preparatory steps for filming in China were taken in 1925, shortly
after diplomatic relations were established between the two countries.
The release of *The Great Flight* in 1925 demonstrated audiences' interest
in China, but Vertov's crew was deported from Xinjiang on suspicion of
espionage.[13] Their journey to Western Europe was cancelled due to budget
constraints, forcing Vertov to rely on found footage. He noted that the lack

of foreign material damaged the original concept, which was a 'film about our relationship with other states', and made it instead 'locked in a circle of internal digestion', which forced him to search for a new film structure.[14]

Gostorg's budget soon became a bailout for other undermined studio projects and therefore could not accommodate all of Vertov's ambitious plans.[15] However, even if the territory covered by Vertov's 'scouts' during the expeditions of 1925–26 did not match the director's initial ambitions, the extent of their travels was unprecedented in Soviet cinema. By March 1926, footage had been recorded in Novaya Zemlya, Pechora, the Northern Urals, Siberia, Turkestan, the Crimea, Novorossiisk, Kuban and Dagestan.[16] Yet delays in obtaining both equipment and funds created recurrent scheduling problems, forcing Vertov to constantly rethink the structure of the film:

> When there was enough time, we spoke about one cine-race on a circular itinerary with two cameramen. When we had less time left, we considered two summer and two winter itineraries with two cameramen for all four journeys. Further delays forced us to send a third cameraman to Novaya Zemlya. It is currently obvious that the filming of the circular race will turn, under the force of circumstances, into the 'radial' [*luchevaia*] race, which I did not favour since I originally considered our available staff and did not want to lose on quality.[17]

While the amount of footage for the film on the USSR grew steadily, Vertov fell behind or missed many scheduled Gostorg filming activities due to the belated arrival of the cameramen who were filming elsewhere. Coming under increasing pressure from both the studio and the commissioner, he considered using amateur 'correspondents' to capture the necessary footage. However, this attempt to see the world filmed 'through the eyes of the millions' could not solve the film's growing problems.[18]

In response to many mounting challenges, Vertov continuously reframed the film's focal point. His early notes contemplate the role of the state trade monopoly in relation to consumer 'luxuries'. He condemns the seductive pleasures of consumerism in an imaginary address to Soviet small clerks and 'bohemians':

> You dream about a foreign tie, and you about laces for your blouse. You are typing a business letter and all of a sudden you

insert: Coty [...] as if you think only about that. If we listened to you, typists, and to you, assistant directors and actors, hanging around Kultkino, we would flood Moscow and other Soviet towns with such rubbish [*drebeden*][...] Ladies' underwear or a tractor? This is the title we should have given to the film we are currently making.[19]

This appeal to reject personal comfort, redefined as excessive luxury, carried the imprint of early Soviet avant-garde asceticism, clashing with the consumerist NEP policies.[20] However, Vertov did not discard the market and publicity altogether. In March 1923, he wrote an outline for an article 'Kinoreklama' (Advertising Films),[21] which contained an elaborate classification system – from a 'most elementary advertisement' to a 'special-effects advertisement', a 'cartoon advertisement' and even a 'detective advertisement'.[22] Beyond cinemas, these films were to be screened using specially-equipped film-cars, film-steamers, cinema-barges and even cine-automobiles which would 'work on call, wherever, whenever needed'.[23] In the spirit of the NEP, advertisement became the engine of trade and industry, forcing Vertov to answer the question, 'What can be advertised?' in the most decisive way:

> Everything – from lottery loan tickets to hair-growth ointment [...] and back again, from 'Sanagri' tooth powder to the Donbass coal industry. Gostorg, syndicates, trusts, cooperative agencies, private individuals – all can advertise their products on the screen, choosing the most suitable form of film advertising. Traction and oil engines, tractors, sages, furniture, footwear, pianos, textiles, headgear – everything can be broadcast through the special-effects film, can be made amusing by a humorous film, witty by a cartoon or exciting in a detective film.[24]

The tension between exerting the power of advertisement and condemning the practices of consumerism was resolved by channelling all efforts towards advertising a political concept framed by market logic. Vertov was commissioned to create one of the paradoxes of the 'regulated economy' – the promotion of a state monopoly which disregarded the preferences of individual consumers in favour of the 'interests of the state'. Advancing such a controversial concept required creativity and rhetorical mastery. While it is anyone's guess how the films would have turned out had Vertov had the chance to realize his concept of 'The USSR' separately from the Gostorg promotion, the ultimate solution of combining the two ideas in one film was a creative child of necessity.

In the final version of the film, the anti-consumerist drive is transformed into an attack on petty-bourgeois tastes relocated to the 'West', where Vertov projects the consumerist 'bacchanalia'. By contrast, the Soviet universe sells its goods to purchase machinery and to further increase production with the help of an extensive Gostorg network. Vertov's emphasis on the communication network paradoxically resembles that promoted by the British Empire Marketing Board, which envisaged itself as 'a pedagogic project intended to completely overhaul the ways of the colonised'.[25] The Soviet state trade monopoly represents a chain connecting countryside producers with the industrial world abroad, and features the Soviet Union as an organic part of the global economy. Gostorg thus becomes a synecdoche for the wholesale promotion of the ideological and political foundations of the new regime. Hence, while corresponding to the mercantile ideology of NEP, the unorthodox idea of 'selling' the image of the developing Soviet Union to the broadest possible audience required, from the director's point of view, an equally revolutionary visual form.

Vertov's original optimism with regard to the scope and quality of production waned by the end of 1925. He qualified these difficulties as a 'paper mess' [chekharda bumag],[26] which turned the cine-race into a hurdle race. On 22 October 1925, Vertov noted:

> For two months I have not been working on the 'cine-race.' For about four months I have not been paid. The expedition, Zotov, to be precise, is not going to Astrakhan. The same with Bezhetsk. Since 20 October, Kaufman has been filming without my guidance, without filters, without lenses and possibly without willingness, just out of despair. Benderskii is asking for money and filters. Shurka Lemberg asks for a camera and money. The trip abroad fell through. The footage filmed by Zotov in Dagestan is still in danger of being destroyed. [...] The situation is extremely confusing. Gostorg is also not very

45

Figure 2.1 Advertisement for *A Sixth Part of the World* in *Sovetskii ekran* (1926). Mapping and cataloguing as structuring principles of the film.

decisive. They are only talking to Kultkino. Anyway, no matter how you push an empty cash desk, nothing can be squeezed out. […] Will I find the strength to pull myself together, to channel my own blood to the drained blood of the film and to defend it from a growing number of its already triumphant enemies? Kino-Eye is in danger.[27]

In December 1925, frustrated by constant delays, financial difficulties and lack of equipment, Alexander Lemberg left the film crew. In March 1926, Vertov wrote yet another request to Nikolai Baklin, the Head of Production and Commercial Director of Kultkino, asking him to send Kaufman and himself abroad for one month to collect material.[28] The request was never approved. To make matters worse, in April 1926, a series of dismissals and arrests took place in film circles. Baklin was among those arrested on charges of mismanagement and sabotage. Oleg Kapchinskii researched the relationship of the secret services with cinema in the 1920s. He interprets the 1926–27 'Film Affair' as part of an ongoing struggle between the All-Union State Political Administration (Ob'edinennoe gosudarstvennoe politicheskoe upravlenie, OGPU, and Dzerzhinskii, the head of the Soviet secret police and ODSK) with Narkompros (and its head, Anatolii Lunacharskii) for the upper hand in cinema affairs.[29] While the political charges were soon lifted from all of the accused, Vertov's ability to carry out his work became considerably more difficult due to changes to the studio's management, related uncertainties, and the reform of the studio system which led to Kultkino's demise in 1926.

New Imperial Catalogue: Surveying Ethnic Bodies

Sovkino took over the Goskino and Kultkino premises and released the feature-length film *A Sixth Part of the World* in December 1926. The film did not in the least resemble an advertising film; it combined the ideas originally reserved for 'The USSR' cine-race with the promotion of the state trade monopoly. The footage for this composite film was recorded by numerous cameramen, but some material was borrowed or taken from other film-makers.[30] Though Vertov's cameramen often worked in unfavourable conditions that did not match the original filming plan, they nevertheless brought to the screen a new credo of the Soviet newsreel and non-fiction. With its radical angles, enhanced panoramas, extreme close-ups, and rhythmic editing pace, *A Sixth Part of the World* is a manifesto and an open-ended catalogue of the new ways of filming. As such, it developed a visual vocabulary for representing Soviet unity and revised the concept of the Soviet travel film. It was called, at once, a monumental, epic, lyrical, and poetic vision of the Soviet Union.

The first reel of the film represents the external, alien, distant 'land of Capital.' It opens with an aerial shot from uncredited, found footage and is accompanied by the intertitle, 'I see'. The shot establishes a sense of global domination: the visualization of the utopian-conquest drive of revolutionary culture. The aerial shot, the epitome of a 'global vision', emphasized the inherent connection between airplane, camera and reconnaissance established during World War I.[31] In the 1920s, the airplane was the most modern means of conquering space, which, as Scott Palmer wrote, 'overturned conventional notions of time and space, compelling young and old, citizen and statesman alike, to reconsider their relationship with the natural order.'[32] Martin Stollery has underlined the role of aerial cinematography in confirming colonial tropes by 'marking out the boundaries, which separate and connect the Western and the non-Western world.'[33] In a different context, Karen Frome has discussed the use of aerial photography and its ethical implications during the Italian colonial enterprises of the 1930s, stressing that '[t]he aerial perspective, like that of the cartographer, objectifies the target, making mass destruction psychologically viable.'[34]

In Soviet cinema, too, aerial shots mapped, ordered and expressed control over the landscape. Emma Widdis has dated the Soviet 'cinematic adulation of the airplane' to the mid-1930s, contrasting it to the earlier 'linear mode' of cinematic explorations exemplified by train rides.[35] However, in 1923 *Kino-Fot* had already praisingly reported on the aerial recordings of cameraman Zheliabuzhskii, who mounted a camera on a military airplane in place of a machine gun.[36] Viktor Pertsov has interpreted an aerial perspective of the first Soviet travelogue, *The Great Flight*, not only as a radically new way of seeing, but also as a way to demonstrate technological and political dominance:

> In *The Great Flight*, two opposite cultures constantly clash their foreheads. Soviet airplanes impregnate the masses of the peoples of the East not only politically, but technically. This union of two bases [*dvukh nachal*] is a historical symbol.
>
> It would be desirable to lift the whole of peasant Russia up in the air and shake it a little. It would help to eradicate

patriarchal ways of thinking [...] [In order] to help feeble, verbal propaganda, special film-hangars should be created all over
the country, where the new generation would learn the audacity
of flying.[37]

A Sixth Part of the World challenges 'Western' aerial dominance. The establishing shot sets up a global optical domination. The bird's-eye view of the
reconnaissance aircraft creates a setting wherein the 'West' is positioned
as an ideological battlefield to be surveyed, dominated and transformed.
The establishing shot demonstrates the vertical taming and controlling
perspective present in Vertov's early works, and challenges the relationship
with the West as a technical and industrial donor. The drive to 'outwest' the
West[38] is fulfilled by reversing the assumed hierarchy and locating the audience in a position of visual and conceptual dominance. Vertov's manifesto,
which ascribed the camera's perfected mechanical eye the ability 'to ascend
with an airplane' and to show an unseen and inexperienced world, received
a visual embodiment.[39]

The film's establishing aerial shot is followed by images of a 'bourgeois'
party, a jazz performance, a dance hall and the daily routine of a steel
factory – contrasting leisure and work, spending and construction, and
the exploiters with the exploited. In contrast to linear expedition films,
wherein a forward-moving itinerary helps to create a unity of time and
space at each particular moment, Vertov sought to ascribe symbolic significance to spaces, identifying them not by their geographical locations
but by their political and economic conditions. His 'World of Capital'
represented an economic system which loosely covered Western Europe
and the US. The structure of the scene is reminiscent of Vertov's unreal-
ized études, 'Hands,' 'Legs,' 'Eyes'.[40] Demonstrating the Constructivist
potential of cinema, Vertov 'take[s] the most agile hands of one, the fast-
est and most graceful legs of another.' Yet he creates not 'a man more perfect than Adam'[41], but his exact opposite: the people of the passé world
of capitalism. Their fragmented world is opposed to the image of a new
Soviet unity.

The image of the Soviet Union – shown as a site of spatial variety,
economic diversity, and cultural richness – is created through multiple
lists, both highly determinant and open-ended. Analysing archiving

principles, Ernst van Alphen has pointed out that lists 'seem to miss the possibility of rendering subjective vision'.[42] Indeed, although Vertov's lists are presented by the first-person account of an omnipresent, invisible, and God-like observer, the 'non-character-bound focalization in this film strengthens the idea of objectivity of the record, emphasizing the distance between the observer and the observed – between "I" and "you"'.[43] Produced in the heyday of indigenization, identified by Hirsch as a crucial moment in the 'conceptual conquest of lands and peoples',[44] *A Sixth Part of the World* embraces Soviet federalism, transforming it into a new unity based on a paradigmatic declaration of collective rights addressing the whole population of the USSR:

> You, / who bathe / your sheep in the surf of the sea /
> And you, / who bathe your sheep in a brook /
> You / in Dagestan villages /
> You / in a Siberian virgin forest /
> You / Careful not to get lost /
> You / in the tundra /
> On the Pechora river /
> On the ocean /
> And you / who have overthrown the power of capital in October /
> Who have opened the road to new life /
> For the nations earlier oppressed in this country /
> You / You Tatars / You / You Buryats / Uzbeks / Kalmyks /
> Khakkass /
> Mountaineers of the Caucasus /
> You, Komi people of the Komi region /
> And you, of a distant village /
> You / taking part in the deer race / and you /
> playing goat polo [*kozlodrańe*]
> [...]
> You, suckling at your mother's breast /
> And you, hale one hundred-year-old /
> [...]
> You, the owners of the Soviet land / Hold in your hands
> a sixth part of the world.[45]

Figure 2.2 Still from *A Sixth Part of the World* (1926). Soviet ethnographic catalogue: 'You, the Buryats'.

The fast-paced montage gives the viewer a glimpse of figures and faces
in different, mostly outdoor, settings. The visual list represents an ethnographic taxonomy which contains mixed classification principles. Along
with nationality (Tatars, Buryats, Uzbeks, Kalmyks, Khakkass), Vertov lists
localities (on the Pechora river), age (hale, one hundred-year-old), and
practices (bathing the sheep), with occasional markers of exoticism reinforced in the intertitles ('you who use your feet to do the laundry'; 'you,
who are eating your venison raw'; 'you playing goat polo'). While the 'taxonomic impulse' of Vertov's work exemplifies features shared with the early
travelogues, its editing and intertitles reverse the traditional power axis as
minorities are shown as masters and owners, rather than passive recipients
of the mastering gaze.

The list of nationalities is intentionally open, allowing the viewer to
imagine a growing community that subscribes to Vertov's charter of collective rights. At the same time, appearing as part of the 'Soviet project',
like items in a collection as opposed to items in storage – assuming that

51

a collection 'is dependent on principles or organization and categorization, whereas storage is not' – they acquire significance as a unity.[46] As van Alphen argues, 'when the objects in a collection are listed, the resulting ordered structure is no longer inherent to the collection but imposed on it.'[47] 'United borderlands' offered a radically new ordering of Soviet space.

This visual all-Soviet catalogue also includes images of an audience watching the film in a cinema, featuring a self-reflective gesture of an active community-builder and emphasizing the role of the cinema as the 'integrator' of the new, unified space.[48] These images extend the community of Vertov's addressees and highlight the role of cinema in transforming its audience. The pronoun 'you' is central to the understanding of the principles of community building. While Vertov challenges internal hierarchies and unifies culturally diverse groups into a single entity, the intertitles play the role of the omnipresent and omnipotent 'voice-of-god', which mirrors the hierarchical power relations of the establishing aerial shot. Elizabeth Papazian has argued that Vertov 'seeks to transform individuals through the participatory surveillance' of the Kino-Eye.[49] While the film seeks to erase the border between the observers and the observed, it simultaneously reinstates the power of the camera to bring such 'communities of vision' to life.

The image of the Soviet Union as a mosaic of exotic subjects draws on the extensive imperial visual legacy. Analysing the visual representation of imperial subjects in eighteenth-century Russia, Elena Vishlenkova has examined albums from that period containing engravings that visualized, for the first time, a multinational empire 'stretching from the Lopars to the Kamchadals'.[50] She points out the importance of ethnic bodies as a form-defining element in space, catalogued hierarchically in imaginary geographic landscapes and sometimes engaged in various activities such as horseracing, hunting, dog-sledge riding or shamanic dance.[51] Further reproductions of these patterns in different media, from porcelain figures to maps, facilitated the survival of these visual topoi into Soviet times.

With his vision of a new unity of multinational borderlands, Vertov sought to refashion the centralized imperial legacy by underlining a horizontal communications network. Vertov's film omits references to the centre, addressing mainly the peoples of the Soviet borderlands, in contrast with the mainstream image of a centralized Soviet Union.[52] The film also challenges the original meaning of 'one sixth of the world', a meta-phor introduced in Sergei Esenin's poem, 'Rus' Sovetskaia' ('Soviet Russia', 1924). Esenin's notion of Rus' refers to a homogeneous Russian space – the disappearing, rural-patriarchal world of traditional culture.[53] While Esenin elegiacally opposes himself to 'other youngsters who sing other songs', Vertov rejects idealized homogeneity and, instead, stresses a new, unified mosaic stretching 'from the Kremlin to the Chinese border [...] from the beacon beyond the Arctic Circle to the Caucasian mountains'. The realm shown in *A Sixth Part of the World* is not only geographically heterogene-ous, but also culturally fragmented, wherein the Kremlin walls become one geographical reference among many.

Network Community:
Gostorg and the New Soviet Unity

In contrast to the enclosed spaces in the film's section on 'Capital', Vertov depicts Soviet sites as vast outdoor spaces; fields, rivers, mountains, seas, oceans, forests and other natural vistas constitute the new entity. This pre-sented Vertov with the challenge of creating a unified Soviet landscape. Sergei Tretiakov, a journalist and playwright affiliated with the *LEF* cir-cles of left-wing radical artists, described the landscape as 'nature seen through the eyes of a consumer', and saw the relationship with landscape as overtly possessive, capitalist, and non-Soviet. The Soviet avant-garde saw in nature a 'visual ballast' awaiting transformation through industrial intervention (see Chapters 6 and 7). Vertov's take on nature and moder-nity was to create a composite unity of diversified landscapes through the idea of movement; movement provided the main principle in the con-struction of unity, and served as the main source of thematic and visual rhyming in editing.

The unity of the mosaic world is created through montage, exemplify-ing Vertov's 'interval theory' derived from the contrapuntal structure of a musical phrase: 'The organization of movements is the organization of intervals in each phrase. Each phrase has its rise, peak, and decline. A film is, therefore, composed of phrases [shots] as each phrase is composed of intervals.'[54] The reviewers unanimously pointed to the unusual rhythmic organization of the film, described on various occasions as 'musical' or 'poetic'.[55] Yet Vertov remained loyal to Constructivist principles even when falling short of footage.

While the second reel of the film is structured by the address 'you', calling on the variety of nationalities and ethnicities of the Soviet universe, the third reel concentrates on the possessive pronoun 'yours', which visually enumerates the natural and industrial resources in the possession of the Soviet, collective owner. 'Yours' reinforces the cataloguing principle with intertitles paralleled with images of the enumerated resources: 'Your factories / your plants / your oil / your cotton / and sheep / wool / your butter / fish / your flax / your tobacco'.[56] However, the enumeration of the collective riches does not translate into individual prosperity. Instead, these riches are declared export goods set to cross vast spaces in order to reach their foreign buyers. It is here that Gostorg finally enters the narrative.

The fourth reel of the film focuses on the role Gostorg plays as the provider of the vital communication infrastructure, without which the country's treasures would remain scattered and isolated, bringing no benefit to anyone. The communication network is introduced in the first shot of the fourth reel through a close-up of the rolling wheels of a steam engine, a favourite modernist image, and the intertitles: 'Export goods are moved along all the routes of the Soviet land'. Gostorg emerges as the engine and the demiurge of this perpetuum mobile. It triggers the union's motion and secures its smooth functioning and further development: 'Where no roads exist at all / where in the span of hundreds of miles / you may not encounter a single soul / through severe frosts / through the snow-drifted limitless tundra / they are moving towards the nearest post of State Trade / to deliver their pelts / to be exported to the lands of Capital.' In one scene, the intertitles and image merge into a single composition; the large letters of Gostorg overlap with the railways, literally turning it into the primary means of communication within the USSR.

An obvious fascination with a variety of local customs coexists in *A Sixth Part of the World* with a linear, progressive worldview. According to Vlada Petrić, Vertov differentiated the functions of the recorded image within the film: 'Vertov wanted the screen image of man to be truthful to his prototype in reality on an ontological level, while the new vision of man (different from that existing in reality) had to be conceived on the

structural level.'[57] A combination of reality footage and visionary structure is achieved through editing and intertitles. Advocating 'active seeing',
'Vertov argued that the film-maker should organize life facts into new
cinematic structures, which would reflect his own ideology.'[58] In this cinematic reality, 'the spectacular value of each distinct image in its relations
to all the others engaged in the "montage battle" becomes crucial'.[59] Thus,
the image/text construct allows him to create a desired 'film-thing' with
utopian dimensions.

This utopia is enhanced by the use of special effects: the speeded-up
motion of the first reel represents the agony of 'Capital', while the abundance of the Soviet Union is illustrated by the use of split screens and
superimpositions in scenes portraying factories, agricultural technology,
harvesting, as well as the extensive Gostorg network. Movement across
space is complemented by anticipated future changes. In the final reel of
the film, Vertov marks some cultural practices as belonging to the world of
the past, which can only temporarily survive in the present. The intertitles
envision a break with old customs, the arrival of new forms of media and
the triumph of technological progress:

> I see the woman has cast away her *yashmak* [veil] / another
> woman educates the women of the East / a young Communist
> Samoed is reading the *Northerner* newspaper / Buryats and
> Mongols are reading the *Buryat-Mongol Pravda* / Mongol chil-
> dren join the Young Pioneers / The deer-herds are assisted by the
> Polar laboratory / Irrigation canals / help the waterless steppes /
> The electric bulb illuminates the peasant hut / the reading hut /
> and the radio-report / The Volkhov electric plant.[60]

The edited sequence illustrates each statement with a short visual account
directly following the intertitles, using the indexical photographic potential
to construct a visionary world of the future. Having presented the Soviet
Union as a multinational state with countless natural resources, the film
closes with the centrifugal expansion of the Soviet ideology and economic
model, spilling over the borders of the Soviet Union to incorporate the
rest of the world, from the West to its colonies. The film's finale points to
changes in the world at large; the intertitles introduce footage of mass protests in Germany and colonial travel films as support for the Soviet cause
and a sign of ongoing global transformations.[61]

Was Vertov's film, avowedly emancipatory and anticolonial, able to fully escape the colonial gaze that dominated early cinematic representations of 'exotic' peoples and places? Approaching colonialism not as a fixed practice but, rather, as a set of rhetorical *topoi* used in fiction as much as in non-fiction, allows for a new reading of power relations.[62] Although Vertov's film does not square well with the notion of the colonial 'other', it can be revisited from the perspective of colonial discourse that, as David Spurr points out, bears 'an inherent confusion of identity and difference, a simultaneous avowal and disavowal of its own authority. ... [it] makes for a rich profusion of rhetorical forms, which often clash with one another, and yet, which all enter equally into the matrix of relations of power that characterizes the colonial situation.'[63] While Vertov emphasized the equality of the represented subjects, repeatedly portraying the world on behalf of and from the perspective of ethnically diverse subjects, an analysis of the camera gaze demonstrates that his modernist ideology incorporates a set of colonial topoi.

The fifth reel of the film provides a quintessential example of the ambiguous engagement of Soviet modernism with colonial aesthetics and exemplifies Vertov's interpretation of the nationality question. In the Far North, Nenets (referred to as Samoeds) are filmed motionlessly sitting on the deserted ocean shore. The image of static Samoeds carries a heavily loaded message embodying remoteness and backwardness. The natives of the Far North are implicitly contrasted to the modern and further modernizing population of the Soviet Union, evoking the imperial hierarchy by portraying the peoples of the North at the bottom of the civilizational ladder. It was not the first time Nenets had appeared on the screen. Already in the early 1910s, a number of travelogues featured their everyday life and customs.[64] Apart from cinematographic interest, in the nineteenth and early twentieth centuries the 'Samoed Question' was a topic of intensive discussion of the public policy necessary to 'support, develop or change a group of people defined by their primitiveness'.[65] Vertov introduces the Samoeds as living in a semi-mythical place 'where the sun stays in the sky for half a year and the night lasts for the other half.' Waiting for the ship, which once a year brings necessary food and other goods in exchange for furs, the Samoeds are shown as fully dependent on external supplies. Their time spent on the ship is presented as their sole contact with the external, distant, and 'progressive' culture.

Vertov's spatial representations reflect the legacy of the nineteenth-century, colonial travel accounts introduced by Mary Louise Pratt as a three-fold rhetorical structure: 'The landscape is first aestheticized, then it is invested with a density of meaning intended to convey its material and symbolic richness, and finally it is described so as to subordinate it to the power of the speaker'.[66] The appropriation of the landscape is first under-taken by the camera, whose panoramic high-angle shots establish power relations before they are introduced in the intertitles. The power relations are clearly unequal; the Samoeds are dependent, backward, and merged into nature, and the Soviet world enters their patriarchal life as a techno-logically advanced, progressive and modern force 'conquering' the space through industrial goods and technology, while also bringing ideological dominance. As the Samoeds listen to a gramophone recording (allegedly of Lenin's speech), the film creates a sender-recipient, active-passive relation-ship, establishing a cultural hierarchy and a normative direction for both technological and ideological development.[67] The scene resonates with a structurally similar episode from *Nanook of the North* (Robert Flaherty, USA, 1922), wherein an Inuit family is introduced to the gramophone. Yet rather than being awed by the technological 'miracle', the Samoeds appear subsumed by the ideology of the Soviet 'civilizing mission', which is inherently close to the legacy of French colonialism with its emphasis on cultural superiority.[68] At the same time, the Samoeds, whose life is shown conditioned by external supplies, feature as a necessary element in the Soviet Union's economic machine; they 'advance the future' by trading furs for the machines needed for the country's development.

The final reel unifies all entities exposed to the total vision from an imaginary, aerial perspective:

> I see you
> the Black Sea
> and you, the sea frozen at the Baltic Coasts
> the ships stuck in the ice
> and you
> the ice-breaker Lenin
> who breaks the ice with her breast
> we break the way…

for our ships
to trade our grain…
to trade our furs…
for machines that are necessary for us.[69]

A Sixth Part of the World channelled Vertov's earlier experiments with creating a unified image of space through a cine-race towards reformatting the image of the Soviet Union as a new, fully surveyed entity. It is in this sense that we can understand Vertov's film as 'more than a film … [it was] the next stage after the concept of "cinema" itself'.[70]

The relationship of the camera with the filmed subjects remains ambiguous. The film features both intrusion into private spaces and domination over the masses via close-ups and high-angled panoramas. It also creates an equal 'camera-subject' relationship that gives the filmed subjects their right to an autonomous gaze. The distance between the camera and its focal points alternates as the camera demonstrates various degrees of mobility. While stylistic discrepancies could partially be explained by the individual styles of the numerous cameramen working on the film, the ambiguity is also inherent in the structure of this visionary film, hailing diversity and awaiting its 'overcoming'.

Although Vertov's plan to initiate a series of films on the USSR fell through, a number of shorts on different minorities were released along with *A Sixth Part of the World*, such as *The Tungus* [*Tungusy*], *Dagestan* and *The Hunting and Reindeer Practices in the Komi Region* [*Okhota i olenevodstvo v oblasti Komi*] (all 1927). *Dagestan*, edited by Sergei Liamin (see Chapter 6), repeats Vertov's structure of a cine-race within the borders of one republic. *The Tungus*, a one-reel sketch filmed by Petr Zotov and edited by Elizaveta Svilova, zoomed in on one of the minorities in Northeast Siberia (after 1931 referred to by the ethnonym Evenk)[71] to present a conventional 'ethnographic' collective portrait. The film introduced its anonymous protagonists as medium close-ups of 'types' of men, women and children, which were followed by demonstrations of habitat, construction of a tent, cooking, hunting and trading activities. The collective Tungus portrait emphasized regular interaction with state traders. Bearing residual structural elements of the Gostorg promotion, the short includes a visit to the state cooperative and features a Tungus hunter trading furs for manufactured goods. Originally shot to empha-size the extension of the Gostorg network, the film presents the new trad-ing 'contact zone' as mutually beneficial, and, at the same time, it seals the visual imagery of a developmental hierarchy that resonates with Vertov's portrayal of the Samoeds.

By contrast, *The Hunting and Reindeer Practices in the Komi Region* does not have a well-defined structure. This sloppily edited film shows a range of Komi activities from hunting to deer-racing and uses numerous repetitions. The film includes an image of a man setting off for the hunt accompanied by his dog. The same shot, which here is presented as straight-forward and unambiguous, was included in *A Sixth Part of the World* with the intertitle 'someone departs into the distant icy unknown', which led Shklovskii to criticize the film for turning an indexical sign into a symbol. While the 'auxiliary' films did not receive much attention, the release of *A Sixth Part of the World* and the film's inherent ambiguities evoked a con-troversial reception among film professionals and broader audiences.

Figure 2.3 Still from *The Tungus* (1927). A composite shot demonstrating the ben-efits of state cooperation: the goods exchanged for pelts.

Rhetorical Battles over Modernity and Backwardness

Vertov's hopes that *A Sixth Part of the World* could not possibly encounter criticism within the borders of the USSR since 'both the opponents and the supporters of the film are also its participants', remained wishful thinking.[72] Sovkino, which had taken over Kul'tkino's productions, released the film in December 1926. The union of 'exotic minorities' presented as the masters of the Soviet Union, evoked a controversial reception. Many praised the film as a formal and thematic achievement.[73] Critic Izmail Urazov, an early and enthusiastic viewer, stated that the film 'has managed, perhaps for the first time, to show all at once the whole sixth part of the world; it has found the words to force us to be amazed, to feel the whole power, and strength, and unity; it has managed to infect the viewer too with lofty emotions, to throw him [sic] into the screen'.[74]

The professional audience was polarized. While newsreel veteran Grigorii Boltianskii did not hesitate to declare it the birth of a new film type, 'a poem about the Earth',[75] another critic saw in this work no more than 'the first remotely significant ethnographic and newsreel film'.[76] In January 1927 a series of critical articles, often written anonymously or under pseudonyms, appeared in the press. Some such articles deemed the 'ethnographic' material as the main value of the film, while others were disturbed by what they perceived as signs of Soviet backwardness.[77] Praising the authenticity, spontaneity, and genuineness of the recorded episodes, reviewers criticized Vertov's editing as 'pretentious, fanciful, and obscure'.[78] Some even accused Vertov for being behind the times, stating, 'It is absurd and ridiculous to believe that the example of deer, pigs, goats, and those who "slash live goats" and "drink warm blood" could be a convincing construction of socialism'.[79] In a similar vein, other critics protested the film's 'unnecessary exoticism' and claimed, 'Samoeds, furs, camels, and Uzbek robes are not the core of our economy'.[80]

Thus, criticism was concentrated either on the film's formal/aesthetic aspects or on its content. The former targeted its complex structure and fast montage sequences, lamenting the film's 'oratorical repetitions', 'monotonous intertitles', 'moving photographs', and misplaced 'artistic nature photography'.[81] The latter focused on the schematic portrayal of both the capitalist system and the Soviet world, and on the absence of achievements within the Soviet Union. Osip Beskin was particularly critical of the 'frivolous game of contrasting the working life of the peoples of the USSR with fox-trotting Europe [...] failing to give us a sense of all the power and the huge scale of European technology, its individual trading apparatus'.[82]

In the West, Vertov's painstaking presentation of the Soviet economy as an essential part of the world remained unconvincing, even for Soviet sympathizers. In his overview of contemporary Soviet cinema, Walter Benjamin described *A Sixth Part of the World* as the 'filmic colonization of Russia' which he saw as 'misfiring'. He concluded, 'What [Vertov] has achieved, however, is the demarcation of Russia from Europe'.[83] In the Soviet Union, Vertov was further attacked for the absence of an approved script. The criticism ignored the conditions under which the film was produced and eclipsed Vertov's insistence on detailed planning, which 'does not stop from the very first observation to the finished film'.[84] The absence of a strong narrative coordinating the verbal and the visual was considered a cardinal sin.[85] The film's emphasis on a variety of cultural practices within the multinational state made it difficult to use the film to promote the generalized requirements of the five-year plan.

Vertov actively responded to the criticisms, although his prophesy about the 'great days, which are beating with hammers against the empty heads of our conservative comrades'[86] did not win his work any greater appreciation. While the representation of the multinational and resource-rich Soviet Union became a standard trope, the film itself did not receive broad distribution, which undermined Vertov's hope that 'by the tenth anniversary of October there must not be a single Tungus who has not seen *A Sixth Part of the World*'.[87] Vertov, on the pretext of budget overspending and refusal to follow the 'iron script' policy, was fired from Sovkino.[88]

After the curtailed distribution of *A Sixth Part of the World*, movement began to acquire different overtones for Vertov. Having lost his job at Sovkino, he joined the VUFKU studio in Kiev where he continued experimenting with travel motifs.[89] All three of the films he made in Ukraine – *The Eleventh Year* [*Odinnadtsatyi*, 1928], *Man with a Movie Camera* [*Chelovek s kinoapparatom*, 1929] and *Enthusiasm. Symphony of the Donbass* [*Entuziazm. Simfoniia Donbassa*, 1930] are 'cine-races' that unite diverse sites into a single film space.[90] *Man with a Movie Camera*, conceived during the filming of *A Sixth Part of the World*, became Vertov's most radical experiment in constructing a quintessentially urban Soviet space and placing cinematographic practices at the heart of modernity.

Upon his return from a trip to Western Europe, where *Enthusiasm* was screened with success, Vertov became one of the main targets of an organized state campaign against so-called 'documentarists'.[91] The campaign and its consequences deeply affected not only Vertov's career, but also his reflections on the role of non-fiction and his approach to film. The more the state restricted Vertov in physical and artistic terms, the more his filmed subjects began to move. In his last feature, *To You, Front!* [*Tebe, front!*, 1942], the camera crosses the vast steppes of Kazakhstan and united the West, North, Centre and East of the Republic in a single entity based on the pattern used in *A Sixth Part of the World*.

Vertov's 'laboratory of vision' produced an ideologically up-to-date and cinematographically original visualization of the Soviet Union. *A Sixth Part of the World* was followed by a growing number of expedition and ethnographic films aimed at familiarizing the audience with the ethnographic diversity of the Soviet Union, many of them commissioned and distributed by Sovkino, which strengthened its positions of near-monopoly on distribution by entering film production. Ironically, Vertov's primary critic, Sovkino Deputy Head Ilia Trainin, was formerly the editor of *Zhizn' natsional'nostei* (*Life of Nationalities*), and a long-term advocate of the multinational approach. He actively supported the 'ethnographic principle' of the organization of the Soviet Union and wrote extensively on the role of the Bolsheviks in transforming 'nonhistorical people' into nations.[92] While seemingly unappreciated in the short run, Vertov's vision of the multinational Soviet Union had a lasting impact which reverberated in dozens of cinematographic versions of the Soviet multinational landscape, some of which are considered in the following chapters.

3

Arctic Travelogues: Conquering the Soviet Far North

Imagine a huge, endless snowy plane, blinding the eyes
and stretching as far as the eye can see – to the right, to the left,
ahead and behind! Across the plane runs a man.
He runs easily – like a deer, like the wind.
His chest moves evenly and powerfully.
His sharp eyes look ahead. He hardly touches the earth
with his feet, so strongly and skilfully he pushes himself,
jumping, and he runs in amazing leaps stretching ten,
twenty, forty kilometres, which he covers without stopping…
That is how reindeer herders run in Chukotka.
And that is how Chukotka itself, in an immensely short period
of time, made an enormous leap from the most primitive
clan-based system to the most perfect state regime.

Dmitrii Nagishkin, *Chukotka Fairy Tales*[1]

A Sixth Part of the World depicted Nenets according to an existing representation pattern for the people of the Soviet Far North [*Krainii Sever*] –
as the beneficiaries of the technologically advanced and culturally
dynamic industrial centre. Early Soviet policies towards the numerically
small, indigenous populations of the North and Far East emerged from a
nineteenth-century Populist framework that saw cultural extinction as
a major problem.[2] Romantic primitivism fused with positivism resulted

63

in a peculiar way of viewing indigenous populations: a 'combination of the contemptible and the admirable' by which, as Yuri Slezkine put it, 'the native might be rebuked for eating rotten fish, abusing his wife, and killing his elderly parents, but he absolutely had to be praised for his simplicity, generosity, and stoicism'.[3] Thus, indigenous people were simultaneously presented as primitive societies awaiting modernization and as complex cultures in need of research and preservation.[4] Furthermore, contributing to the 'well-being' of indigenous peoples became an important element of the 'progressive' identity of the new state, distinguishing it from 'exploitative and destructive' imperial policies.[5]

In 1922, a Polar Subdivision was established within the People's Commissariat of Nationalities; two years later, after the dissolution of the latter, the Committee for the Assistance to Peoples of the Northern Borderlands, known also as the Committee of the North, was formed.[6] These state-run institutions faced the inherent challenge of combining the homogenizing effects of modernity with the anticipated 'flourishing' of cultures under socialism.[7] Anatolii Skachko, who left the Vostokkino board to take the position of Deputy Head of the Committee of the North, argued for an emancipatory and assimilationist policy:

> The Soviet government does not intend to preserve the peoples of the North in a primitive state, as rare ethnographic specimens, or to keep them as helpless charges of the state in special areas reserved for them and isolated from the rest of the world like zoological gardens. On the contrary, the government's goal is their all-around cultural and national development and their participation as equal [...] and active partners in the socialist economy.[8]

Cinematography, as the Bolsheviks well knew, provided a powerful tool for visualizing diversity and demonstrating desired developments and achievements. In the Soviet context, 'disappearing' minorities benefitted from the new regime, at least on screen. The landscape they inhabited was imagined as a complex composite: a territory rich in material resources and underdeveloped land, a home to endangered people, a vulnerable frontier and the futuristic venue for an anticipated economic miracle. The ethnographic principle underlining early Soviet reforms and attitudes towards the peoples of the North shaped the first visual representations of northern minorities.[9] Officially registered ethnicities were deemed the elementary units of a new socialist structure.

This chapter traces the transformation of the ethnographic principle in representing both landscapes and nationalities in the Far North. I compare representations of the Arctic in the works of Vladimir Erofeev, Olga Podgoretskaia, Vladimir Shneiderov and Mark Troianovskii as paradigmatic examples of the evolving representation of the Far North in Soviet cinema of the 1920–30s. In the scope of just a few years, the Far North transitioned from a borderland with a variety of exotic cultures to a harsh and resourceful frontier that provides a liminal space for testing individual qualities, and in which the image of the indigenous population is reduced to the operatic features of generic backwardness.

The Contact Zone: National Variety beyond the Arctic Circle

In 1927, Erofeev teamed up with experienced editor, Vera Popova,[10] to make the montage film *Beyond the Arctic Circle* [*Za poliarnym krugom*, 1927]. The film offered a paradigmatically different image of the North from that of *A Sixth Part of the World*. Erofeev and Popova used pre-Revolutionary film stock from the Khanzhonkov studio (an inexpensive way to make a film compared to Vertov's costly cine-poem). However, like Vertov, Erofeev and Popova sought to create an engaging travelogue for the wider audience and to advance the genre of travel film in Soviet cinema. The editors faced numerous challenges in constructing a coherent and ideologically intact narrative from footage recorded without their involvement and in a different historical context. Erofeev saw it as an opportunity to demonstrate that the geographical and ethnographic expedition films, which he celebrated in writing, could be a financially sustainable and ideologically beneficial genre in the Soviet Union.[11] Popova provided the inexperienced Erofeev with invaluable editorial know-how in creating their 'cultured' film.

Fedor Bremer, an experienced cinematographer who had worked on a number of high-budget productions including the historical drama *1812* (1913), as well as on newsreels about royalty, recorded the footage used in the film.[12] In 1913, crossing the Polar circle on the *Kolyma* to film the

Bering Strait, the Far East and Kamchatka, Bremer became trapped in the Arctic ice. Three lives were lost on that winter expedition and the whole crew suffered from scurvy. Upon his return, Bremer published accounts of his travels in Khanzhonkov's film magazine, *Pegas*. A few short films were edited from his footage, including the one-reel *Life of the North* [*Zhizn' severa*, 1914] showing the *Kolyma* and interaction between her crew and the indigenous circumpolar population. The bulk of the footage, however, had not been edited prior to Erofeev and Popova's undertaking.

Bremer's account in *Pegas* opened with the dramatic scene of the ship's encounter with an iceberg. Later, the text shows a meeting with the Chukchi, one of Russia's northernmost indigenous populations whose territory spans coastal areas and interior tundra. Bremer painted nature as hostile, powerful and overwhelming; in contrast, he described the locals as 'miniature, fragile, pitiful'.[13] Bremer's account of the ensuing exchange emphasized the cultural gap between the crew, the passengers and the indigenous population. His description of the physical appearance and material goods of the Chukchi further underscored the writer's contempt: '[their] eyes are not visible, in their place there are only narrow purulent slits [*gnoinye shchelki*]'. Furthermore, he described their objects of trade as 'useless goods: broken walrus fangs, dirty and worn-out seal skins, rather bad lemmings'.[14] The trade thus turned into the crew offering condescending 'rewards' of small portions of tobacco and tea to the locals. Bremer's text lumped together the northern ethnicities, contrasting them with what he saw as the superior, civilized white race:

> All these Yakuts, Yukagirs, Chukchi greatly value all the beautiful and useful objects that our ship brought to them. Listen to what a Chukcha is singing at a bear hunt: 'Bear, bear, I'll kill you, your fur will give me beads for adornment. The merchant will give me alcohol, threads, needles, axe, tobacco, tea, kerosene, bullets, primus stove, etc.' Could anyone possibly offer better praise to the cultural and technological progress of the great races?'[15]

Although he found the Far North 'repetitive' and 'monotonous', Bremer took his assignment seriously, and diligently filmed and photographed his long journey, assembling an extensive visual archive.[16] Appropriating

Bremer's gaze, Erofeev and Popova made use of the principles of 'created geography' to produce a holistic image of the North which preserved the editing pace of the early travelogues but invested the landscapes with new meanings.

The footage offered numerous narrative options. The editors thus needed to decide on the structuring principles for the film, and relied on commentary which Soviet film-makers routinely employed to formulate 'correct' ideological messages. They structured *Beyond the Arctic Circle* chronologically, using the *Kolyma*'s itinerary as the backbone of the narrative. The editors did not draw attention to their use of archaic 1913 footage, nor did they credit Bremer's camerawork.

Downplaying the temporal gap, *Beyond the Arctic Circle* features continuous movement – from the opening scenes of the hustle and bustle in the port of Vladivostok to the movement of individual people – following the conventions of early cinematographic travelogues which moved 'into landscape via technology'.[17] The aesthetic penetration of space is accompanied by time-travel – the audience of 1927 watches footage shot in 1913 using a range of archaic visual conventions of the landscape films of the 1910s. Bremer's camera remains largely static; it stays at eye level and keeps a significant distance from the objects it records. The camera pans slowly left and right, rarely making use of the vertical axis, and avoids dramatic angles. This enables the viewer to enjoy the picturesque space, 'to enter a scene safely and to be charmed by its novelty or its awe-inspiring grandeur'.[18] Panoramic and long tracking shots taken from the moving ship dominate the presentation of the landscape. Bremer employs the conventions of turn-of-the-century ethnographic photography to record 'ethnographic scenes' by focusing on the de-individualized static figures within the landscape.[19] *Beyond the Arctic Circle* avoids fast-paced cuts, makes extensive use of continuity editing and firmly anchors the viewer in space – equating the viewer's gaze with that of the camera. The film thus masks the mechanical nature of filming that Vertov so eagerly emphasized. As a 'phantom ride', *Beyond the Arctic Circle* follows the visual convention of 'viewer as passenger'.[20]

Beyond the Arctic Circle begins with the image of a map with the Far East and the Pacific Ocean in its centre. As Tom Conley has argued, the map not only 'underlines what the film is and what it does, but it also opens a rift or brings into view a site where a critical and productively interpretive relation with the film can begin'.[21] The emphasis on a region rather than on the country as a whole – on the borderland rather than the centre – zooms the audience in on the territory and avoids a 'hierarchical' landscape. The interpretation of the north thus starts with its localization; fragmenting the general and zooming in on the particulars, it approaches a part as a whole. The animated map further supports the film's optical mastery over the territory, but features it as a self-sufficient region rather than a dependent borderland, thus transforming Bremer's views of the area as the remote and backward North. Through trade and intermarriage, the inhabitants of the Far North are shown in constant interaction with the Cossacks tracing their roots back to the seventeenth-century expeditions of Semen Dezhnev, Alaskan gold-diggers and the Inuit. The representation of local cultures as products of centuries-long interaction correlates with the ethnographic research of the day, which was instrumental in formatting the optics of virtual travelling across the Soviet Union.[22]

The film's emphasis on the primacy of geographical conditions in shaping cultural practices and economic activities echoed the work of Vladimir Bogoraz – former political exile and one of the founding fathers of Soviet ethnography, who devoted great attention to the peoples of the Soviet North in the 1920s. Bogoraz conducted extensive research among the Chukchi and advocated the holistic and systemic study of a 'cultural area'.[23] His theoretical position was inspired by the work of Franz Boas and was rooted in the Humboldtian tradition.[24] Under the umbrella of the Jesup North Pacific Expeditions headed by Boas, Bogoraz undertook research on the Chukchi.[25] Opposing full assimilation, Bogoraz insisted 'that the Northern peoples live apart so that they might avoid the inevitable devastation of Russianization' and argued 'in favour of the North American and Scandinavian experiences of creating territorial reservations'.[26]

Flaherty's *Nanook of the North* proved another important influence on Erofeev and Popova's work. The film established a number of the visual and conceptual conventions of the ethnographic cinema, and received a warm welcome from Soviet film-makers.[27] *Beyond the Arctic Circle* used a structure similar to *Nanook* by introducing activities around the house, family life, hunting and trade. While Flaherty's work created the image of a primeval world ruled by the primary instincts of survival, and underplayed both the complexity of the Inuit social structure and the encroachments of the modern world, Erofeev and Popova continuously emphasized the permanent communication across ethnic, cultural, or political borders and put their emphasis on local, particular and geographically determined activities.

Nanook of the North also introduced the 'primitive meets technology' motif that resonated with both *A Sixth Part of the World* and *Beyond the Arctic Circle*. All three films followed the tradition of depicting technical curiosities as 'signs of ingenuity and advancement' and proof of 'a more homogeneous, civilized, and scientific empire' – an image eagerly shared by the Soviet regime.[28] When exposed to a gramophone, Nanook observes it with theatrical awe and fascination. Although already familiar with up-to-date technological devices including the film camera, he plays the ascribed role of the 'child of nature' and bites the record with naïve surprise.[29] Vertov also used a gramophone record as a metaphor for the discursive power of technology carrying the dominant voice of official ideology. Erofeev and Popova referred to the Chukchi's introduction to a film camera with the intertitle, 'first meeting with a cameraman', and followed it with a long shot of women and children looking at the camera with curiosity and attention, suggesting both attraction and unspoken fear that becomes palpable as some of the women and children withdraw to the tent.

The concept of the North as 'a place of dearth' was not exclusively Soviet, nor was it limited to the 1930s alone.[30] By the early 1920s, Nordic cinemas had developed elaborate semantics for snow, used both as a marker of the landscape and a narrative characteristic of representing 'purity'.[31] Marina Dahlquist has argued that in Swedish films, a white background denotes the space as the 'North' and simultaneously removes the specific visual markers of the landscape.[32] Snow was an important constitutive element for national cinemas identified as 'Nordic' and served as a metaphor for purity and perfection. Richard Dyer has described this notion as 'the idea of the excellence of white people seen as a heritage from the Romantics' admiration for remote, cold and "pure" places, and the virtues that it brings'.[33] Contrary to pairing the whiteness of men and snow, *Beyond the Arctic Circle* reassigns the space to the indigenous population and uses the relationship between humans and their habitat to redraw asymmetrical power relations; Erofeev and Popova emphasize how the Chukchi routinely manage the elements while the crew and ship's passengers struggle in the face of extreme and deathly difficulties.

The ambiguity of the snow and the imagery of death returns in the hunt scene wherein the crew kills a polar bear, a staple ingredient of northern travelogues. The fur of this 'lord of the Arctic' is proudly presented to the camera, embodying, as John McCannon has pointed out, domination over the region itself.[34] Yet the death of three crewmembers inadvertently places animals and humans on the same plane, denying both a rhetoric of linear progress and an ethnographic salvage paradigm. This hunt also offers an interesting contrast to the walrus-hunting scene in *Nanook of the North*. While Flaherty demonstrates the beauty of the 'primitive body' in nature, untouched by modern hunting practices, Erofeev and Popova interpret Bremer's footage as an ambiguous commentary on the relationship of travellers with the hostile and dangerous environment.[35]

Figure 3.1 Still from *Beyond the Arctic Circle* (1927). The hunted trophy as a metaphor of dominating the space and its resources.

A comparison of *Beyond the Arctic Circle* with *A Sixth Part of the World* brings up important points of divergence. Vertov assigned the North an economic functionality, yet perpetuated the discourse of dependency – both material and ideological – on the advanced centre. Erofeev and Popova, on the other hand, combined travelogue, adventure and ethnography to feature the landscape of the Far North as a space of diverse habitual, economic and ethnic practices emphasizing its cultural plurality. The dated footage allowed them to omit references to the Soviet-induced change that, although required of all contemporary productions, was just not possible to identify in the available material (and was hardly visible in the Soviet Far North at the time of the film's release). Instead, the film presented a paradigmatic 'contact zone' described by Mary Louise Pratt as 'the space in which peoples geographically and historically separated come into contact with each other and establish ongoing relations, usually involving conditions of coercion, radical inequality, and intractable conflict'.[36] The specificity of the contact zone in *Beyond the Arctic Circle* is enhanced by the extreme conditions of the Far North; this liminal environment tested the adaptability and skills of all the protagonists. At the same time, rather than imposing the traditional rhetoric of backwardness on the local inhabitants, Erofeev and Popova consistently emphasized cultural predispositions of the indigenous population towards successful adaptation. The film shows locals as better equipped than travellers and explorers in mastering the elements as part of their daily routine.

Difficulties in organizing expeditions postponed active cinematic exploration of the Far North until new approaches to landscape construction developed in the 1930s. Olga Podgoretskaia, the film student who criticized Erofeev for his 'non-dialectical' approach to documentary (see Chapter 1), directed a two-reel short released under the same title, *Beyond the Arctic Circle [Za poliarnym krugom]*, in 1931. Podgoretskaia worked in cooperation with three cameramen (Grigorii Donets, Boris Chechulin and Iurii Stilianudis – the latter worked with Erofeev in *Towards the Safe Haven [K schastlivoi gavani*, 1930]) and offered a radically different image of the North. Surveying the Khibinsk Mountains, which are rich in apatite ores, the film emphasized the active industrialization of the region. The opening panoramic landscapes were followed with footage of the mountain industry and chemistry plants in the region, the newly built town of

Khibinogorsk (after 1934, Kirovsk) with its broad streets and new resi-
dential buildings, bank, hotel, railway and factory, proudly presenting the
modern transformations in the Soviet Far North. The film, Podgoretskaia
argued, had to bracket off any sign of 'unfitting' reality.[37] Although a
1930 ethnographic expedition studying the indigenous population of the
region concluded that there was 'no real evidence "of a break [perelom]
from the old to the new"', the film nevertheless visualized the desired
Soviet utopia.[38]

Arctic Tales: From Contact Zone to Icy Desert

The ice block floats the heroes around the ocean,
They know not what direction they are headed,
Fires of all sorts burn on the ice block,
Flowers bloom on it, blue as the sky.
Yet it is no wonder, there is no marvel to it:
For now the weather is made for our homeland
By Soviet heroes with their wisdom,
Their wisdom made by great knowledge!
Marfa Kriukova, 'Tale of the Pole' (1937)[39]

A year after the release of Erofeev and Popova's film, international media
attention focused on the Arctic, specifically on the efforts to save Umberto
Nobile's expedition after his polar airship *Italia* crashed.[40] Several countries,
including the Soviet Union, took part in the rescue mission. The crash and
rescue operation became the subject of Georgii and Sergei Vasilievs' com-
pilation film, *Exploit in the Ice* [*Podvig vo l'dakh*, 1928]. The film started
with footage of Georgii Sedov's 1912 expedition and incorporated later
newsreels and material shot by a film crew on board the Soviet's icebreaker,
Krasin, during the rescue.

Unfolding industrialization accompanied by a wide media campaign
ensured growing attention paid to the Soviet Arctic as a new frontier of the
symbolic spatial politics of the 1930s. The 1932 expedition of the *Sibiriakov*
icebreaker in the Arctic Ocean received heavy coverage in this media campaign, resulting in a film with a captivating visual vocabulary that promoted the government's policy of exploring the Soviet Far North. The film

played a prominent role in highlighting the regime's successes and demonstrated an important transition towards resource-centred explorations.[41]

Otto Shmidt, explorer and scientist who completed consecutive expeditions on the *Sedov*, the *Sibiriakov* and finally the *Cheliuskin*, was one of the masterminds behind and a central figure of the explorative campaigns. Shmidt, keenly aware of the public image of his explorations, used his broad network of cultural connections to invite reporters, artists and film-makers to join his polar expeditions and craft accounts of his heroic undertakings.[42] Shmidt planned to complete, in a single season, an expedition on the icebreaker *Sibiriakov* along the northern shores of Russia from Arkhangelsk to the Pacific Ocean. He asked Vladimir Shneiderov, whom he had met during the 1928 Pamir expedition, to film the journey.[43] Like Erofeev, Shneiderov had launched his career re-editing films and made a name for himself after the success of his first air travel film, *The Great Flight*. His later films, shot in the Pamir and in Yemen, shaped his views on expedition cinema prior to his northern journey (*At the Foothills of Death* [*Podnozhie smerti*, 1928], *El'-Yemen*, 1930, *4,500 Metres High* [*Na vysote 4500*, 1931].[44] Shneiderov believed in controlled, organized filming and argued that 'expedition film should be prepared the same way as a fiction film shot in a studio is prepared. It needs a detailed, well-developed script'.[45]

Anticipating the success of Shmidt's mission, Mezhrabpomfilm commissioned the film upon realizing its ideological and commercial potential in the Soviet Union and abroad. The film would showcase Soviet-bred bravery and mastery over the Far North, and was largely scripted prior to the vessel's departure to include both reporting and staged episodes. Expedition participant and writer Boris Gromov believed the expedition's aim was to bring to 'previously unseen heights the economy of our remote borderlands [...] breath[ing] life into the deserted and unpopulated, but very promising [*perspektivnye*] regions.'[46]

Two Oceans [*Dva okeana*, 1933] was a sound film that centred on the *Sibiriakov*'s treacherous journey. It used extensive dramatization to fuse the expedition and adventure film genres. Shneiderov's ambition was 'not to make a reportage of the expedition, not a film diary [...] but to try to build a narrative film, with the expedition team as the film's protagonist, fighting with the ice of the Arctic, with the obstacles which unexpectedly arise in their path'.[47] Shneiderov recruited Mark Troianovskii as cameraman and

Figure 3.2 Cameraman Mark Troianovskii, assistant Iakov Kuper, director Vladimir Shneiderov during the making of *Two Oceans* (1933) on board of the *Sibiriakov*.

Iakov Kuper as his assistant during the expedition.[48] For all three, the journey offered their first work experience in the extreme conditions of the Far North. Troianovskii had acquired experience in camera work in Alexander Ptushko's animation and special effects workshop and later made several *kulturfilms* on agricultural activities and the construction of the Moscow metro. His experience across various genres and his sharp sense of composition proved decisive for the film's success.

The *Sibiriakov* launched in June 1932. In the first two months of the expedition, the ship sailed across the Kara and Laptev Seas, but the vessel got caught in the ice near Kolyuchin Island, damaging the ship's propeller blades. Following unsuccessful attempts to repair the blades, the ship drifted and eventually reached the northern passage to the Bering Strait. While the *Sibiriakov* suffered serious damage along the journey and could only partially complete its mission, the backbone of the resulting film becomes the story of the Soviet explorers successfully mastering the elements. The premise of completing, in a single season, a northern navigation route is presented not only as economically rational, but as a step towards political and economic autarchy. The existential struggle with nature and the maximum exertion of human capacities provide the driving force of the narrative. As a result, *Two Oceans* represents the union of a romantic blueprint with the modernist conquest of nature, situated within the framework of nascent socialist realism. The film's closing scene, showing a map with the original itinerary and Shmidt reading the Soviet government's congratulatory telegram, reinforces the expedition's success.

The number of structural similarities between Erofeev and Popova's *Beyond the Arctic Circle* and *Two Oceans* only highlights their conceptual differences. In both cases, the directors depict a linear voyage aboard an icebreaker through a visual diary of sorts. Both journeys enhance and extend the communication network used to supply the circumpolar population with goods and to facilitate the transportation of resources from the Far North to industrial centres. If *Beyond the Arctic Circle* shows a long and difficult winter on the ice, *Two Oceans* concentrates on mastering time and space at any cost; the focus on a geographical periphery with its 'ethnographic' practices is replaced with an attack on nature. The use of maps further underlines the films' differences; while Erofeev and Popova focus on a region, Shneiderov cuts across empty space with progress measured in kilometres. In *Two Oceans*, the indigenous population makes only a cameo appearance during a brief stop at the Yakut port of Tiksi, wherein a few general shots of reindeer and their riders portray the population mastered along with nature. The timing of *Two Oceans* accentuates the expedition's linear progression; the precisely dated entries in the ship's log intensified the narrative in contrast to the seasonal activities of the crew and the local population in *Beyond the Arctic Circle*.

The distanced observation of *Beyond the Arctic Circle* gives way to the subjective perspective of *Two Oceans*. The mobile camera's close-ups and Troianovskii's dramatic angles differ radically from Bremer's panoramic shots.[49] In *Two Oceans*, the most dramatic indoor scenes were re-enacted in the studio with synchronized sound. Despite use of re-enactment, Shneiderov described the film as a document that caught 'life unaware', as the first intertitle stated. The film climaxes with the crew's attempts to change the damaged propeller – a single mobilizing effort needed to transport several tons of ballast in order to lift the stern of the ship by sinking its bow. Powerful low-angle shots of the icebreaker during the dramatic episode of unloading the stranded ship with a broken propeller visualize the might of the iron giant and the role of a larger-than-life polar explorer.

Dramatized reportage in cinema, along with novels, songs, poems and paintings, established a set of recognizable conventions powering a specific genre of Soviet *novina* (a neologism created as an alternative to *bylina* – heroic epic poem – and emphasizing its 'novelty'), where 'the motifs and poetic devices of traditional folklore were applied to contemporary subjects'.[50] Shmidt, a tall, bearded man, was baptized by the Soviet balladist Marfa Kriukova as 'Beard-to-the-Knees'. He was later described by John McCannon, historian of the Soviet Arctic, as a character who is 'tailor-made to fit into the roles of the giant Sviatogor' or 'an even more famous alter ego, that of "Grandfather Frost" (*Ded Moroz*).'[51] Shmidt became a model Soviet hero embodying a courageous struggle against a hostile environment.

The symphonic soundtrack and intertitles of *Two Oceans* further emphasized the emotional impact of the narrative. The film's script was written by poet and writer Boris Lapin, an adventurer-traveller-writer known for his essays on the Soviet border areas from the Pacific Ocean to Central Asia and the Caucasus.[52] His 1931 essay, 'American Border', poeticized the Soviet frontier, which was described through the lens of colonial adventure novels.[53] Although Lapin described a limited Soviet presence in the Far North in his essay, declaring that the 'RIK [Regional Executive Committee] lives by itself, and the Chukchi by themselves',[54] in the film he declared the full and ultimate Soviet triumph over nature and the metamorphosed and poeticized Far North.

To further emphasize this mastery over nature, *Two Oceans* extensively used the perspective of the mounted camera's phantom ride – its impact and meaning transformed from the early travelogues of the 1910s. The Soviet films of the 1930s used the tracking shots to show the triumphant feats of icebreakers and airplanes actively penetrating the landscape and feeding a 'fantasy of total visual dominance.'[55] However, rather than emphasizing the heterogeneity of space, the film facilitates its subjective appropriation on a personal affective level.

The Far North in *Two Oceans* lost elements of a 'cultural zone' and became a liminal space for individual heroism, a testing ground for one's physical and spiritual strength. Appearing in newspaper reports and on photographic albums and posters, the film's motto borrowed Stalin's quote: 'There are no fortresses that the Bolsheviks cannot storm.'[56]

A visually engaging and challenging adventure became a new way of showing the Soviet Arctic. The affective experience created by dramatic camerawork and a narrative structure transforms the 'montage of attractions' to a
new type of visual engagement with the travelogue. Rather than representing an exotic space, the film creates space for the individual projection of
fantasies and excitement, as well as gratification evoked by the collective
achievement.

Tragedy into Triumph: The Rise of Affective Travelogues

> *Ever since the first airplane landed*
> *in the taiga for the furs – the taiga itself*
> *is no longer the one we had known before;*
> *and since the Cheliuskin's crew,*
> *drifting as they did on their ice floe,*
> *became heroes, the sea is not*
> *the same old sea any more* [...]
>
> Mikhail Prishvin, *Diaries*[57]

The regime's 'love affair' with industrialization in general and polar exploration in particular reached its zenith in 1934.[58] Two years earlier, the Main
Administration of the Northern Sea Route (Glavnoe upravlenie Severnogo
Morskogo Puti, GUSMP) replaced the Committee of the North, becoming
the main institution dealing with the territories of the Russian Far North.
The Administration pursued the non-preferential treatment of northern
minorities and concentrated on exploring the natural resources of the area,
facilitating large-scale media exploration campaigns in the circumpolar
region. The Administration supported another expedition along the path
taken by the *Sibiriakov*, on a cargo ship called the *Cheliuskin*, again under
Shmidt's leadership.

   This expedition gave rise to one of the most extensive Arctic media
campaigns. Shmidt again took care of the propaganda of the voyage by
inviting journalists, writers, painters, and film-makers to document the
success of the mission. The *Cheliuskin* set sail in the summer of 1933.
The film crew consisted of Troianovskii and Arkadii Shafran. They were

provided with approximately 4,500 metres of raw stock and had three possible scenarios in mind:

1. The *Cheliuskin* reaches Wrangel Island – the best outcome in every cinematographic and non-cinematographic sense.
2. The *Cheliuskin* does not reach the island and goes out to the Bering Strait.
3. The *Cheliuskin* does not reach the island and does not go to the Bering Strait.
   We have to film prudently [*ekonomno*], so that the available 4,500 meters of the stock would be enough for any of these variants and so that from the filmed material we could make a film from any combination of the elements.[59]

They could not foresee the worst-case scenario; in October 1933, the *Cheliuskin* became caught in the ice. The vessel was unequipped for such an incident and, finding himself short of supplies, Shmidt decided to send a group of 18 people back to the continent, 400 kilometres on foot across snowy planes, accompanied by local Chukchi guides. Lacking proper facilities for developing the film on board and facing a shortage of raw stock, Troianovskii chose to return to the continent with some of the filmed material while Shafran stayed on board and filmed with the remaining stock. Troianovskii's diaries mention the invaluable help the local guides provided, as well as their numerous misunderstandings due to the lack of a common language.[60]

In the resulting film, the audience sees some of the crew depart on sledges, yet the logic of the division of the film-making team is not made apparent; neither is the role the Chukchi guides played in the crew's survival. The film's version of the cross-country trek emphasizes individual courage and persistence; meanwhile, Troianovskii's diaries included accounts of a different nature, contrasting the dexterity and proficiency of the locals with the problems of those whose lives depended on the experience and orientation of their guides.

Unfit for its purpose, the ship could not resist the increasing pressure of the thickening ice; it was crushed and finally sank at the entrance to the Bering Sea on 13 February 1934. One person died in the process of abandoning the ship, but 104 people successfully disembarked and settled in a makeshift camp on the ice. Shafran succeeded in recording the sink-ing of the *Cheliuskin* and the rescue mission led by Soviet pilots.[61] Lost in the arctic desert, the 'Cheliuskinites' survived on an ice floe, making head-lines in all of the Soviet newspapers and much of the international media. A special Committee was created to help evacuate the drifting camp, and a coordinated evacuation took place two months after the sinking. The evacuation gave rise to a new media campaign celebrating the pilots and praising the political leadership for its prompt and efficient guidance of the rescue effort.

Contemplating the significance of the *Cheliuskin* campaign, Mikhail Prishvin perceptively noted:

> The destiny of the *Cheliuskin* [...] [is] intertwined with our state-ship: no-one dared to voice the most important signifi-cance of this whole 'epic'. [...] But this is how it should be: the state is made strong by its people and the triviality of the motif disappears in the significance of the demonstration: there is something to *show*.[62]

The rescue turned into one of the largest and most well-orchestrated cam-paigns of the 1930s and was branded by some as the epitome of Stalinist cultural politics. 'Cheliuskinites are the parade',[63] concluded Prishvin laconically, emphasizing the visual dimension of the campaign. Turning failure into triumph required creativity, and again the cinema played an active role in constructing the heroic image of the *Cheliuskin* and 'Cheliuskinites'.

Numerous published accounts by eyewitnesses and photo albums formatted the story of the 'Cheluskinites' in a self-congratulatory mode. The film, *Heroes of the Arctic* [*Geroi Arktiki*, 1934], made from the foot-age recorded by Troianovskii and Shafran, became the key account of both the expedition and its rescue. The film credits Iakov Poselskii as dir-ector, and Troianovskii and Shafran as cameramen. The film was released within nine days of the rescue of the ship's crew and passengers, which was possible only because Troianovskii had delivered a large part of the footage to Moscow earlier for developing and editing. The film did not use re-enactments, although Shafran's memoirs are full of regrets over the scenes he left out.[64] Nevertheless, the film was instantly hailed as a day-by-day chronicle of the *Cheliuskin* expedition, including the sinking of the ship and the arrival of the rescue planes.[65]

The final version of the film contains elements of the three potential scripts developed by Troianovskii and Shafran. *Heroes of the Arctic* opens with the cheering crowd bidding farewell to the ship in Leningrad, and includes references to the government and the Party who 'demand hard and daily struggle for the exploration of the Great Northern Way.' It also shows press headlines in multiple languages declaring the international importance of the exploration.

Several scenes are reminiscent of *Two Oceans*, including collective efforts to repair the vessel. Additionally, the *Cheliuskin* expedition performed cartographic surveys, undertaking measurements both on land and in the air. Recurrent images of the mapped itinerary highlight the conflict between the original plan and natural forces. Life in the camp is shown as organized work during which the exploration and topographical surveys continue undisturbed. The radio operator keeps constant contact with the continent, ensuring a direct link with the caring centre and emphasizing the unity of the state. Icy camp panoramas include a Soviet flag waving in the background, thus marking ownership over the territory. The flag remains flying over the evacuated camp after the completion of rescue operations, reminding viewers that the northern territories were to be seen as ubiquitously and unconditionally Soviet.

The film concludes with an extended episode of the celebrations held for the polar explorers and pilots. It fuses the expedition and rescue into a single undertaking presented as a triumph. Introduced as the 'heroes of the nation', the rescued explorers cross the country by train from Petropavlovsk-Kamchatskii to Moscow, where a final parade in 'the heart of the motherland' shows the country united in celebrating the rescued and the rescuers. A high-angle shot from the roof of the Bolshoi Theatre shows long rows of cars and people in the ceremonial uniforms of the army. The abundance of flowers, confetti, laughter and festive white dresses in the high-angle shots of the crowds creates an atmosphere of carnival, merged with that of a military parade on the Red Square. The rows of tanks, planes and sportsmen marching in symmetrical rows extend the heroic rhetoric and ascribe to it straightforward militant overtones.

A combination of tracking and aerial shots of moving trains and cheering people, merging into a single cross-country crowd of indistinguishable faces but recognizable emotions reinforces the Soviet collective identity. The low-angle close-ups monumentalize the 'country's heroes' as exemplary role models. Coverage for the most part avoided reporting on the several months Shmidt spent in the US recovering from pneumonia, but declared him an 'iron-cast man'; the loss of the ship was overshadowed by the praise of the achievements of Soviet aviation. At the same time, the crew of the *Cheliuskin*, with the exception of Shmidt and a few others, remained anonymous.

The appeal of the 'Cheluskinites' was global. The Soviet poet Ilia Selvinskii, who was part of the expedition and left together with Troianovskii, heroicized the mission in a poem entitled 'Cheliuskiniana'. The émigrée Marina Tsvetaeva, following the rescue mission from her home in France, also took pride in the Cheliuskinites:

> Today – long live
> The Soviet Union!
> With every muscle
> I support you –
> And take pride in you:
> For the Cheliuskinites are Russian![66]

In the films on polar exploration, the images of celebration became an important aspect of emotionally charged narratives. The cathartic happiness, pride and satisfaction following tense, threatening images of life endangerment ensured the film a strong emotional response and a high audience turnout.

The self-congratulatory happy ending usually took the expedition to the symbolic centre of the country to complete the spatial hierarchy. This pattern featured prominently in later films about the 1937 'conquest' of the North Pole by the 'Papaninites', a group of explorers named after Ivan Papanin.[67] In the summer of 1937, the media continued its campaign by greeting the pilots on their return from the North Pole. A series of films on Papanin's expedition was released in 1937–38, including *At the North Pole* [*Na severnom poliuse*, 1937], *We Conquered the North Pole!* [*Severnyi polius zavoevan nami!*, 1937] and *Papanin's*

Team [*Papanintsy*, 1938] which depicted the explorers heroically over-coming inhospitable conditions.[68]

These films exemplified the disappearance of the dichotomy between the 'documented' landscape and the mythological space of larger-than-life Soviet achievements. The use of total aerial surveillance matched the complete domination of the land and sea as 'the inhospitable periphery' was successfully mastered.[69] The transformation of the landscape corre-lated with the disappearance or marginalization of the indigenous popu-lations of the northern territories. Soviet expedition films emphasized the emptiness of the space and the emotional gratification of its success-ful conquest.

Fiction cinema followed the path of *kulturfilms*, relegating the native population of the Far North to the background and presenting oper-atic heroes or villains in line with class logic. A growing number of film-makers transferred their experience with *kulturfilms* to fictionalized portrayals of the Soviet borderlands. Shneiderov, for example, moved towards fiction film-making, using his experience in the Far North and Far East in the adventure tales *Golden Lake* [*Zolotoe ozero*, 1934], *The Alamas Gorge* [*Ushchele Alamasov*, 1936] and *Gaichi* (1938). Another pioneer of *kulturfilms*, Alexander Litvinov, also filmed extensively in the Far North and Far East, moving towards fiction following several popu-lar *kulturfilms* (as discussed in the following chapter). Surveying these changing representational strategies offers insights into the entangle-ment of non-fiction and fiction filming modalities within *kulturfilms*. The next chapter compares the films of Litvinov, Amo Bek-Nazarov and Mikhail Slutskii, and examines the evolving image of the Far East as a definitive Soviet frontier.

4

Forest People, Wild and Tamed: Travelogues in the Far East

In the Union there are many
Long roads,
The longest of them
To the Far East.
              Evgenii Dolmatovskii, *'For those going to the Far East'* (1937)[1]

The Soviet Far East, as seen from the Soviet political and cultural centre and exemplified in Evgenii Dolmatovskii's popular song, was often
described in superlatives as the most remote region. As such, it was recur-
rently portrayed as home to the most exotic and backward ethnic groups
in need of the greatest amount of help from devoted Soviet citizens to leap
into the modern future.[2] At the same time, the Soviet citizens became
increasingly fascinated with the Far East as a space charged with 'fantasies
of discovery, progress, reinvention, freedom, and adventures'.[3] The region
joined Soviet Russia in 1922 after a protracted period of war followed by
intense attempts to fully appropriate it on behalf of the Soviet state.[4] This
distant territory became one of the favoured, although challenging, destinations for film expeditions. The Soviet films set and filmed in the Soviet
Far East during the 1920s and 1930s constructed an appealing image of the
area and its 'exotic-looking' natives. These films refashioned the imperial
vocabulary of progress and conquest and elaborated a sophisticated visual

83

language for demonstrating the region's diversity, its multi-ethnic character and 'organic' belonging to the Soviet Union.[5]

This chapter traces the changing image of the region and its inhabitants in the films made between 1928 and 1936 by Alexander Litvinov, Amo Bek-Nazarov and Mikhail Slutskii. Presenting their largely forgotten films, I focus on the emerging hybrid genre built on representational conventions found in *kulturfilms* and its impact on mainstream film production of the time. This chapter also presents a diachronic development of the topoi of wilderness, remoteness, resourcefulness, and exoticism, and demonstrates the coexisting plurality of ways of representing and integrating the region into the Soviet film-universe of the 1920–30s.

The First Blueprints: Following Arsenev's Trail

One of the first film-makers to become involved in extensive travel and filming in the region in the early Soviet period was Alexander Litvinov.[6] Litvinov developed an interest in cinema, travel and adventure in cosmopolitan Baku. He served as film administrator, director, scriptwriter and actor at the nascent republican film studio, and took part in several films on workers' leisure and work, as well as 'red detective' and adventure films: *Miners Rested and Cured* [*Gorniak-neftianik na otdykhe i lechenii*, 1924], *Oil* [*Neft'*, 1926], *An Eye for an Eye, Gas for Gas* [*Oko za oko, gaz za gaz*, 1924], *Red Pinkertons* [*Krasnye Pinkertony*, 1925], *On Different Shores* [*Na raznykh beregakh*, 1926].[7] In 1927, he joined the Moscow-based Sovkino studio. A year later, inspired by a short article in *Vecherniaia Moskva* on the Udege tribe, Litvinov and a small crew – cameraman Pavel Mershin and assistant Efim Feldman – set out on a distant and exciting expedition.

The expedition resulted in two features, *Forest People* [*Lesnye liudi*, 1928] and *Through the Ussuri Area* [*Po debriam Ussuriiskogo kraia*, 1928]. Transporting the audience over thousands of kilometres, these films offered a journey back in time, merging spatial and temporal distance within the established tradition of travelogues about the lives of 'primitives'. Both films were made in cooperation with Vladimir Arsenev (1872–1930), a well-known explorer of the Ussuri area, who influenced both films' itineraries and the outcome.[8] A former military officer, topographer, and self-trained ethnographer, Arsenev's expeditions combined military reconnaissance with ethnographic research. He had been a member of the Society for the Study of the Amur Region since 1903. His most appraised expeditions took place in 1906, 1908–10, and 1912–13, and served as the basis for his numerous writings on the indigenous peoples of the region.[9] His travelogue *Through the Ussuri Area* (first published in 1921) was continuously republished in the Soviet Union and favourably received by the ideologues of the 'literature of fact'.[10]

Precisely located and dated, Arsenev's novels are powerful literary fictions that contain a composite and idealized portrait of several guides whom Arsenev had befriended during his expeditions.[11] One of the main characters in *Through the Ussuri Area* is Arsenev's guide Dersu, later powerfully visualized in Akira Kurosawa's film adaptation *Dersu Uzala* (1975). Arsenev's novels make extensive use of the romantic image of the noble savages, ascribing to the 'children of nature' a unique way of seeing. Dersu speaks the tongue of nature and lives in organic unity with the pantheistic world. Arsenev describes how his guide aptly reads traces on the ground – broken branches, the colour of the sky in the taiga; all of these vital signs kept him informed, but remained invisible to urban travellers. Identifying Dersu as part of nature emphasized the modern character of the imperial travellers. However, the romantic image of the Udege as a compact cultural unit isolated from the world contrasted with Arsenev's own earlier research findings, which emphasized multiple Udege subcultures differentiated by their level of assimilation to Chinese, Russian, Gold and other cultures.[12]

Both *Forest People* and *Through the Ussuri Area* incorporate Arsenev's views on the region and its people, and take their titles from his monographs; the explorer himself makes a cameo appearance as the mouthpiece of the minorities in *Forest People*. Inspired by Arsenev's vision of the Udege culture, *Forest People* projects the notions of cultural distance, territorial compactness, remoteness, isolation and the self-sufficiency of the Udege community.[13] It suggests an indigenous scopic regime contrasting 'natural signs' with the written language of 'civilization'.

The archival print of *Forest People* at RGAKFD starts with a German-language map of Europe and Asia (presumably from a copy prepared for export) which shows the distance from Berlin to Moscow, and further on to Kharbin and Vladivostok, all connected by a railway line. The rest of the print uses Russian intertitles. Following the introduction of this 'wild' environment through an establishing panoramic shot of the taiga with close-ups of animals, the Udege appear masterfully navigating narrow rivers with dangerous rapids and crossing 'impenetrable' spaces as part of their daily routine. Their skills seem akin to those of the wild animals with whom the Udege share the secrets of survival in this hostile environment.

The film embodies a 'salvage' paradigm, presenting the disappearing practices of the Udege and demonstrating 'a relentless placement of others in present-becoming-past'.[14] It aims at a holistic, 'taxidermic' approach.[15] By the 1920s, the salvage paradigm was an established perspective in ethnographic studies and colonial photography, exemplified by Flaherty's *Nanook of the North*.[16] In that vein, Litvinov turned an ethnographic lens on everyday life, including subsistence practices and household activities. Like Erofeev and Popova, he included an episode with a bear hunt, offering the excitement of enjoying the celluloid trophy from the safety of dark cinemas. The episode of the bear hunt was, as Litvinov recalled, prepared for three days while the bear was chased to a place chosen to shoot the scene. Litvinov's memoirs ironically describe a retreating animal, demonstrating the reversal of roles as the guide became the scene's director.[17]

Litvinov's recurrent use of mid- and close-up shots created an illusion of intimacy with the protagonists and facilitated emphatic observation. To achieve the impression of observational immersion, he utilized a range of strategies to accustom the Udege to the presence of the camera, which later became classical elements of ethnographic film-making.[18] In cooperation with the cameraman and translator he negotiated with the locals, carefully planning each scene in order to develop 'an entertaining form which would incorporate educational material'.[19] Furthermore, he sought to avoid cultural taboos and unfitting shooting conditions with the help of advance preparation and, whenever necessary, re-enactment of certain scenes. However, occasional gazes into the camera, as well as the reciprocal recognition between the cameraman and protagonists, revealed camera's invisible presence.

The first part of the film uses the modality of an ethnographic present, within which the subjects are 'explained in the present tense but conceived as remnants of the human past, and thus [...] represented as timeless, without history'.[20] By contrast, the second part of the film implies an evolutionary, progressive development from 'savages' into a 'modern' ethnic unit, and reinserts the Udege into a teleological narrative with references to Soviet power. Signs of transformation, ascribed to the new regime, are indicated by the opposition of nomadic to settled cultures, and the diffused presence of Russian sedentary cultural practices. Young Udege women and men at the Khabarovsk Pedagogical University visualize the goal of indigenization, 'to create national proletarian cadres on whom the Soviet government could rely wholly and unequivocally'.[21] A mixed-gender student group of various nationalities emphasized equality as an important component of this ideological programme. The elements of salvage rhetoric and of modernization created a continuous, yet tacit tension within the film's narrative.

From an isolated tribe in the primordial forests, the Udege gradually become an agricultural community dependent on external help. The Committee of the North appears as the benevolent centre, sending goods and providing the resources necessary for survival. The film features a number of middlemen between the centre and the indigenous population. The community delegates a messenger to Vladivostok to report the community's quests and grievances to Arsenev, who appears as the local protector of all indigenous communities, mediating their interests to the central authorities. This benevolent 'cultural broker', who had offered his expertise on the region's natural and human resources to the new regime while remaining under the surveillance of the OGPU until 1924 and who held a number of important positions during the Soviet era, was instrumental in transforming the Udege's image from savage to modern.

Towards the end of *Forest People*, Arsenev takes the Udege messenger, Suntsai, to see *Through the Ussuri Area* in a cinema. In addition to providing a self-reflexive estrangement of the film medium, the scene creates a space for the protagonists to encounter their cinematic doubles as film characters. It contrasts the film-makers' trained gaze to Suntsai's naïve viewing, exemplified by the excitement and expressive body language of the latter upon identifying his screen persona (Litvinov and Mershin also appear on screen holding a photo and a film camera in the film's closing credits). The inability of Suntsai and, by extension, the 'forest people', to understand the transformative power of cinema allowed Litvinov to emphasize the gap separating the 'naïve' viewer from the visually savvy consumer of media products. Litvinov's memoirs, however, describe a different situation; Arsenev insisted Suntsai evaluate the film and invited him as an expert rather than an inexperienced viewer.[22] The audience saw Suntsai's emotional excitement upon recognizing himself on the screen, yet it was Arsenev and the crew who were anxiously awaiting for his verdict on their work. Suntsai's approval, recorded in Litvinov's memoirs in broken Russian, 'Everything filmed truly [*vse pravda snimai*]', subverts the screen hierarchy of the 'backward' versus 'civilized' and exposes instead a complex web of mutual projections and anticipations.[23]

Self-reflexive Tale: Film-diary and Subjectivity

Although the discipline of visual anthropology developed only in the post-World War II context, *Through the Ussuri Area* is an early example of a self-reflexive visual diary. Histories of documentary cinema usually attribute the emergence of self-reflexive, ethnographic film-making to the performative modes of the 1960–70s.[24] Subtitled 'diary of the film expedition', this 1928 film shows the activities and itinerary of the Sovkino crew on their mission to film the natural world and inhabitants of the Soviet Far East. The film opens with a panorama of a town introduced as 'one of the largest ports of the Soviet Union'. The next intertitle, following a slow panning shot from the water, over the port and large commercial vessels, takes the audience by surprise and introduces a Chinese toponym, Hai-Shen-Wei, subtitled 'the great city of trepangs'. In the 1860s, this town became a military fortress and took on the name Vladivostok, meaning 'overlord of the East', a possessive military term that appears later in the film to replace the Chinese, 'sea cucumber cliffs'. Following the dual identification of the film's setting, Litvinov uncovers layers of the urban fabric, incorporating both Asian and European cultures; narrow streets lead to vistas of the main, Europeanized broad avenue (Lenin Street, formerly known as Svetlanskaia) with its modern tram lines and tall stone buildings. One building carries the insignia of the Sovkino Far East office, positioning cinema and its representatives at the heart of European modernity.

Highlighting the constructed nature of the film, the visual diary includes close-ups of team members involved in the film production: Arsenev, Litvinov, Mershin, Feldman, and Mikhail Firsov (the Scientific Secretary of the Vladivostok Geographical Society). Gathered around the map, the crew follows Arsenev's confident military topographer's hand as it traces the expedition route. Maps, used extensively in *kulturfilms* to facilitate and advance spatial appropriation, play a double role in the construction of the Soviet landscape; they present an appropriated territory by erasing the uncharted areas, the 'blank spots', and overwrite the (pre)existing ways of structuring space by renaming, rebuilding, and rearranging sites as the principal outcome of the exploration process.[25]

Through the Ussuri Area concentrates on the travellers' experiences through motifs of exploring and taming – with extensive attention paid to their interactions with the indigenous population. The diary structure foregrounds the film's authority over time and space, but in fact conceals the crew's abandonment of the preconceived pacing plan determined by their indigenous guides. The film's itinerary leads from urban sites to the taiga, from civilization into wilderness, from multicultural modernity to archaic practices and implies the existence of a progressive 'scale' from savagery to civilization. The expedition moves gradually backwards in time, discovering a variety of exotic-looking cultural practices. The map reappears to mark the cinematic journey and locate the audience in space, equipping them with the modern means of spatial conquest. The cartographic dominance of the 'civilizers', however, is challenged by an alternative image of space in the episode where an Udege draws a map that subverts the toponymic domination of both the travellers and viewers. The Udege's improvised map structures the space through networks of rivers, providing an alternative way of seeing and mastering it through the indigenous communication system.

The motif of taming offers an important structural component to the film. From the first scenes within a nature reserve, the beneficial use of taming expands to the film expedition. The crew's movement into the 'untrodden' depths becomes both a symbolic and a medial conquest strengthened by the parallels between film-maker and hunter, and is accentuated by the use of paramilitary clothing, weapons, flags and references to the expedition as a 'squadron'.

Through the Ussuri Area introduces the communities of the Gold (Nanai) and Udege as part of a complex communication network which includes other inhabitants of the region. Gradually moving from more to less densely populated areas, Litvinov presents a variety of settlements and cultural practices to demonstrate the process of active transculturation. The film brackets off the religious beliefs and customs of the Gold and Udege, presenting a shaman as a local trader pursuing commercial interests. The exploration of resources resurfaces as a dominant motif. Looking around with the eye of an explorer trained within the Western taxonomic system, the camera points out trees, animals and plants by their Latin Linnaeus-based classification as valuable assets for trade, construction, or medicine. Cinematographer Mershin reproduces the iconography of Vertov's Kino-eye, suggesting a reference to the self-reflexive film-maker striving to grasp life 'as it is' using images of animals 'caught unaware' interspersed with those of the cameraman and photographer at work. Litvinov's double take on the single expedition is an early reflection on the multifaceted nature of non-fiction and the role of the crew as interpreters and active agents of the filmed narratives, as well as masters of filmed spaces.

Terra Incognita: Exploring the Frontier

Litvinov's first expedition films earned him international success and a favourable comparison with Flaherty.[26] The studio rewarded the film crew and financed their next expedition. That expedition, to Kamchatka, began in April 1929 and lasted for eighteen months. It covered close to 8,000 kilometres from Vladivostok – Petropavlovsk-Kamchatskii – the Commander Islands – Ust-Kamchatsk – Korfa Bay – Penzhina Bay and back to Vladivostok, returning to Moscow in 1930.[27] The film expedition was equipped with two large film cameras, Bell-Howell and Debrie, and two mobile ones – Kinamo and Sept, along with a photo camera and a mobile film projector.[28] The film credits reveal that high-ranking Soviet political commissar Sergei Natsarenus, who headed the Kamchatka Joint-Stock Company in 1927–29 and was responsible for developing the resources of the peninsula, took part in the film. His role as an 'editor' ensured that the film carried the proper ideological message and secured the administrative support the crew needed to facilitate crossing the peninsula. The ambitious, and in many ways unprecedented expedition resulted in four films. Two films, *Terra Incognita* [*Nevedomaia zemlia*, 1931] and *Mysterious*

Peninsula [*Tainstvennyi poluostrov*, 1931] covered Kamchatka, while two other films focused on its indigenous ethnicities: *Deer Rider* [*Olennyi vsadnik*, 1931] on the Lamuts and *Tumgu* (1930) on the Koriaks.[29] The latter three are considered lost, but a surviving fragment from *Deer Rider* shows the Lamut taking part in an ecstatic, eroticized feast with shamanistic chanting combined with sensual images of semi-nude females and animal furs, exemplifying Litvinov's increased use of re-enactment in filming indigenous communities, as well as his search for refashioning the modes of portraying 'the primitive'.[30]

Litvinov's *Terra Incognita* shows strong continuities with the imperial literary tradition of representing the peninsula. Starting from the seventeenth century, Kamchatka had been described primarily as a remote and hostile land rich in resources. In seventeenth-century travel descriptions, Kamchatka's remoteness carried the imprints of both the physical and temporal periphery of the Russian empire. In the nineteenth century, the term 'Kamchadal' connoted the whole indigenous population of the peninsula, who were placed at the bottom of the civilizational hierarchy.[31] Soviet films about Kamchatka inherited several of these topoi. Nikolai Konstantinov's short travelogue *Kamchatka* (Sovkino, 1926) reinforced the literary continuity by referencing Stepan Krasheninnikov's eighteenth-century text in the film's opening quote: 'As for Kamchatka, it is hard to say which are greater: its drawbacks or its advantages [...] One would say that these lands are better suited to animals than people'.[32] Litvinov's expedition film both reflected on and altered the existing representative canon.

Terra Incognita opens with a short animation that frames the title with moving waves, flashes of light in the sky and a deserted mountainous plateau in the background, all of which suggests a remote and mythical land. 'Far, far away…where the mainland washes its shores in the cold waters of the great ocean' – begins the opening inserts, much like a folk tale. Picking up the established trope, the film offers the audience the comfortable role of discoverers and explorers taken across this *terra incognita*, or as the working title suggests, the 'forgotten land' [*zabytyi krai*]. The opening scene shows Kamchatka as a resource-filled space laid bare to the appropriating gaze of the audience and awaiting a 'civilizing' input. Furthermore, the Kamchadals are introduced as part of nature, in a 'backward' state and

Figure 4.1 Still from *Terra Incognita* (1931). The state's trade network as an assimilating agent.

in need of education and guidance. The absence of visible markers of ethnic or cultural difference makes the 'civilizing mission' seem all the more urgent and relevant.

The second part of the film breaks away from the image of a remote and autonomous space and situates the territory within the broader Soviet universe. A map of the Asian part of the Soviet Union visualizes the peripheral status of the peninsula. The label 'Soviet' above the geographical area of 'Kamchatka' marks the political status of the territory and creates an ideologically charged spatial palimpsest. Like the Samoeds in Vertov's *A Sixth Part of the World* who receive help and supply goods,[33] the Kamchadal and the Koriaks appear as the beneficiaries of Soviet policies and part of their global economic network. A Soviet ship arrives loaded with textiles, flour, and other supplies for the local co-op (ironically, the flour bags they carry are stencilled in English, coming from the United States). While contemporary accounts reported constant shortages of essential items,[34] the cinematographic Soviet universe depicts a world of plenty. The film shows

Figure 4.2 Still from *Terra Incognita* (1931). Expanding the Soviet media network.

two indigenous hunters trading furs at a state co-op for a teakettle and a rifle – marking the economic exchange with the paradigmatic symbols of combined cultural and military domination.

The interaction between the centre and the periphery went beyond commercial exchange. An extensive communication network, including the most modern technological means, radio and cinema, made the indigenous population of Kamchatka a part of the Soviet world. A Kamchadal woman with headphones and a community watching a film on a make-shift outdoor screen provide tangible examples of a shared communicative space and demonstrate the change in cultural practices in the new, ideological 'contact zone'.[35] Litvinov's crew also became part of the expanding communication network by bringing the first radio and projection equipment to the remote settlements on Kamchatka. Radio transmissions and film screenings connected audiences to the 'big land' and introduced cinema as a major agent of change both on and off screen.

The final reel of *Terra Incognita* fuses the motif of resourcefulness with that of political modernization. Visually captivating footage of fishing in the open sea, reminiscent of John Grierson's *Drifters* (1929), works as a rhythmically edited sub-plot of conquest and perseverance. The abundance of nature and its technological conquest is reinforced through images of semi-automatic processing at a new canned-food factory. The film brings together tradition and modernity in a visionary union. In the animated finale, a five-pointed star covers the screen with its shining rays, depicting Kamchatka as a utopian space: traditional and modern, remote and close.

The film strengthened Litvinov's reputation as a proficient expedition film-maker and Vostokkino commissioned him to write the script for a film on the 'collapse of the old ways of life among the Chinese workers in Soviet territory'– a central question for the 'toiling minorities' in the Far East.[36] Developed under the working title *Li-Van-Yu*, the script told the story of a Chinese woman in Vladivostok and addressed two hot issues – domestic violence and prostitution. The studio management, however, grew wary of such sensitive topics and rejected it.[37]

In 1932–33, Litvinov undertook another ambitious expedition to Chukotka, where he worked as consultant and director on three Moskinokombinat[38] films: *On the Shores of the Chukotka Sea* [*U beregov Chukotskogo moria*, 1934], *Dzhou* [aka *Syn khoziaina zemli*, 1934] and *I Want to Live* [*Khochu zhit'*, 1934].[39] The films used elements of expedition films and narrative drama to various degrees. In *On the Shores of the Chukotka Sea*, Litvinov combines location footage with professional actors from the Vladivostok Workers' Youth Theatre (TRAM). *I Want to Live* stars Dzhan Fun-Tiun and Iun Shao-chin, along with actors from central Russia, and tells a tale of sabotage and *kulaks* transposed to the circumpolar setting. *Dzhou* is even more of a fiction, schematically contrasting the commercial and religious exploitation of the American Chukchi with the idyllic life of the Chukchi in a Soviet circumpolar *kolkhoz*.[40]

Reviewing *Dzhou*, film critic Konstantin Feldman accused it of having 'all the marks of a "Moscow production", meaning that it was probably completed before the crew ever set foot on Chukotka'.[41] While unfairly accusing the director of being unfamiliar with the region, the critic pointed out an increasingly schematic application of pre-fabricated schemes of class warfare, which became a prescribed theme in Soviet film and literature.[42] Feldman also criticized the film's casting and argued for the use of non-professional actors with their facial *typazh* (types) and unique 'bodily memory' of gestures.[43]

Land of the Golds: Amo Bek-Nazarov's Two Versions of Progress

Many directors of both *kulturfilms* and fiction sought to explore the exotic imagery of the Far East, redressing the 'ethnographic gaze' in new ideological garments.[44] Following the success of Litvinov's Sovkino productions, Vostokkino also decided to make films in the Far East. While they found Litvinov's script on prostitution and the Chinese minority in the Soviet Union too controversial for production, the studio chose a 'safer' theme from the life of 'small peoples'. The studio planned a full feature on the Gold minority (present-day Nanai) in 1928. They commissioned Litvinov together with a member of the studio Artistic Council, Sergei Vitkin, to write the script.[45] However, in 1929, possibly due to Litvinov's involvement with the Sovkino expedition, Amo Bek-Nazarov was contracted to direct the film. Bek-Nazarov, a pre-Revolutionary film star, began his directing career in 1923, and by 1930 was credited as one of the founding fathers of Armenian cinema. His previous features were shot in the Caucasus against the exotic backdrops of nomadic Kurds [*Zare*, 1926], Turkish harems [*Natella*, 1926] and Persian bazaars [*Khas-Push*, 1927], which looked, according to one film critic, 'like a good opera'.[46] The invitation of an established director and the film's comparatively high budget testify to the studio's desire to produce a 'blockbuster' for export as well as broad circulation in-country.[47]

Bek-Nazarov joined Vostokkino at the invitation of the Head of its Board of Directors, Berd Kotiev. As a result of the expedition to the Far East, Bek-Nazarov made two films: the drama *Igdenbu*, and a *kulturfilm*, *Land of the Golds* [*Strana Gol'dov*]. Both were filmed by Georgii Blium, the cinematographer of *The Great Flight*. They were released in 1930. Rather than following Arsenev in pointing out the differences between the 'scopic regimes' of modern travellers and pre-modern locals, Bek-Nazarov portrayed the Gold community using the romantic topoi he tried out in the Caucasus.

Igdenbu refashions a classic love triangle within an imposed class narrative. To justify sharp class distinctions, the feature introduces Golds as hunters economically dependent on fur traders. The narrative is set in 1923, the beginning of Soviet domination over the area. A Chinese merchant and 'old-timer' Siberian Cossack enslave the villagers, but Red Army soldiers come to the villagers' aid. The protagonist's wife, Naoja, is sold and an extensive chase scene follows with dynamic parallel editing. Liberated, Naoja is sent to Nikolaevsk, where she studies and becomes a model Soviet woman. Her inner transformation is matched by her changed appearance: she replaces her embroidered indigenous robe with a plain dark suit and a peaked cap, and removes the exotic-looking nose-ring that is common among Gold women of older generations. Despite the ethnographic details, Naoja emerges as a Far Eastern 'cousin' of Bek-Nazarov's Caucasian beauties, who have fallen prey to vicious rich men before being saved by idealized (proto)-communist heroes. Her husband suffers an accident while trying to help his community, but is saved by a Soviet steamship and finds himself in the city as well. By the time Naoja and her husband Igdenbu meet, both have been transformed internally and externally – in his striped sailor's shirt the hero is indistinguishable from other mariners on board. Reunited in the city, the couple sets off to help transform their community.

Bek-Nazarov's hunting scenes and panoramic shots of the taiga are reminiscent of Litvinov's expedition films. Both *Igdenbu* and *Land of the Golds* include the same footage, depicting a chanting shaman, the cooking of a festive meal, the processing of fish and dramatic flood scenes that add 'authentic' texture and provide credibility to the narrative. Yet they were edited very differently and thus fulfilled different functions: *Igdenbu* emphasizes the inherent dependency and weakness of the indigenous population, presenting the Gold as in need of help and guidance, and exposed to abuse unless offered protection by the Soviet regime. This allowed Bek-Nazarov to demonstrate the benefits of the Soviet regime and show changes (a new dress and body language) as a proxy of the coming modernity. Despite the schematism of the script, the 'ethnographic appeal' of the footage ensured the film's successful distribution in the Soviet Union and abroad.[48] Although a Soviet critic noted the division between 'fiction' and 'documents' in the film, he praised *Igdenbu* for showing the Golds in a 'detailed, truthful, and cinematographically effective way'.[49]

Figure 4.3 Still from *Land of the Golds* and *Igdenbu* (1930). The appeal of the exotic: Bek-Nazarov's scene of *kulturfilm* also enters his fiction.

Using the same 'documentary' footage in the *kulturfilm*, Bek-Nazarov demonstrated proficiency in formatting meaning within different narrative sequences. In contrast to the dependent Golds in *Igdenbu*, *The Land of the Golds* emphasized the autonomy and self-sufficiency of the ethnic group. While the *kulturfilm*'s foregrounded statistical and ethnographic data strove for a strictly impartial, objective presentation of material, it is a carefully composed piece with re-enacted scenes. Bek-Nazarov used continuity editing to portray the annual life cycle of the Golds at the Naikhin settlement, structuring the film as a series of episodes arranged by the seasonal changes of activities. While *Igdenbu* emphasized the harsh living conditions and constant hunger of the Golds, the *Land of the Golds* used long tracking shots of the Amur River – serene and abundant nature mastered by the Golds.

Fishing scenes in *Land of the Golds* show the community working in unison and preparing supplies for the winter months. The intensified editing rhythm creates dramatic tension to emphasize the accumulated energy of a collective undertaking. The recurrent appearance of the fishing nets – being prepared, used, mended, dried and used again – works as an embodiment of a cohesive social network and a visual metaphor of the community unified by common activities. Harmonious communal life is rooted in the successful division of labour – images of fishermen are followed by those of women, from the elderly to young girls, processing the catch together. Children are shown becoming socialized into their gender roles and involved in everyday activities on a par with adults. Even the shaman is shown playing an important role in the community, securing a successful catch. The images of Golds fishing are edited together with episodes of animals fishing, reinforcing the 'children of nature' topos. Images of a flood, which occurred during the expedition in 1929, poignantly capture the natural disaster to enhance the emotional impact of the episode. Scenes of half-submerged houses, a boy with a dog on a roof and a woman with a baby in a boat, build up the audience's empathy and add a sense of ambivalence towards a harmonious coexistence with nature.

To introduce the arrival of Soviet-marked modernity, the traditional lifestyle is framed as primordial 'ignorance'. To justify the sudden turn in the narrative, Bek-Nazarov includes scenes of an arranged marriage and a male drinking party in order to supplant the viewers' empathy with feelings of cultural superiority and condemnation of 'backward' social practices. Discussions on alcohol dependency among natives and the responsibility of 'white' traders appeared in the ethnographic literature of the pre-Revolutionary years, but during Soviet times it became the main characteristic of the 'degenerating' influence of old traders and smugglers.[50] Locating the evil influence beyond Soviet borders (the Chinese smuggler) and in the past (the Siberian Cossack), the film frames 'salvation' in political terms: Soviet modernity breaks away from an archaic lifestyle and eradicates the declared vices of the past.

The film's closing episode features a young teacher lecturing her indigenous students with a book in her hands. Challenging the traditional gender divisions and introducing the printed word as a carrier of knowledge overruling traditional oral practices, the Soviet cultural revolution assigned the role of 'the real and most authentic proletarians of the north' to women.[51] Presenting a woman as the new 'cultural revolutionary', the film highlights the role of education in an optimistic promise 'to defeat the darkness and backwardness of the remote borderlands'.

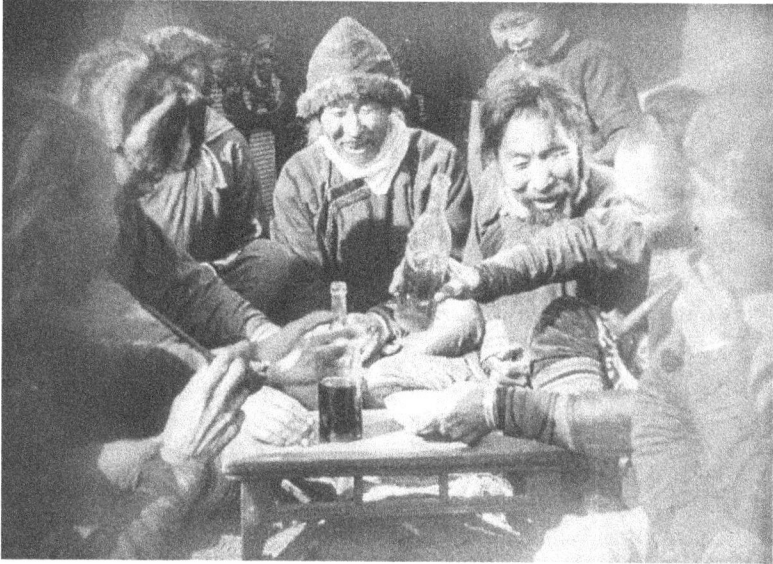

Figure 4.4 Still from *Igdenbu* (1930). The corrupted local: moral disintegration under the influence of alcohol

The structural and ideological differences between *Land of the Golds* and *Igdenbu* highlight the divergence of travelogue and drama filming modes. In both cases, however, Soviet modernity appeared as a gendered concept in which education provides a desirable path of transformation. Filmed during the massive literacy campaign, Golds (along with other 'small peoples') subsequently 'received' a codified version of alphabet and written language, and were renamed Nanai. In a matter of a few years their image, as well as the representation of the Far East, transformed dramatically.

Babylon Re-enacted: The Nanai, the Chinese, and the Jews in Mikhail Slutskii's Far East

We have entered a space of endless advance
across the land of the socialist fatherland.
The Cossack expansion turned into the Bolshevik one,
and this is the whole point.

Mikhail Prishvin[52]

An extensive media campaign was launched in the 1930s to 'popularize' the Far East and attract a new working force to the area from across the country.[53] Four years after Bek-Nazarov's expedition, Mikhail Slutskii, a graduate of the State Film Institute, came to the Far East to contribute to the visual imagery of the dynamically developing area. Slutskii made four short films, all released in 1934, enhancing the changing image of the region.[54] These films anticipated many of the themes that came to dominate fiction cinema in the second half of the 1930s, and demonstrate the changing modalities of minority representation.

Slutskii's aesthetics combined the poetics of enthusiasm and optimism with an attempt at individualized portraits. His film *A Nanai from the Tunguska River* [*O nanaitse s reki Tunguski*, 1934] is a portrait of a Gold, described in 1934 by the ethnonym Nanai. Following the shift towards actors and psychologically driven narratives, Slutskii chose to focus on a Nanai student rather than portray an anonymous community or 'ethnic type'. In contrast with Litvinov's immersive observation and tracking shots and Bek-Nazarov's carefully composed scenes of collective, rhythmic effort, Slutskii makes his hero synecdochical for the whole community and, by extension, for the peoples of the North.

Cinematographer Mikhail Glider collaborated with Slutskii on all four of his films on the Far East. The Slutskii-Glider tandem developed a coherent visual vocabulary which included static shots with dramatized high and low angles, sun-bathed panoramas and low-angle close-ups.[55] *A Nanai from the Tunguska River*, built as a succession of largely static frames, highlights cinema's photographic nature and zooms in on the protagonist's emotions. Slutskii replaced the dramatic narratives of struggling for survival and dependency on nature with idyllic images of a peaceful and abundant existence. The use of static *tableaux vivants* reflected a shift away from montage aesthetics towards didactic presentation of normative ethnic development in Soviet expedition film-making and emphasized the photographic nature of filmed material.

A Nanai from the Tunguska River was the first expedition film wherein a local subject left their 'assigned' region. Accompanied by a symphonic soundtrack, the young Nanai Aka leaves his native village for the 'city of Lenin', where he is introduced to the 'riches of civilization' and undergoes a major transformation. The protagonist arrives to the Institute of the People of the

North, where he studies together with students from different minorities, all of whom are uniformly dressed in modern, urban clothes. Under the guidance of the faculty, the students study arts and sciences. In 1934, a total of 148 representatives of the small peoples of the North graduated from various professional schools and became 'official "soldiers of the cultural army" responsible for spreading education farther afield'.[56] The Nanai protagonist attends art class where he learns casting, carving, sculpting and easel painting. He casts deer and paints landscapes according to the Renaissance perspective conventions. The depicted opposition of 'before' and 'after' receiving a Soviet education emphasizes the dislocation of the main protagonist from the shores of his native river. His future 'happy life' is thus conditioned by his departure for the symbolic centre, where the formation of 'a new person' takes place. Rather than Moscow, this centre is Leningrad, represented by its iconic sites – the Bronze Horseman (the equestrian statue of Peter the Great) and the Palace Square – emphasizing its imperial 'civilizing' legacy.[57]

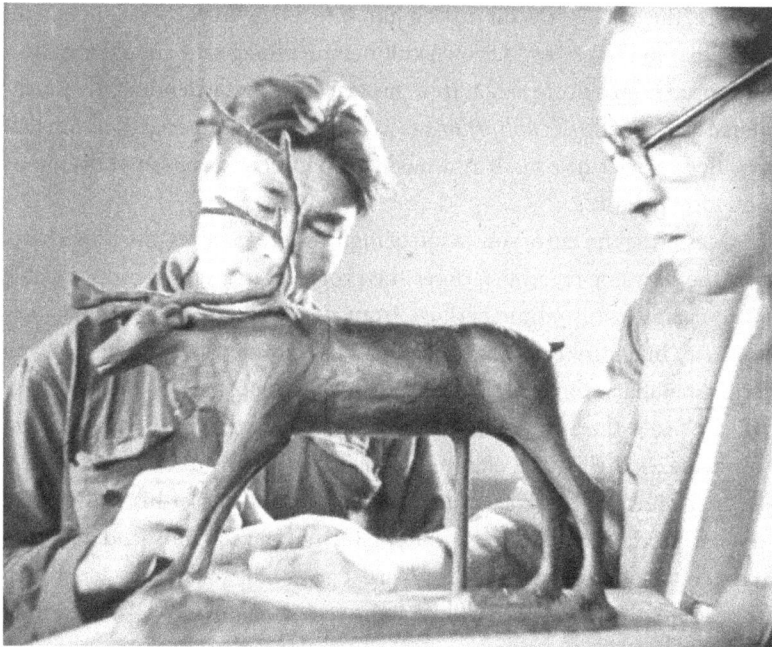

Figure 4.5 Still from *Nanai from the Tunguska River* (1934) Learning the national craft in the centre.

With the introduction of sound, the use of an off-screen narrator became a dominant feature in documentary movements across the globe, including Grierson's Film Reform movement, Pare Lorentz's cinema of the New Deal and Joris Ivens' left-wing activist films. Soviet film-makers also relied on the narrator to transmit the voice of official power. Combining intertitles with a diegetic soundtrack, Slutskii uses 'voice-of-god' narration at crucial turning points to announce change and predict the future. This invisible *deus ex machina* merges individual and collective desires. In line with the optimistic political slogans of the time, the narrator promises the hero that 'happiness will be your friend', while claiming the discursive power over the future of its subjects.[58]

Crucial to Slutskii's interpretation of the Nanai's transforming identity is not only the acquisition of new skills or knowledge, but a new way of seeing, which allows the subjects to refashion their surrounding world according to a 'proper' perspective. As the protagonist works on creating 'socialist realist' artefacts by copying his natural environment, turning nature into culture, the state works on casting him into a new form. Slutskii makes it clear that to understand his own culture, the protagonist should acquire a European high culture canon from his teachers, thus extending the educational aspect of Soviet *kulturfilms* as well as the long, imperial tradition that positions Soviet discourse as a mediator between European conventions and local practices.

Mastering the European canon of high culture 'civilizes' the Nanai hero, and the narrator thereby declares the protagonist 'a new person' capable of re-narrating his ethnic heritage from an internalized Eurocentric perspective. In a stroke of cinematographic fancy, ethnic identity is equated with imaginary folklore. Slutskii portrays the peoples of the North as initiated into the Soviet 'family' through education, which estranges and aestheticizes their living culture as a mythologized and folklorized past.[59] Furthermore, as the protagonist returns to the shores of his native river, the narrator announces 'the awaited return of the son, husband, father as a new man'. A close-up of the fresh artist gives him a name and identity in contrast to the other Nanai villagers who remain anonymous – thus sealing the cinematic prophecy.

On the same journey, Slutskii also made the short film *Liu-Fu* on the Chinese minority in the Far East. The film told the story of a Chinese migrant finding a 'new motherland' in the Soviet Union's eastern-most corner in the 1930s. To exemplify the benefits of Soviet nationality and military policy in the Far East, Slutskii again applied a 'before' and 'after' contrast. The film opens with re-enacted events depicting the main character earning a hard living as a rickshaw puller in China in 1925. After a fade-in, Liu-Fu and his friends appear in a Soviet *kolkhoz* of 1934. Close-up scenes of the Chinese peasants are accompanied by an intertitle introducing Liu-Fu's 'new motherland'.

In *Liu-Fu*, the Soviet Far East is depicted as an aggregate of the modern 'achievements' of the regime: farms, urban landscapes and industrial sites. It culminates with the May Day celebrations, crowned by a military parade portrayed as the pinnacle of strength and technological progress. The footage of the parade documents the abundance of political images on the streets; including the monumental portraits of Lenin, Stalin, Voroshilov and Marx on buildings decorated with flags and electric light bulbs, the film underlines the transition towards the cult of Stalinist prosperity.[60] Visualized security and prosperity make happiness a condition of life, and the exuberant demonstration of joy becomes a rule of conduct. Alternating laughing (predominantly female) faces with tanks and planes in Khabarovsk, Slutskii exemplifies the transformation of representational strategies taking place across the Soviet visual arts in the mid-1930s. The cult of the smile emerges as a new visual canon to represent 'the new entity – Soviet people'. Slutskii with his consistent attention to feasts and holidays, reveals himself as a prolific contributor to the emerging canon, helping to shape what Galina Orlova aptly branded the 'hegemony of the positive [*gegemonia pozitiva*]' in his Soviet cultural products of the 1930s.[61]

Birobidzhan: Civilizing the Wilderness

Slutskii's double-edged talent for being at once a loyal follower and a creative interpreter of the emerging socialist realist conventions became even more visible in his film promoting the newly established Jewish Autonomous Region in Birobidzhan.[62] The Soviet Jewish organizations launched a campaign in 1928 to advance the institutionalization of the Jewish minority as a titular nation, which, according to the Soviet understanding of nationality, was impossible without a clearly defined territorial ascription.

Film-makers and other artists were called upon to provide visual support for the campaign. Slutskii's contribution, *Birobidzhan. Far-Eastern Region.* [*Birobidzhan. Dal'ne-vostochnyi krai*, 1934], transposed the conventions used to represent national minorities in *Liu-Fu* and *A Nanai* to the representation of Jewish settlers.[63] *Birobidzhan* promoted the establishment of the Jewish Autonomous Region. The Birobidzhan project was the regime's last attempt to establish Jewish agricultural settlements in the Soviet Union to 'serve as an alternative to Palestine and resolve a variety of perceived problems besetting Soviet Jewry'.[64] This nationalizing experiment took place just as the indigenization policy was reversed and the repressions of 'bourgeois nationalists' began.

Slutskii's *Birobidzhan* bears a number of similarities with Abram Room's *Jews on the Land* [*Evrei na zemle*, 1927]. Room's film, released seven years earlier, was commissioned by the Society for Settling Toiling Jews on the Land (Obshchetsvo zemleustroistva evreiskikh trudiashchikhsia, OZET) with the aim of promoting agricultural Jewish communes in the Crimea. Made in cooperation with Shklovskii, Mayakovsky and Lilia Brik, Room's film criticized the lifestyle in a traditional Jewish borough (*shtetl*) and proposed an alternative to the Zionist project of resettlement to Palestine.[65] *Jews on the Land* opens with a panorama of a vast steppe, a bare frontier where the eye slips undisturbed into the distance; here the colonists face only the dry land, the hot wind, and tumbleweed. This imagery gives a visual counter-argument to the local authorities' objections of appropriating the Crimean steppe as 'the territory of others'. Starting with harsh, uncomfortable conditions, the film emphasizes the stages of improvement over three months, one year and three years – from a single tent to the visibly better conditions of the communes.[66] A straight furrow running across the screen towards the horizon offers a recurrent visual motif and a materialized metaphor for new life.

Birobidzhan opens with an animated map. The map locates the region between the rivers Bira and Bidzhan, outlines the state border, and depicts a railroad to demonstrate the region's connection to the rest of the country. The first intertitle hails 'the abolition of the centuries-long homelessness and rightlessness of the Jewish toiling masses'. The first scene features a group of three men and two women, shot frontally and from below, praising their life in Yiddish (their speech is not translated).[67] The synchronized sound, plain clothing and obvious stiffness of the speakers mark them as amateurs, adding credibility to their words. A Russian language intertitle appears praising the Party and government 'for their attention and love'. The next episode offers a bird's-eye view of the taiga, followed by a tracking shot along the riverbank, both surveying the territory and emphasizing its emptiness. The caravan of the settlers, accompanied by Jewish songs, cuts across this 'wild' space. The combination of Russian intertitles with spoken Yiddish and Jewish folk songs makes *Birobidzhan* a characteristic example of the multivocal nature of early sound cinema in the Soviet Union.[68] It also implies that the film was aimed at audiences both within and outside the Soviet Union.

Despite an active international campaign to attract Jews from all over the world to the Soviet Far East, the number of settlers in the first decades did not exceed 40,000. The planned agricultural resettlement failed: by 1939, only 25 per cent of the total Jewish population in Birobidzhan lived in the countryside, and not all of them engaged in agricultural pursuits.[69] Yet to enhance the agricultural resettlement movement, *Birobidzhan* and other visual propaganda works – including a 1935 issue of the journal *USSR in Construction* – promoted the Soviet policy of resettlement offering photographic proof of the happy lives given to the settlers.[70]

In order to make the *Birobidzhan* message more convincing, Slutskii involved a team of Jewish luminaries to work on the film. The soundtrack was produced by Lev Pulver, an acclaimed composer and violinist known for his sophisticated use of Jewish folklore in theatrical and cinematic productions. The text was written by poet Peretz Markish, an active supporter of the Soviet attempts to institutionalize the Jewish minority.[71]

While the Soviet authorities quickly abandoned the Crimean project and its settlers, the visual vocabulary developed by Room's crew was reincorporated into Slutskii's film. *Birobidzhan* contrasted the vast taiga to the crowdedness of the *shtetl*, the freshness of nature to the stench of towns, calmness and tranquillity to urban hustle and bustle. The taiga of Birobidzhan, as much as the Crimean steppe, was shown as virgin soil populated by occasional indigenous hunters who were presented as an organic part of nature, and thus seemingly in need of transformation. At the same time, the meaning of the landscape, earlier used to emphasize the backwardness of its inhabitants, exemplifies the ideal living conditions for primarily urban settlers. The contrast between Jews as civilizers and the empty, uncultivated land excluded references to all other ethnic groups in the region.

Images of the successful conquest of nature did not square well with the harsh material conditions and technical shortages endured by the settlers.[72] The film articulates the idealized present, showing manual work of stonecutting, bee-keeping and gold prospecting as ways to amplify the natural riches of the country and advances manual, agricultural labour as the settlers' primary occupation, valuing primordial manual labour over technology. The factographic aesthetics of life-constructors is substituted by the pictorial and expressionist camera work. Where Room's film speaks of bareness and emptiness, Slutskii emphasizes the abundance of nature. A low-angle, expressionist long shot of a man chopping a large uprooted tree, filmed with dramatic back-lighting, stands out as a metaphoric rendering of nature undergoing a profound transformation.

Figure 4.6 Still from *Birobidzhan. Far-Eastern Region* (1934). The earth in turmoil: a new take on the land and landscape

Despite fulfilling its promotional aims, Slutskii's film was overshadowed by a high-budget fiction that also focused on Birobidzhan and its inhabitants. *Seekers of Happiness* [*Iskateli schast'ia*, 1936], an adventure film made by Vladimir Korsh-Sablin at the Belgoskino studio, focused on a Jewish family coming from abroad and settling onto one of the Birobidzhan *kolkhoz* farms. A happier Soviet counterpart to Sholem Aleichem's *Tevye's Daughters* (1894), *Seekers of Happiness* was made within the paradigm of institutionalizing the Jewish territorial minority. It created a virtual utopian landscape by mixing location footage with studio reconstructions. Furthermore, *Seekers* advanced the ideas of collective ownership and assimilation, and anticipated the coming '*sliianie*' [merging] of nationalities exemplified by the marriage of Roza, a Jewish settler, with Kornei, a Russian hunter. The 'back-to-the-land' ideology in both *Seekers of Happiness* and *Birobidzhan* was rooted in the Soviet interpretation of nationality as 'belonging' to a certain territory.

The Birobidzhan campaign, despite its international scope and the considerable number of enthusiasts it attracted from all over the world, waned quickly.[73] Yet four years after the release of Slutskii's film, another short feature entitled *Birobidzhan* (1938) was released. Without credits or attribution, it partially recycled the imagery of Slutskii's *Birobidzhan*, but the overall message of the film was markedly different. Avoiding any reference to the conquest of or struggle for the land, and lacking personal commentary, the film showed rather than spoke about the happy conditions of life in Birobidzhan. The later *Birobidzhan* depicted people in urban parks during leisure time as 'proof' of the successful acculturation of the space. This change in visual language underlined the shift in the target audience: instead of speaking to Jewry worldwide, the film addressed Soviet viewers outside of Birobidzhan to demonstrate the successes of a failed project. The ultimate failure of the territorial Jewish republic left Soviet Jews outside the established hierarchy of Soviet nationalities, while aggressive attacks on religion and religious education gradually excluded references to Jewish culture from public discussion.

In addition to his three films on national minorities, the prolific Slutskii also made *City of Youth* [*Gorod iunosti*, 1934], a film that focused on the 'sovietization' of the landscape *per se*. Created as part of another campaign to populate the territory of the Far East, it also depicted a virgin land awaiting cultivation and mastery. But while *Birobidzhan* emphasized the agricultural potential of the land, *City of Youth* focused on industrial construction sites, the emergence of urban spaces and masses of settlers marked by their political rather than national identity. The film coupled images of monumentalized anonymous heroes and heroines of industrial labour with a materialized utopian landscape where young men and women dressed in festive urban clothes enjoyed their leisure time in cafés to a smooth jazz soundtrack.

Slutskii introduced a number of *topoi* characteristic of the thinning conceptual borderline between fiction and non-fiction. Along with an emphasis on the transformative power of education, he fused performative and observational filming modes and elevated vision as a privileged form of obtaining knowledge, foregrounding the role of the centre, which was underplayed in the films of the 1920s. The four films Slutskii produced in 1934 demonstrated the variety of rhetorical frames available for interpreting the landscape of the Far East. His work paved the way for imagining the Far East as a tabula rasa as it gradually lost its 'ethnographic' qualifiers.

Playing the Native: Transformation of Expedition Films

We are sending you a film script about Romanian life.

If necessary, it can be easily reworked into Georgian life.

Sergei Tretiakov, 'Production script' (1928)[74]

In 1934, in the emerging era of socialist realism, Litvinov returned to the Far East to make a fiction film based on a script by the celebrated 'old-school' writer Mikhail Prishvin.[75] Litvinov had met Prishvin in the Far East in the early 1930s.[76] Based on this journey, Prishvin later wrote a novel *The Root of Life* [*Zhen'-Shen' – koren' zhizni*], which was hailed by critics as an exceptionally masterful representation of nature and the transformation of individual despair into constructive activity.[77] Shortly after its publication, Prishvin was approached by both the head of the Soviet film industry, Boris Shumiatskii, and Party functionary and Chair of the Film Commission, Alexei Stetskii, to rework the novel into a script, which

Litvinov, following the new trend of scripted, narrative expedition films, was invited to direct.[78]

Prishvin and Litvinov shared a fascination with Arsenev and looked forward to a joint venture, aspiring to create a film 'better than *Chang*'.[79] Working on the script, Prishvin reflected intensely on cinema's relationship with truth, image and literature. Scriptwriting required new skills, and Prishvin made extensive use of his collection of photographs taken during his travels in the region. He defined scriptwriting not as a 'reworking [of a novel], but a return of the author to the "*Ur*-images" created on the basis of the photographs', which communicated a 'distinctiveness of cinema as the art of special truthfulness'.[80] Interpreting a photographic image as a 'truthful' account, Prishvin fantasized about 'the play which would emerge directly from the photo' transformed by a subjective vision, and thus reaching out to a new 'artistic truth'.[81] These reflections ran parallel to the 'anti-documentarist' campaign in which Litvinov, Erofeev and Vertov were accused of 'fetishizing reality' (see Chapter 1). Prishvin described documentarism as 'naturalism', and discussed the relationship of 'realism' and 'truth' as intertwined with that of 'beauty'.[82]

Prishvin and Litvinov's film, *Old Luven's Hut* [*Khizhina starogo Luvena*, 1935], centres on the creation of a deer nursery in the Far East. The transition from novel into film makes the plot structure more schematic, foregrounding themes of individual sublimation, territorial exploration and the conquest of 'wild' nature. The central conflict addresses the tension between socialist construction and traditional practices, embodied in the character of the Chinese healer Luven, who resembles Arsenev's Li-Tsun-Bin and is portrayed as the bearer of traditional wisdom.[83] The motif of taming nature structures a triangular relationship of 'oriental' primordialism (Luven, played by Si Tu-Mon), the technological rationality of the West (Avgust, a settler from the Baltics, played by N. Pokhorni), and the Soviet transformative energy (Alexei, played by P. Smirnov). The male triangle is complemented by a melodramatic relationship between Alexei and Avgust's daughter, Mina (Hilde Jennings). Domination over nature and people acquires imperial overtones as the film strives to present the Soviet male 'civilizer' as a synthesis of traditional (Eastern) wisdom and modern (Western) knowledge.[84]

Although *Old Luven's Hut* is considered lost, its reception can be partially reconstructed.[85] The reviewers praised it as 'a masterful representation of the beauties and riches of the Far East', reinforcing the image of the
Far East as an open and boundless space.[86] Litvinov combined the principle
of *tipazh* with professional acting, casting a German actress to play the
daughter of a German colonist and a Chinese actor for Luven; he also cast
locals as extras. Prishvin emphasized a new use of landscape and identified
the need for rigorous visual retraining to transform oneself from a simple
'inhabitant' [*obyvatel'*] into a 'proper' member of society who can see in
unison with the new 'masters of the landscape'.[87]

After finishing *Old Luven's Hut*, Litvinov once again returned to
Kamchatka. The frequency of his expeditions increasingly acquired the
overtones of escape in the context of the growing waves of purges. But even
a geographical withdrawal from the political centre could not ensure his
safety. In the 1930s, arrests and prison sentences increasingly befell those
involved with cinema and the arts, as well as those identified as 'nationalists' or belonging to an 'undesirable' minority, and several of Litvinov's colleagues fell victim to the purges.[88]

In 1935, Litvinov stayed a year in Kamchatka to shoot an adventure film
with an 'ethnographic' background – *The Girl from Kamchatka* [*Devushka s
Kamchatki*, 1936]. Mikhail Dubson, a Soviet film director married to Hilde
Jennings, the female lead of *Old Luven's Hut*, wrote the film's script. Unlike
Prishvin and Litvinov, Dubson had no first-hand knowledge of the region
and composed a story easily adjustable to any part of the Soviet Union. The
film features a young woman, Natasha, returning to Kamchatka after earning an engineering degree in the capital. Natasha chooses a professional
career over marriage. The young graduate joins a research expedition to
explore the natural resources of the area. And, although her disaffected
boyfriend abandons the team, endangering the mission of the expedition,
the group succeeds in finding an oil deposit, proving the area's richness.
Hence, the film's protagonist follows the romantic literary lineage of the
native female warriors represented as 'independent-minded, strong-willed,
free-spirited, and defiant', whose ultimate function was to 'bring the rest of
the tribe under Russian protection'.[89]

Zana Zanoni (born Zinaida Nikolaenko) and Mikhail Viktorov, both
experienced with playing various Soviet indigenous heroes, played the

young Kamchatka natives. Zanoni had played the roles of an Uzbek wife in a harem, a Turkmen teacher, a Chinese philanthropist, and an Udmurt kulak girl. Viktorov, an emerging cinematographic persona of the new 'Soviet indigenous hero', had played a talented Mari musician in *Song about Happiness* [*Pesn' o schast'e*, 1934] and exemplified an 'ethnic' type without evoking an immediate visual 'othering'.[90] Yet the reviews for *The Girl from Kamchatka* mixed lukewarm compliments for its outdoor photography with harsh criticism of the actors' work and 'too much artifice [*remeslennost'*] and sloppiness'.[91] Litvinov's strengths, including knowledge of the area and local customs, were overshadowed by a psychological drama for which he had little directorial experience. The crew filmed on location without the necessary sound-recording equipment and all of the dialogues had to be synchronized in Moscow upon their return.[92] The film suggests a new way of representing ethnic minorities in the Soviet Union. The emancipated heroine, who discarded her private life for professional satisfaction, was envisioned as an example for women all over the Soviet Union, resonating with Valentina Khetagurova's campaign to attract young female settlers to the underpopulated region in order to enhance its development.[93]

The image of the Far East as a space of diverse archaic cultures proved transitory and was replaced by that of a resource-rich frontier marked by distance, yet firmly bearing a symbolic Soviet imprint over the entire territory. The growing militarization of Soviet culture, along with the pervasive concern over external aggression, assisted in developing the imagery of a fixed and closely guarded border, to which Litvinov provided an important alternative.[94] A short travelogue, *On Kamchatka* [*Na Kamchatke*, 1936], reasserted Soviet rights over the territory and emphasized the need for border protection; the travelogue's closing scene depicts a battleship sailing in the open sea whilst a solemn symphonic soundtrack plays, presenting the land and sea as inherently Soviet.

The evolution of the Soviet *mission cinématographique* in the Far East remained rooted in the intellectual and representational legacies of late imperial culture as well as romantic literary *topoi*.[95] Yet in contrast to the early travelogues, which portrayed the Far East as a cultural frontier featuring a unique mix of ethnic and cultural identities, later films depicted uniformed Soviet subjects sealing off the Soviet representational canon of cultural differences. In their films of the late 1920–30s, Litvinov,

Bek-Nazarov and Slutskii utilized three different approaches – 'civilizing', 'domesticating' and 'assimilating' – to portray the nationalities of the Far East. Gradually, non-institutionalized minorities, such as Koreans and Chinese, disappeared from Soviet screens just as they were, to a large extent, swept away by the unfolding purges in the Far East that targeted populations on a national basis.[96] When Litvinov returned to the Far East to repeat the journey he had undertaken in 1928, his films *Udege* (1947) and *On the Far Eastern Roads* [*Po dorogam Primor'ia*, 1957] relied on a rigid visual vocabulary of Soviet 'multinationalism', making all the more palpable the impossibility of returning to the earlier representational genre.

The motif of a resourceful frontier re-emerged in a number of fiction films made about the Far East, including Alexander Dovzhenko's *Aerograd* (1935), David Marian's and Efim Aron's *In the Far East* [*Na dal'nem vostoke*, 1937], Gerasimov's *Komsomolsk* (1938), and Konstantin Iudin's *Girl with a Character* [*Devushka s kharakterom*, 1939]. Both fiction and non-fiction homogenized the space and reproduced the topoi of a bountiful and generous land, replacing the discourse of scarcity, backwardness, and dependency with that of abundance, harmony and picturesque folklore. The creation of such a landscape required constant effort and continual adjustment. Dovzhenko painstakingly recalled working on achieving the proper image:

> Cleaning up the taiga was a common phenomenon during shooting, for almost each and every shot. We had to correct nature to achieve proper composition and lighting. In a word, we had to ascribe to [nature] as much expressivity as it possesses only in its full entirety, but never in its separate parts. We had to select proper details of the taiga, select from an endless variety. […] to show this region as an inseparable part of our socialist motherland.[97]

The concentration on the border went along with the elimination of the concept of the borderland as a space of cultural melange, turning it into a closely guarded resource-rich and fully controlled space. Film-makers from different studios and parts of the country were contributing to an 'all-Soviet' visual vocabulary of progress, national peculiarity, and socialist development; as all Soviet nations were expected to enter socialism, their 'backward' traces were to be eliminated, while their specificity was to be made visible through recognizable visual markers.

The early Soviet expedition films made in the Far East embodied and visualized the Soviet outreach vector from the centre to the periphery, and emphasized the Soviet Union's expanding communication network. The cinematographic records of the Far East created by Litvinov, Bek-Nazarov and Slutskii inscribed the region as part of the Soviet state discursively and conceptually, and presented it in increasingly affective terms such as pride of 'possession' and fears of intrusion. Their films exemplified continuity with nineteenth-century thinkers and explorers, who were, as Mark Bassin has pointed out, 'identifying a population that clearly stood in need of the very civilization and enlightenment that they and their compatriots were desperately seeking to provide'.[98] At the same time, they demonstrate that Soviet film-makers mastered a range of transnational representational strategies that inscribed the ideas of progress and ethnic difference within a paradigm of colonial film-making.[99] Film expeditions across the Far East and Kamchatka reinforced the image of ethnic minorities as beneficiaries of the Soviet regime. The 'ethnographic gaze' was supplanted by a new hybrid genre of docudrama with scripted narratives of monolinear progress.

5

Diagnosing the Nations: Nationalizing Dirt and Disease on the Screen

Wash your face and scrub your hands
When the day begins and ends
Chimney-sweep with dirty face –
Howling shame
And such disgrace!

Kornei Chukovskii, *Wash 'em clean* (1923)[1]

In 1926, the young film-maker Alexander Dubrovskii made a film with the 'Vertovian' title *Life As It Is* [*Zhizn', kak ona est'*], about the importance of timely medical intervention for treating tuberculosis. The film, made with amateur actors in their work and home environments, wraps an educational message inside a fictionalized story about a young female factory worker. The film received chilly reviews as 'a mechanical combination of the Kino-Eye method with fiction cinema', but was deemed 'quite acceptable for workers' clubs'.[2] Dubrovskii's unappreciated attempt to fuse educational and visually engaging forms to promote new practices of bodily hygiene was but one example of a large task on the agenda of Soviet hygienists, educators, artists, and film-makers.[3]

Soviet hygienists focused on tuberculosis because not only was it highly contagious and widespread, but because of its exemplary socio-economic roots as well; it mostly affected members of the working class who lived in improper conditions. Translating health issues and illness into class categories was characteristic of the early Soviet period when 'the imposition of a hygienic order became the way of promoting a political one'.[4] Research on Soviet hygiene policies tends to foreground the activities and discourses of the hygienists who shaped prescriptive policies for the 'collective body' of Soviet subjects.[5] The visualization of diseases linked their causes to class oppression and 'corrupt civilization' (e.g. tuberculosis, alcoholism, or venereal syphilis), or 'backwardness' (e.g. plague, malaria, trachoma or endemic syphilis), and played a crucial role in establishing normative ideas of 'health'. The social hygienists, Susan Gross Solomon has argued, insisted on the social roots of both disease and health: 'Health was not simply the absence of disease; it was the active promotion of the well-being of the population at large'.[6] However, promotion of uniformly prescribed hygienic behaviour conflicted with the indigenization policy, which lauded cultural plurality. The emancipatory Soviet discourse faced the challenge of integrating medical universalism and national pluralism.

This chapter considers the entanglement of two concepts, 'national particularity' and 'hygienic universalism', by looking at expedition films which depicted endemic illnesses as affecting ethnic groups. Analysing travelogues which address health issues, I approach the Soviet hygienic discourse as a relational process which translated into national and cultural policies beyond the questions of disease and treatment. Soviet concepts of health incorporated a number of earlier imperial legacies and borrowed from the visual patterns of colonial representation – both rejecting and drawing on traditions in German, British and French colonial cinema. Beyond the primary goal of raising awareness about broad issues of public health, Soviet *kulturfilms* addressing issues of minorities' health performed a dual function of presenting an implicit cultural hierarchy of ethnic minorities on the basis of their health practices, while also attempting to introduce and standardize new rules of hygienic behaviour.[7]

The use of scientific equipment in exploring and charting the body can be paralleled to the exploration of land, extending the concept of modern mapping to the level of the body. Valerie Traub, who has studied early modern cartography, proposes a concept of 'cartographic bodies' arguing that '[m]iming the grammar of latitude and longitude that organizes the cartographic idiom itself, [...] [maps] begin to imply that bodies themselves may be terrain to be charted'.[8] The parallel of charting space and the body by modern means could be extended further: just as maps reference space as 'a geometrical net of lines of longitude and latitude', the representation of human bodies can be quantified and standardized with the help of developing medical science.[9] Normative images of a healthy and clean body circulated in a variety of media – from children's poems to popular films – thus strengthening the dividing line between the observer and the 'other', the modern (in possession of the latest medical technologies) and the backward (applying traditional healing practices). Metaphors of individual health projected to collectives contribute to a visual standard of norm and progress. At the same time, ideas and understanding of individual beauty gradually come 'to have significance as a sign of the healthiness of the race'.[10]

European encounters with unknown cultures used the markers of health, disease, and dirt to construct a civilizational hierarchy. In nineteenth-century Germany, the East was perceived as dirty, 'marked by chaos and disorganization, and yet also a land of future possibilities'.[11] Such a conceptualization, as Vejas Gabriel Liulevicius has pointed out, went along with customizing the main concept of *Kultur* – originally 'a value identified with Germaness, opposed to barbarism and oppression in the East' and that of *Bildung*, equating education with cultivation.[12] Liulevicius has further emphasized that the German concept of *Kultur* carried associations that 'ranged all the way from the cultivation of land to the cultivation of the spirit', retaining an 'organic' dimension.[13] Linda Hogle, who has highlighted the role of epidemiological techniques in public surveillance, tracked the transfer of biological approaches from individuals to groups.[14] As a result, society can be described in organic terms, facilitating the application of the concepts of 'health' and 'illness' to collective entities:

Increasingly, biological terms and metaphors were applied to social and political concerns, culminating in the unique concept of the *Volkskörper* (literally, the body of the people, or society as a body). The nation was idealized as a highly integrated community of *Volksgemeinschaft*, and represented the moral regeneration of family and Volk. Families were seen as elemental cells of the state organism, and the alarming decrease in family size [...] was described as cellular degeneration.[15]

Films propagating individual health and hygiene, like the German *Wege zu Kraft und Schönheit* (directors Wilhelm Prager, Nicholas Kaufmann, 1925) or the Soviet *Abortion* [*Abort*, 1924], carried important implications for the 'body of nation'.

Physical appearance and attention to the body 'overwhelmingly framed European encounters with other cultures'.[16] Robert Grant reminds us that 'underneath these formulations of racial difference lay contemporary European embodiments of normative behaviour, dress and taste, as well as countervailing anxieties about potential licentiousness, moral abasement and miscegenation'.[17] Rather than drawing unsurpassable borders, Soviet film-makers used health markers to point out the direction of progress. Discussing the image of Siberian indigenous peoples, Bruce Grant has stressed the weight and consequences of such cultural projections:

> If Siberian peoples were considered to be a blank slate on which to inscribe a new Soviet identity, their experience perforce would be one of the most lucid markers of the new culture. In their gradual progress from people of a different land, to people of a different birth, to people of a different faith, to natives, to small peoples, and to peoples of the North, the representation of Siberian native peoples has been predicated on distance. Both of the dominant mythical constructions that defined them over the last seventy years have been obstacles to a discourse that fosters a self-definition consistent with the specificity of their lived experience.[18]

Normative representations of health and illness provide yet another dimension for sustaining the notions of distance and cultural hierarchy.

References to 'deviant' illnesses surfaced in numerous films not directly devoted to medical or hygienic topics. In Soviet cinema, illness was repeatedly projected to the borderland, befalling film characters who travelled to remote underexplored spaces as a personality test, an initiation ritual, or a marker of martyrdom. At the same time, representations of illnesses dwelt on the 'healing' potential of the centre in possession of medical expertise and technologies. The relationship between the centre (with its medical knowledge and modern equipment) and the periphery (using traditional healing practices) reinforced the power asymmetry and relationship of dependency. Such a relationship is exemplified in the 1929 *Kaan-Kerede*, directed by Vladimir Feinberg. In this adventure feature, the Altai population suffers from malaria, attributing their sickness to having angered a winged deity. An 'iron bird' from the Society for the Assistance to Aviation and Chemistry (Obshchestvo sodeistviia oborone, aviatsionnomu i khimicheskomu stroitel'stvu, Osoaviakhim), solves the problem by transporting medical assistance from the centre.[19]

The motif of illness re-emerges in numerous Soviet fiction films of the 1930s. Perhaps the most memorable example is the early sound film by Grigorii Kozintsev and Leonid Trauberg, *Alone* [*Odna*, 1931], which presents a dramatic clash of civilizations and implies the backwardness of the Altai people. The plot centres on a young female teacher sent to a remote village where she falls ill due to a malicious conspiracy by local *kulaks*. As in *Kaan-Kerede*, help comes via an airplane which carries the sick teacher back to the centre. Beyond the celebration of the utopian omnipotence of modernity, however, the film presents Altai as a space of alterity, embodying distance and difference. Shamanistic healing was among the first markers of this difference creating a lasting visual argument to claim authority over the right to cure.

This chapter continues by surveying *kulturfilms* on the inhabitants of Southern Siberia (the Buryats, the Oirots, the Khakass and other Altai peoples) and the peoples of the Volga region (the Chuvash, the Mari and the Bashkirs), and focuses on the entanglement of dirt, disease and nationality. It traces how syphilis and trachoma became cinematographically the most endemic diseases in the context of minority representation. The imposition of prescribed behavioural norms allowed the Soviet regime to advocate a radical transformation of cultural practices in minority communities and to impose a 'Western' understanding of hygiene and cure within an indigenization paradigm that otherwise declared to accommodate ethnic and cultural plurality. This perspective foregrounded 'backwardness' as a descriptive characteristic and presented health and hygiene as the central elements of Soviet modernity.

Syphilis Against Socialism: Medical Expedition As a Bearer of Social Progress

The age-old motif of health and illness in travel accounts to little-known lands also featured prominently in the cinematic travelogues produced in the early twentieth century by all major colonial powers. Fatimah Tobing Rony has argued that early anthropologists, while 'exemplifying a linear evolutionary history, believed that the "Primitive" was a "pathological" counterpoint to the European'.[20] The imagery of dirt and, by extension, human disease, highlighted the principles of 'a systematic ordering and classification of matter, in so far as ordering involves rejecting inappropriate elements'.[21] The definition of a community through a particular set of illnesses carried on into the twentieth century. Visualizing the prescribed course of progress, the makers of Soviet *kulturfilms* in the late 1920s and early 1930s made extensive use of the 'pathologizing' approach. Mary Douglas' classic formula 'where there is dirt there is system' used the concepts of dirt and pollution for pitting 'primitive' societies against 'modern' ones.[22] Soviet film-makers used the imagery of dirt and disease to visualize an evolutionary developmental model in portraying nationalities in the Eastern part of the Soviet Union within the civilizing framework. As Tricia Starks has noted, 'pushing into Siberia, Central Asia and the countryside, cultural workers promoted Soviet values to counteract what they considered the bizarre, unhygienic customs of the natives'.[23]

Representations of the indigenous population of the Far North repeatedly made references to dirt to describe their living conditions. Such references did not relate directly to the issue of disease, but marked the border between modernity and primitivism, which would be portrayed with the romantic flavour of 'healthy wilderness' seen as an alternative system of health coordinates.[24] Rony has explained that the fascination with the 'primitive body' developed as a reaction to advancing modernity and emerging theories of the degeneration and overstimulation of the modern urban citizen for whom '[t]he "ethnographic" Other was thus not only "savage" and pathological, but was also physically closer to the genuine and authentic in man'.[25]

The imagery of disease features prominently in Lidia Stepanova and Vasilii Beliaev's *Across Buryat-Mongolia* [*Po Buriato-Mongolii*, 1929], which recorded the activities of the 1928 Soviet-German medical expedition.[26] The expedition took place in a period of intensive scientific cooperation between Germany and the Soviet Union, facilitated by the marginalization of the two academic communities in Europe in the aftermath of World War I.[27] It set out to explore the problem of syphilis among the indigenous population of the Buryat-Mongolian Autonomous Republic in 1928. Since the nineteenth century, syphilis had been perceived in Russia as a social disease, which – together with tuberculosis and alcoholism – '"disfigured" the body politic through the "infection" of the individual'.[28] As Laura Engelstein has persuasively argued, the non-venereal transmission of syphilis, which plagued entire districts in imperial Russia, was considered a definitive marker of backwardness: 'In its endemic guise, in fact, syphilis served Europeans as an exact index of cultural deprivation: its prevalence mirrored existing levels of filth, poverty, malnutrition, and overcrowding.'[29] In *Across Buryat-Mongolia*, the ethnic ascription of illness becomes the backbone argument for acculturation, enforced sedentarization and control over sexual practices.

The aim of the medical team, consisting of eight Soviet and eight German medics, was to study endemic syphilis among the indigenous population. The Soviet and German groups had different agendas: the German scientists' aim was to test the impact of the anti-syphilis drug, Salvarsan; the Soviet researchers intended to determine the socio-cultural causes of the spread of syphilis and concentrated on conducting interviews with the local population regarding their everyday culture and sexual practices.[30] The film went beyond focusing on the activities of the medical expedition to make far-reaching conclusions about Buryat culture. Intertwining the evolutionary paradigm with geographical determinism, the film presents syphilis as 'endemic' to a particular environment and lifestyle. In this context, the impact of an international scientific expedition, which since the eighteenth century had become 'a source of some of the most powerful ideational and ideological apparatuses through which European citizenries related themselves to other parts of the world',[31] was amplified by the cinematographic projection of pathology and disease onto an ethno-national framework.

Rejecting an immutable racial approach, Soviet *kulturfilms* emphasized that cultural practices can be transformed through a communal lifestyle, the forcible elimination of religion and intensified educational campaigns. To justify the need to transform the nomadic lifestyle to a sedentary one, which was enforced by the Soviet regime as a part of the imposed vision of stadial development, the Buryats' customs were presented as infectious and unclean. Buryat daily practices – collective eating and dwelling – were shown as rooted in religious activities, and the hygienic discourse was applied to accuse Buddhism and Lamaism of impurity and of spreading diseases. The release of the film coincided with an accelerated attack on Lamaism; on 26 December 1928, the Organizational Bureau of the Bolshevik Party forbade meetings of Tibetan medics, decreed tighter control over the activities of the lamas and assigned journalists to prepare a series of publications discrediting Tibetan medicine.[32] Straightforward and negative evaluations of the nomadic lifestyle were part of a larger campaign described in *Pereklichka narodov* (*Roll Call of Nations*) as the 'everyday life which should not exist [*byt, kotoryi ne dolzhen byt'*]'.[33]

Anti-religious discourse frames the first reel of the film, and is reminiscent of Douglas' classification of 'primitive religions' within which 'rules of holiness and rules of uncleanness were indistinguishable'.[34] Soviet-marked progress features in the film as a proxy for 'Western' medical modernity, shown as a conceptual alternative to monasteries that traditionally preserved practices of hygienic arrangements.[35] In the Soviet context, the appropriated legacy of international science, which inscribed Soviet 'civilizing' efforts within universalized Eurocentric health standards, allowed the state to create its own self-image as an advanced and modern nation in contrast to the 'backward' indigenous population. The Buryats were portrayed as patients, united by a shared disease, awaiting an externally provided cure. The solution to their health problems was shown stretching beyond the medical realm.

By bringing together disease and lifestyle, *Across Buryat-Mongolia* argues for a uniform set of hygienic customs to ensure the emergence of perfected and culturally homogeneous Soviet bodies. The film opens with close-ups of outdoor Buddhist sculptures attributed to a Lamaist monastery, followed by domestic scenes of nomadic Buryats. Both daily and religious activities, such as communal meals or the feast of Maitreya Buddha, are introduced as 'unhygienic'. Such an introduction to the Buryats' 'hazardous' practices paves the way for the arrival of the medical expedition. Their interaction with the local population evolves in four stages: an official meeting, a festive reception, demonstration of medical equipment to excited children and, finally, work with patients in a makeshift clinic. A strict division of roles marks the communication with the medics. Surrounded by equipment, doctors in white robes stand in sharp contrast to the anonymous native bodies whose disturbing signs of illnesses are emphasized by medium- and close-up shots. The film does not distinguish between Soviet and German expedition members, but unites them as the 'bearers of progress' surrounded by signs of technological modernity: X-ray equipment, microscopes, syringes and other modern medical tools.

The contrast of the black-and-white film images further enhances the healthy/ill and 'clean'/'dirty' assumptions supported by the European symbolism associating white with purity. The power asymmetry between observers and observed is laid bare as patients, men and women alike, are stripped naked in front of the camera. The medics' dominant gaze is identified with that of a camera, which further radicalizes the contrast between the ill and the healthy, knowledgeable and ignorant, advanced and backward. The mechanical camera-eye allows the audience to follow the medical examination, identifying spectators with the modern surveying gaze of the medical personnel and recording equipment.

Nakedness – particularly in contrast to the uniformed, white outfits of the medics – becomes an important marker separating the 'primitive' from the 'modern'. This episode includes numerous close-ups of patients' skin and facial deformities, and points out blind patients or those with impaired vision, emphasizing the primacy of the camera as a proxy for the normative gaze, in identifying disease and marking the lower 'civilization level' of the 'other'. Furthermore, the film frames issues of sexuality and health by contrasting the modern Soviet way of seeing to the deficient eyesight of the indigenous population. As Sander Gilman has pointed out, 'the image of the "deformed" face of the ethnic group parallels the social anxiety about the sexual. Society's notions of physical deformity are virtually always associated with notions of moral difference.'[36]

Indeed, sexuality and sexual practices were a focus of the Soviet expedition's research.[37] If films on disease and health focused on an individual rather than an ethnically-defined group (as, for example, *A Shame to Admit* [*Stydno skazat'*, 1930], an agitfilm that focused on the importance of treating venereal diseases by telling a fictionalized story of a sailor hiding his illness from his wife and comrades), they tended to downplay or altogether avoid ethnic ascription. For 'the Buryats', however, their collective conversion to the Soviet lifestyle (presented as a proxy for a 'Western' one) and political framework appeared as a prerequisite for a cure.

The medics' interaction with the population follows the patterns of standardized medical practices aiming at collecting large sets of data. The emerging landscape of a peculiar medical 'contact zone' brings to the fore the underlying power relations between the indigenous population and the Western 'progress bearers' translated into a hierarchical representation of traditional and modern healing practices. In the film, scars and other body marks are introduced as the 'results of the Lamas' healing', implying – without further visual 'proof' – the possession of an alternative and successful medical treatment.

The film puts its emphasis not on the patients suffering from acute forms of diseases, but on the impact of the lifestyle on the younger generation. The medical examination of the population is followed by images of youths studying and collectively doing physical exercises, presenting 'visual evidence' for the transformation of the Buryat culture. The socialization of the young is shown as a way to institute change. The closing scene depicts uniformed, muscular bodies freed from their 'ethnic diseases' and united with the other nationalities of the Soviet Union through the common denominator of health. This image embodies the successful transformation of the religious, cultural and sexual practices, which in turn ensures their seamless integration into the Soviet body politic. The healthy and fit national body is posited as a prescribed model for all the inhabitants of the Soviet Union, bringing together the mission of

Figure 5.1 Still from *Altai-Kizhi* (1929). Pagan sacrifices: exhibiting the markers of radical cultural 'otherness'.

the *kulturfilm* with 'the Soviet mission of *kulturnost*'.[38] The healthy and assimilated youth are also presented as an alternative and proper master of the country's natural riches.

Other *kulturfilms* also include references to indigenous lifestyles from the perspective of their impact on hygienic practices. Vladimir Stepanov's *Altai-Kizhi* (1929) focuses on the transformation of the nomadic practices of the Altai people.[39] Opening with spectacular panoramic landscape, the film presents the nomadic Altai population (referred to as Oirot prior to 1948) accompanied by their cattle.[40] The film's most memorable shots feature a communal prayer, a ritual horse sacrifice and an ensuing feast wherein the horse's skin is left out to dry. At the same time, the intertitles comment on the lifestyle as 'tedious and devoid of feasts' and denigrates local cultural practices, advocated settling and the establishment of *kolkhozes* and *dekulakization* with the prescribed logic of class struggle.[41] A central episode of the film features the arrival of a sanitary

124

Figure 5.2 Still from *Altai-Kizhi* (1929). The civilizing mission on record: the medical station.

camp and medical examination. Three years later, the visually arresting images of the dried horse skin were shown as a powerful metaphor of cultural otherness in Grigorii Kozintsev and Leonid Trauberg's *Alone*. *Altai-Kizhi*, however, used this image as a visual argument for erasing cultural differences.

Commentary on nomadic culture also appears in Nikolai Kudriavtsev's *Lake Baikal* [*Baikal*, 1929], another travelogue shot in Southern Siberia. Filmed by Vasilii Beliaev, the cameraman of *Across Buryat-Mongolia*, the film begins in Irkutsk, the unofficial capital of Eastern Siberia. Natural vistas and town panoramas merge the natural and the historical image of Siberia as exemplified by a visit to a regional history museum. Placing Buddhist art and ritual objects within the museum framework, the film-makers mark them as elements of the past, withdrawn from the network of daily interaction, aestheticized and estranged. The museum visit precedes an overview of a food market, which demonstrates the natural riches of the area.

125

The dynamic tension between images of nature and culture is the underlying theme of the film. The western shore of Lake Baikal is introduced as a realm of 'untouched' nature. As the camera slowly pans across to show pristine panoramas, the indigenous population appears to be an organic part of the lake and the surrounding taiga. The entrance to a Buryat village is again marked by a dried horse skin, a reminder of the pagan beliefs of the community shown later attending a religious feast in honour of Maitreya Buddha. Images of a neighbouring Russian village are accompanied by statistics emphasizing the minority (39 per cent) presence of Russians in the area compared to the Buryats (61 per cent).[42]

Like *Altai-Kizhi*, *Lake Baikal* oscillates between an ethnographic gaze and a normative evolutionary rhetoric. While the religious and daily practices of the Buryats in *Lake Baikal* were not outwardly branded 'unhygienic', their museum status inherently implied their obsolescence. Together with the natural resources of the region, the health issues described in the film emphasize the touristic potential of the area, highlighting a refurbished

Figure 5.3 Still from *Lake Baikal* (1929). The 'caught unawares' observation subverted by the intense gaze of one of the guests.

126

sanatorium for rheumatism and tuberculosis at the Arshan springs which had been in use since the late nineteenth century. The opposition of old versus new lifestyles is highlighted through references to growing health tourism.

In the 1930s, the emphasis on disease in *kulturfilms* receded. As one of the indirect results of the 'cultural revolution', hygienic concerns were relegated to the realm of the past. In 1933, *The Law of the Steppes* [*Zakon stepei*, 1933, director Alexander Slobodnik] produced by Vostokfilm, contrasted the life of the Buryats before and after the Revolution. By the time the Oirot Autonomous Republic celebrated its tenth anniversary, themes of hygiene and health acquired a standard model of representation. The anniversary film *Oirotia* (1932) opened with Lenin's quotation stating that nomadism was a precondition for 'patriarchate, semi-wildness, and real barbarism'. This 'great Oirot', as Lenin was named in the 1924 fiction film, *The Valley of Tears*, marked a historical watershed, contrasting 'barbarism' to life under the Soviet regime, and thus implied a profound transformation of living conditions and practices. An important part of this transformation included the consolidation of the norms of individual body hygiene which, along with literacy and the *kolkhoz*, were presented as an achievement of Soviet power.

The image of the ideal Soviet body, irrespective of its national belonging, accommodated Western patterns of health and beauty.[43] Soviet heroes and heroines were portrayed as healthy and young, devoid of visual markers of illness or signs of cultural differences such as traditional clothing, piercings or 'excessive' decorations. The final scene of another jubilee film, Nikolai Anoshchenko's *On the Asian Border* [*Na granitse Azii*, 1930], highlighted this pattern in a series of close-ups with smiling faces introduced as Bashkir, Tatar, Russian, and Chuvash. During the short screening time, the filmed subjects of travelogues journey across condensed time from 'backward' individuals into the modern, healthy Soviet future.

Clearing the Vision: Eye Diseases and Constructions of New National Bodies

Skin was not the only part of the body marking both purity and danger. Other bodily portals carried the threat of contamination and thus presented potential or actual danger. As Tricia Stark has pointed out, early Soviet culture and its self-proclaimed guardians – social hygienists – 'concerned themselves with bodily purity and the protection of those areas subject to penetration – the mouth, the eyes, and other orifices'.[44]

Eyes and eyesight were central to the advancement of the new optics of the Soviet regime, making representation of eye diseases on the screen a rich trope extending beyond its immediate medical interpretative framework. Emphasizing the role of cinema in developing new mechanisms of visual perception was the starting point of Vertov's manifesto. He ascribed the machine eye the power to liberate and emancipate 'weak' and 'imperfect' human vision. His experiments with this new vision aimed at liberating as much as directing the way spectators see. For Vertov, the acquisition of a new vision was considered *sine qua non* of a future, 'perfected' human.

Along with emphasizing the empowering impact of the camera on the human eye, film-makers repeatedly revisited the other side of vision, namely its deficiency. Among early experiments with 'imaginary films' which Kinoks worked on to develop observational skills, Vertov composed a written etude 'Eyes', which comprises forty-one different forms and ways of seeing:

1. Blind (groping on the street)
2. Short-sighted
3. Sleeping
4. Dead eyes
5. Kinok-observer eyes
6. Editors' eyes
7. Eyes, armed with binoculars
8. Looking through a spyglass on a boulevard
9. Sweet eyes peeping through a crack
10. Prostitute's eyes calling a man
11. Man's eyes
12. GIK female student – exercise 'eyes'
13. Eyes of a worker at a machine
14. Newborn's eyes
15. Madman's eyes [...][45]

Rather than striving for total description of vision, the list relies on 'the principle of etcetera' characterized by ultimate expandability.[46] Thinking in visual categories, Vertov contrasts normative and particular, and employs an eccentric collection principle to assemble cases which represent altered, obstructed, estranged, or altogether blocked vision.

The formation of the normative Soviet way of seeing was undertaken in cinema along with photography, cartography, and other fields of visual production. Thematizing blindness gave imperfect vision new political connotations.[47] Fighting eye diseases such as trachoma implied not only medical interference, but the transformation of a lifestyle, which served as a powerful old/new opposition in *kulturfilms*. The normative expectations of the 'new sight' is shown through the representations of anomalies of vision. The latter highlights new dimensions of the Soviet visual vocabulary and redefines the notions of norm and deviation, inscribing bodily representations to political and ideological agendas.

Indigenous vision and practices of seeing were not always associated with the motifs of disease and illness. Chapter 4 discussed the construction of a peculiar native scopic regime in Alexander Litvinov's films inspired by Vladimir Arsenev's writings. Dersu possessed advanced visual skills for 'reading nature'; Arsenev represented this visual capacity as a unique feature of the 'forest people'. Just like the collective 'advantages' of vision, eye deficiencies as well as representations of blindness were used to impose hierarchical taxonomies, legitimize the models of cultural development, and naturalize a politically-defined identity.

In the 1920s, eye diseases were considered to have reached an epidemic dimension in several areas in Central Russia. This problem is addressed in *The Chuvash Land* [*Zemlia chuvashskaia*, 1927], produced by the short-lived Chuvashkino studio, and is an exemplary case of evolving *kulturfilm* conventions.[48] Commissioned to celebrate the tenth anniversary of the Revolution, *The Chuvash Land* was directed by an aspiring journalist-turned-film-maker, Vlad (Vladislav) Korolevich. The commissioner, the Chuvash Commissariat of Enlightenment, expected a standard jubilee film, contrasting the dark past with the bright present.[49] Korolevich rejected this scheme and appealed to the 'Chuvash masses' through the local newspaper to send in ideas for the film. This initiative allowed him to later argue that 'the authorship of the film belongs to them [the Chuvash people]. It is their film, they should create it and take responsibility for it, and the film crew only fulfils the technical tasks'.[50] The director further stated that the advice the crew received from the local Komsomol, Women's Society, Public Health Department and from peasants and workers was incorporated into the script. In fact, Korolevich opens the film with images of marching crowds introduced as 'the authors of the film'.

The Chuvash Land postulated the compactness and specificity of Chuvash culture. Some critics, based on scenes of traditional work practices and festivities, wrote about it as an 'ethnographic film [...] [which] could be convincing and impressive for the mass audience'.[51] Despite, or perhaps due to, the advice the director received, the film narrative did not fully abandon a schematic structure; instead, it reproduced a triad of idyllic nature, past sufferings and contemporary progress. The director re-enacted historical episodes, fusing elements of melodrama, action and comedy from the repertoire of fiction productions. The eclectic outcome was defined by Boltianskii as 'a lyrical film with epic elements'.[52]

Despite the upcoming anniversary of the Republic, Sovkino management deemed the film of poor quality and refused to distribute it. To challenge this decision, the director initiated a public debate, which somewhat unexpectedly grew into a vivid discussion. Two public screenings with discussions were organized by the Organization of the Friends of Soviet Cinema (ODSK) and by film professionals in the Association of Revolutionary Cinematography (ARRK).[53] The comparison of the two debates sheds light on the contemporary reception of a hybrid film that cut across the conventions of 'fiction' and 'non-fiction'. The debate at ODSK gathered a mixed crowd of journalists, Party functionaries and select workers who focused on the film's political message. The studio was praised for the 'agitational' value of the film which fulfilled 'the practical objective of presenting a cinematographic report for the tenth anniversary of the October Revolution', but at the same time was criticized for the film's schematic approach and low professionalism.[54]

The discussion at ARRK took a different turn. The audience of 135 people – unusually large for a run-of-the-mill jubilee *kulturfilm* from a regional studio – used the occasion to debate the nature and principles of non-fiction. The professional community concentrated on the perceived violation of the conceptual division between fiction and non-fiction. Erofeev was among the most active critics of the film, arguing against the 'contamination' of material: 'this film is built as a fiction film with actors appearing as in a provincial theatre, with mood and tears – one does not trust this film. This film was criticized as a fiction film, but it should be [criticized] as a non-fiction one.'[55] The result, he concluded, is that 'without achieving the goal of emotional impact on the viewer, it undermines [the] spectator's trust in documentary material, [while] at the same time evoking suspicions in its authenticity'.[56]

Tretiakov rejected the film's 'pathetic style' and remarked on the 'competition between the material caught unaware and the theatrical (re-enacted) parts, which appear in patches'.[57] In 1927, the pastiche nature of the material made film-makers and film critics judge the hybrid film as 'compromising'. Within just a few years, the anti-documentarist campaign revised these views, reinstating the legitimacy and priority of such hybrid genres that became a dominant mode of documentary representation (see Chapters 1 and 4).

While film-makers and critics argued about ways of seeing the film, the film itself centred on questions of vision. Adhering to the principles of 'screen authenticity' in which the filmed subjects were shown unaware of the camera, Korolevich wrote at length on the difficulties he had in achieving this illusion.[58] He had to consistently prevent his subjects from entering a dialogical relationship with the camera by, at the least, establishing eye contact with a film-maker or cameraman behind the camera. To these undisciplined and untrained film subjects, Korolevich contrasted the 'perfect eye' of the blind and the deformed eyes of the ill. The contrast laid bare the power relations between the recorded and the recording equipment operated by the film crew. In a short article, 'Look at the Camera!', Korolevich describes the painstaking efforts it took to teach the Chuvash workers not to look at the camera during filming. He compared the dozens of takes needed to secure the impression of authenticity to the experience of filming patients suffering from trachoma. In this case, Korolevich remarks, the intentions of the cameraman and director were the opposite: to record an extensive number of close-ups of the blind, going after the most visually shocking footage of the 'purulent, red, swollen eyes of the elders, the young, the children. Successions of the blind with trachoma-eaten walleyes.

Mothers, infecting their children with trachoma'.[59] The camera was used as a training device for both the film's subjects and the audience, coached to see illness and health in both national and political terms.

The director contrasts the unruly healthy eyes of the workers to the immobilized and impaired eyes of the ill: 'Tired by the work with watching eyes, we went to film trachoma'.[60] The bodies deprived of the active power of vision were meant to teach the importance of a hygienic lifestyle to viewers and to condemn their traditional lifestyles. They also inadvertently demonstrated how bodies deprived of the individual capacity for sight are docile, easily manageable and able to project an act of seeing on a political framework of 'proper' vision. Korolevich's ideal subject is blindly unaware of the camera, but at the same time possesses an ideal body not marked by the signs of a disease connected with the past. The 'infectious' and 'contaminated' old lifestyle is replaced by Soviet modernity.

The prominence of the imagery of hospitals and maternity wards is intended to demonstrate the achievements of the new regime and to connect individual health with the political regime. Hospitals stand not only in opposition to disease, but to traditional healing as well. Korolevich mentions the difficulties the crew encountered in their search for an 'authentic' and sufficiently exotic-looking, local, traditional healer (*iomzia*). Shamanism and its healing methods are placed in opposition to modern medicine, which the Soviet regime united with industrialism, collectivization, and cultural revolution.[61] Korolevich's account creates a symbolic competition over the 'correct' way of seeing when he contrasts the blind Chuvash grandmothers with the sharp-sighted, young Komsomol members.[62]

The director invites the audience to identify with the ideologically and politically 'healthy' Soviet subjects through the one-way communication established by the camera. The schematic opposition of old vs. new, advanced by Korolevich with the impeccable zeal of the neophyte, spotlighted the markers of health – identified with correct and controlled vision – as having broader implications for Soviet film production. His approach adapted the Kinoks' desire for 'the perfect electric man'[63] and made the eyesight a primary battlefield for the correct vision of the future. Transforming ways of seeing are accompanied by changes in lifestyle and outlook, which presume a new, uniformed identity. Similarly to *Across Buryat-Mongolia*, *The Chuvash Land* includes episodes with gymnastic exercises and military drills, leading to a straightforwardly militant agitational ending. The film closes with a simulated military attack featuring ranks of uniform-dressed, healthy and armed bodies marching straight at the camera.

The loss and return of eyesight is a recurrent motif in films featuring other minorities such as the Mari, Mordvins, Bashkirs, Chuvash and Udmurt (*The Mari people* [*Mariitsy*, 1928], *Legacy of the Past – Fighting Trachoma* [*Nasledie proshlogo – bor'ba s trakhomoi*, 1930], *Scourge of Time* [*Bich vremeni*, 1931], *On the Asian Border* [*Na granitse Azii*, 1930], *From the Darkness of Centuries* [*Iz t'my vekov*, 1934]). The emergence of a new, 'politically healthy' eyesight underlies the transformation of both the body and the landscape.

The representations of national minorities on film follows a normative representation of the individual body. Korolevich depicted the prescribed transformation of the national body to that which is healthy, athletic, unmarked by signs of cultural difference and imbued with political loyalty. The transformation of the masses from 'ethnographic' to 'militant' subjects emphasized the acquisition of a new, correct vision, which implied the ability to identify and see the enemy. It was straightforwardly exemplified in *From the Darkness of Centuries*, made by another former Kinok, Alexander Lemberg, Vertov's associate and cameraman on *A Sixth Part of the World*.[64] His own film on the Mordvins, a Finno-Ugrian minority, cast amateurs to perform a scripted narrative, which highlighted the blurred genre conventions. Lemberg also incorporated scenes with original animation to teach viewers to identify political enemies behind a seemingly innocent façade.

Journeys of Health: Tourist Bodies in Motion

Ideal bodies, free of disease and ethnic 'peculiarities' alike, increasingly populated Soviet screens throughout the 1930s.[65] The emergence of a new body canon in the late 1920s to early 1930s took place along with the development of a tourist infrastructure in the Soviet Union.[66] In January 1927, on the initiative of *Komsomolskaia pravda*, the Committee on Tourism began work, and a year later the shareholding society SovTur was created. A growing touristic network and active support of tourist initiatives rationalized a new understanding of travel which, according to the early Soviet tourist doctrine, was to educate and physically train Soviet subjects. Striving to direct travel impulses, the Soviet tourist movement prescribed not only concrete routes, but also offered a model of desired behaviour to tourists.[67]

Soviet tourism was perceived as a matter of health and a state priority, and involved officials like Nikolai Semashko, the People's Commissar's of Public Health, as well as Nikolai Krylenko, the People's Commissar for Justice and Nikolai Gorbunov, Secretary of the Council of People's Commissars of the USSR. Irina Sandomirskaia has noted that the establishment of state control over individual mobility went along with marginalizing alternative forms of travel, such as religious pilgrimages and wandering. At the same time, new forms of travel fused the 'administrative tone with the voice of individual desire, institutional voice with folklore motifs, articulation of power with the counterpoint of high cultural value'.[68] The Soviet ideologies opposed socialist tourism to the 'bourgeois' idea of travel (understood as the practice of a privileged subject). Socialist tourism provided new forms of spatial appropriation and was presented as 'a form of cultural revolution' and 'one of those steps, on which the masses perform their ascendance to the heights of culture'.[69] The Soviet tourist emerged in parallel with the formation of a tourist gaze.[70]

Soviet tourism in the 1920s sought to give a class twist to pre-Revolutionary Russian practices and offer a new, proletarian and 'multinational' interpretation of the sights exposed to the tourist gaze. Films featuring the Soviet tourist combined advertisement with education, as they not only attracted attention to new itineraries, but also offered a narrative and a role model. The Soviet tourist perspective gradually came to replace that of the hygienist. Information on tourist routes was regularly published in central newspapers. In 1929, a new journal *Na sushe i na more* (*On the Land and on the Sea*) was established as a platform for developing new discourses and visions of spatial explorations. The tourist, presented as a new type of explorer, also appeared in the *kulturfilms* of the 1930s to offer new behavioural codes while transforming and commodifying the landscape in line with the new forms and practices of travel.[71] This new spatial mapping is exemplified in Nikolai Prozorovskii's *Four in a Boat. From Nizhnii Novgorod to Astrakhan* [*Chetvero v lodke. Ot Nizhnego do*

Astrakhani, 1930], which followed three men and a woman visiting historical, natural and industrial sites along the Volga river.

Rivers and seas were among the most favoured sights for constructing tourist optics. In late nineteenth century Russia, the Volga was constructed as an axis structuring and organizing Russian identity discourses,
and emerged as a tourist destination in the 1890s.[72] Multiple actors – government officials, early entrepreneurs, painters and writers – contributed
to packaging the attractive and 'consumable' idea of traveling down the
river. Western European tourist patterns were also creatively adapted in the
Russian and, later, Soviet context. Multiple German *kulturfilms* films, such
as *Der Rhein in Vergangenheit und Gegenwart* (1922), *Die deutsche Nordsee*
(1925), *Die deutsche Ostsee* (1928), and *Die Donau – Vom Schwarzwald bis
zum Schwarzen Meer* (1929) portrayed rivers and seas as symbolic arteries
and reservoirs unifying German culture both historically and spatially. In
Soviet cinema, too, boats constituted 'a key site of a new kind of travel',
which were associated primarily with leisure.[73] Transferring the concept
of a river travelogue into the Soviet context required an 'adjustment' to

Figure 5.4 Still from *Four in a Boat* (1930). Soviet tourists set off to explore the
country.

a multinational framework, transforming both pre-Revolutionary and the imported legacies.

In *Four in a Boat*, model factory employees receive travel vouchers for their exemplary work. The group includes three men – a worker, an accountant and a young club instructor – and a young female editor of the factory newspaper, spending their well-deserved holidays in a 'cultured' manner. Travelling down the river in a small motorboat, the four tourists visit historic monuments, factories and *kolkhozes*, and spend time fishing, hunting and camping fireside. As prescribed by the ethos of proletarian tourism, their itinerary expands the range of traditional cultural heritage sites cultivated by the *kraevedenie* (local lore) tradition to incorporate new venues, and thus introduces information on industry and agriculture as a component of edifying recreation.[74]

An animated map shows the group's itinerary, highlighting sites embodying modernity and change, like a cement factory in Volsk and a *kolkhoz* in the vicinities of Saratov, over the pastoral landscapes. In the Mari Region, the tourists are introduced to the forestry industry. In Cheboksary, the capital city of the Chuvash Republic, the group visits a local museum occupying the building of a former Orthodox church. In Kazan, they observe monuments commemorating the fall of the Khanate of Kazan to Moscovite Russia and tour a printing house publishing in Tatar. The legacy of the Russian Empire is both reinforced and challenged, presenting the Soviet Union as a 'better heir'. At the same time, new *lieux de mémoire* emerge: the museum in Lenin's birthplace, Ulianovsk, and industrial construction sites in Stalingrad, for example, are shown as new loci of symbolic power.

Sites of religious veneration change their meaning in the symbolic spatial hierarchy. In Kalmykia, the tourists visit a functioning Buddhist temple which is introduced as a monument of and to the past and the monks are described as 'lazy-bones' in opposition to the *kolkhoz* workers. The combination of socialist, rural, urban, Orthodox and Buddhist references portray the Volga as a micro-universe, and allow viewers to gain the experience of cultural otherness for which, as an intertitle states, 'one does not need to go to Mongolia'. Finally, the boat reaches Astrakhan in the delta, from where the group takes a train home after this model edifying trip; 'educated' and 'strengthened' they return 'to the hot daily work [*v goriachie budni!*]'.

Offering an image of a cultured and class-conscious tourist as a role model, Soviet *kulturfilms* encouraged viewers to consume the country's landscapes in a prescribed way. Soviet tourism fulfilled the pragmatic function of sustaining the able and fit bodies which were required of the Soviet heroes of the 1930s, while its representation demonstrated the ideological transformation of body and space. References to disease and deformity were relegated to the past and ascribed to ideological opponents. Originally a characteristic of 'backward' minorities, medical metaphors of impaired health and vision became political markers. The tourist gaze perpetuated the consumption of 'exotic' visual sites, but it was framed as an alternative to the logic of individual travellers and relied on the notion of a shared Soviet identity. *Kulturfilms* encouraged viewers to identify with the screen tourists who appropriated the picturesque scenery and ethnic markers as part of the commodified landscape. While the tourist industry re-mapped space by designing new paths, some of the most popular routes led to the most 'uncanny' imperial region, the Caucasus, where the next chapter takes us.

6

Touring the Caucasus

Here I see streams at their sources up-welling,
The grim avalanches unrolling and swelling!
                    Alexander Pushkin, 'The Caucasus'[1]

Located between the Black and Caspian Seas, and defined by a mountain range that divides it into Northern and Southern parts (the latter known as Transcaucasia), the Caucasus has been described by Bruce Grant as 'a babbling tower of religions, languages, peoples, and conflicts'.[2] Following its incorporation into the Russian Empire, the Caucasus became one of the most 'uncanny' imperial spaces; its mountainous landscapes inspired poetry, prose and a large visual corpus of works.[3] Carrying the legacy of conflict and subjugation, as well as contradictory romantic imprints of noble and ignoble savagery, it was imagined as a space of violence and unrestrained military bravura, and mythologized as a territory for free minds in exile. Early twentieth-century cinema found nourishing sources in the romanticized images of freedom and wilderness concocted in the memoirs of the officers stationed in the Caucasus, as well as romantic travelogues, *luboks* (cheap lithographic prints), orientalist paintings and pulp-fiction novels.[4]

How could *kulturfilms* enter, utilize and reconstruct the elaborate imagery that had already developed in literature and the visual arts in and about the Caucasus? Despite resolute rhetorical attempts to establish a break with the imperial past, the policies targeting ethnic minorities in the region – as well as other Soviet nationalities – combined imprints of romanticism and missionary traditions reformatting the belief that 'alphabets are always adopted along with faith' in a Bolshevik tone.[5] The mosaic ethnic portrait of the North Caucasus in *kulturfilms* combined the legacy of the nineteenth-century, missionary, educational paradigm with the logic of indigenization, enhancing and actively constructing ethnic identities and national languages in the region.

Soviet power in the region was established through a protracted conflict that depended on a combination of force and diplomacy in which the trump card of national self-determination was played out to the Bolsheviks' advantage.[6] Following the consolidation of Soviet power in the North and South Caucasus, the region's history was rewritten in anti-colonial fashion, describing the nineteenth-century anti-Russian forces as national-liberation resistance fighters. At the same time, a campaign to promote tourism in the Soviet Union was launched. *Kulturfilms* played an active part in shaping the popular Soviet image of the Caucasus (both the mountains and its coastline) as one of the primary destinations for leisure, relaxation and health resorts, as well as alpinism, a new form of proletarian tourism.[7]

Among the first Soviet journalists travelling across the mountainous regions in Georgia in 1923–24, Zinaida Richter reflected in her book *Kavkaz nashikh dnei* (*Caucasus Today*) on the difficulties of navigating between the Scylla of propaganda and the Charybdis of exoticism when writing about the Caucasus:

> I was most afraid to make a 'Soviet candy' out of the Caucasus. But at the same time I did not want the readers to get a wrong impression of the Caucasus and the Soviet authorities [there] on the basis of my description of the Upper Svanetia and Khevsureti, where there is still a lot of darkness and where blood vengeance rages.[8]

Rikhter wrote critically of both the imperial travellers of the past as well as the 'Western' tourists who, she argued, missed the essence of the area and the people. The 'correct' way of seeing could only be achieved by developing a new and properly Soviet perspective:

> Contrary to the titled presidents of imperial societies, who supported the Russification policy in the area while traveling with all the comforts in governors' carriages, we see now what was invisible to them. We not only see archeological antiquities and beautiful views from the 20,000 feet high, but first of all genuine, unvarnished life – our new Soviet way of life. [...]
>
> English and American tourists would be jealous of such a journey. But they would be surprised even more if they saw how Soviet journalists travel across mountains and glaciers. A western tourist looks like a Christmas tree in his special hiking boots, with alpine trekking poles, loaded with flags, binoculars, tents, footbridges and so on. Nonsense! No American mountain boots can be compared with the indigenous goat-skin shoes [...] and a felt cloak [burka] – nothing else is needed in the mountains.[9]

The makers of Soviet non-fiction shared this determination to show the space and its inhabitants in a novel way. To this end, *kulturfilms* experimented with various strategies of 'sovietizing' the space, from turning their lens towards the region's diverse ethnic groups, to promoting new tourist optics, or by radically transforming space in line with the industrialization policy. In addition, these films constructed new versions of the past and present, and sought to reframe long-term conflicts in the language of the socialist 'friendship of nations', thereby inscribing the region within the Soviet multinational 'family'.

In the Mountains of the Caucasus [*V gorakh Kavkaza*, 1927], filmed by Elmurza Tlatov,[10] provides an example of the new rhetoric of the multi-ethnic Caucasus. Personifying the external audience for whom this presentation was intended, the film features Henri Barbusse on his first visit to the Caucasus. Barbusse travelled across the Soviet Union and returned to the Caucasus on several occasions in the 1930s. It was his first trip, however, that made him most enthusiastic about the Soviet nationality policy, which he hailed as a primary revolutionary achievement distinguishing the regime not only from tsarism, but also from a social-democratic alternative suppressed by the Bolsheviks in Transcaucasia.[11]

In the Mountains of the Caucasus uses the external perspective of this important 'witness' to present ethnic groups of the North Caucasus (the film introduces Chechens, Ingush, Ossetians, Kabardins, Karachaevs, Cherkess, Nogais, Adyges and Mountain Jews). The film follows the structural principle of a photographic travel album, showcasing memorials, construction sites and panoramas of different towns (Vladikavkaz, Grozny and Nalchik). The film positions Barbusse as the bearer of the external gaze, creating a context and a frame for a 'self-portrait' that normalizes the image of the North Caucasus as a modern, dynamically developing and fully Soviet region.

National film studios in the Republics of Georgia, Armenia and Azerbaijan produced an increasing number of films displaying mountainous backdrops and exploring traditional cultures.[12] Yet the picturesque

Figure 6.1 Still from *In the Mountains of the Caucasus* (1927). Observer and observed in front of the camera: Henri Barbusse in the North Caucasus.

141

landscapes of the Caucasus did not cease to attract film-makers from the central studios. By 1926, the growing number of 'mountainous' films prompted a sarcastic remark from one film critic:

> Caucasian films begin to disappoint with their repetitiveness. They are usually based on some suspicious 'folk' legends, where a tall and perfectly shaved *abrek* [outlaw] who widely rolls his eyes on any occasion takes revenge on an exploitative duke with a marvellous moustache and lion's hair. Women are of course raped. This is their destiny. [...] The whole plot centres on a woman, everything else is just a matter of decency – fragments of ideology, ethnography, and so on. [...] What is almost always good is landscape. But this is not really an achievement of our film-makers. The beauty of Caucasian nature is just made to be filmed.[13]

The Soviet press called upon film practitioners to find new ways of filming the Caucasus 'without embellishment'. The head of Vostokkino's Board, Berd Kotiev directed his indignation towards a range of 'oriental' films such as *Eyes of Andozia* [*Glaza Andozii*], *Abrek Zaur* and *Under the Burden of Adat* [*Pod vlast'iu adata*] (all 1926), and argued for replacing the romantic tales of *abreks* (outlaws) with contemporary materials showing socialist achievements and the ongoing modernization of the region.[14] Even after the *abreks* transformation from romantic outcasts to class-conscious freedom-fighters struggling against the colonial expansion of the Russian empire in the Caucasus, these fictional mountaineers were still seen as an obstacle for getting to know the 'Caucasus as it is'.[15]

Early Soviet historiography used a straightforwardly anti-colonial rhetoric to frame the imperial history of the nineteenth-century wars in the North Caucasus as a national-liberation struggle for independence, and promoted the Soviet regime as a solution to long-term conflicts.[16] Vladimir Bobrovnikov has pointed out how the discursive coordinates for imagining and narrating the Caucasus changed from the pre-Revolutionary opposition of 'civilization' and 'wilderness' to that of 'domination' and 'resistance' in the early Soviet years.[17] Along these lines, early Soviet films reframed the conflicts within an anti-colonial framework, often with the help of film-makers and writers from the capital.

Sergei Tretiakov, for example, who channelled the ideas of *LEF* to Georgian artists, was among the important influences in 1920s Georgian cinema.[18] Tretiakov's scripts were made into films by Nikoloz (Nikolai) Shengelaia (*Eliso*, 1928), Mikhail Chiaureli (*Khabarda*, 1931) and Mikhail Kalatozishvili (who changed his name to Kalatozov) (*Salt for Svanetia* [Sol' Svanetii, 1930]) – providing a formative experience for a new generation of film-makers in Georgia. *Eliso* is an adaptation of Alexander Kazbegi's novel on the 1864 forced expulsion of the Chechen community to Ottoman Turkey from the territories conquered by the Russian Empire. Interested in the masses as 'the engine of history', Tretiakov and Shengelaia reworked the tragic love story of a Chechen, Eliso, and a Khevsur,[19] Vazhia, into a study of the social forces underlying ethnic conflicts to show the impossibility of private happiness in the context of discriminatory imperial politics.

Critics in Moscow hailed the film for its 'authentic' representation of 'local conditions' that 'show and characterize this [indigenous] life'.[20] Ironically, Tretiakov himself confessed the 'insignificant historical value of the film', pointing out 'those clichés, which constantly reappear' on film: *lezginka* (Caucasian dance), men in epaulettes, people with bullock carts and torches.[21] The misrepresentations of Chechen customs were also noticed by a local film critic who lamented that the film had no Chechen actors or consultants; he concluded that it 'is not showing the real East with blood, nerves, and flesh, but a pale, cachectic, and sugary-operetta fabrication'.[22]

Kulturfilms were seen as an alternative to bring the 'real Caucasus' to the screen. Made by film-makers from central studios, *kulturfilms* differed in the ways they aligned the conflictual past with the official nationality policy, but converged in reinforcing Soviet legitimacy and territorial unity. This chapter introduces films on Dagestan and Chechnya in the North Caucasus, and touches upon representation of two highland regions, Khevsureti and Svanetia (Svaneti), the highest inhabited areas in Georgia. This comparison brings to the forefront different ways of framing ethnic variety and difference. It also points to the emerging 'tourist optics' in presenting the landscape for external consumption by Soviet audiences outside of the region, as well as audiences abroad.

Kulturfilms played an important role in inscribing the diverse ethnic landscape within the Soviet modernization project and presenting it as a different, yet *natural* part of the Soviet Union. Film-makers and cinematographers who travelled from Moscow to film the Caucasus – Nikolai Lebedev, Petr Zotov, Iakov Tolchan and Iurii Zheliabuzhskii – were not equally familiar with the region, but aimed to strengthen the legitimacy of the new regime by emphasizing the conceptual divide between the Soviet Union and the Russian Empire. However, as the films demonstrate, certain conventions of representation challenged this rhetoric.

Dagestan: The Space of Diversity

Within the North Caucasus, Dagestan is marked by the most concentrated cultural diversity, which induced policy-makers to avoid selecting a single titular nationality and to preserve the multinational character of the republic.[23] The non-ethnic name Dagestan – translated as the land of the mountains – remained in use throughout the Soviet era. Dagestan took pride in its exceptional ethnic diversity, which included the Avars, Aguls, Azeris, Chechens, Dargins, Kumyks, Laks, Lezgins, Nogais, Russians, Rutuls, Tabasarans, Tats, Tsakhurs and others as its 'official' ethnic groups.[24]

The suppression of anti-Soviet uprisings and the proclamation of the Dagestan Autonomous Republic required further work to enhance the regime's power through symbolic means.[25] The first short travelogue *Dagestan* (1927) was edited by Sergei Liamin from footage filmed by Iakov Tolchan and Petr Zotov for *A Sixth Part of the World*. Following Vertov's ideas of spatial diversity and unity, Liamin made a cine-race within the borders of one republic. The film started in the capital Makhachkala (the former Port Petrovsk), and took its viewers across the republic to industrial sites and remote mountainous villages, constructing the image of Dagestan as a diverse and rapidly industrializing land. Images of a barrel factory, fishing cooperative and oil tankers were complemented by traditional crafts, agricultural activities and 'mountainous' feasts.

While the film highlighted the ethnic diversity of the territory, the communities on film were not identified. Close-ups of 'mountaineers' did not use ethnic classifiers, while traditional festive practices such as wrestling and tight-rope walking were introduced as generic 'mountaineer' activities. Preserving Vertov's legacy, *Dagestan* further emphasized the unity of the republic through industrial developments, irrigation pro-grammes and modern factories, foregrounding a new foundation for the Soviet Dagestani identity. This modernist discourse reframed the moun-tainous landscape from its associations with romantic freedom-fighters towards an identity of an enlightened citizen. The mountains remained a primary spatial identification that secured the common past, shared future and multi-ethnic coexistence.

The final destination point in *Dagestan* was a remote highland village visited by a representative of the Dagestan Central Executive Committee. Visualizing the presence of the Soviet legal order in the most distant cor-ners of the republic, the film emphasized the full sovietization of the land-scape. Striving to create distance from the Russian imperial legacy, the film redressed the anti-imperial resistance in a positive light. In line with active

Figure 6.2 Still from *Dagestan* (1927). Away from an ethnic identity: a village fair in Dagestan.

historiographic rewriting, Imam Shamil (political and religious leader of the anti-Russian resistance in the nineteenth-century Caucasian war), was referred to not as a religious leader, but as a social revolutionary.[26] The film omitted the religious dimension of the confrontation, but included the site identified as Shamil's tombstone (in fact, the place of his capitulation) as a memorial to the anti-colonial cause.[27] While the role of Islam and especially *sharia* within the Soviet legal system were central among debates in the North Caucasus from 1920 through the early 1930s, references to religion were markedly missing from expedition films on Dagestan. The 'tomb' established a visual and spatial continuity between the rejected past and the glorified present, and became a potent *lieu de mémoire*, a reminder of the bloody conflict and a material sign of imperial victory and dominance.

The mountains continued to serve as a common denominator for representing Dagestan throughout the 1930s. Seven years after *Dagestan*, Mezhrabpomfilm's cameraman Georgii Bobrov made the short travelogue, *Across Dagestan* [*Po Dagestanu*, 1935]. The film largely repeats the main spatial references of Zotov and Tolchan; it opens with a view over the mountains and mirrors the diversity of languages and cultures through variegated landscapes. The region's ethnic groups are likewise not introduced in *Across Dagestan*, enhancing instead a generic, 'mountainous' identity. Bobrov shows Dagestan as a micro-universe of its own with deserts, hills, mountains, valleys and even 'Martian' landscapes, and refers to historical legacies of particular sites by introducing the landscapes of war in the North Caucasus, the place of Shamil's capitulation and a rotunda with his 'tomb'. Bobrov uses these *lieux de mémoire* to unite the mountaineers' opposition to colonial oppression.

One of the film's intertitles describes the developmental path leading 'from mountainous nature to a European city'. Like Zotov, Bobrov demonstrates the creation of modern citizens through images of the construction of schools, health centres and sanatoriums, and by showing newspapers in various local languages. The film also includes a reference to gender equality policy, interpreted as a necessary component of Soviet identity. Traditional habits and crafts retain their picturesque value in 'ethnographic' scenes with jewellery and weaponry craftsmen making elegant pottery and colourful (albeit filmed in black-and-white) carpets, yet they no longer appear central to the lifestyle of a modern citizen.

The image of Dagestan as a modern, multicultural shop-window of the Sovietized Caucasus was also created for export; in 1938, the short film *Dagestan* was produced with French intertitles and without credits to emphasize its impartial newsreel status. This film combined images of nature with Soviet-driven modernity to showcase the republic's abundance of natural resources. It also advanced a strong emancipatory rhetoric that showed women at work, as well as everyday comforts and new consumption patterns. The images of an electric iron and a boiler in a village, however exceptional in mountainous households at the time, and champagne produced at a local factory fought the concept of backwardness and intended to demonstrate emerging Soviet consumerism to the West.[28] The film made no references to the ethnic composition of the republic. The absence of ethnic references also marked *Dagestan* (1946), which showed the Dagestanis as a collective body enjoying the festive cornucopia of the present. In this later film, the image of Stalin emerges as the ultimate metaphor of unity.

The republic was visualised as an ethnically diverse space without listing ethnicities or introducing ethnic 'types' but through the metaphor of a mountainous landscape as a space of diversity. Images of nature replaced potentially more explosive images of religion. A supra-ethnic discourse was exceptional in Soviet *kulturfilms* employing nationalizing optics. By comparison, the filmic representations of Chechnya demonstrate the emergence of a radically different pattern for showing the 'mountaineering' identity.

Chechnya As It Is: Native and Tourist Gazes

Among the many images of the Caucasus, the films about Chechnya evoke particular interest as sensitive indicators of changing visual and nationality politics in the Soviet Union. Shifting Soviet administrative borders first made the territory of Chechnya part of the multinational Mountain [Gorskaia] Republic. Later it was included in the Chechen-Ingush Republic before finally becoming institutionalized as an Autonomous Republic of the RSFSR. The historiographic narratives reflect these changes; at various points Soviet historiography portrayed Chechens as romantic children of nature, dangerous rebels, honourable freedom fighters, and religious fanatics.[29] Two travelogues by Nikolai Lebedev represent the attempts to reformat the image of Chechnya and the Caucasus in line with the new policies of Soviet nation-building. Following his debut *Across Europe* [*Po Evrope*, 1925], and attempts to provide a theoretical overview of *kulturfilm* as a film form, Lebedev aspired for more hands-on experience.[30] In 1928, he undertook a trip to the Caucasus, which resulted in two expedition films: *Land of the Nakhcho* [*Strana Nakhcho*, 1929] and *Gates of the Caucasus* [*Vorota Kavkaza*, 1929], both Sovkino productions.[31]

Without knowledge of the local context, Lebedev involved Khalid Oshaev as his consultant. Oshaev was the Head of the Department of Public Education in Chechnya and a rising writer and playwright, as well as a creator of the Latin-based Chechen alphabet. In 1928, Oshaev published *V serdtse Chechni* (*In the Heart of Chechnya*), which largely influenced the film's line of argument and could be seen as a reason behind changing the Sovkino working title 'Chechnya' to the ethnonym 'Nakhcho', which emphasizes the 'insider's perspective' adopted in the film.[32]

Land of the Nakhcho speaks to the viewer in the first person through the voice of a local 'guide'. The film opens with a close-up of a narrator – an anonymous *tipazh* whose expressive mimic and passionate eyes accompany viewers throughout the film to establish a personal connection and to facilitate the audience's emphatic attention. The narrator is introduced as a 'real' Chechen. The 'tour' starts by denouncing popular stereotypes about the Caucasus, such as General Ermolov's notes on the Caucasian War, Mikhail Lermontov's poem about an 'evil Chechen' and the 'Caucasian' melodramas, all of which are mocked and discarded. The viewers are promised instead a ride across the authentic Chechnya.

Introducing a subjective voice was an unorthodox decision for expedition films, which conventionally relied on anonymous and objective commentary presenting 'universal' and 'scientific' facts as introduced by an omnipotent external observer. With Oshaev, Lebedev radically revised this stance and argued for the inherent authenticity of an indigenous perspective amplified by the non-fiction status of the footage which allowed audiences to 'see for themselves'. However, a Moscow-based crew with limited knowledge of the local context had control over the film's production. Lebedev described the complexity of the situation in a note to a local Party cell at Sovkino:

Figure 6.3 Still from *Land of the Nakhcho* (1929). A Chechen guide introduces 'Chechnya as it is' to the viewers.

I left for Chechnya on 9 April 1928. I went without a script, without preliminary study of the location (I considered such preparations necessary, but they were not allowed), with a very sketchy and approximate shooting plan, with an unsatisfactory budget and even less satisfactory schedule, without adminis-trator and assistant. On 22 April, the cameraman arrived. We spent three weeks in April studying the region, establishing connections and making the plans.[33]

At the same time, when reporting about the expedition to the leading film journal *Sovetskii ekran*, Lebedev tried to appear in full control of the situation while reiterating the colonial stereotypes the local 'guide' intended to subvert:

Chechnya – the wildest and least researched and visually most bare corner of the North Caucasus. Our aim was to give concrete examples as to the heavy economic, everyday [*bytovoi*] and cultural heritage we received from the tsarist regime in the national borderlands.[34]

Shooting without a script, without prior knowledge of the area and without time for proper research, Lebedev reverted to rigid editing to combine an established ethnographic perspective with an unorthodox local voice. Vertov's associate and earlier a member of the Kinok group Ivan Beliakov filmed the details of Chechen life using close-ups of everyday activities in a Vertovian vein. These multiple influences explain the eclectic texture of the film, which combines a primordial rhetoric with an ethnographic perspective and elements of constructivist visual aesthetics confined by the staple imagery of 'Soviet achievements'. Both subjective and objective perspectives converged in constructing Chechnya as a homogenous territory inhabited by the Chechens. Maps are used to back up the guide's statements and enhance subjective claims with cartographic authority.

The film introduces the lowlands of Chechnya, expropriated by the imperial forces, as the natural habitat of the Chechens. Images of the valley precede panoramas over the mountains, which are introduced not as a space of freedom, but rather of forced and unwelcome refuge from imperial advances – the last resort of an exploited population. The intertitles explain that the mountains have shaped a martial people forced to resort to guerrilla warfare under colonial rule. At the same time, the valley landscape underscored the 'organic' unity of Russia and Chechnya by comparing the Terek River valley with rivers in Russia. Mixing romantic ideas reminiscent of the nineteenth-century popular writer Alexander Bestuzhev-Marlinskii with the Soviet historiography of Mikhail Pokrovskii's school, the film identifies the roots of military conflict in the imperial policies in the Caucasus.[35] It further emphasizes the shortage of agricultural lands as a justification for the otherwise peaceful peasants' and shepherds' struggle with Russian settlers.

The role and views of the narrator change over the course of the film. The anti-colonial rhetoric of the guide gradually gives way to patronizing comments made from an outsider's perspective. Half-way into the film, the agency of the proud local is supplanted by the perspective of an outsider, a male traveller who surveys and harshly judges the local inhabitants:

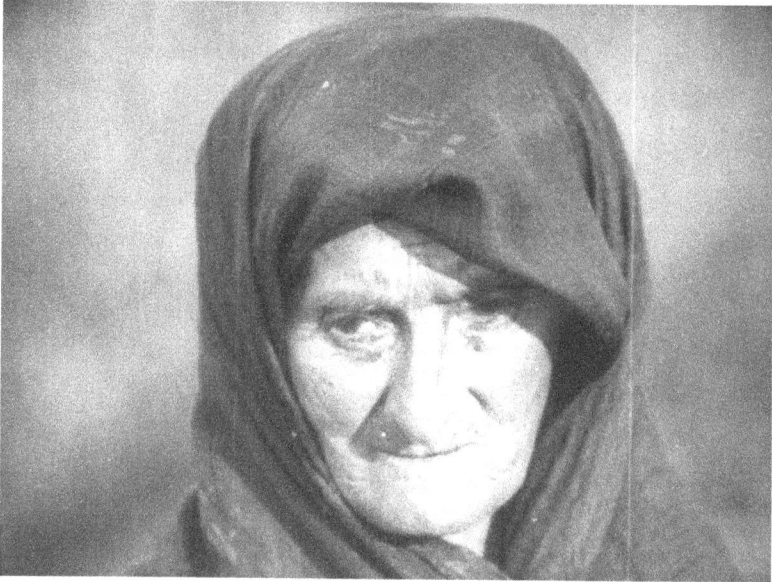

Figure 6.4 Still from *Land of the Nakhcho* (1929). The outsider's gaze: 'Aged 40, a Chechen woman is an old rack'.

'the men here are lazy and do not like to work', 'women are preoccupied with household duties and age quickly', 'life is poor' and 'syphilis and tuberculosis are endemic'.

Following this cultural indictment, Lebedev introduces the Revolution as a watershed, showing the present as a steady modernization. He excludes references to the traces of a recent war and conflicts in the region. Replacing the communal pride of a local with the pejorative commentary of an external observer, the film highlights changes brought by Soviet power, such as schools and kindergartens operating in the vernacular, as well as the growing use of industrial and agricultural equipment. The final intertitle returns to the first-person narrative, evaluating changes from the perspective of the local population – 'We work, we build. The new, young Chechnya is growing up'. The intertitle is accompanied by images of young sportsmen in uniform. Their outlook downplays any visual 'othering' and encourages the viewers' optimism regarding the successful integration of Chechnya (shown as ethnically homogeneous territory) into the multinational USSR.

As the Soviet regime intended to overcome religious practices by attributing them to the past, Soviet *kulturfilms* of the 1920–30s addressed questions of religion in a mocking and pejorative way, often discarding them as deviant and backward practices. *A Sixth Part of the World* branded all religions as a practice of the past. Buddhism was presented as the manipulation of the masses in *Across Buryat-Mongolia*, and as a remnant of the past in *Four in a Boat*. Christianity was associated with drunkenness and excess in Vertov's *Enthusiasm* and in Kaufman's *Spring* [*Vesnoi*, 1929]. Sects were ridiculed in Vladislav Korolevich's *Sectarians* [*Sektanty*, 1930]. Old Believers were mocked in *On the Merry Hills* [*Na veselykh gorakh*, 1929], and shamanistic rituals were shown as a sign of backwardness in Litvinov's *Forest People* and Bek-Nazarov's *In the Land of Golds*.

In this anti-religious campaign, Islam was one of the central targets. But in comparison to straightforwardly vilifying fiction films,[36] Lebedev showed Muslim practices as a popular prejudice by combining images of prayer with scenes of the ecstatic circular dance, *zikr*.[37] This most expressively filmed and edited episode referred to this practice as a 'marginal ritual', but later described it as having 'tens of thousands' of followers. Panoramic shots of the richly decorated graves of the Muslims who died fighting the 'infidels' followed the dance scenes to remind viewers of the social cost of a religious confrontation.

Perhaps Oshaev, whose first drama *The Law of the Fathers* [*Zakon ottsov*, 1924] addressed the question of vendetta, convinced the director to include themes of religious conflict, customary law and blood feud in the film. The film demonstrates the first steps towards 'civilizing' Chechen culture by addressing the practice of blood feud still practiced in the North Caucasus at the time of filming.[38] The public renunciation of the blood feud intended to demonstrate the progressive impact of the Soviet regime on the community. The final episode of *Land of the Nakhcho* features a mediation ritual between two clans to end a long-standing feud.[39] The male representatives of the families stand in front of a special committee that includes clan elders to surrender their weapons and sign a declaration of peace on camera. The episode also promotes new gender roles by emphasizing the active position taken by women in this discussion.

This episode fused the insider's perspective with the Soviet authoritative gaze that directed and controlled the political, economic, cultural and religious development of the community. *Land of the Nakhcho* represented Chechnya as a compact territory inhabited by a single ethnic group. Correlating ethnicity with territory fell in line with the Soviet indigenization policy and established a synecdochal relationship between the 'guide' and the community. As opposed to the multinational Dagestan, the portrait of Chechnya made no reference to other nationalities or plurality of cultures in the region. *Nakhcho*'s landscape was constructed as belonging exclusively to the Chechens.

While *Land of the Nakhcho*, which relied on Oshaev's insights, established a straightforward connection between nationality and territory, Lebedev's *Gate of the Caucasus*, made during the same expedition, constructed landscape in a markedly different way. The crew for *Gate of the Caucasus* travelled from Vladikavkaz to Tiflis (Tbilisi) by way of the Georgian Military Highway built in the nineteenth century as the main traffic artery across Northern Ossetia, Ingushetia and parts of Georgia. By taking this route, the film self-consciously reproduced military and touristic perspectives on the Caucasus and drew on a dense literary legacy identifying the Darial Gorge as the symbolic entrance to a 'mysterious' world. Citing Pushkin's 'Journey to Arzrum' ('Puteshestvie v Arzrum', 1835), the film established a romantic literary legacy and emphasized the imperial dimension of their travel. It also pointed to a literary Caucasus, which was by and large the only point of reference for 'cultured' Russian audiences, as an anonymous Chechen guide argued.

Gate of the Caucasus repeatedly points out the presence of tourists and reflects on its own mediatized status of travelogue by including images of a 'man with a movie camera' *en route*.[40] Changing the film's point of view from that of a local to that of a tourist, Lebedev captured the Russian graffiti covering the mountains as well as the burgeoning tourist network of private bridges, a funicular railway and places like the site of the legendary Princess Tamar palace – a 'must see' for tourists. Following the conventions of travel cinema, the travellers' location is shown on a map.

Like the *Land of the Nakhcho*, the film uses a double-edged rhetoric: it promotes and ironizes the evolving tourist infrastructure, mocks and reproduces the tourist gaze appropriating the mountainous landscape as an attractive tourist site, and thematizes filming and amateur photography as an important part of the tourist experience. On visits to local communities, the ethnographic optics determine the markers of 'backwardness', but also reflect on the impact of the growing tourist industry by showing visitors from 'Leningrad, Moscow, Kharkov'. Arriving to a highlanders' village, the film contrasts the 'Khevsurs as they are' and the 'Khevsurs as they dress for tourists', challenging the essentializing approach of a conventional ethnographic perspective while reinforcing its role as an impartial observer penetrating beyond the 'surface'.

The film's travel route ends in the capital of Georgia, where the camera offers a bird's eye view over the city and merges the travellers' figures with the landscape. Before arriving in Tbilisi, the crew attends a seasonal feast where Orthodox Christian rituals are mixed with animal sacrifices. Accompanied by a moralizing commentary, the fast-pace editing turns the celebration into a 'wild' happening that, through parallel editing, is metaphorically 'washed away' by a new hydroelectric power-station. The finale reinstates the victory of Soviet-driven modernity with images of the power station, Lenin's monument and the travel map – fusing technology, ideology and cartography as the foundation of the new vision and demonstrating the successful transformation of lifestyles as well as the camera's mastery over the landscape.

Whether speaking on behalf of an ethnic group in *Land of the Nakhcho* or looking at the landscape with the eye of a 'civilized' tourist in *Gate of the Caucasus*, Lebedev demonstrated a discursive flexibility which could be applied in various ideological contexts. While the 'indigenous' perspective remained an exception in Soviet travelogues, the touristic gaze increasingly emerged in visual representations of the Soviet Caucasus. The image of a commodified and exotic space was also increasingly marketed to foreign audiences. The travelogue *Foreign Tourists in the Soviet Land* [*Inostrannye turisty v strane Sovetov*, 1930] showed one such group of Western tourists following the beaten track through the Darial Gorge to a Khevsur village, eagerly consuming the images of exoticism and backwardness which the tourist industry and cinema generated all too willingly.

The Heart of the Mountains: Svanetia Wild and Conquered

'My home is my fortress' – say the Brits. Probably this
proverb was invented when they lived like Svans.
Sergei Tretiakov, 'Old Svanetia'[41]

Svanetia, a remote mountainous region in Georgia, increasingly gained the attention of Soviet writers, film-makers, and tourists in the second part of the 1920s. Sergei Tretiakov wrote of the area: 'Geography threw it under the fence of the Caucasian ridge. Across this fence the smooth Elbrus is looking at its greyish meadows. History locked it in the tenth century, paucity and austerity of medieval feudals look down from the mouldy, smoky merlons of twenty-meter high Svan towers'.[42] Tretiakov, an advocate of literature of fact and a powerful castigator of metaphors and aestheticization, could not resist a poetic description of Svanetia. Susan Layton identified the 'aesthetics of dread and splendour' as a romantic discourse constructing a literary image of the Caucasus in nineteenth-century Russian literature.[43] This flamboyant style referred only to the 'old Svanetia', while the new one was presented by Tretiakov as striving to put nature to use and was described in terms of kilowatt of energy from prospective power stations, and cubic meters of timber for construction purposes.[44]

Film-makers were increasingly drawn to Svanetia. Tretiakov ironically reported on two film expedition crews from Moscow and Georgia, arguing over the 'rights' to picturesque sites. The film crews reached a compromise: 'Moscow expedition films in Svanetia from the top till the waist – the glaciers and mountain tops, not touching human settlements, while Tiflis [Tbilisi] film-makers film from the waist to the toes – the inhabited Svanetia.'[45] Indeed, numerous film crews toured the Caucasus at the same time. Mezhrabpom-Rus sent one of the first Soviet film expedition crews to Svanetia. Iurii Zheliabuzhskii and his team spent two months in the mountains producing the romantic melodrama *Dina-Dza-Dzu* (1926), which told a story of love and revenge, and used ethnographic and landscape footage as cinematic seduction.[46] Subsequent *kulturfilms*, *Heart of the Mountains. Svanetia* [*Serdtse gor. Svanetia*, 1926] and *Across Mountains and*

155

Glaciers of the Caucasus [*Po goram i lednikam Kavkaza*, 1926] were edited from the footage filmed by cameraman Arkadii Ialovoi. *Dina-Dza-Dzu* included all of the attributes of a so-called 'Caucasian film', an adventurous and dramatic plot and select Georgian theatre actors. *Kulturfilms* were made alongside of this high-budget production as side-products. While the critics condescendingly and critically reviewed the drama, the accompanying travelogues received praise as a great achievement and 'justification' for the cinematographic expeditions which made the 'discovery of a fascinating and totally unknown to us land – Svanetia'.[47]

Svanetia is a film diary of the expedition, introducing the lifestyle and traditions of the Svans. Preparing for the expedition to Upper and Lower Svanetia, Zheliabuzhskii consulted Pimen Dvali's publications in *Dawn of the East* [*Zaria Vostoka*] in 1923 and a photo album of Svan types which reflected nineteenth-century ethnographic conventions.[48] Transferring these stylistic and compositional conventions to the screen, Zheliabuzhskii presented the Svans as a society of primitive equality that exhibits some of the 'republican' values in the remote mountains.[49]

The film opens with a map and descriptions of the differences between Upper and Lower Svanetia. Svans are depicted in accordance with the ethnographic conventions in medium and medium-long shots reminiscent of the pre-Revolutionary film series *Picturesque Russia* [*Zhivopisnaia Rossiia*]. The film avoids dramatic compositions, but Svans pose for the camera with 'photogenic' objects – icons, musical instruments and objects of daily material culture. The film introduces the Svans' everyday life, work, housing and family, as well as central communal events, such as a wedding, funeral, and a religious feast. The optics of filming placed an emphasis on the communalism of the Svans. Most scenes are shot from the position of a non-participant observer and are interspersed with static, medium close-ups of anonymous Svan 'types'. Zheliabuzhskii uses medieval Christian references to emphasize the Svans' connection to a 'civilized' world, and to stress the distance between Soviet modernity and this traditional society. The mountain range hinders the development of the community, but at same time acts as a 'natural reserve' for centuries-old cultural traditions.

The demonstration of the collective exercise of authority is central for the film, creating a romantic image of a society of proud and equal people

Figure 6.5 Still from *Heart of the Mountains. Svanetia* (1926). Svans seen through the eyes of a 'civilized' traveller: exploring the cultural treasure.

with a sharp sense of justice and friendly hospitality. *Svanetia* includes several episodes demonstrating collective decision-making in the community, implying the ancient collectivist traditions of the mountaineers. Religion also appears under the control of the community, with local priests held accountable by the elders. The patriarchal, communal power of traditions extends to the Svans' relationship with the Soviet authorities in the closing scene, wherein a member of the Georgian Central Committee attends to the needs of the Svans. Rather than following the convention of elevating or singling out the figure of authority, the committee representative stands on a par with the locals in a circle.

Zheliabuzhskii's romantic portrayal of the Svans contrasts with Kalatozov's modernist approach. Celebrated as a highlight of Soviet avant-garde cinema, *Salt for Svanetia* was based on Tretiakov's script. It incorporated parts of Kalatozov's earlier films: a 'scenic' film about Svanetia and a drama, *The Blind Girl* [*Slepaia*] (also scripted by Tretiakov and created with the participation of Paris-trained painter David Kakabadze), which was banned from distribution.[50] Connecting blindness with cultural backwardness, *The Blind* featured medical practices as a proxy for modernity. While this narrative line was lost in the reedited travelogue, a number of compositionally dynamic scenes acted out by the cast of *The Blind* were incorporated into *Salt for Svanetia*.

The combination of bird's eye panoramas with a subjective camera, powerful, diagonal, low-angle shots and dynamic editing emotionally affected the viewer with images of isolation in picturesque and austere conditions. Contemplating the nature of montage, Shklovskii made a passing reference to Kalatozov's film, adding some information to the story of its reediting and taking credit for the restructuring decision:

> In silent cinema, one director made a film based on Sergei Tretiakov's script. This film was pathetic, beautiful, full of exoticism. I don't want to name the director here, we also have our 'medical secrets'. The film was not released. And this director-cameraman, for whom it was the first film, was told that he would never again work in cinema. I suggested to re-edit the film. I was turned down. Then I promised to re-edit it for free and without additional shooting. This was allowed. But I knew one secret which [Maxim] Gorky once shared with me: one cannot do a staircase without landings: the landings provide a chance for rest. One cannot make a drama made up only of the most pathetic parts – a person's emotions need rest. One cannot make a comedy where people would constantly laugh, because one laugh would overpower the next comic episode, its exposition; laughter would suffocate laughter. I consulted the director and suggested to find the filmed parts […] and dilute his film, introducing 300 metres of footage where nothing happens.[51]

Salt for Svanetia indeed combines location footage 'where nothing happens' and a straightforward narrative – atypical for most *kulturfilms* with the notable exception of *Turksib*, which was released a year earlier (see Chapter 7).

In *Salt for Svanetia*, isolation and lack of salt endanger the community and impede its development, conditioning the need to build roads and modernize the Svan lifestyle. This theme was formulated in Tretiakov's essays and reportages from Svanetia in 1927–29.[52] Observations made along the way towards 'development' were projected onto the Ushkul (aka Ushguli) community in the Upper Svanetia, who were pitted against Lower Svanetia in a straightforward opposition of freedom/slavery. In the film, nature is shown as the main obstacle on the Svans' way to freedom. Thus, instead of their natural habitat and a picturesque backdrop, the mountains are portrayed as their main enemy. The Svans are presented as a 'people of the past', retaining medieval practices and living a natural economy. Kalatozov creates an ethnographic fiction with authentic medieval towers and re-enacted events, such as a lavish funeral, visualizing Tretiakov's indictment of 'three locks that keep the Svans in the dark middle ages: houses, roads, and the dead'.[53] The representation of their daily struggle culminates in a dramatic episode wherein a young mother loses her child due to the alleged practice of 'expelling' pregnant women from the community.

Despite the similarities between *Heart of the Mountains* and *Salt for Svanetia*, they could not be more different visually and conceptually. Compared to Zheliabuzhskii's authorial distance, Tretiakov and Kalatozov created a highly engaging form aimed at changing the audience in line with the *LEF* manifesto: 'the creation of a New Man by using art as one of the means of production'.[54] At the same time, the rhetorical form of the film and its 'ethnographic' setting classified it as a *kulturfilm*, and later a documentary. Zheliabuzhskii's celebration of cultural heritage and traditional lifestyle stood in marked contrast with Kalatozov and Tretiakov's attack on tradition. *Salt for Svanetia* found tradition 'unnatural', challenged the patriarchal society and reframed a Biblical allegory ('Ye are the salt of the Earth', Matthew 5:13) in the language of an agitation film arguing for the radical transformation of Svanetia.

While Lebedev juxtaposed the 'unnatural' lifestyle in the mountains to the 'natural' sedentary lowland life of the Chechens, Tretiakov and Kalatozov argued that 'natural' and 'native' landscapes should be mastered by technology in order to secure the very survival of the community. The landscape presented an obstacle for progress. Subverting a romantic myth about the independence of the mountaineers, Kalatozov and Tretiakov replaced it with another powerful illusion, identifying modernity with freedom for the 'Caucasian prisoners'. The film's powerful visuals drove the point home: traditional society, with all its picturesque beauty must give way to the new world; the patriarchal society must be replaced by the futuristic, modernist utopia constructed by 'the assembly of youngsters'.[55] Kalatozov's film paradoxically incorporated his fascination with nature and Tretiakov's condemnation of landscape:

> Repulsive is the primeval forest, untilled steppe, unused water-falls, falling not when they are told to, rains and snows, ava-lanches, caves, and mountains. Beautiful is everything, which carries an imprint of an organizing human hand.[56]

The last reel of *Salt for Svanetia* provides 'visual evidence' of the ongoing transformation of the landscape. The scenes of road construction, punctuated by explosions literally and symbolically undermining natural obstacles, show the conquest of space by connecting Svanetia to the Soviet world. The landscape, originally portrayed as hostile and dangerous, becomes subsumed and domesticated through active interventions, explosions, and the penetration of technology. The film put women at the forefront when advocating an explosive change to the immobile life of the Svans, and the conquest of nature to develop Svanetia. Creating a radical rupture with the past implied replacing an organic rural cycle with future-oriented modernity. However, it is the image of expressively masculine Bolshevik workers in the closing scene that visualizes a modernist utopia.

The director chose to leave out a different type of transformation taking place in Svanetia – the increase in tourist mobility. In 1930, Tretiakov wrote of the 'colossal flood' of tourists, including many foreigners, in Svanetia.[57] Brought about by the expansion of the communication network and overall travel infrastructure allowing increased mobility, the image of Svanetia also entered the traveling circuit. Information on the distribution of *kulturfilms* is rarely available, thus making all the more interesting Tretiakov's passing remark on the Mestian church bells calling the Svans to watch the first film: 'On the screen the viewers saw themselves moving. They were watching *Svanetia* filmed by Zheliabuzhskii in 1925'.[58] The experience of consuming their own image was part of the Soviet transformative project of 'visual alphabetization' that intended to teach the audiences their 'place' in the Soviet landscape.

The Soviet policy to 'reload' the image of the Caucasus took various forms. *Kulturfilms* replaced a romantic poeticizing discourse of noble/ignoble savagery with a factographic, modernist perspective, but at the same time developed a tourist gaze which framed ethnographic differ-ence in a visually attractive and consumable way. *Kulturfilms* can be seen as a platform for a variety of discourses – from assuming an indigenous perspective to promoting a 'cultured' version of travel and tourism, or lobbying for an accelerated transformation of the landscape through a communication network. Touring the Caucasian mountains, *kulturfilm* directors included the obligatory attributes of modernity: schools, hospi-tals, industry, travel and communication infrastructure, as well as gender emancipation. With the experience of wars increasingly bracketed off and contained, the mountainous Caucasus emerged as a picturesque yet fully domesticated area and invited viewers to explore the simultaneously 'wild' and 'tamed' borderland.

7

Camels and Railways:
Reframing Central Asia

Incidentally, a line of camels was visible on the horizon, behind
the machinery. All of it, the tractors and the camels, were framed
perfectly in a shot that could be entitled Old and New *or* Who'll
Beat Whom?
Ilia Ilf and Evgenii Petrov, *The Little Golden Calf*[1]

Alongside the Caucasus, Central Asia was another attractive and challenging space for the film industry.[2] Film-makers from the central studios
travelled to Central Asia armed with their best anti-colonial intentions to
replace imperial stereotypes with unembellished images of daily life. In
1925, as the campaign to break away from the 'oriental' filming conventions
of Russian cinema was at its height in the Soviet press, the Russian-Bukharan
joint stock company, Bukhkino, released the oriental drama *The Minaret of
Death* [*Minaret smerti*, director Viacheslav Viskovskii], complete with las-
civious scenes in a harem and sabre dances.[3] Chastised as an 'artificial East',
the film was used as a negative example of commercial film-making. Films
made on location were called to replace such 'orientalist' dramas. The first
attempt, *A Muslim Woman* [*Musul'manka*, 1925], was made by Proletkino,
which set off to make a film on female emancipation 'understandable to
the Uzbeks and other peoples of the East'.[4] The critics, however, remained

162

sceptical of the film due to its non-local (Moscow) cast, the incessant the-atricality and lack of local 'socio-biological types'.[5] Despite spending two weeks observing the people and places of Bukhara, the actors perpetuated the colonial optics of cultural superiority, commenting on the 'semi-wild, poorly cultured population' that was 'never exposed to film-making [and] observed our work with [the] curiosity of real Asians'.[6]

Soviet travel films sought to break away from the colonial framework by 'documenting' reality. Several film crews arrived in the region on the heels of national delimitation, which changed the administrative arrangement and promoted new cultural elites. In 1924, the Turkestan Autonomous Soviet Socialist Republic, at that time part of the RSFSR, was rearranged into a cascade of Republics, Autonomous Republics and Oblasts: the Uzbek and Turkmen Soviet Socialist Republics (SSR), the Tajik Autonomous Soviet Socialist Republic (ASSR), and the Kyrgyz and Kara-Kalpak Autonomous Oblasts (AO).[7] The new delimitation followed the 'ethno-national' princi-ple, cutting across areas with ethnically mixed populations and disregard-ing cases of hybrid and mixed identities by imposing a rigid normative grid over spaces and cultures.[8]

Ethnographers actively participated in the reform by defining ethnici-ties and nations on the basis of language, cultural practices and territorial settlement. They imposed distinctions over the palimpsest of local and reli-gious identities in Central Asia and applied these to communities without a strong sense of national identity.[9] Arne Haugen has perceptively demon-strated how the oppositions of settled versus nomadic, urban versus rural and Turkic versus Iranian enhanced boundaries which previously had not been ascribed ethnic connotations.[10] The indigenization policy under-mined the pan-Muslim and pan-Turkic movements in the region and was based on a mix of coercion and complex negotiations between central and local elites wherein the category of nationality played an important role.[11] Official decrees, howerver, were not enough to create new communal soli-darities. Cinema played an important role in the cultural work that pro-moted the 'creation' of ethnic communities; it simultaneously instilled new boundaries, reinforced prescribed identities, and helped to naturalize and visualize ethnic categories.

Throughout the 1920s, cinema was one of the most productive experi-mental grounds, functioning as a laboratory for developing new ways of *seeing* Central Asia. Like the cinematographic Far North, the Caucasus and the Far East, the filmic representations of Central Asia exhibit both continuities and ruptures with the pre-Revolutionary literary and visual representations of spaces and peoples. This chapter shows how *kulturfilms* were used as a modernizing force that developed formulae visualizing practices of territorial appropriation and new categories of identity. National delimitation in Central Asia resulted in a set of concepts and topoi that transformed discourses of shortage, backwardness, passivity and dependency in characterizing the local populations, and created new visual conventions for representing Central Asia.

The following three examples foreground the complexity of the visual and discursive practices developed by the Soviet film industry. The first case focuses on two expeditions to the Pamir Mountains undertaken in 1928–29, and demonstrates a co-existence of an ethnographic paradigm with the representation of space as a resource. The second case surveys the production and reception of *Turksib* as the centrepiece of a media campaign accompanying the construction of the Turkestan-Siberian railway – reading it as a hybrid statement combining modernizing and (officially suppressed) pan-Turkic discourses. Finally, by addressing the representation of veiling and unveiling, used as a metonymy for a changing Central Asia, I demonstrate how Vertov reflected on the possibilities and limits of Kino-Eye as a documentary method, and how he elaborated the mechanics of producing a new Soviet community in *Three Songs about Lenin*. Bringing together well-known works and unduly forgotten releases of the late 1920s and 1930s demonstrates the coexistence of alternative visual traditions challenging the notions of uniformly 'colonial' Soviet visual representations.

Views from the Roof of the World: Mapping the Pamir Mountains and its Peoples

In the summer of 1927 the Sovkino studio and the Geological Committee sent a joint expedition to Pamir, an unexplored region of Central Asia referred to as the 'Roof of the World'. This was the first time a film expedition had crossed a border area close to Afghanistan, India and China – an area at the core of the 'Great Game' between the British and Russian

Empires, where the underlying tension between political allegiance and cultural plurality remained tangible.[12] The journey resulted in *The Roof of the World* [*Krysha mira*, 1927], Erofeev's expedition film that featured culturally heterogeneous spaces and communities with archaic cultural practices. Setting off from Osh, the expedition proceeded across the Taldyk pass to the Alay valley, the Eastern and Western Pamir, across Murghab (the former Russian military fort Pamirsky Post), Khorugh (the capital of the Badakhshan Mountainous Region), along the Panj, down to the villages in the foothills of Western Pamir, from where it finally reached Dushanbe, the capital of the Tajik Autonomous SSR.

Erofeev travelled with cameraman Vasilii Beliaev, who had previously filmed in Soviet Turkestan, and a team of natural scientists who studied the area's resources. Numerous equipment caddies and translators remained uncredited in the film. The film credits mention instead, as was deemed appropriate for an 'artless' *kulturfilm*, the two scientific advisers: ethnographer Mikhail Andreev,[13] whose ethnographic map of the region became instrumental in the national delimitation of 1924; and geologist Dmitrii Nalivkin, a mastermind of Soviet geological cartography. Andreev and Nalivkin helped design the itinerary and conceptual framework for representing places and peoples through 'ethnographic' and 'cartographic' lenses. As a result, the film combined the motif of spatial exploration with attentive observation of ethnically defined cultural practices. This approach was markedly different from another account of the same region seen in the expedition film *At the Foothills of Death* [*Podnozhie smerti*, 1928], directed by Vladimir Shneiderov.

The Roof of the World made no note of the new internal Soviet borders, but resonated with the official Soviet nationality policy, which, as Francine Hirsch has argued, 'should be understood as a manifestation of the Soviet regime's attempts to define a new (and presumably non-imperialistic) model of colonization'.[14] Given the paucity of knowledge about the region, the film presented an authoritative image of the Pamir to viewers across the Soviet Union. The map, which covers distances and geographical locations, constituted the linear progression of the film. It performed multiple functions and used cartographic authority to secure territorial rights, orientate the audience and emphasize the 'documentary' status of the footage. The film introduced ethnic communities as divided by nomadic versus sedentary lifestyles, but emphasized processes of cross-ethnic communication and acculturation in the borderland space.

The film placed the sedentary inhabitants of the Pamir under the general description of Tajik, unifying them with the sedentary urban population of the Tajik ASSR at a time when most urban dwellers in Central Asia did not define themselves by ethnic categories. The urban population of the former Turkestan was bilingual and often referred to themselves as Sarts (sedentary Turkic and Iranian speakers), a demographic that was abandoned in the 1926 Soviet census.[15] While most Sarts were registered as Uzbeks during the 1926 census, the classifier 'Tajik' was ascribed to the peoples of Iranian origin, which included the mountainous Pamir peoples who spoke various Iranian languages.[16] Soviet ethnographers remained divided on how to define the Tajik – as 'a non-nomadic Muslim, regardless of language' or as 'a person who spoke a dialect of the Farsi language, regardless of religion'.[17] As Haugen has put it, 'even though the group labels "Uzbek" and "Tajik" were given priority in the 1920s and made the basis for the reorganization of Central Asia, they did not refer to groups that could easily be traced back in time, not even for a rather limited number of years'.[18] After the delimitation, the Turkic vs. Iranian people emerged as the major dividing line, which allowed for unification of the Tajiks both ethnographically and administratively.[19]

The Roof of the World begins in Osh, introduced as an Uzbek town with no mention of its inclusion in the recently established Kyrgyz ASSR.[20] It crosses the territory of Uzbekistan, focusing on the nomadic and sedentary Pamiris, whom the film presents as mountainous Kyrgyz and Tajiks. The film provides details on the nomadic lifestyle, such as tent construction, animal herding, the making of dairy products and other gender-specific tasks filmed in long and medium shots with occasional close-ups. The image of a mobile medical station demonstrates the 'civilizational superiority' and benevolent care of the new authorities. Posing syphilis and trachoma as the most acute problems of the Kyrgyz, the film also reinforces the idea of state control over sexual practices and vision problems as part of the discourse on bodily hygiene as a pre-requisite of the modern Soviet identity.[21]

The camera remained in continuous movement and joined topographic and cinematographic reconnaissance. Erofeev combined a pioneering exploration of 'virgin lands' with a detailed examination of the indigenous inhabitants' lifestyles. While showing spectacular mountainous vistas, waterfalls, glaciers, gorges and blooming valleys, *The Roof of the World* presents an extensive communication network tying the region together. Both visually and in the intertitles, the film emphasizes the centuries-old human presence in and mastery over the area by highlighting ancient rock paintings, ruins of an old fortress and ancient pagan sanctuaries. While remoteness, unapproachability and 'roadlessness' were recurring characteristics of the region,[22] Erofeev paid special attention to traditional routes across handmade bridges, wooden ladders and the fragile *ovringi* (the artificial narrow wooden trails or ledges along the mountains), which allowed for extensive mobility and cultural contact within the region.

Murghab, administrative centre of the Murghab district of the Gorno-Badakhshan area and a township in east Tajikistan, was described by an inter-title as 'the centre of trade between the Pamiris, Kyrgyz, and Chinese'. Such a description broke away from an established way of charting the region. Between 1894–5, following a dispute between the British and Russian Empires in the region of Eastern Pamir, a border between Russia and Afghanistan was agreed upon. At the same time, Sven Hedin, a renowned Swedish geographer, topographer, photographer and travel writer, undertook his first expedition to Pamir and spent several days at the newly built Russian military garrison on the right bank of the Mughrab where he saw a 'little outlying fragment of mighty Russia'.[23] Hedin poeticized life in a military unit while justifying the Russian 'mission' as a 'civilizing' influence:

> Fort Pamir often reminded me of a ship at sea. The outer walls might be likened to the bulwarks; the wide, open, sweeping valley of the Murghab to the sea; and the courtyard to the deck. Up and down the latter we used to walk day after day, stopping every now and then to gaze through our powerful field-glasses towards the far-distant horizon – a view which never varied in its dull lifelessness, except on one day in the week. That was Tuesday, when all eyes were early on the alert for a single, solitary horseman, the post-courier (*jighit*), who brought the eagerly-expected mails from far-off Russia. His arrival was the great event of the week.[24]

In 1927, Erofeev omitted references to the military presence when depicting Murghab as a vivid cultural space with the imprint of the Silk Road trading legacies – a place where the Pamiri people came into contact with the merchants of Kashgar as well as Soviet representatives. Emphasizing an active economic exchange over Hedin's perception of 'wide emptiness', the film portrayed Chinese merchants and a state co-op competing for the attention of local clients shown as participants of a global economic network. *The Roof of the World* ultimately features a space of communication and contact unrestrained by political borders.

Although lumped together with Vertov during the 'anti-documentarist' campaign, Erofeev's filming, just as his first montage film, proved different from Vertov's Kino-Eye active scouting. Discussing Erofeev, Alexander Deriabin has introduced the idea of a '*weak* camera', implying the dominance of non-participant observation as well as 'aversion to tricks, montage effects, and [...] attention to reality untainted by the presence of the camera'.[25] But the director was well aware of the impact the camera had on its subjects.[26] He compared the arrival of the crew in a new community with that of an 'invasion' and emphasized the importance of allowing sufficient time for the people to become accustomed to the 'strange equipment' [*dikovinnyi apparat*].[27] His written accounts also challenged the illusion of the observational mode, but at the same time expressed his 'mistrust of re-enactments'.[28] Erofeev's films come closest to the practices of ethnographic documentary film-making, including the ethos of respect for alternative cultural coordinates.[29]

One episode, filmed in a village in Western Pamir, exemplifies how Erofeev created conditions for filming and anticipates the later practices of 'exits' from observational realism.[30] In his published account, Erofeev emerges as an active creator of the filmed 'documentation', as demonstrated by an episode of opium-smoking, which he arranged with the help of his guide-translator and a local smuggler:

> Calling the Tajik to my tent, I explained to him why we are interested in opium. I told him that we were only going to film the smokers and were not going to report them anywhere. At the end of the conversation, I hinted that I would also like to smoke. [...] In half an hour [after the return of the smuggler] we were back in the village. This time the locals greeted us in

a more friendly fashion. Several men gladly agreed to demonstrate how they smoke opium [...] We busied ourselves with the
camera, the smokers quickly put down the carpets and made
candles from cow fat. In a few minutes, everything was ready
for shooting [...][31]

The Roof of the World, like *Beyond the Arctic Circle*, stood out among the
growing number of self-congratulatory films on Soviet-driven changes
due to its conspicuous downplaying of the motif of change and novelty. On a visit to Khorugh, the capital of the Badakhshan Mountainous
region in Western Pamir, the film's only fragmentary Soviet elements are
marching pioneers, a school under construction, a Soviet representative
and a bust of Lenin – demonstrating the region's inclusion into a broader
Soviet space. At the same time, close-ups of the 'Little Octoberists' (a
Bolshevik political youth organization) in torn clothes, and a Soviet

Figure 7.1 Still from *The Roof of the World* (1927). Opium-smoking session: constructing observational realism.

functionary on a donkey create an ambiguous contrast between the image and its alleged ideological impact.

Unlike most Soviet expedition films, *The Roof of the World* does not end with the arrival of Soviet-inspired changes. Following their visit to Khorugh, the crew attend a harvest festival in a Western Pamirian village where wrestling, a partridge fight, traditional games, and costumed dances are recorded. Moving further along the Panj, the expedition visits settlements where the majority of inhabitants suffer from iodine deficiencies. Close-ups of goitre-afflicted youth and elders subvert the image of an archaic paradise and, at the same time, avoid the ethnicization of the disease.[32] Classifying and arranging both spaces and peoples, Erofeev constructed a visual portrait of Tajik culture using an authoritative ethnographic blueprint. Advancing the perception of a national entity, the film refers to the sedentary Pamir population as Tajik and presents them as ethnic subjects lacking personalities or individual histories. The close-ups detail and catalogue their traditional practices, such as butter-making and thread-spinning, as well as ethnographic prototypes, which exemplify the 'taxidermic' dimension of ethnographic films.[33] At the same time, Erofeev's account visually unifies the Tajiks into a single, sedentary culture.

The film concludes in Dushanbe with glimpses of a bazaar and a field where the crew board a plane. Erofeev makes a cameo appearance in a fleeting scene wherein the expedition horses are sold to a local merchant. The director energetically shakes hands with the buyer to seal the deal, breaking the established convention that relies on the 'invisibility' of the traveller – identified by the camera's gaze and, by extension, with the audience. For all its briefness, the appearance of a crewmember – albeit uncredited in the intertitles and filmed three-quarters from the back, encapsulates the ambiguity of the filmic and filmed relationship of the travellers. They had come from the capital of the new state equipped with modern technologies to film their subjects, interlocutors, partners and co-travellers, who at the same time were classified and visualized through a grid of categories that determined the ways in which they were seen.

The handshake undermines the opposition of the observer and the observed; it shows two male figures of different cultures united by a common interest. Entering the filmic space, Erofeev assumes the role of the

Figure 7.2 Still from *The Roof of the World* (1927). Stepping into the frame: the director as the film subject.

'other' in a setting traditionally reinforcing the authorial position of 'men with cameras'. As a representative of the Soviet centre, he exhibits the ambiguity of expedition film-making, which transformed recorded reality as well as the very world it filmed. This scene points to the entanglement of Soviet policies with imperial legacies and the power of expedition cinema to embody the abstract categories of identity using 'documentary' images. It further exemplifies the ambivalence of 'otherness' described by Homi K. Bhabha as 'at once an object of desire and derision, and articulation of difference contained within the fantasy of origin and identity'.[34] Regardless of whether the horse merchant identifies himself as Tajik, Uzbek, or Sart (or would have declined any national denominations as irrelevant) within the context of this film, audiences across the Soviet Union learned to identify him with a 'Tajik type', thereby reinforcing the 'ethnographic' logic of national delimitation.

In 1928, another film crew offered an alternative to Erofeev's ethnographic portrait of the Pamir Mountains and the 'nationalization' of its population. *At the Foothills of Death* is an account of the Soviet-German expedition of 1928 wherein scientists and alpinists set off to explore the alleged 'last blank spot' on the map of the Soviet Union. The Soviet-German expedition came about through cooperation between the Association for the Emergency Funding of German Science (Notgemeinschaft der Deutschen Wissenschaft), which was seeking to overcome the international isolation of German science after World War I, and the Soviet Academy of Sciences, which was eager to utilize German expertise.[35] The film was made by Shneiderov and Tolchan, and was released by Mezhrabpomfilm in the Soviet Union and abroad.[36]

The expedition aimed at exploring little-known parts of Western Pamir in order to create maps and photogrammetry of the unexplored mountainous area, and to collect information on its climate, natural resources and population. Alpinism, although still a budding practice in the Soviet Union, was an important constitutive element of the expedition; the members of the German and Austrian Alpenverein joined forces with Soviet amateur alpinists.[37] Willi Rickmer Rickmers, a scholar and alpinist who had taken part in the Pamir explorations of 1913, led the German team.[38] The Soviet group included a range of scientists, many of whom had extensive pre-Revolutionary track records of research in the area. It also included prominent functionaries Nikolai Krylenko, the Commissar for Justice and Prosecutor General of the RSFSR; his wife, Elena Rozmirovich, a former member of the revolutionary tribunal; and Otto Shmidt, introduced in Chapter 3, who was at this point Deputy Commissar of Statistics, and editor in chief of the *Great Soviet Encyclopedia* [*Bol'shaia sovetskaia entsiklopediia*]. All three were devoted amateur alpinists. Nikolai Gorbunov, Lenin's former secretary, who played an active role in the formation of Soviet scientific institutions, headed the Soviet expedition team.[39] As their plans evolved, the expedition's scope grew more ambitious. Originally, the team consisted of five German scientists, five alpinists and five Soviet participants, but eventually it grew to 11 Germans and 26 Soviet members who departed from Stettin and Moscow to Osh in the spring of 1928.[40] A caravan of 200 horses and 205 camels set off from Osh to the new Soviet borderland to bring 'the natural and cultural realms of the mountainous Pamir within the system of coordinates of European science'.[41]

The expedition had multiple objectives, including research of the 'last blank spot', an important reconnaissance mission facilitating the exploration of resources, as well as territorial integration and control. The Soviet team aimed to improve the regime's image abroad and debunk 'the defamations of bourgeois slanderers of the USSR about the degradation of scientific thought and cultural degeneration of the Soviet Union'.[42] Although the Soviet and German units spent most of their time divided, only occasionally convening for meetings at camp,[43] the film depicts them travelling together, sharing the mission, equipment and activities of the expedition. However, Krylenko, Rozmirovich, the medic Efim Rossels and Shmidt arrived a month after the departure of the main Soviet-German group, using their summer vacations for an exciting alpinist tour at the expense of the state. The German and Soviet expedition leaders are introduced in the beginning of the film, and both groups make a collective appearance in a panoramic shot prior to their departure in small teams for explorative trips in different directions. The unity of the expedition is one of the most powerful illusions the film creates.

The motif of territorial appropriation offered a key theme for the Soviet functionaries in the group. Commissar-alpinist Krylenko fantasized about the expedition's goal by mixing romantic language with the colonial discourse of mastery:

> We will have to find unknown passes and climb the yet unknown peaks the height of which is not yet known, but definitely not less than 6,000 meters, or 500 metres higher than Elbrus, to cross the mountains where passages are unknown, and peaks without names that not only no one has visited before, but no one has even seen.[44]

In the meantime, the German expedition lead by Rickmers considered their research 'scientific avant-garde', demonstrating a new form of knowledge advancement and a shift in contemporary travelling from a form of 'discovery' to one of 'investigation'. It also highlighted the roles of surveyor [*Vermesser*] and statistician [*Statistiker*] in spatial exploration and creation of maps as a total form of land description.[45]

Soviet and German expedition participants applied a colonial system of reference to space. The expedition medic Rossels saw the landscape through the lens of a cultured civilizer:

> Unwittingly one starts to think, how people live here, in what difficult conditions they lead their toiling life [which is] monotonous like this desert, how the youth is brought up here, where their gaze rests after a baking hot day. And one clearly realizes the main reason of the cultural backwardness of this borderland, cultural reticence [*zabitost'*] of the people inhabiting the desert. All the desert romanticism, which has so often and so beautifully been written about by some writers, turns into a bitter mockery and scorn when facing reality.[46]

Rossels' account established a strong continuity between the imperial Russian and Soviet ways of perceiving the Pamir and its peoples.[47] He also made explicit references to Sven Hedin's legacy by 'baptizing' his fellow travellers and expedition guards, the Red Army soldiers Nagumanov and Sakhutdinov, Sven and Hedin.[48] Ironically, while the Soviet travellers looked at the 'Eastern' landscape through the eyes of civilizers, the German participants felt that 'Asia' began much earlier, although they did not come to a unanimous opinion as to whether it began in Tashkent, at the east bank of the Volga, or in Moscow.[49] Yet both the Soviet and German expeditions shared the idea that the scientific study of the space constituted the ultimate borderline between the East and the West.

Filming the Kyrgyz in the Alay valley, Shneiderov and Tolchan, like Erofeev, emphasized the gender divisions of work and observed leisure practices, including a festive meal, music and dancing. Nevertheless, while Erofeev included both the nomadic and sedentary lifestyles of the Kyrgyz and Tajiks respectively, Shneiderov made reference to the Tajiks simply as equipment carriers devoid of knowledge of the area or any individuality. Tolchan filmed frontal and profile close-ups of the nomads, omitting personal details or individual identities. The alleged disinterest of the locals in exploring the Pamirs set them apart from the 'civilized' travellers and justified the symbolic appropriation of 'blank spots' by the carriers of knowledge equipped with the latest technologies for measuring and exploring the territory. Furthermore, the film shows Rossels in a makeshift clinic, enhancing the gap between the travellers and the locals, and demonstrating the 'civilizational' dominance of the expedition, which was in possession of the latest Western medical technologies.

Although Shneiderov described his intention 'to cross Tajikistan so that the camera could capture all the exotics of the half-Soviet, half-Asian world,' *At the Foothills of Death* primarily showed 'the primeval and unexplored Pamir'.[50] The endeavour was envisioned as a 'full-feature geographic film with elements of ethnography and alpinism', which was 'documentary and educational as well as captivating and exciting'.[51] To achieve this goal, Shneiderov and Tolchan prepared a script outline 'adaptable' to the expedition circumstances. To ensure quality footage, the film crew used technical equipment of the highest standards. Three cameras, a massive Askania-Bamberg with a set of lenses, and a compact Sept and Kinamo provided a range of possibilities for shooting vast panoramas, quick action and individual portraits. Their Agfa film stock included tropical and aerial types to ensure image quality.[52] Mezhrabpomfilm saw great potential for

Figure 7.3 Still from *At the Foothills of Death* (1928). The cartographic mission of cinema: exploring the 'blank spot'.

the mountainous expedition film in both international and internal film markets and made sure to secure adequate technical conditions for it. A common practice of the time, domestic and foreign versions of the film were made.

Mastering the vast, empty frontier was the main motif in all versions of *At the Foothills of Death*. Topographic and meteorological measurements, zoological and botanic collection building and geological observations justified and supported this appropriation by a team of explorers that represented a union of Western knowledge and the Soviet political system. Omitting any references to earlier research conducted in the area, the film portrayed the expeditioners as pioneers giving structure to the space. The deadly hot sands and the deceptive ice cracks bestowed a sense of pride and heroism on the 'conquerors'. Perceived as primarily a male task and duty, the filmed expedition registered Rozmirovich's presence on only two occasions.

To make the film engaging, Shneiderov and Tolchan carefully planned and composed each episode to grasp only the most dramatic moments of travel.[53] To this end, the crew actively engaged in preparatory work and organized special 'film ascents' [*kinovoskhozhdeniia*], exploiting the work of the expedition members for the goals of shooting.[54] Tolchan's ingenious camera work, original compositions, attention to detail, and subjective camera angles provided the dramatic tension. He combined panoramic shots with detail-rich close-ups, bird's-eye panoramas with subjective point-of-view shots, and used reportage filming techniques to enter the thick of the dynamic action. Spectacular mountain panoramas not only conferred a sense of the pristine beauty and sublime aesthetic to the viewer, but also visualized the 'unclaimed' status of the space, facilitating its appropriation through discovery and exploration.

A scene concerning a radio transmission highlighted the act of appropriation through exploration. As both Krylenko and Rossels emphasized, the radio unit of the expedition had an important mission to test the short-wave communication network.[55] Radio, along with cinema, provided one of the most modern media technologies employed in the 1920s to transform the cultural landscape; it compressed time and unified the space.[56] The film visualizes radio waves as concentric, expanding circles that covered the sky, crossed the mountains, lakes and forests to

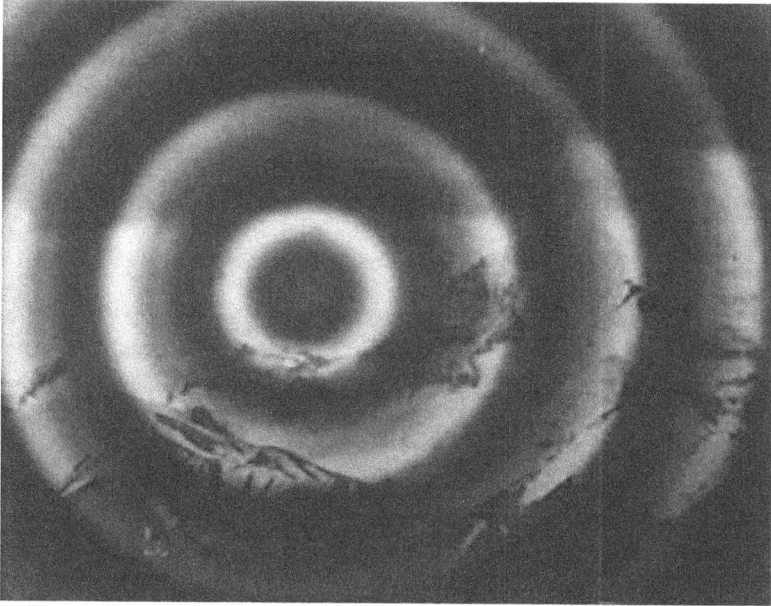

Figure 7.4 Still from *At the Foothills of Death* (1928). Extending the communication network: the Pamir as part of the Soviet world.

make visible the invisible. These circles actively penetrate and dominate the frame, connecting the Pamir plateau with Moscow and Berlin. Thus, the expedition's medial dimension brought the Pamir into an expanding Soviet technological orbit. The modern travellers created a new network unrestrained by physical boundaries or cultural differences. The film's final scene enumerates the achievements of the expedition: the discovery of 'the greatest glacier in the world', identification of gold deposits and ascent to the highest peak of the Pamir, 'Lenin's Peak'.[57] Both the expedition and the film received praise as great successes, and Soviet scientists and alpinists continued to make annual Tajik-Pamir expeditions, led by Gorbunov, until 1936.[58]

The film's success was attributed to the effective presentation of the recorded material. A reviewer for the Soviet military newspaper *Krasnaia zvezda* (*Red Star*) praised it as 'a new style of the Soviet scientific film' possessing 'sharp and precise editing' without 'unnecessary shots'.[59] But for Shneiderov, the experience also pointed out the limits of the film-making initiative. Following *At the Foothills of Death*, he insisted that expeditions be organized specifically for the purposes of shooting films and that they not be 'attached' to teams with different missions and tasks.[60] With the following production *4,500 Metres High* [*Na vysote 4500*, 1931] and the even more popular *Dzhul'bars* (1936), both made in the Pamir, he developed the genre of adventure travelogues by combining dramatic narrative with extensive use of the location footage – a combination which earned broad audiences' approval.

The film's title, *At the Foothills of Death*, acquired tragic overtones several years later with the unfolding of the great terror, initiated in part by Krylenko; Gorbunov, Krylenko, and their co-travellers were later arrested and executed on charges of espionage. Active involvement with alpinism was among the accusations held against them. Today, *At the Foothills of Death*, with its uncanny title, commemorates the use of film as a strategy for spatial domination, which helped make the Pamir a part of Soviet space.

The Roof of the World and *At the Foothills of Death*, made within a year of each other, exemplify different models of representing the territory and its inhabitants. Erofeev utilized ethnographic optics, reduced narrative engagement, and kept a distance between the observer and the observed. *The Roof of the World* demonstrated the incongruity of cultural and political borders, emphasized cultural plurality and archaic practices within the region, and inscribed it within a broader Soviet and regional economic network. Shneiderov, on the other hand, used the logic and language of natural science to classify and measure the phenomena of natural history, downplayed existing cultural alternatives, and highlighted the appropriation of 'empty' and 'unknown' spaces with the help of a Western scientific vocabulary. Yet the range of conceptual possibilities for depicting the Soviet 'East', formatted by pre-existing colonial, ethnographic, and broader global trends in politics and science, was not limited to these two options alone.

The Iron Unity: Conquering Turkestan

Pristine nature, archaic practices, and traditional cultures were not the only themes explored by Soviet film-makers in Central Asia. In the 1920s, Central Asia became a laboratory for Soviet modernization projects designed to prove that, with Soviet help, the region could leap straight into a brave, new, industrial world. The construction of the Turkestan-Siberian railroad (Turksib), undertaken between December 1926 and January 1931, inspired one of the largest Soviet media campaigns. The pinnacle of this campaign, Viktor Turin's *Turksib* (1929), is considered a classic documentary film fusing political changes with new technologies for mastering space. *Turksib*'s portrayal of Soviet Asia's industrial transformation is particularly important as it generated a set of clichés establishing a long-term Soviet visual vocabulary.

The Turksib stretched 1,400 kilometres and exemplified the Bolsheviks' commitment to create a modern, industrial society which eliminated both class and ethnic enmities.[61] It was intended to transform Turkestan, labelled by Stalin as the 'Achilles heel of Soviet power' into 'a showcase republic, a revolutionary outpost in the East'.[62] By the time construction began on the railway, Turkestan ceased to exist as an administrative category, and its territory was divided into republics whose administrative status, structure and internal borders continued to change until 1936.

Top Soviet politicians supported the Turksib project. Perhaps the most active of them was Turar Ryskulov, a Russian-educated Kazakh Communist who had supported pan-Turkic ideas and advocated the creation of the Turkic Communist Party in his early career. Benjamin Loring has argued that despite the salience of colonial elements, such as the complementary relationship between 'periphery' and the industrialized 'centre', resource extraction at low prices and economic dependence on markets outside the region, the relationship between the Soviet political centre and Central Asian local authorities and its population developed a 'qualitatively different' subordinate relationship from the one that had existed in imperial Russia.[63] Ryskulov's career is a case in point. He saw the Soviet regime as a natural ally for promoting pan-Turkic ideas. Having joined the Bolsheviks in Tashkent in 1917, he held the post of Chairman of the Muslim Bureau of the Communist Party in Turkestan two years later. Paolo Sartori has identified Ryskulov as one of the most influential local politicians in Tashkent.[64] Yet in 1920, Ryskulov faced criticism for his pan-Turkic views, was removed from his post in the Turkestan Muslim Bureau and expelled from the Bolshevik Party. In 1922, after publicly renouncing his 'deviation', he was appointed Chairman of the Council of People's Commissars of the Turkestan ASSR. After the national delimitation, he became the Kazakh representative to Sovnarkom of the RSFSR and acted as the driving force behind the Committee to Assist the Construction of the Turkestano-Siberian Railroad attached to Sovnarkom (Komitet sodeistvia postroike Turkestano-Sibirskoi zheleznoi dorogi pri Sovnarkome) under the auspices of Sovnarkom.[65] As its Chair, Ryskulov supervised finances, recruitment policies and a media campaign to popularize the construction effort. As part of this campaign, Vostokkino was encouraged to produce a *kulturfilm* to celebrate the grandiose project.

On 9 April 1928, Vostokkino's Artistic Council received the film outline, signed by Turin and Efim Aron, for approval. The script opened with British and US stock exchanges and focused on textile shortages attributed to capitalist speculation. Having spent ten years in the US studying at MIT and working for Vitagraph studio, Turin had first-hand experience of market economy functions.[66] References to the global market remained a legacy of the NEP and appeared in the films of Vertov, Litvinov, and Erofeev. Like them, Turin envisaged his film as a product of global appeal that could popularize the Soviet cause beyond its borders. The director's note that accompanies the application to the State Repertory Committee (Glavrepertkom) emphasized his intention to create 'a *kulturfilm* that could exist on a par with a fiction film' and find a 'dramatic collision for the non-fiction material without introducing a standard plot to it'.[67]

On 11 June 1928, Vostokkino's Artistic Council approved the script and suggested that Turin focus on the difficulties in constructing the railway and on the workers' everyday life.[68] Two days later, Vostokkino sent a request to Glavrepertkom, whose approval was required to start production.[69] At this point, the script evoked the objections of the political editor, who warned that 'a clear idea of the usefulness of this road [may be] drowning in a Vertovian hodgepodge [*kasha*] of imperialists, dreadnoughts, factories [...] moving trains, mountains of construction material and *the whole Soviet Union* seized with the "construction rush"'.[70] In response, Vostokkino emphasized the film's subject as a matter of state priority and claimed the support of Ryskulov, one of the founders and ideological masterminds of the studio.[71] The counterattack worked, and on 26 June, Glavrepertkom gave the production the green light with the added request that the studio not 'overemphasize the dependency of our textile industry on foreign markets' and 'remove the scenes with queues in a village cooperative'.[72]

Originally, the production cost was set at a modest 29,000 roubles, but the final budget, together with promotion costs, went over 96,000 roubles.[73] Cameraman Evgenii Slavinskii completed filming of the southern part of the construction in mid-November of 1928, just as Boris Frantsisson was sent to film the northern part of the Turksib.[74] On 20 May 1929, a year before the official, ceremonial opening of the railroad, the studio filed a request with the State Repertory Committee for distribution permission.[75] As opposed to most *kulturfilms*, *Turksib* offers a dramatic linear narrative which, as Bill Nichols has emphasized, 'allows documentary to endow occurrences with the significance of historical events'.[76] The narrative leads the viewers from backwardness to modernity, from traditional values to the industrial future. A closer reading, however, brings out several additional layers of meaning.

Showing the construction *ex nihilo* allowed Turin to downplay the continuities with Tsarist 'railway imperialism' in Central Asia which, not unlike the Soviet authorities, viewed the railway network as a crucial means of securing territorial integrity, border protection and the advancement of cultural homogeneity.[77] The film structure follows a classical advertising, 'problem-solution' scheme. The first reel graphically demonstrates water shortages and dependency on the seasonal cycles, which constrained the development of the region. The second reel outlines the inefficiency of traditional communication and shows, with powerful visuals, how natural obstacles such as a desert sandstorm could obstruct the development of the area. The railroad appears as a solution to both insufficient cotton production and the integration of the Soviet Union into a single economic organism. The land is measured and surveyed during the construction of the railroad, and the sleeping nomadic population awakens to the benefits of modernity. The railroad also wins over its 'natural' enemies – desert and frost. The film ends with the promise that Turksib's construction will be complete by 1931, two years after the film's release. While the railway became functional only in 1931, construction officially ended by 1930, and the intertitles of the export copies were adjusted to reflect this.

Unlike many *kulturfilms* discussed in this book, *Turksib* reached instant acclaim as a uniquely powerful film understandable to the millions – an 'epic poem' of remarkably 'clean simplicity'.[78] *Turksib* was praised as a 'useful and cultured, as well as exciting and moving film'.[79] Instructions for accompanying activities to enhance the film's impact were published.[80] The film played with success to audiences in Germany, England, the US, the Netherlands, Denmark and France, and was described by a *Bioscope* critic as 'one of the most thrilling chapters of screen history ever written in the language of the eye'.[81]

Several versions of *Turksib* can be found in circulation and differ significantly in length and intertitles.[82] The discrepancies between prints might reflect the dispute between Turin and Vostokkino's administrator, Shimanovskii, who insisted that Turin provide a longer copy of the film.[83] The differences in length and editing sequences of the existing copies, however, are remarkable. For example, the British Fim Institute's (BFI) release contains scenes within the sandstorm episode, considered one of the most difficult to film from a technical point of view (its production cost grew tenfold, much to the dismay of the Vostokkino administrator), that were left out of the version distributed in Russia. Following the sandstorm, viewers are transported thousands of kilometres north to Siberia, introduced as 'helping' the 'deficient' Asia. The Russian-language version here cuts to images of horse-drawn carts filled with timber awaiting the railroad. This is followed by sights of trains ready to carry construction materials south. Steam whistles blow and locomotives, those engines of modernity, appear in dynamic diagonal compositions, embodying the revolutionary energy of Soviet Russia. By contrast, this episode is preceded in the BFI version with the image of a vast, snowy plane crossed by countless sledges, 'rhyming' with the caravans in the desert. The snowy plane, followed by images of woodcutting and grain collection, emphasize natural resources rather than technology, resonating with George Curzon's notorious statement of 'an Asian colonizing an Asian' in Russia.[84]

The British intertitles for *Turksib* emphasize a 'civilizing' rhetoric. For example, in the first contact of workers and locals, the latter are awakened by the dynamic arrival of the land-surveying team, who are equipped with modern instruments for taking measurements. The term 'civilization', altogether absent in the Russian version,[85] appears in the intertitles prepared by John Grierson, filmmaker and active promoter of documentary film as well as head of the Empire Marketing Board Film Unit. The intertitles describe the land-surveyors as 'the vanguard of the new civilization' and introduce the industrialization as 'civilization breaks through'. Grierson's translation makes use of the established British colonial language of cultural superiority, streamlines the orientalizing discourse of the film and places it within the European colonial context. However, *Turksib* does not square with the binary logic of 'civilizer/civilized', but constructs a more complex image of the region.

Matthew Payne has pointed out two central omissions in *Turksib*: references to 'nativization' (indigenization) and class struggle.[86] However, both themes are indirectly addressed, although not in line with the mainstream Soviet policy of the time. The motif of class struggle is sublimated into the struggle with nature, which is introduced as an enemy, north (frost) and south (desert). Two communities make up the cinematographic 'Turkestan': sedentary cotton-growers and nomadic cattle breeders. The two are portrayed remarkably differently: agricultural workers in the cotton fields are not introduced in ethnic terms, while the nomads are identified as Kazakhs.[87] The film makes geographical references only to 'Siberia'

Figure 7.5 Still from *Turksib* (1929). Ethnographic exoticism: a 'sleeping community' awakened by Soviet modernity.

and 'Turkestan', omitting any mention of the new Soviet Republics. No borders separate Turkestan internally, yet the contrast between the sedentary versus nomadic Asian population is made visually palpable: the land workers passively suffering from heat and the caprices of nature are filmed frontally or from above, while the Kazakhs are monumentalized through a series of low-angle shots. Celebrating the nomadic lifestyle, wool is mentioned on a par with cotton as a vital resource for the Soviet economy. The picturesque and powerful images of mass movements of animals through space recall Vertov's poetic narrative in *A Sixth Part of the World* and make similar 'ownership' claims over the space.

'Turkestan' thus emerges as a metonymy for Central Asia, seen as a unique cultural amalgam, giving politically banned pan-Turkic ideas a new visual formula. After the official denunciation of pan-Turkism, Ryskulov rechannelled his ideas into cultural activities. The creation of Vostokkino was to supplant the lack of political initiative with an attempt to shape a cultural discourse safely reframing the pan-Turkic dream of a united Asia within the narrative of industrial development. Industrial unification is paralleled with the unity of educated minds, as the conquest of nature is paired with the campaign against illiteracy – described as the 'conquest of the word'. Scenes from a school for adults where the future Kazakh proletariat reads Arabic-script books containing the image of Lenin translate the Jadids' educational paradigm into the class content in 'national form'.[88] Like Vertov, who called for a new 'decoding of the world', Turin's film depicts the shaping of the landscape of the mind along with that of nature, and thus fuses the enlightenment legacy with the logic of catching-up modernity, for which Central Asia stands in a metonymic relationship to the whole Soviet project.

Turksib as a Media Campaign

The reception of *Turksib* should be seen in the context of a grand-scale media campaign that accompanied the construction of the railroad. Numerous books, poems, paintings, newsreels and even a symphony glorified Turksib's achievements.[89] Ryskulov published a monograph and authored several articles and introductions to other publications, investing them with the authority of a high-ranking state functionary.[90] In April 1930, a group of

Soviet and foreign journalists, writers and photographers was sent to tour Central Asia and attend the unification (*smychka*) of the northern and the southern parts of the construction. Ilia Ilf and Evgenii Petrov, quoted at the beginning of this chapter, immortalized the event in *The Little Golden Calf* (*Zolotoi telenok*), a peculiar travelogue across Soviet space of a Soviet trickster, Ostap Bender.[91] Ironically reversing the factographic vogue of the time, they focused on the construction of Turksib's media image, parodying the clichés recycled by Soviet writers and artists on the occasion.

Visuals – photographs and maps – routinely accompanied publications on the Turksib. The most recurrent among them was the image of a camel at the rails. Shklovskii, who according to Alexander Feduta might have served as a model for Bender,[92] claimed authorship over this image, which he allegedly 'presented' to Turin.[93] Despite lack of proof for this auto-hagiographic account, camels and rails certainly became the most standard visual construction in representing a modernizing Central Asia. *Turksib* also visualized another rhetorical cliché, 'who gets whom' (*kto kogo?*), in the scene where locals race with the train and, predictably, lose to the mighty machine.

Turin's film became the most celebrated contribution to the Turksib media campaign. It developed a paradigmatic 'visual inventory' for representing the Soviet way of modernizing Asia. It also presented an image of Central Asia as a single, undivided whole. Thus, it stood out as a utopian vision for the region's unity at a time when 'in Moscow and Tashkent, Soviet officials were drowning in a sea of claims and counterclaims to contested regions on or near the Uzbek-Kirgiz, Uzbek-Turkmen, Uzbek-Kazakh, and Uzbek-Tajik borders'.[94] While the film's intricate detour from an official nationality policy might have been lost on many domestic and foreign spectators, its orientalist appeal – drawing on the long legacy of colonial representation and pacifying the anxieties of cultural difference with the promise of cultural superiority – was not. By the time Vostokfilm closed in 1935 and the film was removed from Soviet distribution, it had already firmly entered film history.[95] It continues to inspire audiences worldwide, overshadowing the plight of Central Asian nomads, whose forced settlement and collectivization, which lead to the large-scale destruction of the pastoral economic base, came shortly after the film triumphantly announced the coming of modernity.[96]

Future of the Desert

Turksib was the last popular Soviet *kulturfilm* that featured Turkestan as a territorial unity. In the second half of the 1920s and further into the 1930s, the ascription of ethnic identity and the logic of national delimitation became the driving principle for most films made in Central Asia. Cinematographic exploration of Central Asia proceeded with increasing speed as film-makers from the central studios arrived in Uzbekistan and other republics 'to capture the new expanses and entertaining exoticism of the new territories'.[97] The 'new look' of Soviet Central Asia is exemplified by Iulii Raizman's 1930 release, *The Earth Thirsts* [*Zemlia zhazhdet*, aka *The Soil is Thirsty*]. This fiction film made ample use of 'couleur locale' and incorporated many of the filming conventions characteristic for expedition *kulturfilms*. Scriptwriter Sergei Ermolinskii combined the themes of water shortage with class struggle by placing the story in the Karakum desert, where exasperated Turkmen villagers suffer from lack of water. In a formerly blooming oasis, only the elderly head of the tribe, Aman-Durdy-bai, has plentiful water and everyone else must struggle for meagre portions from underground wells. Help comes from five freshly graduated engineers, who blow up the hills to access water. While the *bai* forbids any contact with the 'Russians', the impoverished Turkmen join the expedition which, after a series of explosions, brings water to the village.

Filming on location with a mix of professional actors and local extras, Raizman created a peculiar hybrid film. Cameraman Leonid Kosmatov's location footage, including a sandstorm and memorable desert landscapes, is reminiscent of *Turksib*'s visual aura. The dynamically edited scenes exemplify a modernist fascination with technology; the visually arresting scenes of working bodies and the mechanics of the underground wells belong to the formalist photographic tradition and subvert the motifs of industrial production in a dramatic and surreal way. There are structural parallels between *Turksib* and *The Earth Thirsts* as well: the local population is presented as passive and immobile as they suffer from scarcity of natural resources and cannot solve their subsistence problem without external help in the form of expertise and technology. 'Help' comes along with land surveillance, and locals play the role of apprentices lacking agency and knowledge.

There are, however, profound differences in the way this story is narrated and framed, marking another transition from expedition *kulturfilm* towards hybrid cinema. *The Earth Thirsts* fuses an imaginary conflict with historical references – from Timur's empire to the 1916 uprising. As opposed to *Turksib*, Raizman brings both class struggle and Soviet nationality politics to the forefront. The local population is identified as Turkmen; they, in turn, describe the arriving engineers as 'Russians'. This, the film argues, is false imperial logic, as the young group features a multinational unit attentively constructed according to the guidelines of the Soviet 'affirmative' empire: Senia, a Russian (Dmitrii Konsovskii); Misha, a Ukrainian (Mikhail Vinogradov); Leva, a Jew (S. Sletov); Niko, a Georgian (Nikoloz Sanishvili); and Kurban-Geldy, a Tatar (Yuldash Agzamov). Along with local extras, Kira Andronikashvili played a young class-conscious Turkmen woman, Dzhamal. The five friends work harmoniously and repeatedly demonstrate their unity by collectively embracing.

Figure 7.6 Still from *The Earth Thirsts* (1930). Embodying the Soviet nationality policy: a multinational group of young engineers sets out to transform the desert.

The film consciously emphasizes the rupture between the imperial past and the multinational Soviet present: upon arrival, the group pauses by an obelisk commemorating a Russian officer killed by a 'wicked Turkmen' in 1916. The animosity is relegated to the past and the team of explorers are joined by the most 'progressive' (and of course, poor) Turkmen. A growing attraction between Senia and Dzhamal' hints at new prospects for the Soviet multinational future. The ethnic classifiers are scrupulously crafted, yet declared irrelevant for the identity of future Soviet generations.

The film received mixed reviews; it was found both too simplistic and not sufficiently ideological.[98] The imperative ascription of ethnicity, territorial belonging, anti-colonial declarations and multinational unity emerged as obligatory in Soviet cinema. Furthermore, the bright new world which the film envisaged appeared increasingly detached from real lives. In Turkestan, the filming coincided with growing protests against forced collectivization, which imposed harsh demands on the peasants.[99] Those who participated in the film were not spared either; within several years, many from Raizman's crew would be arrested in the purges.[100]

Paraphrasing Vertov, Raizman's film can be called 'a drama in *Turksib*'s trousers'.[101] It testifies to the emergence of a new visual form that embeds authenticity cues within a rigid narrative reifying national categories. These films classify the Central Asian population in line with the institutionalized nationalities that are compact, non-overlapping and indicated by recognizable markers such as garments, houses, everyday household objects and languages (referenced in silent films in images of classrooms, books and newspapers in local languages). To approach these early Soviet productions in and on Central Asia today as 'a first step towards national cinema'[102] points out the lasting continuity of the nation-centred logic of representation.

Imagined Community: Unveiling the Kino-Eye

My Kino-Eye is on death row.
Dziga Vertov[103]

Along with speeded modernization, gender emancipation was another recurrent motif in representing Soviet Central Asia. Filming for Vertov's *A Sixth Part of the World* in Bukhara in 1926, Tolchan recorded a demonstration of veiled women in support of the Revolution. This episode, together with other scenes from Central Asia and the Far North, came under attack for what were seen as signs of 'backwardness' unfitting for the industrial and modern image of the Soviet Union.[104] The intertitle and footage at the end of the film transpose the viewer into a utopian future created by Vertov's visionary gaze. The comment 'I see the woman cast off her veil'[105] is accompanied by a medium close-up of a mixed group of women, veiled and non-veiled, marching under a banner with an inscription in Arabic and Russian: 'Join us under the flag, everyone who cherishes Lenin's legacy.'[106] One woman, filmed in a monumentalizing medium close-up low-angle shot, lifts her veil and smiles proudly.

The film-maker's desire to match reality with an idealized image had practical consequences. On 8 March 1927, International Woman's Day, Party activists in Tashkent announced *hujum* (assault) – a campaign against gender inequality and segregation that turned unveiling into a mediatized, performative act.[107] Albeit falling short of its goals, the mediatized *hujum* enshrined the veil and veiling as a metaphor of political and cultural backwardness.[108] Gender equality was one of the pillars of Bolshevik rhetoric; just as the desert was a potentially rich space to be 'revolutionized' by technological intervention, the women 'of the East' were seen as a 'surrogate proletariat' in need of profound transformation.[109] Clothing was one of the primary markers of female emancipation: a growing number of screen heroines had their national garments replaced by a modern, urban dress-code to reflect their awakening to a 'revolutionary consciousness'.[110]

In the Orientalist visual canon, veiled women held a prided place of attraction and contention, naturalizing 'the mythology of Oriental eroticism'.[111] The representation of (un)veiling by Western artists exhibited an inherent ambiguity, combining the rhetoric of emancipation with the desire to possess and dominate.[112] The Soviet discourse denounced colonial representational conventions, but perpetuated the tension between the rhetoric of 'liberation' and 'domination' in the name of Communist ideology and modern values. Soviet *kulturfilms* about ethnic minorities commonly emphasized the oppressed status of women. However, in the representations of Central Asia, the gendered discourse became a *sine qua non* element of the Soviet rhetoric where images of veiled women were used to depose romanticizing discourse and present a 'dying out' cultural practice, eventually abandoned with the help of a civilizing cultural force. While the *hujum* campaign largely failed and was called off in 1929, the performative practice of unveiling continued throughout the 1930s. These images circulated within the Soviet Union and abroad (in special Soviet-sponsored media outlets like *USSR in Construction*) to demonstrate the modernizing course of Soviet development.[113]

Vertov returned to the motif of the veil and unveiling in *Three Songs of Lenin [Tri pesni o Lenine]* in 1934. Introduced as 'Soviet folklore of the East', the film relied on the 'new folklore' promoted by the Soviet press, as well as on the material collected in the expedition.[114] The rehabilitation of folklore, defined as 'oral poetic creations of the broad folk masses', started in the early 1930s following a period of aggressive criticism by RAPP activists and *LEF* writers who condemned it as 'vestiges of the past'.[115] The renewed attention to the folklore movement was promoted in Maxim Gorky's speech at the first Congress of Soviet Writers on 17 August 1934. The speech framed folklore as a forerunner of socialist realism, treating it as a semantically unambiguous 'truth' ascribed to 'the people'.[116] Rather than striving to distinguish between 'authentic' folklore and its 'fake' imitations (or 'fakelore', to use an apt category coined by Richard Dorson),[117] Konstantin Bogdanov has argued that Soviet folklore should be studied as a new form of collective 'ideological (self)-representation', a communicative tool and a means of mediatized identity discourse.[118]

Structured as three 'songs', the film monumentalized the life and deeds of Lenin in a hagiographic account featuring the life-death-transfiguration of the sacralized leader.[119] The commemoration of Lenin's legacy combined folklore anonymity with a constructed subjectivity of a composite subject. *Three Songs* marked the performative act of unveiling as a rite of passage equivalent to acquiring a new identity; the intertitles describe unveiling as the acquisition of the new (and proper) vision required to join a socialist emancipated community. The film demonstrates how such a community is generated by various medial interactions, creating new forms of connectivity and collectivity through the constant circulation of visual and aural ideological messages.

Three Songs of Lenin made ample use of visual 'otherness', but avoided introducing these Soviet subjects in ethnic terms. The film's footage was shot during expeditions to Uzbekistan, Turkmenistan and Azerbaijan.

While Douglas Northrop has argued that the Soviet anti-veiling campaign helped format a way of cultural resistance and sealed the veil as one of the primary markers of 'Uzbekness' used for delineating ethnic boundaries,[120] for Vertov and many other travellers, veiled women embodied the generic idea of the 'East' and were associated with the past.[121] This non-differentiated view of the former Turkestan exemplified a long-lasting rhetorical and visual colonial legacy.

Mezhrabpomfilm commissioned *Three Songs of Lenin* for the tenth anniversary of Lenin's death. The film's plot underwent considerable transformations prior to its realization, and continued to change after its release, and even after Vertov's death.[122] Originally released as a sound film, it was later re-edited into a silent film for distribution to places without sound projecting equipment.[123] At first, the film was not solely set in Central Asia; Vertov originally planned a 'cine-race' showing 'workers from Stalingrad, Kharkov, Tiflis, the Urals, Turkestan, Siberia, and the kolkhoz members from all the ends of the Soviet Union'.[124] The original plan resembled a mighty fresco featuring the Soviet spring and rebirth, including Central Asia as one of its elements:

> Spring of a desert turned into a garden, spring of the land which welcomes a tractor, spring of a woman who takes off her veil, spring of the Moscow river which joins the Volga, spring of an illiterate becoming literate, spring of the most enslaved and terrified, spring of the most suppressed and darkest ones, spring of the weak, helpless, blind and deceived, spring of an enslaved man and a slave-woman, eastern and western spring, spring of the Turkmen and Uzbek women, spring of the Turks and Samoed, Russians and Ukrainians, Tatars and Tungus, all-people spring, pioneer, Komsomol, worker-peasant, Lenin's, socialist spring.[125]

The 'Asian' focus that came out of Vertov's plans resonated with an 'orientalizing' trend in Soviet culture of the 1930s and a growing interest in new epic forms.[126] The film merged aural, textual and visual layers into a historicized narrative that combined expedition material with *Kino-Pravda*.[127]

The first song uses the first-person narrative: 'My face was in a black prison'. It equates the veil with blindness and unveiling with the ability to see. John MacKay has perceptively pointed out that the editing visualizes the subjective experiences of the protagonist, making her 'arguably the closest thing to a "character" to be found in any major Vertov film'.[128] This composite character is created not through a montage of elements, as Vertov's early 'cinematic Adams', but through consecutive editing of multiple veiled and unveiling women who speak with a single voice. The Soviet 'East' is likewise created by mixing images from Central Asia and the Caucasus, and by fusing archaic and modern communicative forms.[129] The spatial distance between the 'East' and the Soviet core – Lenin's body in Moscow – is eliminated through parallel editing that creates not only a 'synthetic space' but also a new form of subjectivity that escapes ethnic ascriptions.[130] The composite identity is forged through partaking in a collective emotional experience of mourning and celebrating.

Mourning – the underlying motif of the second song – is mediated participation in a commemorative ceremony following Lenin's death. The second song combines footage of the living and dead Lenin as seen in 'the mind's eye' of the women of the Soviet East. The song opens with a panning

Figure 7.7 Still from *Three Songs of Lenin* (1934). Synchronized emotional experiences create a shared identity across ethnic divides.

192

shot over a hall of women dressed in urban designs sitting in silent, pensive concentration. The film does not identify the location of the women as they metonymically embody the whole country. Extreme close-ups of meditative and sad eyes are edited together with Lenin's funeral ceremony, taken from *Kino-Pravda 21* – thus changing its authoritative status from newsreel to archival record. Such recontextualization replaces the actuality of the footage with the status of a unique historical record, 'reality at second hand', capable of generating new meanings.[131] The ceremony turns participants into witnesses, constituting a community through their emotional participation in a mediatized event. The collective affect is presented as formative in shaping group unity.[132]

Vertov's crafted geography brings together Lenin's funeral and the mourning women 'of the East' (filmed a decade after Lenin's death) into a single spatial-temporal event. The women, who 'never saw Lenin', epitomize the changing function of vision as they incorporate his mediatized presence.[133] To be Soviet, the film suggests, is to be part of an 'imagined community' which shares sufferings and joys, evoking Ernest Renan's idea of nation:

> Having suffered, rejoiced and hoped together is worth more than common taxes or frontiers that conform to strategic ideas, and is independent of racial or linguistic considerations. [...] A nation is therefore a great solidarity constituted by the feeling of sacrifices made and those that one is still disposed to make.[134]

Along with an internalized perception, the forging of a shared identity requires an extensive media network which transmits and unifies culturally heterogeneous groups into a new unity. *Three Songs of Lenin* highlights the construction of the Soviet media universe that synchronizes emotional experience and generates 'new ideas of simultaneity', described by Benedict Anderson as a precondition for a nation state – a new form of 'a solid community moving steadily down (or up) history'.[135] While Anderson emphasizes the role of print-languages and print-capitalism as the best glue for the national social fabric, Vertov achieves a supranational unity and overcomes linguistic boundaries with the help of the omnipresent camera-eye, as well as radio, newspapers and books in multiple languages. New Soviet subjects, young and old, are exposed to print and broadcast images of Lenin: an illustrated journal

Figure 7.8 Still from *Three Songs of Lenin* (1934). 'My face was in a black prison': veil as a metaphor of obstructed vision.

informs women in Baku of Lenin's death, and a radio broadcast transmits the experience of the Red Square parade to a nomadic family in a yurt. Vertov's close-ups of the women's eyes is not only a rhythmic leitmotif of the episode, it is a new model of an 'inner vision' shaped by media technologies.

The comparison of the sound and silent versions of the film foregrounds the primary elements of the imagined Soviet identity. The sound version creates a composite portrait of a Soviet 'woman of the East' whose transformation is shown as a subjective reminiscence through the eyes of a female protagonist, Melkiu.[136] The silent version preserves the subjective perspective, but strengthens the educational motif in scenes where identically dressed boys and girls in a kindergarten learn to recognize and value the image and name of Lenin.[137] In contrast to *A Sixth Part of the World*, which listed Soviet minorities following a Soviet ethnographic classificatory system, *Three Songs of Lenin* mentions no ethnic or national identities, yet includes a variety of facial types, living arrangements and garments that emphasize the ethno-cultural diversity of the Soviet people.

The third song praises Lenin's posthumous transformative imprint on the country. The invisible, collective, nomadic protagonist promises to sacrifice 'all their steppes and their tents' for the lost leader, who also acquires nomadic characteristics, resting in a 'tent on a square in a big stone city'. But the tone changes as Lenin's sacralized body is transformed into water and light for the Soviet subjects.[138] The leitmotif of this section of the film – 'if only Lenin could see our country today' – is accompanied by images of industrial construction and military activity: army units, tanks and military planes. The new collectivity is visualized through a high-angle shot of masses dancing on Red Square in Moscow and Palace Square in Leningrad. Tchaikovsky's 'Flower Waltz' and military marches gradually replace Iurii Shaporin's arrangement of oriental tunes. Central Asia is made Soviet through full submersion into 'Lenin's universe', described through a mediatized fusion of 'eastern', 'industrial', and 'military' themes. The Soviet identity emerges by generating its own 'invented traditions'.[139]

Making the film in the wake of the campaign against 'documentarism', Vertov reassessed his film-making method and connected the themes of 'veil' and 'blindness' with reflections on the Kino-Eye as a filming method.[140] Film-makers advocating the importance of non-fiction cinema were accused of 'fetishizing facts', yet Vertov continued to explore the relations between truth, knowledge and Kino-Eye as a film-making mode. The integration of *Kino-Pravda* as part of 'folklore' made it anonymous, timeless and unique, as well as exposing its subjective impact on the viewers.

The film's parallel emancipation of women and mediatization of their inner vision draws on an extensive iconographic tradition of aligning veiled women with truth. Madeleine Dobie has elaborated on the role of veiling in the literary tradition, showing how from the late seventeenth century 'the allegorical figure of truth as a veiled woman became intertwined with ethnographic representation of Oriental women'.[141] The establishment of the veil as a primary signifier of Islamic women in orientalist representations nourished beliefs that 'to unveil the woman is to know her, and to know the woman is to render the entire culture transparent'.[142] The insistence on 'seeing' was entangled in controversial drives to gain understanding and ownership. The unveiling is at the same time a quest for liberating the eye and the primacy of seeing over other forms of knowledge – and by extension the rehabilitation of the Kino-Eye's explorative and explosive potential – which restores the camera's dominance over spaces and bodies.[143]

As the obstacles mounted, Vertov increasingly identified with the subjects of his emancipatory quest – the camera and women. He formulated his frustration as the worries of a 'mother-director' about the proper 'delivery' of the 'film-child', and assumed the position of the 'surrogate proletariat' that he strove to transform with his film.[144] But essentially, his Kino-Eye method also became transformed. Arlette Farge has evoked the metaphoric qualities of the veil in describing the archival 'effect of the real', created by a 'naïve but profound feeling of tearing apart a veil, of cutting across the opaqueness of knowledge and of entering, as if after a long and uncertain journey, the essence of beings and things'.[145] In Vertov's film the opposition of suppressed/empowered vision is exemplified by the contrast of veils with the image of a female sharpshooter. This scene features the film's only non-Russian dialogue (in Azeri) between a young woman with a rifle and a military officer offering advice and controlling her movements.[146] Provided it could (re)gain its all-penetrating capacity of seeing, the Kino-Eye, like the Soviet woman, could become liberated and armed.

The parallels between *A Sixth Part of the World* and *Three Songs of Lenin* underline the differing spatial logic of the two films, as well as the radical new model of unity in the Soviet Union that emerged in the 1930s. Both films use a form of collective address, but *Three Songs of Lenin* replaces the interactive 'you' with the composite 'me' marking collective possessions: 'my country, my land, my university, my factory, my kolkhoz'. In this new unity, ethnicity is submerged within a larger totality commanding collective loyalties. The logic of a (gendered) mosaic offered an alternative to the 'ethnographic cataloguing' of *A Sixth Part of the World*. Emma Widdis has characterized this new community as 'a single, homogenous national subject', pointing out the salience of the vertical spatial movement of an 'almost mythical grandeur', in which the future is already achieved.[147] This new unity goes beyond ethnic ascriptions, and the film shows a Soviet identity produced and conditioned by mediatized discourses.[148]

The studio prepared to distribute *Three Songs* across the Soviet Union and internationally.[149] Before its simultaneous release in forty Soviet towns, the film was screened at the Venice International Film Festival. It also appeared in the supplementary programme of the First Congress of Soviet Writers, and was shown in a closed screening to William Bullitt (first US Ambassador to the Soviet Union) and British socialist Sydney Webb on arrangement through the offices of the Commissariat of Foreign Affairs.[150] There was also a special public screening at the Moscow Publishing House [*Dom Pechati*] with Karl Radek and Nikolai Bukharin present.[151] Yet, following the film's release on 1 November 1934, Stalin objected to the image of Lenin as 'a leader of Asians', and the film was withdrawn from distribution.[152] The alleged 'orientalization' of Soviet culture had its limits; the political leadership continued to identify the 'East' with 'backwardness', and 'progress' with industrial modernity. Vertov created new sound and silent versions of the film in 1937–38, emphasizing the role of Stalin as a legitimate 'heir' to Lenin, but it did not improve the film's distribution chances.[153] Both versions, however, preserved the perceptive emphasis on the centrality of the communication network in generating the affective dimension of Soviet identity, where the 'East' served as a laboratory for developing a new Soviet way of seeing.[154]

Three Songs of Lenin demonstrates a transformation of the expedition film practice of the 1920s. By the time of its release, film studios in the Central Asian Republics were by and large established, and the Soviet film industry had grown increasingly wary of 'uncontrollable' expeditions:

> The expedition, which is not justified, should not be allowed, especially when there is not even a working script; that is, it is not even known what to film. [...] Expeditions, as is well-known, are the most expensive part of the production. They are expensive not only because a lot of money is spent on travel and accommodation, or because time is used extremely unproductively, but especially because *in the expeditions the film crews get away from studio control with all the related consequences.*[155]

The expeditions did not stop completely. In 1935, Shneiderov returned to the Pamir to make the feature film *Dzhulbars* (1936). The film, an adventure drama about Soviet border guards set against a spectacular, mountainous background, became an instant hit. It presented the successful 'creation' of Soviet Pamir, conveying the idea of a fully controlled space. Professional actors were cast in all the roles, including supporting ones. At the same time, *Dzhulbars* used *kulturfilm* realist cues to preserve ethnographic authority and to enhance its ideologically streamlined narrative.[156]

The films discussed in this chapter developed a set of visual idioms presenting Central Asia as an integrated, developing, resource-rich, 'natural' part of the Soviet Union. Today, they provide an opportunity to gain insight into the reshaping of a colonial borderland space into a set of non-overlapping, national units following the new, ethnically-defined dividing lines. Turin's formula of making emotionally engaging films that could be 'both artistic and a little unplayed [*chut'-chut' neigrovaia*]' proved a winning solution for Soviet films framing – and taming – ethnic diversity.[157]

Epilogue: Day of a New World

– 'Do you see?'
– 'I see!'

   Day of a New World (1940)

'Today's child is a Soviet citizen, an engineer, mechanic, teacher, doctor, member of the Soviet in 1940', wrote Sergei Tretiakov when discussing the importance of cinema for shaping every child as 'a 100 per cent activist' in 1926.[1] Tretiakov, arrested and executed in 1937, did not live to see the new 'masters of life' develop, but his insistence on the primary role of cinema in shaping a vision of a shared Soviet identity took root. On 24 August 1940, 97 Soviet cameramen set out across the country to record a day in the life of the Soviet world, filming glimpses of the lives of 'simple citizens'. The resulting film, *A Day of the New World* [*Den' novogo mira*, 1940], directed by renowned Soviet film-makers Roman Karmen and Mikhail Slutskii, was a monumental fresco that accumulated and condensed the themes and motifs developed by Soviet *kulturfilms* over the preceding fifteen years. As World War II entered its second year, the film offered Soviet citizens an optimistic image of the future secured by growing militarism and the incorporation of new territories following the Winter War with Finland and the Molotov-Ribbentrop Pact, which extended the Soviet sphere of influence to the west. A design of immense ambition, it returned to the idea

199

of a cine-atlas to legitimize the new borders of the Soviet Union. The official success of this cinematographic mission was confirmed when Karmen and several cameramen were awarded the Stalin Prize, the highest-ranking Soviet award.[2]

Karmen and Slutskii's film resonated with Maxim Gorky's idea to make a 'snapshot atlas' of the world, which he had put forth at the First Congress of Soviet Writers in 1934. Gorky imagined a collage of simultaneous experiences, written down and photographed by hundreds of contributors. This first 'crowdsourcing' idea was widely discussed in the press and promoted internationally, resulting in the massive volume, *Day of the World*, which contrasted the peaceful land of the Soviets with the conflict-torn capitalist and colonial worlds.[3] In 1935, Gorky advised film-makers to film a 'typical day across the [Soviet] country, starting from the Arctic and ending with the southern borders of Central Asia – up to the Pamir, from Vladivostok to Odessa, Astrakhan or Yerevan.'[4] Vertov, the first to enthusiastically pick up on Gorky's vision, proposed a composite film – an 'anniversary anti-fascist survey of the capitalist world'.[5] But his proposal did not meet with support, and a film based on Gorky's idea only came to fruition five years later.

Made without Vertov's participation, *Day of a New World* both perpetuated and transformed the composite multinational image of the Soviet Union first articulated in *A Sixth Part of the World*. Creating a virtual catalogue of 'citizens of the year 1940', the film constructed an affective image of the Soviet people integrating diverse 'borderlands' into a hierarchical structure. Soviet unity was presented as ideological and stylistic, and images of variety were attentively crafted to fit the imposed ideological framework.[6] The choice of the film's first protagonists, a 'random' sample of Soviet citizens on the Vladivostok-Moscow train, emphasizes spontaneity and chance. This structure seemingly repeats the associative 'threading' of motifs reminiscent of Vertov's cine-race organizational principle, but Karmen and Slutskii carefully selected their 'random' subjects. The passengers – introduced by name and a brief overview of their social status – represent a variety of citizens by occupation, status, and reason for travelling, and emphasize the convergence of happy and well-off members of society drawn to Moscow as the symbolic centre of their shared space.

Set between dawn and sunset, *Day of a New World* uses an organic temporal framework and presents a spatial totality through a combination of panoramas and individual stories. Opening with the sunrise in the Far East, the camera effortlessly moves between the distant parts of the Soviet Union to 'integrate' Western Ukraine, Lithuania, Latvia and Estonia into the Soviet universe, and legitimize and naturalize the territorial expansion.[7] The film visualizes the prescribed 'merging' [*sliianie*] of nations into a single 'Soviet people' portrayed as prosperous, content, rewarded for their work and enjoying the fruits of high culture. At the same time, it emphasizes the national character of the Soviet republics and the closely guarded state borders. The towering Kremlin creates an image of a prominent centre associated with military might and a rich cultural life.

The edges of the empire are 'stitched together' by tested visual formulae featuring a catalogue of representational means for this spatial construction: tracking shots from trains and aerial surveillance, land measurements, road construction, maps, newspapers printed and circulated across the Soviet Union as well as all-Soviet radio broadcasts announcing the 'Moscow time'. Yet, purely cinematic means are no less important for creating a sense of Soviet spatial unity. Contrary to the pastiche and uneven texture of footage filmed by less than a dozen cameras in *A Sixth Part of the World*, the alleged ninety-seven cameramen filmed *Day of a New World* in a uniform style to visually unite the space through their shared vocabulary. Their cameras avoid dramatic angles, for the most part use frontal compositions, rely on natural lighting, alternate panoramas with long and medium shots and low-angle uplifting individual portraits.

The soundtrack creates an additional dimension of unity. The recognizable off-screen voice of Soviet radio anchor Iurii Levitan, known for his controlled pathos, melds with Tchaikovsky's symphonic scores, which in turn are merged with folk songs and a march about the 'big motherland' by Daniil Pokrass and Vasilii Lebedev-Kumach. The latter is the leitmotif of the film, reinforcing the organic metaphor of a family which punctuates and structures the acoustic universe:

> Greetings, big Motherland
> My beloved
> Working, fighting
> Boundless Family.[8]

Both the visual and aural layers are structured as loops, materializing the anticipated future. Taking over and reformatting the Kino-Eye method with which Vertov intended to impose order on the viewers' sensory impressions and to ensure the 'unity [of] all the participants through the film screen', Karmen and Slutskii devised a new way of framing authenticity cues into a controlled narrative identified as 'documentary'.[9]

The film demonstrates a triumph over the factographic method and new standards of documentary films in Soviet cinema. As Vsevolod Pudovkin argued in 1940:

> The knowledge of truth is not born from the mechanical assembly of 'facts' and 'little facts' ['*faktov' i 'faktikov'*]. Naturalism is dangerous, as it forced the artists to represent single characters precisely and in a detailed manner, mechanically reconstructing small and miniscule 'truths'. Only penetrating the deep connection of the events, creative foregrounding [*vyiavlenie*] of this connection takes an artist away from the mechanical enumeration of naturalistic 'truths' and leads him [sic] to show the great truth of real life, leads him to realism.[10]

Day of a New World generated 'deep connections' to legitimize the inclusion of new territories into the 'big motherland'. Following Soviet territorial expansion, the new 'borderlands' were shown enjoying national freedom (a Ukrainian wedding in Northern Bessarabia described as 'free for the first time'), job security (an unemployed Jewish worker in Western Ukraine receiving a job) and the right of self-determination (the Estonian parliament voting for the Soviet Constitution). This carefully scripted footage epitomized the transformation of Soviet non-fiction through the process of 'total intervention' which subsumed 'facts' and 'little facts' into a well-crafted documentary fiction.[11] Yet this painstakingly crafted, cinematic construct has its own 'excess of mimesis over meaning', as formulated by Tom Gunning.[12] The film shows Soviet passengers boarding a German plane with a swastika, bearing witness to the cooperation between the two dictatorships which has since then been shyly suppressed from the Soviet public discourse. While this menacing 'shadow of the future' is visible only with the benefit of hindsight, the questions of visible and invisible community boundaries are essential to the film.

In its compositionally and semantically central episode, a 'simple woman', Natalia Lysak, is shown regaining her vision following eye surgery. She is filmed nine days after the operation; her symbolic 'rebirth' is documented from the moment of taking off the bandages to the cathartic moment of seeing. The episode refashions the Kino-Eye legacy to make 'children and adults, literate and illiterate open their eyes as if for the first time'.[13] In this scene, the camera assumes a subjective perspective, first blurred and insecure, reminiscent of Vertov's scene of awakening in *Man with a Movie Camera*; Natalia's eyes are embodied by the camera which gradually focuses as she 'sees' the Soviet world of festivities and achievements. The return of an individual's sight represents the birth of a new Soviet subject into a community united by a shared way of seeing; obtaining 'corrected' sight is a precondition for joining the Soviet community.

'I see' – this emotional exclamation presents the heroine's ambiguous status as the subject and object of an ambitious experiment to unite Soviet women and men in a community of vision. This community was defined

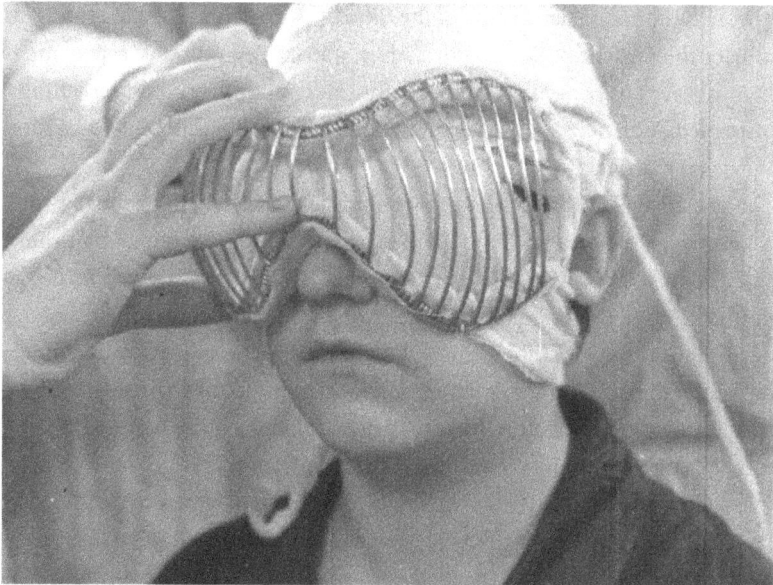

Figure 8.1 Still from *Day of the New World* (1940). Acquiring a Soviet vision through new eyesight.

by a particular optical regime that relied on affective engagement with the images of happy life that were invariably recognized as objective reality. This new epistemic model elevated vision as a privileged form of obtaining knowledge. Cinema played a central role in developing new mechanisms of visual literacy. Vertov's visionary concept of the emancipatory function of the 'machine eye' aimed at liberating as much as directing the way spectators see. Multiple agents – directors, cameramen, film administrators and critics – used the 'camera-eye' to shape the normative way of seeing expected of a Soviet citizen.

The screen space exemplified the plasticity of the very category of reality, which is graphically demonstrated in Rafail Gikov and Lidiia Stepanova's *Road to the Future* [*Doroga v budushchee*, 1940]. The film shows the stages of socialization into the 'new vision', culminating in university graduates stepping out into a landscape that seamlessly fuses the never-built Palace of Soviets with the Moscow urban fabric. These 'citizens of 1940' possess the visual skills for interpreting and navigating the hybrid space of the utopian future-as-present. 'Landscapes of Stalinism', as Eric Naiman put it, required that Soviet citizens master the skill of 'steering through the virtual landscape of the future by projecting it on the topography of the present'.[14] Soviet *kulturfilms*, watched by millions as accompanying pieces in composite film programmes and full-evening screenings, provided audiences with extensive training for a 'dialectic' interpretation of visual material.

The image of the USSR as a composite unity, which gradually took shape over the 1920–30s, embodied a variety of representational traditions. It is this plurality that invites us to think of the USSR, as well as of the foundations of the 'documentary' genre itself, in plural rather than singular terms.[15] Multiple paradoxes ensued with the Soviet category of 'documentary'. On the one hand, there were active attempts to distinguish – conceptually and visually – fiction from non-fiction. On the other hand, a growing number of hybrid *kulturfilms* fused the non-fiction and fiction representational conventions. The co-existence of these tendencies added tension and internal controversy to the history of documentary film. Between 1925 and 1940 film-makers advocating the creation of a non-fiction film studio were castigated with the label 'documentarists'. *Kulturfilm* as a concept was finally abandoned following a period of fervent criticism. Yet the production of hybrid films fusing non-acted and acted scenes within a documentary framework became a common practice in Soviet cinema. The condemnation of the 'documentarist' approach co-existed with the insistence on 'objective facts' in films. Similar tensions can be seen in the contents of the films as well. An emphasis on the plurality of Soviet nationalities went along with the demonstration of assimilation into a modern, 'Soviet' collective. Statements on the inviolability of borders coexisted with the celebration of their 'extension'.

The promotion of a particular way of seeing requires an extensive media network that transmits and unifies culturally heterogeneous groups. In this context, non-fiction cinema emerged as a training platform for both the films' subjects and audiences. The preceding chapters have analysed individual contributions towards creating cinematic portraits of particular regions structured, for the most part, as national spatial units. These films juxtaposed pre-Revolutionary 'backwardness' with Soviet 'modernization', whether by visualizing ethnic differences or by depicting the 'merging' of nations. Through *kulturfilms*, various regions of the Soviet Union – the Far North, Far East, Siberia, the Volga Region, Caucasus and Central Asia – acquired a set of recognizable visual features that both presumed and justified their 'natural' belonging to the Soviet world. However, while the Soviet Union emerged as a visual and discursive aggregate of regions, the representations of these regions were never brought to a common denominator.

From Vertov's network of ethnically diverse regions, the spaces presented in Soviet *kulturfilms* evolved towards homogenized, imaginative constructions. The Soviet space was constructed as inherently diverse, challenging what Daniel Martin Varisco has described as the orientalist 'binary blame game'.[16] But, at the same time, it reinforced the symbolic hierarchy of the Soviet centre and its multiple peripheries. This book calls attention to the complex entanglement of Soviet film-makers with the global orientalist canon in their early attempts to challenge the image of an idealized 'Orient'. The Soviet film industry relied on modernization logic and metaphors while perpetuating a kaleidoscope of ethnographic differences; it actively established 'national' cinematographic cultures while streamlining patterns of representing ethnic diversity. Not all of these developments were directed from the centre; many originated in the studios of the Soviet republics, where new generations of film-makers had their own reasons to engage with and contribute to the Soviet representational canon. All of this makes the idea of a clearly defined 'subaltern' identity problematic.

At once resisting and reproducing the colonial language of power, as well as the visual grammar of travelogues, Soviet film-makers searched for a new, self-reflexive visual language to describe and depict the 'other'. In this, their work anticipated the epistemic turn in cultural anthropology towards performative documentary.[17] In the early cinematic context, their search brought to the fore the many contradictions of Soviet anti-colonial rhetoric. The coexistence of alternative visual traditions in this formative period challenges assumptions of a uniformly 'colonial' understanding of Soviet visual representations.[18]

The visual mapping of Soviet nationalities in the 1920s and 1930s imbibed the expansive centripetal model of *A Sixth Part of the World*, but replaced ethnographic surveying with a shared symbolic economy of belonging to a unified space. While all of the film-makers discussed in this

Figure 8.2 Still from *Road to the Future* (1940). Seeing Soviet: navigating a utopian space.

book contributed to the formation of the visual grammar of the Soviet land-scape, there was no single road map or master plan for this development.

Among the film-makers discussed previously, Erofeev and Vertov, two intellectual opponents united by their commitment to non-fiction, culti-vated the most elaborate and coherent theoretical views on the relation-ship between reality and its image. Some film-makers developed a credo from participant observation to scripted docudramas and fiction films (Litvinov, Shneiderov). Others moved between fiction and non-fiction, envisaging them as separate fields with non-overlapping filming conven-tions (Zheliabuzhskii, Bek-Nazarov). Yet others actively experimented with re-enactment, but were canonized as the pioneers of Soviet 'documen-tary' (Turin, Kalatozov, Karmen). The studio landscape remained ridden with contradictions; it was marked by a high degree of centralization of control over production and distribution and, at the same time, by a grow-ing number of regional studios that allowed for some digression from the prescriptions of the centre.

The films of the 1920s and 1930s developed the vocabulary of multi-national unity that came to define the spatial imagination of the follow-ing decades. In compliance with the territorial approach of the Soviet nationality policy, these films located the 'family of nations' in 'commu-nal apartments' split into autonomous territories.[19] Nevertheless, the idea of integration through the preservation of national specificity that char-acterized early Soviet *kulturfilms* left significant space for idiosyncratic interpretations of the Soviet nationality policy. Even in the most repres-sive times, the language of non-fiction cinema retained enough variety to accommodate Slutskii's lyrical documentaries, Karmen's reportages and Vertov's Constructivist works. In the long run, however, the career paths of these film-makers radically diverged.

Vertov's career was derailed towards less-than-experimental newsreel editing. Yet the legacy of his revolutionary vision of a unified space cre-ated by and through a modern technological apparatus was rediscovered in the 1960s and 1970s, and powered equally transformative views on the relationship of film and reality by Jean Rouch, Chris Marker, Jean-Luc Godard, Hartmut Bitomsky and Harun Farocki. These film-makers cre-atively translated Vertov's ideas and passion for non-fiction into the prin-ciples of *cinéma vérité* and *Film-Wahrheit*. At the same time in the Soviet

Union, Vertov's legacy experienced a renaissance and resonated in the works of Uldis Brauns (*235,000,000* [*235 millionov*, 1967]) and Artavazd Peleshian (*Beginning* [*Nachalo*, 1967], *We* [*My*, 1969], and *Seasons of the Year* [*Vremena goda*, 1975]).

Two prominent film-makers of the 1920s, Kalatozov and Shneiderov, actively continued to work in the post-Stalinist context, reviving and refashioning the practice of spatial mapping by cinematic means. After spending years as a high-ranking film administrator, Kalatozov directed *The Cranes are Flying* [*Letiat zhuravli*, 1957], which is considered a starting point of 'Thaw cinema' in Soviet film history. He returned to a 'documentary fiction' format in *I am Cuba* [*Soy Cuba*, 1964], which continued the tradition of *Salt for Svanetia* by merging acting and observational illusion, and refashioned an early Soviet post-colonial message in the context of the anti-colonial movements of the 1960s. Shneiderov, on the other hand, reanimated the idea of the cine-atlas in the film series *Puteshestvia po SSSR* (*Travels across the USSR*) in 1946. With episodes filmed in Kazakhstan, the Baltic republics, the Caucasus, the Caspian and the Volga areas, his project perpetuated the legacy of expedition films and reinforced the Soviet Union's right to these spaces by initiating, as Gorky put it, 'the millions to the events in places which their eyes don't reach'.[20] In 1960, Shneiderov pioneered a new twist on the idea of cine-atlas by packaging Soviet space for a television series, *Klub kinoputeshestvii* (*Cinetravellers' Club*), which he directed until his death in 1973.[21] Going on the air in 1960, this programme expanded to include countries across the globe and extended the visual training of Soviet audiences to a new medium: television provided a virtual substitute for the outside world when travelling abroad was not possible for the majority of Soviet citizens.

Litvinov joined the West-Siberian film studio and continued exploring areas and cultures far from the centre. His work in Novosibirsk, and later in Sverdlovsk (present-day Yekaterinburg), inspired new generations of film-makers and contributed to the formation of strong, regional documentary centres. In late Soviet times, Sverdlovsk emerged as an alternative centre of social documentary, and at present, Yekaterinburg hosts festival 'Rossia', the largest documentary film forum in Russia.

In film history, Viktor Turin is remembered as the director of *Turksib*, which overshadowed his earlier and later fiction films. Karmen and Slutskii

stayed in favour with the Soviet establishment, continued to work throughout the war and received numerous awards. Eventually they revived their
modernist legacies in the post-Stalinist period, but they never pushed ideological boundaries or conventions. Bek-Nazarov was canonized for his
work in the film studios in Georgia and Armenia, while his short detour to
the Far East remains largely a forgotten episode of his early career. Nikolai
Lebedev withdrew from film-making in the 1930s and continued his career
as a film historian, shaping the documentary film canon by writing authoritative textbooks and holding administrative positions, including the Head
of the All-Union Film Institute (VGIK).[22]

The legacy of Erofeev who, together with Vertov, was one of the most
theoretically-minded film-makers and thinkers of the early Soviet period,
is perhaps most underrated. Erofeev continued to make expedition films
in Germany, Afghanistan, Soviet Central Asia and Iran (*Towards a Safe
Haven* [*K schastlivoi gavani*, 1930], *The Heart of Asia (Afghanistan)* [*Serdtse
Azii (Afganistan)*, 1929], *Far in Asia* [*Daleko v Azii*, 1933], *Country of Lion
and the Sun (Persia)* [*Strana l'va i solntsa (Persiia)*, 1935]). His untimely
death in 1940, at the age of 42, ended a downward spiral triggered by
aggressive criticism of his works and his increasing dissatisfaction with the
state of documentary production in the second half of the 1930s. Despite
his mounting professional frustrations topped by the increasing rigidity
of film censorship, he – like Vertov – tried to fit with the times. His film,
Country of Lion and the Sun, released after major cuts, lost much of its
political content. The films that followed were conventional to a fault: one
celebrated the opening of the Moscow-Volga Canal, constructed by
Gulag prisoners (*The Way is Open* [*Put' otkryt*, 1937]), another chroni-
cled the stylized Stalinist spectacles wherein jubilant crowds paraded in
generic national costumes across Red Square (*Stalin's Breed* [*Stalinskoe
plemia*, 1937]). A reappraisal of his legacy requires rewriting Soviet documentary film history to include this important antecedent of reflexive visual anthropology and his untimely demise.

Many *kulturfilms* served as testing grounds for new filming methods
including hidden and hand-held cameras, telephoto lenses, slow motion,
aerial photography, synchronized sound, and a combination of animation and non-fiction. Cameramen Mikhail Kaufman, Ivan Beliakov,
Vasilii Beliaev, Mikhail Glider, Pavel Mershin, Iakov Tolchan, Ilia Tolchan,

Alexander Lemberg and Arkadii Ialovoi made important contributions to setting the standards of interpreting and evaluating screen non-fiction. The role of those who shaped the reception of films constitutes another important dimension for understanding the impact and significance of non-fiction. In the absence (or fragmentary state) of sources regarding distribution and audience feedback, texts left by consultants, scriptwriters, editors and critics – such as Sergei Tretiakov, Viktor Shklovskii, Konstantin Feldman, Max Polianovskii and numerous others – fill in missing data on production and bear witness to the active role debates played in under-standing and evaluating 'works of fact'.

No less crucial to the transition from *kulturfilm* to documentary were those who tended to stay out-of-frame: administrators, political function-aries, all those involved in commissioning, approving and distributing films, and those who shaped public opinion in the course of producing and distributing films, among them Ilia Trainin, Anatolii Skachko, Turar Ryskulov and Berd Kotiev. While their political careers received (some) scholarly attention, this book spotlighted, in anticipation of further and more in-depth research, their involvement in the film industry at multiple levels as promoters of the ethnographic principle, advocates of national delimitation or even translators of politically suspect models (such as Pan-Turkism) into visual images. The prevailing tradition of foreground-ing the work and views of film directors tends to overshadow the fact that the meaning of each film emerged in dynamic interaction with people with flexible roles: cameramen became directors, directors served as administra-tors or cameramen, critics wrote scripts, scriptwriters wrote film reviews, and party functionaries, on occasion, ventured onto windy film-making career paths.

Through years of experimenting with the representation of nation-alities as either exotic others to be carefully studied and preserved, or as backward communities in need of civilizing assistance, Soviet cinema remains part of a global history of ethnographic filming. Soviet *kultur-films* shared the exploratory desire and civilizing mission of Western colo-nial empires. Multifaceted cinematic portraits of the composite Soviet state not only made the diversity of the body politic palpably visible, but brought to the fore implicit contradictions in this visualization. Following the pre-established patterns of filming otherness, representing imaginary spatial units like 'East' or 'North', Soviet film-makers searched for ingenious solutions to design new forms of showing and talking about nations as part of a larger political entity. Using the colonial visual *topoi*, they developed new visual languages for filming difference. Developed by Soviet film-makers of the early twentieth century, anti-colonial rhetorical and visual elements were exported to the colonies post-World War II, where they were re-appropriated by anti-colonial movements with active Soviet technical, material and intellectual support in Asia, Africa, and Latin America.

With Soviet space appearing increasingly familiar and tamed, the outburst of interest in mapping the Soviet territory by cinematographic means declined throughout the 1930s, yet the isomorphic relationship between nationalities and 'their' lands persisted. The classification system itself remained a dynamic structure: each new census redrafted the list of Soviet nationalities and gradually reduced their numbers to demonstrate the declared 'merging' of nations on the road to socialism. Starting in the 1950s, the concept of 'ethnos' as a unit of classification with 'objective and subjective qualities' returned to Soviet ethnography, culminating in Iulian Bromlei's 'theory of ethnos' which came to dominate the field of ethnography in the 1970s.[23] This approach refashioned the 1920s ethnographic perspective that classified ethnic and national groups according to 'developmental stages' and further encouraged the 'ethnicization' of visual representation of Soviet citizens. *Kulturfilms* of the early Soviet period offered a convenient visual 'evidence' for this model. At the same time, the notion of the 'Soviet people' was not completely abandoned, but declared to be a new, supranational form of unity. Nonetheless, the late Soviet Union witnessed an increase in the number of nationalities registered in the Soviet census.[24]

New questions on identity and belonging made use of the visual documenting strategies developed by Soviet film-makers. In the context of thematically and stylistically loosening censorship, new generations raised previously suppressed questions of national traumas. When the unity of the empire was questioned by growing social and ethnic tension, perestroika documentaries reframed the image of a happy 'family of nations' (Juris Podnieks' *We* [*My*, 1989], *End of Empire* [*Konets imperii*, 1987–1991] and *People's Gala Concert*, or Semen Aranovich's *Cheyne-Stokes Respiration* [*Bol'shoi kontsert narodov, ili Dykhanie Chein-Stoksa*, 1991]). As the regime's grasp weakened, film-makers set to explore previously suppressed aspects of the Soviet history, such as displaced and collectively penalized nations, and the existence of camps and prisons on the peripheries of the Soviet Union (*Solovki Power* [*Vlast' solovetskaia*, 1988; director Marina Goldovskaia]).

Despite the investment of significant scholarly and medial resources into the concept of a united Soviet people, the construct proved finite, and independent states emerged along the lines ethnographers and film-makers helped designate as national cultures. With the break-up of the Soviet Union, film-makers found themselves facing questions of representation similar to those that emerged in the early Soviet years. Within the independent Russian Federation, the nascent movements for self-determination in Soviet national units reinvested early visual accounts with the authenticity of the document. While the multinational state seemed to be ideologically distancing itself from its predecessor, it continued to use visual topoi and intellectual traditions developed during the Soviet years.

The scope and structure of non-fiction production and distribution is significantly more global and complex today. Yet, in present-day Russia, the representations of various regions still exhibit the optic and intellectual legacies of Soviet times. The contemporary portrayal of the small-numbered peoples of the North fuses an appropriated Soviet discourse with a critical stance towards the Soviet experience, reactivating the 'salvage' paradigm and accusing modernization of the destruction of traditional lifestyles.[25]

The revival of interest in ethnic roots and traditions deemed distorted and suppressed by the Soviet regime (while embodying the Soviet idioms) stimulated the emergence of a significant number of films advancing primordial arguments. These films support Rony's claim about the realism of ethnographic representation being less contested than the realism of historical representation.[26] At the same time, new public platforms developed to screen and debate ethnographic cinema, such as 'Kamera-posrednik' (Camera-mediator), the Visual Anthropology Festival in Moscow, the Russian Festival of Anthropological Cinema (Rossiiskii festival' antropologicheskikh fil'mov) in Salekhard, and Flahertiana in Perm. These events created new forums to revisit the principles of the 'ethnographic gaze' and the multiplicity of its impacts.

Post-Soviet non-fiction has given rise to previously suppressed themes of Soviet crimes against nationalities in such documentary films as Alexei Fedorchenko's *Children of the White Grave* [*Deti beloi mogily*, 2002], or Dmitrii Kabakov's *Brothers* [*Brat'ia*, 2003]. Films on ethnic conflict and discrimination have challenged the sterile Soviet discourse on the 'friendship of nations' and addressed the ambiguous Soviet legacy of inequality.[27] Their imagery became entangled with zones of conflict and danger, primarily in the Northern Caucasus, demonstrating the increasing tensions of the imperial and national registers of identity, and expressing unresolved traumas.[28]

Entering the twenty-first century, Russian cinema continues to devote persistent attention to the entanglement of spatial and national representation. Vitalii Manskii's documentary works revisit shared legacies of multinational unity in the present in *Gagarin's Pioneers* [*Nasha rodina*, 2006] and refashion the themes of natural resources (*Pipeline* [*Truba*, 2013]). Fiction films also continue to rely on 'documentary' footage with borderland spaces and local extras to communicate spaces of alterity and national specificity.[29] The 'local colour' has been appropriated in a new wave of documentary and fiction films produced by regional studios which revive the early Soviet legacies of a nationalized landscape: in the Republic of Sakha, as Marina Kalinina's *Towards the Sun* [*Put' k solntsu*, 2010], and Sergei Potapov's *While the Wind Blows* [*Tual baarun tukaru*, 2010]); in Buryatia, as Bair Dyshenov's *Steppe Games* [*Talyn Naadan*, 2014], or in Kalmykia, as Ella Manzheeva's *Seagulls* [*Chaiki*, 2015].[30]

Discussing the possibilities of a graphic representation of nationalities on a map, Ernst Gellner has contrasted in his *Nations and Nationalism* impressionism with its blurred, evasive contours, to the sharp lines of Amedeo Modigliani.[31] Rejecting the modernist heritage in the anti-formalist campaign, the Soviet regime endorsed the sure hand of a 'modernist cartographer' to draw boundaries between ethnicities and nations and 'their' territories. Soviet *kulturfilms* were instrumental in perpetuating this representational logic which excluded cases of mixed identities or non-overlapping distribution of ethnically defined territories.

This book's discussion of the early *kulturfilms*, as well as their contemporary legacy, identifies three intertwined themes that shaped the Soviet film tradition: the preoccupation with formulating new rules of visual literacy and the epistemic foundations of seeing; the conceptual evolution from the notion of *kulturfilm* towards the concept of documentary; and the shifting Soviet national identity politics which enforced multinational and 'ethnographic' perspectives in representing the Soviet community. Witnessing these multilayered developments, *kulturfilms* both reproduced the prescribed ideological patterns and contributed to the changing field of cultural policies and standards. But despite the attempts to find a general production formula, exemplified by Vertov's idea of a film factory or Shklovskii's suggestion to 'streamline' films as 'on a factory assembly line',[32] as well as the tightening control over production, *kulturfilms* were never reduced to a single prototype.

The multiplicity of approaches rested on the 'documentary' authority of the image. The impact of *kulturfilms* is thus larger than the sum of its individual receptions; formatting the image of nationalities in a 'documentary' language most powerfully affected the epistemological presumptions of Soviet audiences. Despite remaining off the radar of many historical film accounts, Soviet non-fiction planted the seeds of diverse future developments – from immersive ethnographic and anthropological cinema, to self-reflexive performative experiments with identity and difference. Spatializing identities, Soviet *kulturfilms*, identified as non-fiction cinema and preserved in documentary film archives, shaped the way the Soviet period was and continues to be seen and understood. Revisited today, *kulturfilms* present a critical approach to the Soviet 'total vision' project, as well as the means to understand the persistent fascination with its visual formulae.

Notes

Archival references are given as follows:

- RGALI, Russian State Archive of Literature and the Arts (Rossiiskii Gosudarstvennyi Arkhiv Literatury i Iskusstva). Fond / inventory (*opis'*) / document number (*edinitsa khraneniia*): sheet number
- RGASPI, Russian State Archive of Socio-Political History (Rossiiskii Gosudarstvennyi Arkhiv Sotsial'no-Politichekoi Istorii)
- AMK, Archive of the Museum of Cinema (Arkhiv Muzeiia kino)
- GFF, State Film Archive (Gosfilmofond)
- GARF, State Archive of the Russian Federation (Gosudarstvennyi Arkhiv Rossiiskoi Federatsii)

n.p. stands for 'no pagination'

Introduction: Projects of a New Vision

1   Martin Heidegger, 'The Age of the World Picture', in *The Question Concerning Technology and Other Essays* (New York, 1977), pp. 115–154 (p. 134).
2   Valentin Turkin, 'O bumazhnykh zmeiakh i puteshestvii s kino-apparatom', *Kino* (19 August 1924): 2.
3   Turkin, 'O bumazhnykh zmeiakh…'.
4   Al[exander] Abramov, 'Vspomnim o vidovoi', *Sovetskoe kino* 4–5 (1926): 10.
5   N. Korobkov, 'Kinoatlas SSSR', *Sovetskoe kraevedenie* 2 (April 1933): 15–21. Korobkov published two appendices with films which he identified as constituting the 'atlas' project.

215

6 RGALI 1966/1/184: 2–8.
7 On the discursive formation of the concept of 'motherland' in the Russian context see Irina Sandomirskaia, *Kniga o Rodine: Opyt analiza diskursivnykh praktik* (Vienna, 2001).
8 'Kino i politprosvetrabota', *Sovetskoe kino* 4–5 (1926): 3.
9 Benjamin H. D. Buchloh, 'From Faktura to Factography', *October* 30 (1984): 82–119; Elizabeth Papazian, *Manufacturing Truth: The Documentary Moment in Early Soviet Culture* (DeKalb, 2009); Christina Kiaer, *Imagine No Possessions: The Socialist Objects of Russian Constructivism* (Cambridge, 2005); Joshua Malitsky, 'Ideologies in Fact: Still and Moving-Image Documentary in the Soviet Union, 1927–1932', *Journal of Linguistic Anthropology* 20.2 (2010): 352–371.
10 See this Lev Kuleshov's concept discussed in Emma Widdis, *Visions of a New Land: Soviet Film from the Revolution to the Second World War* (New Haven, 2003), pp. 64–65.
11 Dziga Vertov, 'My. Variant manifesta', *Kino-Fot* 1 (1922): 11–12. English translation in Annette Michelson (ed.), *Kino-Eye: The Writings of Dziga Vertov* (Berkeley, 1984), pp. 5–9 (p. 8). For the most comprehensive collection of Vertov's writings see Vertov, *Iz naslediia: Stat'i i vystupleniia*, vol. 2 (Moscow, 2008).
12 Dziga Vertov, 'Kinoki. Perevorot', *LEF* 3 (1923): 135–143 (p. 139).
13 Emma Widdis, 'To Explore or Conquer? Mobile Perspectives on the Soviet Cultural Revolution', in Evgeny Dobrenko and Eric Naiman (eds), *The Landscape of Stalinism: The Art and Ideology of Soviet Space* (Seattle, 2003), pp. 219–240.
14 William Uricchio, 'The Kulturfilm: A Brief History of an Early Discursive Practice', in Paolo Cherchi Usai and Lorenzo Codelli (eds), *Before Caligari: German Cinema, 1895–1920* (Pordenone, 1990), pp. 356–378 (p. 364); Oksana Sarkisova, 'Archäologie eines vergessenen Konzepts: discursive und institutionelle Entwicklung des Kulturfilms in Russland', *Spurensuche* 13.1–4 (2002): 64–89.
15 Khans-Ioakhim Shelegel' [Hans-Joachim Schlegel], 'Nemetskie impul'sy dlia sovetskikh kul'turfil'mov 1920kh godov', *Kinovedcheskie zapiski* 58 (2002): 368–379.
16 Lee Grieveson, 'Introduction: Film and the End of Empire', in Lee Grieveson and Colin MacCabe (eds), *Film and the End of Empire* (London, 2011), pp. 1–13 (p. 3).
17 Timothy Boon, *Films of Fact: A History of Science in Documentary Films and Television* (London, 2008), p. 37.
18 Ronald G. Suny, *The Revenge of the Past: Nationalism, Revolution, and the Collapse of the Soviet Union* (Stanford, 1993); Terry Martin, *The Affirmative Action*

Empire (Ithaca, 2001); Andreas Kappeler, *The Russian Empire: A Multiethnic History* (Harlow, 2001); Jeremy Smith, *The Bolsheviks and the National Question, 1917–23* (New York, 1999); Ronald Grigor Suny and Terry Martin (eds), *A State of Nations: Empire and Nation-making in the Age of Lenin and Stalin* (New York, 2002); George Liber, *Soviet Nationality Policy, Urban Growth and Identity Change in the Ukrainian SSR 1923–1934* (Cambridge, 1992); Yuri Slezkine, *Arctic Mirrors: Russia and the Small Peoples of the North* (Ithaca, 1994); Ilya Gerasimov, Jan Kusber, and Alexander Semyonov (eds), *Empire Speaks Out: Languages of Rationalization and Self-Description in the Russian Empire* (Leiden, 2009); Francine Hirsch, *Empire of Nations: Ethnographic Knowledge and the Making of the Soviet Union* (Ithaca, 2005); Jane Burbank, Mark von Hagen, and Anatolyi Remnev (eds), *Russian Empire: Space, People, Power, 1700–1930* (Bloomington, 2007); Jeremy Smith, *Red Nations: the Nationalities Experience in and after the USSR* (Cambridge, 2013).

19 Martin, *Affirmative Action Empire*, p. 25.
20 Martin, *Affirmative Action Empire*, p. 18.
21 Stefan Berger and Alexei Miller, 'Building Nations In and With Empires – A Reassessment' in Stefan Berger and Alexei Miller (eds), *Nationalizing Empires* (Budapest, 2015), pp. 1–30 (p. 4).
22 David Brandenberger, *National Bolshevism: Stalinist Mass Culture and the Formation of Modern Russian National Identity* (Cambridge, 2002), p. 17.
23 Quoted in Irina Filatova, 'Interpretations of the Dogma: Soviet Concepts of Nation and Ethnicity', *Theoria: A Journal of Social and Political Theory* 90 (1997): 93–120 (p. 97).
24 Hirsch, *Empire of Nations*, p. 7.
25 On the discussion of the conceptual apparatus of Russian and Soviet ethnography see Hirsch, *Empire of Nations*, pp. 36–45; Alexis Hofmeister, 'Imperial Case Studies: Russian and British Ethnographic Theory', in Roland Cvetkovski and Alexis Hofmeister (eds), *An Empire of Others: Creating Ethnographic Knowledge in Imperial Russia and the USSR* (Budapest, 2014), pp. 45–47.
26 Hirsch, *Empire of Nations*, pp. 266–267; Tat'iana Solovei, 'Evoliutsia ponimania predmeta etnografii v sovetskoi etnograficheskoi literature, 1917–1932', *Vestnik MGU Istoriia* 5 (1990): 50–60; Vera Tolz, 'Imperial Scholars and Minority Nationalisms in Late Imperial and Early Soviet Russia', *Kritika* 10.2 (2009): 261–290; Juliette Cadiot, 'Searching for Nationality: Statistics and National Categories at the End of the Russian Empire (1897–1917)', *The Russian Review* 64.3 (2005): 440–455.
27 Francine Hirsch, 'The Soviet Union as a Work-in-Progress: Ethnographers and the Category Nationality in the 1926, 1937, 1939 Censuses', *Slavic Review* 56.2 (1997): 251–278 (pp. 255–256).
28 Hirsch, *Empire of Nations*, p. 10.

29 Iurii Slezkine, 'Sovetskaia etnografiia v nokdaune, 1928–38', *Etnograficheskoe obozrenie* 2 (1993): 113–125.
30 Wendy Zeva Goldman, 'The Internal Soviet Passport' in Marsha Siefert (ed.), *Extending the Borders of Russian History: Essays in Honor of Alfred J. Rieber* (Budapest, 2002), pp. 315–331; Albert Baiburin, 'Rituals of Identity: the Soviet Passport' in Mark Bassin and Catriona Kelly (eds), *Soviet and Post-Soviet Identities* (Cambridge, 2012), pp. 91–110.
31 Hirsch, 'The Soviet Union as a Work-in-Progress', p. 253 (my emphasis).
32 Konstantin Oganezov, 'Kino i etnografiia', *Sovetskii ekran* 19 (1925): n.p.
33 Anatolii Terskoi, *Etnograficheskaia fil'ma* (Leningrad–Moscow, 1930), p. 26.
34 Terskoi, *Etnograficheskaia fil'ma*, p. 87.
35 Nikolai Iakovlev, 'Introduction' in Terskoi, *Etnograficheskaia fil'ma*, pp. 2–13 (p. 2).
36 Terskoi, *Etnograficheskaia fil'ma*, p. 87.
37 Dziga Vertov, 'Kino-Glaz (Kinokhronika v 6 seriiakh)', in Vertov, *Iz naslediia*, vol. 2, pp. 56–57 (p. 56).
38 Ronald Grigor Suny, 'The Contradictions of Identity: Being Soviet and National in the USSR and After', in Bassin and Kelly, *Soviet and Post-Soviet Identities*, pp. 17–36 (p. 24).
39 Brandenberger, *National Bolshevism*, p. 16; Hirsch, *Empire of Nations*, pp. 267–268.
40 Alison Griffiths, *Wondrous Difference: Cinema, Anthropology, and Turn-of-the-Century Visual Culture* (New York, 2002), p. 73.
41 Peter D. Osborne, *Travelling Light: Photography, Travel, and Visual Culture* (Manchester, 2000); Tom Gunning, 'The Whole World within Reach: Travel Images without Borders', in Jeffrey Ruoff (ed.), *Virtual Voyages: Cinema and Travel* (Durham, 2006), pp. 25–41.
42 Tom Gunning, 'Before Documentary: Early Nonfiction Films and the "View" Aesthetic', in Daan Hertogs and Nico de Klerk (eds), *Uncharted Territory: Essays on Early Nonfiction Film* (Amsterdam, 1997), pp. 9–24.
43 Henri Lefebvre, *The Production of Space* (Oxford, 1991), pp. 26–27.
44 W. J. T. Mitchell, 'Imperial Landscape' in Mitchell (ed.), *Landscape and Power* (Chicago, 2002), pp. 5–34; Graeme Harper and Jonathan Rayner, 'Introduction – Cinema and Landscape' in Harper and Rayner (eds), *Cinema and Landscape* (Bristol and Chicago, 2010), pp. 13–28 (p. 16).
45 Brian J. Harvey, 'Maps, Knowledge, and Power', in Denis Cosgrove and Stephen Daniels (eds), *The Iconography of Landscape: Essays on the Symbolic Representation, Design, and Use of Past Environments* (Cambridge, 1988), pp. 277–312.
46 Matthew H. Edney, 'The Irony of Imperial Mapping' in James R. Akerman (ed.), *The Imperial Map: Cartography and the Mastery of Empire* (Chicago, 2009), pp. 11–45 (p. 32).

47 Tom Conley, *Cartographic Cinema* (Minneapolis, 2007), p. 5.

48 Irina Sandomirskaia, 'Novaia zhizn' na marshe. Stalinskii turizm kak "praktika puti"', *Obshchestvennye nauki i sovremennost'* 4 (1996): 163–172 available at http://ecsocman.hse.ru/data/081/714/1216/017_Sandomirskaya.pdf (accessed 20 April 2015).

49 Paula Amad, *Counter-Archive: Film, the Everyday, and Albert Kahn's Archives de la Planète* (New York, 2010).

50 Jean Brunhes directed the Archive between 1912 and 1930. Quoted in Paula Amad, 'Between the "Familiar Text" and the "Book of the World": Touring the Ambivalent Contexts of Travel Films', in Ruoff, *Virtual Voyages*, pp. 99–116 (p. 104).

51 Assenka Oksiloff, *Picturing the Primitive: Visual Culture, Ethnography, and Early German Cinema* (London, 2001). Griffiths, *Wondrous Difference*.

52 Davide Henry Slavin, *Colonial Cinema and Imperial France, 1919–1930: White Blind Spots, Male Fantasies, Settler Myths* (Baltimore, 2001), p. 3.

53 Lee Grieveson, 'The Cinema and the (Common) Wealth of Nations', in Grieveson and MacCabe, *Film and the End of Empire*, pp. 73–113. For further exploration of the notion of 'governmentality' as a complex composite including the reasons, the technics, and the subjects of government in colonial context see David Scott, 'Colonial Governmentality', in Jonathan Xavier Inda (ed.), *Anthropologies of Modernity: Foucault, Governmentality, and Life Politics* (Malden, 2005), pp. 23–49.

54 Fatimah Tobing Rony, *The Third Eye: Race, Cinema, and Ethnographic Spectacle* (Durham, 1996).

55 James Burns, 'American Philanthropy and Colonial Film-making: The Rockefeller Foundation, the Carnegie Corporation and the Birth of Colonial Cinema' in Grieveson and MacCabe, *Film and the End of Empire*, pp. 55–69.

56 Werner Hortzschansky, 'Unterrichtsfilm, Lehrfilm, Industriefilm, Forschungsfilm, Populärwissenschaftlicher Film, Dokumentarfilm: Versuch einer Begriffsbestimmung', *Deutsche Filmkunst* 1 (1955): 3–15; Volker Schulze, 'Frühe kommunale Kinos und die Kinoreformbewegung in Deutschland bis zum Ende des ersten Weltkreises', *Publizistik* 1 (1977): 61–71; Wolfgang Brückner, *Kultur und Volk: Begriffe, Probleme, Ideengeschichte* (Würzburg, 2000); Wolfgang Mühl-Benninghaus, 'Der dokumentarische Film in Deutschland zwischen erzieherischem Anspruch und wirtschaflicher Realität', in Ursula von Keitz and Kay Hoffmann (eds), *Die Einübung der dokumentarischen Blicks: Fiction Film und Non-Fiction Film zwischen Wahrheitspruch und expressiver Sachlichkeit 1895–1945* (Marburg, 2001), pp. 81–102.

57 Barry Alan Fulks, *Film Culture and Kulturfilm: Walter Ruttmann, the Avant-garde Film, and the Kulturfilm in Weimar Germany and the Third Reich*, PhD Dissertation (University of Wisconsin-Madison, 1982), p. 50; Felix Lampe,

'Das geographische Laufbild', in Edgar Beyfuss, A. Kossowsky (eds), *Das Kulturfilmbuch* (Berlin, 1924), pp. 135–140.

58 Hans Schomburgk, *Fahrten und Forschungen mit Büchse und Film im unbekannten Afrika* (Berlin, 1922); Hans Schomburgk, *Wild und Wilde im Herzen Afrikas: zwölf Jahre Jagd- und Forschungsreisen* (Berlin, 1925); Bodo-Michael Baumunk, *Colin Ross: Ein deutscher Revolutionär und Reisender, 1885–1945* (Berlin, 1999); Gerlinde Waz, 'Auf der Suche nach dem letzten Paradies: Der Afrikaforscher und Regisseur Hans Schomburgk', in Jörg Schöning (ed.), *Triviale Tropen. Exotische Reise- und Abenteuerfilme aus Deutschland, 1919–1939* (Munich, 1997), pp. 95–110; Oksiloff, *Picturing the Primitive*, pp. 79–84.

59 Hans Schomburgk produced a series of films under the title *Im deutschen Sudan* (1913–14); Colin Ross, *Der Weg nach Osten: Reise durch Russland, Ukraine, Transkaukasien, Persien, Buchara und Turkestan* (Leipzig, 1924); Colin Ross, *Fahrten- und Abenteuerbuch* (Leipzig, 1925).

60 Ian Christie '"The Captains and the Kings Depart": Imperial Departure and Arrival in Early Cinema', in Lee Grieveson and Colin MacCabe (eds), *Film and Empire* (London, 2011), pp. 21–34 (p. 30); Eric Deroo, *L'illusion coloniale* (Paris, 2005); Tony Chafer and Amanda Sackur (eds), *Promoting the Colonial Idea. Propaganda and Visions of Empire in France* (London, 2002); Martin Evans, *Empire and Culture: The French Experience, 1830–1940* (New York, 2004); Martin Stollery *Alternative Empires: European Modernist Cinemas and Cultures of Imperialism* (Exeter, 2000), p. 153; Annette Deeken, *Reisefilme: Aesthetic und Geschichte* (Remscheid, 2004).

61 Emilie de Brigard, 'The History of Ethnographic Film', in Paul Hockings (ed.), *Principles of Visual Anthropology* (The Hague, 2003), pp. 13–43 (pp. 38–39).

62 Charles O'Brien, 'The "Cinéma Colonial" of the 1930s France: Film Narration as Social Practice', in Matthew Bernstein and Gaylyn Studlar (eds), *Visions of the East: Orientalism in Film* (New Brunswick, 1997), pp. 207–23 (p. 223).

63 Griffiths, *Wondrous Difference*, p. xxix.

64 Shari M. Huhndorf, 'Nanook and His Contemporaries: Imagining Eskimos in American Culture, 1897–1922', *Critical Inquiry* 27.1 (2000): 122–148.

65 Eliot Weinberger, 'The Camera People', in Lucien Taylor (ed.), *Visualizing Theory. Selected Essays from V.A.R. 1990–1994* (New York, 1994), pp. 3–26, esp. pp. 5–6; Scott MacKenzie, 'The Creative Treatment of Alterity: Nanook as the North', in Scott MacKenzie and Anna Westerståhl Stenport (eds), *Films on Ice: Cinemas of the Arctic* (Edinburgh, 2015), pp. 201–214.

66 On 'surplus pleasure' see Anthony Bogues, 'The Colonial Regime of Knowledge: Film, Archives, and Re-Imaging Colonial Power', in Grieveson and MacCabe, *Film and the End of Empire*, pp. 277–280.

67 Vol'fgang Stefan Kissel' [Wolfgang Stephan Kissel] and Galina Time (eds), *Beglye vzgliady. Novoe prochtenie russkikh travelogov pervoi treti 20 veka*, (Moscow, 2000).

68 Dobrenko and Naiman, *The Landscape of Stalinism*; Jeremy Smith (ed.), *Beyond the Limits: The Concept of Space in Russian History and Culture* (Helsinki, 1999).

69 Catriona Kelly and Vadim Volkov, 'Directed Desires: *Kul'turnost'* and Consumption', in Catriona Kelly and David Shepherd (eds), *Constructing Russian Culture in the Age of Revolution: 1881–1940* (New York, 1998), pp. 291–313.

70 Veniamin Vishnevskii, *Dokumental'nye fil'my dorevoliutsionnoi Rossii, 1907–1916* (Moscow, 1996), p. 16.

71 Vishnevskii, *Dokumental'nye fil'my*, pp. 21, 25, 35.

72 Vishnevskii, *Dokumental'nye fil'my*, pp. 96, 119, 139.

73 Samuil Lur'e, 'Stranichka istorii. Kul'turno-prosvetitel'nyi i nauchnyi kinematograf', *Sovetskoe kino* 1 (1927): 8–9.

74 Wolfgang Mühl-Benninghaus, 'Newsreel Images of the Military and War, 1914–1918', in Thomas Elsaesser (ed.), *A Second Life: German Cinema's First Decades* (Amsterdam, 1996), pp. 175–84; Michael Paris (ed.), *The First World War and Popular Cinema: 1914 to the Present* (Edinburgh, 1999); Toby Haggith and Richard Smith, 'Sons of Our Empire: Shifting Ideas of "Race" and the Cinematic Representation of Imperial Troops in World War I', in Grieveson and MacCabe, *Empire and Film*, pp. 35–53.

75 Denise J. Youngblood, *Russian War Films: On the Cinema Front, 1914–2005* (Lawrence, 2006), pp. 12–15.

76 Hubertus Jahn, *Patriotic Culture in Russia during World War I* (Ithaca, 1995), p. 157.

77 For the first years of the Soviet nationalized film industry, see the comprehensive accounts of Peter Kenez, *Cinema and Soviet Society, 1917–1953* (New York, 1992); Denise J. Youngblood, *Soviet Cinema in the Silent Era, 1918–1935* (Austin, 1991); Richard Taylor, 'Agitation, Propaganda and the Cinema: The Search for New Solutions, 1917–1921', in Nils Ake Nilsson (ed.), *Art, Society, Revolution. Russia 1917–1921* (Stockholm, 1979), pp. 237–263; Richard Taylor and Ian Christie (eds), *Inside the Film Factory: New Approaches to Russian and Soviet Cinema* (London, 1991).

78 The decree on the nationalization of the film and photo industry was issued on 27 August 1919 by Sovnarkom of the RSFSR; see Viktor Listov, *Rossia, Revoliutsiia, Kinematograf* (Moscow, 1995). GARF 4085/12/712/75: 239–243verso. Some of the pre-Revolutionary films were re-released by Soviet studios in the mid-1920s; see Vishnevskii, *Dokumental'nye fil'my*, pp. 162–63. For a list of *kulturfilms* in Soviet distribution, see *Kino-spravochnik* (Moscow, 1926); *Nauchnye fil'my* (Moscow, 1927); Samuil Lur'e, 'Kul'turno-prosvetitel'nyi i nauchnyi kinematograf', *Sovetskoe kino* 1 (1927): 8–9.

79 GARF 4085/12/714: 43–75; 'Fil'my, priemlemye dlia rabochikh klubov', *ARK* 2 (1925): 41–42.

80 Until 1928, most *kulturfilms* were available in less than ten copies, distributed among the eleven regional distribution centres (in the RSFSR); see Lazar'

Sukharebskii, 'Nauchno-prosvetitel'skoe kino v SSSR', in Kirill Shutko (ed.), *Kul'turfil'ma* (Leningrad, 1929), pp. 65–73.

81 Alexander Etkind, *Internal Colonization: Russia's Imperial Experience* (Cambridge, 2011), p. 26.

82 Michael David-Fox, Peter Holquist, Alexander Martin (eds), *Orientalism and Empire in Russia* (Bloomington, 2006); Paul W. Werth, 'From Resistance to Subversion: Imperial Power, Indigenous Opposition, and Their Entanglement', *Kritika* 1.1 (2000): 21–43.

83 Elena Kolikova and Birgit Beumers (eds), 'Eurasia as a Filmic Assemblage', *Studies in Russian and Soviet Cinema* 4.3 (2010): 321–344; Irina Sandomirskaia, 'One Sixth of the World: Avant-garde Film, the Revolution of Vision, and the Colonization of the USSR Periphery during the 1920s', in Kerstin Olofsson (ed.), *From Orientalism to Postcoloniality* (Huddinge, 2008), pp. 8–31.

84 Adeeb Khalid, 'Russian History and the Debate over Orientalism', *Kritika* 1.4 (2000): 691–699; David Schimmelpenninck van der Oye, *Russian Orientalism: Asia in the Russian Mind from Peter the Great to the Emigration* (New Haven, 2010); Ronald G. Suny, 'The Empire Strikes Out: Imperial Russia, "National" Identity, and Theories of Empire', in Suny and Martin, *A State of Nations*, pp. 23–66. See also the forum 'The Imperial Turn in Russian Studies: Ten Years Later', *Ab Imperio* 1 (2010): 64–88.

85 Michael Kemper and Stephan Conermann (eds), *The Heritage of Soviet Oriental Studies* (Abingdon, New York, 2011); Vladimir Bobrovnikov, 'Pochemy my marginaly? Zametki na poliakh russkogo perevoda "Orientalizma" Edvarda Saida', *Ab Imperio* 2 (2008): 325–344; Schimmelpenninck van der Oye, 'Orientalizm – delo tonkoe', *Ab Imperio* 1 (2002): 249–264.

86 Melissa K. Stockdale, 'What is a Fatherland? Changing Notions of Duty, Rights, and Belonging in Russia' in Mark Bassin, Christopher Ely, and Melissa K. Stockdale (eds), *Space, Place, and Power in Modern Russia* (DeKalb, 2010), pp. 23–48; Sandomirskaia, *Kniga o rodine*.

87 Philip Cavendish, *The Men with the Movie Camera: The Poetics of Visual Style in Soviet Avant-Garde Cinema of the 1920s* (New York, 2013).

88 Tony Ballantyne, *Orientalism and Race: Aryanism in the British Empire* (Houndmills, 2007), p. 14.

89 James Elkins, *Six Stories from the End of Representation: Images in Painting, Photography, Astronomy, Microscopy, Particle Physics, and Quantum Mechanics, 1980–2000* (Stanford, 2008); W. J. T. Mitchell, 'Showing Seeing: A Critique of Visual Culture', in Michael Ann Holly and Keith Moxey (eds), *Art History, Aesthetics, Visual Studies* (London and New Haven, 2002), pp. 231–250; Jonathan Crary, *Techniques of the Observer: On Vision and Modernity in the Nineteenth Century* (Boston, 1992).

90 Michel Foucault, *Archaeology of Knowledge and Discourse on Language* (New York, 1972); Martin Jay, 'Scopic regimes of modernity' in Hal Foster (ed.), *Vision and Visuality* (Seattle, 1988) pp. 3–23 (p. 4); Valerie Kivelson, *Cartographies of Tsardom: The Land and its Meanings in Seventeenth-Century Russia* (Ithaca, 2006); Elena Vishlenkova, *Vizual'noe narodovedenie imperii, ili "uvidet' russkogo dano ne kazhdomy"* (Moscow, 2011); Widdis, *Visions of a New Land*; Victoria Bonnell, *Iconography of Power: Soviet Political Posters under Lenin and Stalin* (Berkeley, 1997); Valerie A. Kivelson and Joan Neuberger (eds), *Picturing Russia: Explorations in Visual Culture* (New Haven, 2008).

91 Among the Soviet film studios, the Ukrainian VUFKU and Georgian Goskinprom Gruzii were the largest and most autonomous organizations with extensive production and distribution capacities. Throughout the 1920s, Soviet film studios were also established in other Soviet republics, including Azerbaijan, Armenia, Uzbekistan, Turkmenistan, and others. The theme of Soviet Republican studios and their relationship with the central authorities, as well as policies of minority representation falls beyond the scope of this book. For an overview of the early years of the regional studios see I. Vorob'ev, 'Perspektivy razvitiia ukrainskoi kinematografii', *Kino i kul'tura* 2 (1929): 74–78; Vladimir Mislavskii, *Kino v Ukraine, 1896–1921. Fakty, fil'my, imena* (Khar'kov, 2005); Irina Ratiani, *U istokov gruzinskogo kino* (Moscow, 2003); R. Abul'khanov, 'Bukharsko-russkoe kinotovarishchestvo', in *Iz istorii kino*, vol. 5, pp. 53–70; Kh. Abul-Kasymova, 'Organizatsiia kinodela v Uzbekistane', in *Iz istorii kino*, vol. 5, pp. 33–52; Michael Rouland, Gulnara Abikeyeva, and Birgit Beumers (eds), *Cinema in Central Asia: Rewriting Cultural Histories* (London, 2013); Cloé Drieu, *Fictions nationales: Cinéma, empire et nation en Ouzbékistan (1919–1937)* (Paris, 2013); Serhii Trymbach, 'Artistic power vs. state power: Dovzhenko, Savchenko, Parajanov', *Studies in Russian and Soviet Cinema* 6.3 (2012): 357–364; Nino Dzandzava, 'Georgian Kulturfilms', in Susan Oxtoby (ed.), *Discovering Georgian Cinema* (Berkeley, 2014), pp. 16–19; Michael G. Smith, 'Cinema for the "Soviet East": National Fact and Revolutionary Fiction in Early Azerbaijani Film', *Slavic Review* 56.4 (1997): 645–678.

92 Birgit Beumers, 'National Identities through Visions of the Past: Contemporary Russian Cinema', in Bassin and Kelly, *Soviet and Post-Soviet Identities*, pp. 120–153; Nancy Condee, *The Imperial Trace: Recent Russian Cinema* (Oxford, 2009).

1. They Must Be Represented: Kulturfilm and the National Niche in Soviet Cinema

1 Dziga Vertov, "Piatyi nomer Kinopravdy', *Teatral'naia Moskva* 50 (1922); re-published in Vertov, *Iz naslediia*, vol. 2, p. 18.

2 V-skii, 'Inorodtsy i kino', *Kino-gazeta* 9 (24 February 1925): 5.

3 Jeremy Hicks, *Dziga Vertov. Defining Documentary Film* (London, 2007), p. 36; see also Cristina Vatulescu, *Police Aesthetics: Literature, Film, and the Secret Police in Soviet Times* (Stanford, 2010).

4 Vladimir Stepanov, 'Kul't-kino' *ARK* 1 (1925): 38–39; RGALI 2091/1/77.

5 RGALI 2091/1/77: 2.

6 Ilya Gerasimov, Sergey Glebov, Jan Kusber, Marina Mogil'ner, Alexander Semyonov, 'New Imperial History and the Challenges of Empire' in Ilya Gerasimov, Jan Kusber, Alexander Semyonov (eds), *Empire Speaks Out: Languages of Rationalization and Self-Description in the Russian Empire* (Leiden, 2009), p. 25.

7 V. Sytin, 'Kino-atlas' *Kino i kul'tura* 4 (1929): 71.

8 RGALI 645/1/356: 104.

9 Mikhail Yampolsky, 'Reality at Second Hand', *Historical Journal of Film, Radio, and Television* 11.2 (1991): 161–171.

10 RGALI 645/1/368: 131–135, 175–176; published in Varvara Zhdanova, 'K materialam po istorii otechestvennogo kinoprotsessa nachala 1930kh godov. Proekt sozdaniia "Kino-Atlasa SSSR"', available at http://www.esrae.ru/var-varajdanova/pdf/2014/7/6.pdf (accessed 25 May 2015).

11 AMK 26/2/280: n.p.

12 Vladimir Erofeev, 'O fil'makh "vtorogo sorta"', *Sovetskii ekran* 29 (1926): 4; 'Protokol zasedania chlenov ARK po voprosy o kul't-fil'me 10 dekabria 1926', RGALI 2494/1/32: 18; Nikolai Aseev, 'V poiskakh kul'turnoi fil'my', *Sovetskii ekran* 2 (12 January 1926): 4; RGALI 2494/1/32: 18.

13 Nikolai Lebedev, *Po germanskoi kinematografii* (Moscow, 1924).

14 AMK 26/2/3; Nikolai Lebedev, 'Tipy kul'turfil'm', *Kino-Front* 1 (1927): 4 and *Kino-Front* 2 (1927): 5–7.

15 Vladimir Erofeev, 'Ob ekspeditsiiakh voobshche i v chastnosti', *Sovetskii ekran* 25 (1926): 8–9; Erofeev, *Kinoindustriia Germanii* (Moscow, 1926); Erofeev, 'Chemu uchit nas Germaniia', *Sovetskii ekran* 23 (1925): n.p. On the reception of German film culture and industry in Soviet Russia, see Alexander Deriabin, '"Tam ia uvidel neobychainye veshchi." Sovetskie kinematografisty o svoikh poezdkakh v Germaniiu', *Kinovedcheskie zapiski* 58 (2002): 239–285.

16 AMK 26/2/3.

17 GARF 7816/1/2: 120.

18 N. Sh. 'Montazh khroniki', *Sovetskii ekran* 22 (1925): n.p. (original emphasis).

19 RGALI 2494/1/32: 18.
20 Kirill Shutko, 'Kul'turnaia fil'ma k desiatiletiiu', *Sovetskii ekran* 45 (1927): 12–13, esp. p. 12.
21 RGALI 2494/1/212: 18.
22 Nikolai Chuzhak (ed.), *Literatura fakta* (Moscow, 1929).
23 The Kinoks' manifesto was published in 1922; see Vertov, 'My. Variant manifesta', *Kino-Fot* 1 (1922): 11–12. See also Vertov's interview on kinoks in 'U kinokov', *Kino-Fot* 5 (1922): 4, where Vertov mentions 1919 as the year when the Kinoki idea emerged. The manifesto was further developed and published in Vertov, 'Kinoki. Perevorot', *LEF* 3 (1923): 135–143. For an English translation of Vertov's main writings, see Annette Michelson (ed.), *Kino-Eye: The Writings of Dziga Vertov* (Berkeley, 1984). For polemics around Vertov's films, see Yuri Tsivian (ed.), *Lines of Resistance: Dziga Vertov and the Twenties* (Pordenone, 2004).
24 Vertov, 'Kinoki. Perevorot'; Tsivian, *Lines of Resistance*, pp. 22–26. While the principle of being 'caught unaware' came to be associated with a hidden camera, Vertov's argument went far beyond advocating to film in disguise. Rather, his argument went, the camera exposes new, hidden relations that the director brings to the fore and makes visible in the process of filming and editing.
25 Vertov, 'Kinoki. Perevorot', p. 138 (my emphasis); G. B-ii, 'Teoriia i praktika kinokov', *Sovetskoe kino* 4–5 (1926): 12.
26 For an overview of Kino-Eye the method and *Kino-Eye* the film, see Hicks, *Dziga Vertov*, pp. 22–38.
27 Vladimir Fefer, 'Operator khroniki. Smelost'. Smert'', *Sovetskoe kino* 6–7 (1926): 14–15, esp. p. 14.
28 Dziga Vertov, *Stat'i, dnevniki, zamysly* (Moscow, 1966), p. 78.
29 Nikolai Chuzhak, 'K zadacham dnia', *LEF* 2 (1923): 145–146; Devin Fore, 'The Operative Word in Soviet Factography', *October* 118 (2006): 95–131.
30 Fore, 'The Operative Word', pp. 100–101.
31 Nikolai Lebedev, 'Kul'turfil'ma'; manuscript in AMK (Arkhiv Muzeiia Kino) 26/2/3/n.p.; Shutko, 'Kul'turnaia fil'ma k desiatiletiiu', p. 13.
32 Ippolit Sokolov, 'Put' kul'turfil'my', *Kino i zhizn'* 21 (1930): 15–16.
33 Sergei Tret'iakov, 'Chem zhivo kino', *Novyi LEF* 5 (1928): 28.
34 RGALI 2494/1/123: 8.
35 RGALI 2494/1/123: 2.
36 Lazar' Sukharebskii, 'Nauchno-prosvetitel'noe kino v SSSR', in Kirill Shutko (ed.), *Kul'turfil'ma. Politiko-prosvetitel'naia fil'ma* (Leningrad, 1929), pp. 65–73; RGALI 2494/1/123: 9–11; RGALI 2494/1/74.
37 RGALI 2494/1/123: 26–30.
38 'LEF i kino. Stenogramma soveshchaniia', *Novyi LEF* 11–12 (1927): 50–70, esp. p. 69.

39 Sillov's speech at the debate 'On the Crisis in Cinema' at ARRK on 22 November 1928; RGALI 2494/1 /125: 12.

40 D. Levin, I. Maizel', 'Kinokomitet pri Sovnarkome SSSR', *Kino i kul'tura* 4 (1929): 64–67; GARF 7816/1/3: 6–7.

41 Boris Levman, *Rabochii zritel' i kino: itogi I-oi rabochei kino-konferentsii* (Moscow, 1930), pp. 17–22. See also Vladimir Solev, 'Govorit kinozritel'', *Sovetskii ekran* 21 (1929): 10–12.

42 Anon., 'Kul'turfil'mu na ekrany', *Sovetskii ekran* 16 (1928): 3; I. Naumov 'Verno li? (O kul'turfil'me)', *Sovetskii ekran* 18 (1929): 4; Alexander Katsigras, 'Kul'turfil'ma', *Kino i kul'tura* 4 (1929): 10–23.

43 Shutko, *Kul'turfil'ma*, p. 93.

44 *Za fil'my rekonstruktivnogo perioda. Moskovskaia Assotsiatsiia Rabotnikov Revoliutsionnoi kinematografii* (Moscow, 1931), p. 21.

45 Esfir' Shub, 'Neigrovaia fil'ma', *Kino i kul'tura* 5–6 (1929): 6–11 (p. 10).

46 Vladimir Erofeev, 'Ot kustarshchiny k fabrike', *Kino i zhizn'* 20 (1930): 10.

47 'Kakoi dolzhna byt' sovetskaia kino-khronika', *Kino i zhizn'* 20 (1930): 5–10 (p. 7).

48 *Za fil'my rekonstruktivnogo perioda*, pp. 95–96

49 AMK 26/2/73: 134; Vladimir Erofeev, 'Tekhnicheskoe novatorstvo dokumental' noi fil'my', *Proletarskoe kino* 2–3 (1931): 4–13.

50 AMK 26/2/73: 136–137.

51 AMK 26/2/73: 110.

52 *Za fil'my rekonstruktovnogo perioda*, p. 126.

53 Iakov Bliokh and Samuil Bubrik, 'Opyt raboty vyezdnykh kinoredaktsii', *Proletarskoe kino* 12 (1931): 39–47 (p. 39); Nikolai Lebedev, 'Za proletarskuiu kinopublitsistiku', *Proletarskoe kino* 12 (1931): 20–29; Nikolai Lebedev, 'Dva "dokumenta"', *Proletarskoe kino* 5 (1932): 24–29.

54 *Za fil'my rekonstruktovnogo perioda*, pp. 127–129.

55 'Na bol'shevistske rel'sy', *Pravda* (14 December 1931): 1; Richard Taylor, 'Ideology as Mass Entertainment: Boris Shumyatsky and Soviet cinema in the 1930s', in Taylor and Christie, *Inside the Film Factory*, pp. 193–216. Institutionally, the field of production was restructured and a separate studio for the production of newsreels called Soiuzkinokhronika (Union Newsreel Studio, with a number of regional offices) was established on 1 July 1931.

56 Anatolii Lunacharskii, "O sotsialisticheskom realizme', in Lunacharskii, *Sobranie sochinenii: literaturovedenie, kritika, estetika* (Moscow, 1963), p. 359.

57 AMK 26/2/72: 41.

58 AMK 26/2/72: 41–42.

59 Alexander Deriabin (ed.), *Letopis' rossiiskogo kino, 1930–1945* (Moscow, 2007), pp. 86, 111.

60 For the Soviet policy of 'reediting' historical records, see David King, *The Commissar Vanishes: The Falsification of Photographs and Art in Stalin's Russia* (New York, 1997).

61 RGASPI 17/120/349: 23.

62 S. Gekht, 'Minaret smerti', *Sovetskii ekran* 1 (1926): 11.

63 Nadezhda Krupskaia, 'Nam nuzhno tsivilizovat'sia', *Pravda* (11 March 1926): 1.

64 'Kakoi dolzhna byt'' sovetskaia kino-khronika', *Kino i zhizn'* 20 (1930): 5–10; Anatolii Kurs, 'Kino-kritika v SSSR', *Sovetskoe kino* 2–3 (1925): 22–28.

65 Alexander Etkind, *Internal Colonization: Russia's Imperial Experience* (Cambridge, 2011). Catriona Kelly and Vadim Volkov, 'Directed Desires: Kul'turnost' and Consumption', in Catriona Kelly and David Shepherd (eds), *Constructing Russian Culture in the Age of Revolution: 1881–1940* (New York, 1998), pp. 291–313.

66 Denise J. Youngblood, *Movies for the Masses. Popular Cinema and Soviet Society in the 1920s* (Cambridge, 1992).

67 Viktor Shklovskii, *Abram Room: zhizn' i rabota* (Moscow, 1927), p. 14.

68 RGALI 2494/1/125: 25.

69 A. Troianovskii, R. Egiazarov, *Izuchenie kinozritelia* (Moscow, Leningrad, 1928); Vincent Bohlinger, 'Engrossing? Exciting! Incomprehensible? Boring! Audience survey responses to Eisenstein's *October*', *Studies in Russian and Soviet Cinema* 5.1 (2011): 5–27.

70 For examples of early questionnaires see RGALI 2495/1/11; RGALI 2495/1/12; RGALI 2495/1/13.

71 RGALI 2494/1/123: 8.

72 Vitalii Zhemchuzhnyi, 'Moskovskii teatr kul'turfil'my', *Sovetskoe kino* 2 (1927): 21.

73 GARF 8638/2/23: 8–19verso; GARF 8638/2/31: 34; RGALI 2495/1/9: 14; RGALI 2494/1/123: 26–30; N. A. 'My protiv zakrytiia Artesa', *Novyi LEF* 6 (1928): 32–33.

74 Sukharebskii in Shutko, *Kul'turfil'ma*, p. 85; Il'ia Trainin, 'Sovetskaia fil'ma i zritel'', *Sovetskoe kino* 6 (1925): 16–23.

75 Anatolii Terskoi, 'S peredvizhkoi po Kavkazy', *Sovetskii ekran* 19 (1925), n.p.; V. Sh., 'Kino na kolesakh', *Sovetskii ekran* 22 (1925), n.p.

76 Maks Polianovskii, 'Protiv boga', *Sovetskii ekran* 40 (1928): 15.

77 Iz., 'Dva kirgiza', *Sovetskii ekran* 19 (1925): n.p.

78 G. Sh-ii, 'Zhizn' pridvinulas'', *Sovetskii ekran* 24 (1925): n.p.

79 V. Balliuzek, 'Kino na vostoke', *Kino-Nedelia* 6 (3 February 1925): 9.

80 Daniel R. Brower and Edward J. Lazzerini, 'Introduction', in Daniel R. Brower, Edward Lazzerini (eds), *Russia's Orient: Imperial Borderlands and Peoples, 1700–1917* (Bloomington, 1997), p. xviii. See also Larry Wolff, *Inventing Eastern Europe: The Map of Civilization in the Mind of the Enlightenment* (Stanford, 1994).

81 Berd Kotiev, 'Kino sredi natsional'nostei', *Revoliutsiia i natsional'nosti* 5 (1931): 68–73 (p. 68).

82 Anatolii Skachko, 'Kino i vostochnye narody SSSR', *Sovetskoe kino* 1 (1925): 23–25 (original emphasis).

83 Anatolii Skachko, 'Organizatsia vostochnogo kino', *Sovetskoe kino* 2–3 (1925): 16–18.

84 Skachko, 'Organizatsia vostochnogo kino', p. 16.

85 Anon., 'Ne zabyvaite vostoka', *Zhizn' natsional'nostei* 3 (24 November 1918): 1.

86 Anatolii Skachko, 'Vostochnaia kino-fil'ma', *Sovetskoe kino* 6 (1925): 24–27.

87 Dmitrii Bassalygo, 'O vostoke dlia vostoka', *Sovetskii ekran* 24 (1925): n.p. See also E. V-ii, 'Po Kavkazu i Turkestanu', *Sovetskii ekran* 13 (1925): n.p.; E. V-ii, 'Vostochnaia fil'ma. Beseda s rezhisserom D. N. Bassalygo', *Sovetskii ekran* 15 (1925): n.p.

88 Gekht, 'Minaret smerti', p. 11.

89 V. Dvoretskii, 'Abrek Zaur i prochee', *Sovetskii ekran* 5 (1926): 4–5. U., 'Khoroshaia vostochnaia fil'ma', *Sovetskii ekran* 36 (1926): 13.

90 P. Mosiagin, 'Za vidovuiu', *Sovetksii ekran* 50 (1926): 3; Sergei Tret'iakov, 'Dorozhe – deshevle ili deshevle – dorozhe', *Sovetski ekran* 39 (1926): 3; A. Dubrovskii, 'Atel'e i natura', *Sovetskii ekran* 27 (1926): 4–5; Khrisanf Khersonskii, 'Put' na Vostok: "Velikii Perelet"', *ARK* 2 (1926): 22; Nikolai Aseev, 'V poiskakh kul'turnoi fil'my', *Sovetskii ekran* 2 (1926): 4.

91 Viktor Shklovskii, 'Kolumbam – kartu i marshrut', *Sovetskii ekran* 15 (1926): 4

92 Il'ia Trainin, *Iskusstvo v kul'turnom pokhode na Vostoke SSSR* (Moscow, 1930), p. 58.

93 Vance Kepley Jr., 'The origins of Soviet cinema: a study in industry development', in Taylor and Christie, *Inside the Film Factory*, pp. 60–79. On the earlier activities of the Moscow and Petrograd Film Committees, see Listov, *Rossiia, Revoliutsiia, Kinematograf*, pp. 59–76. Anna Lawton, *The Red Screen: Politics, Society, Art in Soviet Cinema* (London, 1992), p. 22.

94 RGASPI 17/60/263; Lev Liberman, 'K voprosu o kino', *Pravda* (1 August 1922): 1; Listov, *Rossiia, Revoliutsiia, Kinematograf*, p. 66.

95 GARF 4085/12/712: 3–14.

96 GARF 4085/12/712: 75.

97 GARF 4085/12/712: 68–89.

98 The Third Factory of Goskino was reformed into Kul'tkino in October 1924. The new studio started its activities on 3 November 1924. Sukharebskii, 'Nauchno-prosvetitel'skoe kino v SSSR', in Shutko, *Kul'turfil'ma*, p. 56.

99 GARF 4085/12/718: 109–110; Vladimir Mikhailov, 'Stalinskaia model' upravleniia kinematografom', in Lidiia Mamatova (ed.), *Kino: Politika i liudi* (Moscow, 1995), pp. 9–25, esp. p. 10; Vance Kepley, Jr., 'Federal Cinema: the Soviet Film Industry, 1924–32', *Film History* 8 (1996): 344–356; GARF, R-8326/1/1:17–18.

100 Natal'ia Riabchikova, ' "Proletkino": ot "Goskino" do "Sovkino" ', *Kinovedcheskie zapiski* 94/95 (2010): 90–108.

101 Sergei Bratoliubov, *Na zare sovetskoi kinematografii* (Leningrad, 1976), pp. 44–45, 135–141; N. Mukhin, 'Pervye gody Sevzapkino', *Kino-Nedelia* 35 (30 September 1924): 9–10.

102 Bratoliubov, *Na zare sovetskoi kinematografii*, pp. 46–56, 105–106, 160–166; RGASPI 17/60/529: 2–5. GARF 8638/2/31; R. Abul'khanov, 'Bukharsko-russkoe kinotovarishestvo', in *Iz istorii kino: materialy i dokumenty*, vol. 5 (Moscow, 1962), pp. 53–70; Kh. Abul'-Kasymova, 'Organizatsiia kinodela v Uzbekistane', in *Iz istorii kino*, vol. 5, pp. 33–52.

103 Rachit Yangirov, 'Le cinema non-joué', in Valérie Pozner, Aïcha Kherroubi, Francois Albéra et al. (eds), *Le studio Mejrabpom ou l'aventure du cinema privé au pays des bolcheviks* (Paris, 1996), pp. 85–92; Günther Agde and Alexander Schwarz (eds), *Die rote Traumfabrik. Meschrabpom-Film und Prometheus 1921–1936* (Berlin, 2012).

104 Barbara Wurm, 'Von Mechanik des Gehirns zu Vierzig Herzen: Meschrabpom-Film und der Kulturfilm', in Agde and Schwarz, *Die rote Traumfabrik*, pp. 120–129; Alexander Razumnyi, *U istokov* (Moscow, 1975), pp. 116–118.

105 Prim, 'General'naia liniia Mezhrabpomfil'ma', *Sovetskii ekran* 20 (1929): 6; Leo Mur, 'Na fabrike Mezhrabpomfil'm', *Sovetskii ekran* 39 (1928): 15; Konstantin Fel'dman, 'Itogi goda Mezhrabpomfil'm', *Sovetskii ekran* 42 (1928): 6; RGALI 2494/1/132: 6; RGASPI 538/3/129: 17; RGALI 2496/2/8: 2–2verso; Oksana Bulgakowa, 'Der Fall Meshrabpom', in Bulgakowa (ed.), *Die ungewöhnlichen Abenteuer des Dr. Mabuse im Lande der Bolschewiki* (Berlin, 1995), pp. 185–193; Jamie Miller, *Soviet Cinema: Politics and Persuasion Under Stalin* (London, 2010), pp. 121–138.

106 Mikhailov, 'Stalinskaia model' upravleniia kinematografom', pp. 10–11; Youngblood, *Soviet Cinema in the Silent Era*, pp. 43–47.

107 Il'ia Trainin, 'Na puti k vozrozhdeniiu', *Sovetskoe kino* 1 (1925): 8–14, esp. p. 12.

108 GARF 8638/2/11: 11; GARF 8638/2/30: 5–6.

109 Trainin, 'Na puti k vozrozhdeniiu', p. 12.

110 M. Kristol' (ed.), *Nauchnoe kino* (Moscow, 1927); Lazar' Sukharebskii, *Nauchnoe kino* (Moscow, 1926).

111 GARF 8638/2/31: 34; Mikhail Efremov, 'O prokatnoi deiatel'nosti Sovkino', *Sovetskoe kino* 4–5 (1925): 42–45; 'Iz deiatel'nosti Sovkino', *Sovetskoe kino* 2–3 (1925): 81–82; 'O polozhenii kino-promyshlennosti i Sovkino', *Sovetskoe kino* 2–3 (1925): 82–83; N. Shapovalenko, 'Ekonomicheskii analiz kino-seansa', *Sovetskoe kino* 2–3 (1925): 73–74.

112 Anon., 'Etno-Mir', *Novyi zritel'* 25 (21 June 1927): 10; RGALI 2489/1/1: 85.

113 RGALI 2489/1/1: 91. The founding members were the Commissariat of Enlightenment of the RSFSR, Autonomous Republics (ASSR) of Bashkiria, Chuvashia, the Crimea, Karelia, Kazakhstan, Kirgizia, Tatarstan, Yakutia, Buryat-Mongolia, Dagestan, Volga German Autonomous Soviet Socialist Republic and Autonomous Oblasts (AO) of Adygeia, Chechnya, Ingushetia, Kalmykia, Karachaevo, Komi, Mari and North Ossetia, and a number of federal organizations. The charter of the shareholding society 'Vostochnoe Kino' was approved on 13 March 1926. V. Vishnevskii, P. Fionov (eds), *Sovetskoe kino v datakh i faktakh (1917–1969)* (Moscow, 1974), p. 38; Anatolii Skachko, 'Vostochnoe Kino', *Sovetskoe kino* 2–3 (1925): 85; 'Vostokkino', *Sovetskoe kino* 1 (1926): 24.

114 Vostokkino was reorganized as a state trust and renamed Vostokfilm in March 1932. I refer to the studio as Vostokkino prior to this date and as Vostokfilm for the period from March 1932–August 1935.

115 RGALI 2489/1/1: 114.

116 RGALI 2489/1/1: 90.

117 RGALI 2489/1/1: 89–90.

118 RGALI 2489/1/1: 95.

119 By the end of 1929 Vostokkino had a staff of 67. For the list of studio employees see RGALI, 2489/1/10: 19verso. The incomplete list of the Vostokfilm staff included in the closing balance already contained ca. 200 names. RGALI 2489/1/111: 27–29.

120 RGALI 2489/1/13: 5, 15, 103, 166.

121 RGALI 2489/1/52: 97.

122 In May 1930 the studio was reformed first into a state trust 'Vostokkino', and in March 1932 renamed 'Vostokfilm'. In March 1933 Vostokfilm trust was taken out of the hands of Soiuzkino and placed under the control of the Council of People's Commissars; its board director Berd Kotiev (later purged) was replaced by Vadim Atarbekov.

123 Among the themes planned for production in 1928/29, for example, were the 1916 uprising in Central Asia, the Bashkir uprising under the guidance of Salawat, the struggle of Shamil against Russian imperialism, and rebellion in Komi. RGALI 2489/1/3: 2.

124 Soiuzkino's first head, Martem'ian Riutin, was promptly removed from his position, after which the studio also underwent a series of purges; see John Arch Getty and Oleg Naumov, *The Road to Terror: Stalin and the Self-Destruction of the Bolsheviks, 1932–1939* (New Haven, 1999), pp. 52–61; Konstantin Zalesskii, *Imperiia Stalina. Biograficheskii Entsiklopedicheskii Slovar'* (Moscow, 2000), pp. 398–399.

125 Boris Shumiatskii, *Kinematografiia millionov* (Moscow, 1935).

126 Mikhailov, 'Stalinskaia model' upravleniia kinematografom', p. 15.

127 Andrei Artizov and Oleg Naumov (eds), *Vlast' i khudozhestvennaia intelli-
     gentsiia. Dokumenty TsK RKP(b)-VKP(b), VChK-OGPU-NKVD o kul'turnoi
     politike. 1917–1953* (Moscow, 2002), p. 202.
128 On 10 August 1935, the Council of People's Commissars of the Russian
     Federation closed Vostokfilm and created the 'Eastern Sector' within the
     Main Administration of the Film and Photo Industry (Glavnoe upravlenie
     kino-foto promyshlennostiu, GUKF), which replaced Soiuzkino after 1933;
     see Alexander Deriabin (ed.), *Letopis' rossiiskogo kino, 1930–1945* (Moscow,
     2007), p. 346. The official reasons for this decision were financial: the closing
     balance of 1935 includes substantial debts and large sums unaccounted for; see
     RGALI 2489/1/110. With the closing of Vostokfilm, the majority of its films
     were removed from distribution by Glavrepertkom, and another 22 were 're-
     worked'; see RGALI 2489/1/111: 194–195.
129 Mikhailov, 'Stalinskaia model' upravleniia kinematografom', pp. 19–20.

2. Absolute Kinography: Vertov's Cine-Race Across the Soviet Universe

1 Vertov, 'Kinoki. Perevorot', p. 140; English translation in Michelson, *Kino-Eye*,
   p. 17.
2 An overview of the Vserossiiskii fotokinootdel (VFKO) activities in 1922 mentions '25 commissions for the total sum over 85 billion rubles' by the agencies Moscow Woolen Cloth Trust (Mossukno), the Ural Chemistry Trust
   (Uralkhim), the Moscow Association of Enterprises Processing Agro-Industrial
   Products (Mossel'prom), and others; see 'Goskino – proizvodstvo i ekspluata-
   tsiia', *Kino-Fot* 5 (1922): 9.
3 For the reception of *Stride, Soviet!* see Tsivian, *Lines of Resistance*, pp. 157–181.
4 RGALI 2091/2/399.
5 The full title of the film is *A Sixth Part of the World. A Kino-Eye Race around
   the USSR: Export and Import by the State Trading Organization of the USSR*
   [Shestaia chast' mira. Probeg Kino-glaza po SSSR: Eksport i import Gostorga
   SSSR]. The title is sometimes translated as *One Sixth of the World* or as *A Sixth
   of the World*.
6 For an overview of *A Sixth Part of the World* in the context of the construction of Soviet space in cinema, see Widdis, *Visions of a New Land*, pp. 108–111.
   The contributions to the debate over the film are translated in Tsivian, *Lines of
   Resistance*, pp. 182–256.
7 Tsivian, *Lines of Resistance*, pp. 22–23.
8 RGALI 2091/1/179:16–17. On cine-trains see Richard Taylor, *Politics of the
   Soviet Cinema, 1917–1929* (Cambridge, 1979), pp. 54–63; Vance Kepley, 'Soviet

Cinema and State Control: Lenin's Nationalization Degree Reconsidered', *Journal of Film and Video* 42.2 (1990): 3–14 (pp. 4–8). Adelheid Heftberger, 'Soviet Agit-Trains from the Vertov Collection of the Austrian Film Museum', *Incite!* 4 (2013), available at http://www.incite-online.net/heftberger4.html (accessed 25 March 2015).

9 *Kino-Pravda* comprised 23 issues produced between 5 June 1922 to March 1925. For a select filmography see Tsivian, *Lines of Resistance*, pp. 403–409. For an overview of *Kino-Pravda* see Joshua Malitsky, *Post-Revolution Nonfiction Film: Building the Soviet and Cuban Nations* (Bloomington, 2013), pp. 93–97.

10 RGALI 2091/2/403: 58verso.

11 RGALI 2091/2/235: 93.

12 RGALI 2091/2/399: 46–49.

13 On *The Great Flight* see reviews and documents compiled and commented by Natal'ia Riabchikova, '"Glaz kino sledoval glazu letchika". *Velikii perelet* Vladimira Shneiderova i Georgiia Bliuma', *Kinovedcheskie zapiski* 98 (2011): 257–290. For the report on unsuccessful expedition to China see RGALI 2091/2/399: 27–28.

14 RGALI 2091/2/403: 53.

15 RGALI 2091/2/403: 93.

16 RGALI 2091/2/403: 52.

17 RGALI 2091/2/403: 58v–59.

18 RGALI 2091/2/403: 61–61verso; Papazian, *Manufacturing Truth*, p. 77.

19 RGALI 2091/2/235: 87–88.

20 Sheila Fitzpatrick, Alexander Rabinowitch, and Richard Stites (eds), *Russia in the Era of NEP: Explorations in Soviet Society and Culture* (Bloomington, 1991).

21 Originally published in *Al'manakh Proletkul'ta* (1925); republished in Vertov, *Iz naslediia*, vol. 2, pp. 26–32.

22 Vertov, 'Advertising Films', in Michelson, *Kino-Eye*, pp. 25–29.

23 Vertov, 'Advertising Films', pp. 29–30.

24 Vertov, 'Advertising Films', p. 30.

25 Aboubakar Sanogo, 'Colonialism, Visuality and the Cinema: Revisitng the Bantu Educational Kinema Experiment', in Grieveson and MacCabe, *Empire and Film*, pp. 227–245, esp. p. 230. For more on Empire Marketing Board, see Lee Grieveson, 'The Cinema and the (Common) Wealth of Nations', in Grieveson and MacCabe, *Empire and Film*, pp. 73–113.

26 Vertov, 'Advertising Films', in Michelson, *Kino-Eye*, p. 91.

27 RGALI 2091/2/235: 89–90.

28 RGALI 2091/2/403: 51.

29 Oleg Kapchinskii, 'Podsudimyi Khanzhonkov', *Rodina* 9 (2008): 13–15. See also Sheila Fitzpatrick, *The Commissariat of Enlightenment: Soviet Organization of Education and the Arts Under Lunacharsky, October 1917–1921* (Cambridge, 1970).

30 Ivan Beliakov, Samuil Benderskii, Nikolai Konstantinov, Alexander Lemberg, Nikolai Strukov, Iakov Tolchan and Petr Zlotov worked as cameramen on the film. 'Vertov's Silent Film. An Annotated Filmography', in Tsivian, *Lines of Resistance*, p. 408. For a conflict over uncredited footage see Nikolai Lebedev, 'A Letter to the Editor', *Kino-front* 7–8 (1927): 32. Vertov reduced the amount of found footage in his film, but the use of uncredited foreign footage continued to worry the studio management; see RGALI 2091/2/399: 61; Tsivian, *Lines of Resistance*, p. 210.

31 Paul Virilio, *War and Cinema: The Logistics of Perception* (London, 1989), p. 1.

32 Scott W. Palmer, *Dictatorship of the Air: Aviation Culture and the Fate of Modern Russia* (Cambridge, 2006), p. 10.

33 Stollery, *Alternative Empires*, p. 164.

34 Quoted in Davide Deriu, 'Picturing Ruinscapes: The Aerial Photograph as Image of Historical Trauma', in Frances Guerin and Roger Hallas (eds), *The Image and the Witness: Trauma, Memory and Visual Culture* (New York and London, 2007), p. 192. See also Ruth Ben-Ghiat, *Italian Fascism's Empire Cinema* (Bloomington, 2015).

35 Widdis, *Visions of a New Land*, pp. 128–129.

36 'S"emka aeroplana', *Kino-Fot* 6 (1923): 5.

37 Viktor Pertsov, 'Podniat' v vozdukh', *Sovetskii ekran* 1 (1926): 14.

38 Yuri Slezkine, *Arctic Mirrors: Russia and the Small Peoples of the North* (Ithaca, 1994), p. 390.

39 Vertov, 'Kinoki. Perevorot', p. 141.

40 Vertov, *Iz naslediia. Dramaturgicheskie opyty*, vol. 1 (Moscow, 2004), pp. 79–86; Alexander Deriabin dates these sketches between 1922–24.

41 Vertov, 'Kinoki. Perevorot', p. 140.

42 Ernst van Alphen, *Staging the Archive* (London, 2014), p. 122.

43 van Alphen, *Staging the Archive*, p. 122.

44 Hirsch, *Empire of Nations*, pp. 101–44.

45 Tsivian, *Lines of Resistance*, pp. 188–89.

46 van Alphen, *Staging the Archive*, p. 55.

47 van Alphen, *Staging the Archive*, p. 91.

48 Widdis, *Visions of a New Land*, p. 14.

49 Papazian, *Manufacturing Truth*, p. 80.

50 Vishlenkova, *Vizual'noe narodovedenie imperii*, p. 62.

51 Vishlenkova, *Vizual'noe narodovedenie imperii*, pp. 14, 51–55, 143–144.

52 James von Geldern, *Bolshevik Festivals, 1917–1920* (Berkeley, 1993).

53 'But yet even then, / When on the entire planet / The animosity of tribes will come to an end, / Lies and sorrow will vanish, / I will glorify / With all my poet's soul / The sixth part of the world / With the short name "Rus" (my translation)'.

54 Quoted in Vlada Petric, 'Dziga Vertov as Theorist', *Cinema Journal* 18.1 (1978): 35.

55 Anna Lawton, 'Rhythmic Montage in the Films of Dziga Vertov: A Poetic Use of the Language of Cinema', *Pacific Coast Philology* 13 (1978): 44–50; Michael Kunichika, 'The Ecstasy of Breadth: The Odic and Whitmanesque in Vertov's "One Sixth of the World"', *Studies in Russian and Soviet Cinema* 6.1 (2012): 53–74.

56 Tsivian, *Lines of Resistance*, p. 190.

57 Petric, 'Dziga Vertov as Theorist', p. 37.

58 Petric, 'Dziga Vertov as Theorist', p. 30.

59 Vertov, quoted in Lawton, 'Rhythmic Montage', p. 45.

60 Tsivian, *Lines of Resistance*, p. 192.

61 Sergei Ermolinskii, 'Shestaia chast' mira', *Komsomol'skaia pravda* (20 November 1926), translated in Tsivian, *Lines of Resistance*, pp. 218–20.

62 David Spurr, *The Rhetoric of Empire: Colonial Discourse in Journalism, Travel Writing, and Imperial Administration* (Durham, 1993).

63 Spurr, *The Rhetoric of Empire*, p. 7.

64 Vishnevskii, *Dokumental'nye fil'my*, pp. 177, 210, 259, 275.

65 Igor Semenov, 'Statistical Surveys of the Kanin Peninsula and the Samoed Question' in David Anderson (ed.), *The 1926/27 Soviet Polar Census Expeditions* (New York and Oxford, 2011), pp. 133–154 (p. 133).

66 Mary Louise Pratt, quoted in Spurr, *The Rhetoric of Empire*, p. 18.

67 Compare, for example, Rudolph Pöch's 'Bushman Speaking into the Phonograph' (1908) and its discussion by Oksiloff, *Picturing the Primitive*, pp. 43–57.

68 Michael J. Heffernan, 'The Science of Empire: The French Geographical Movement and the Forms of French Imperialism, 1870–1920', in Anne Godlewska and Neil Smith (eds), *Geography and Empire* (Oxford, 1994), pp. 92–114 (p. 104).

69 Tsivian, *Lines of Resistance*, p. 192.

70 Tsivian, *Lines of Resistance*, p. 408.

71 The Tungus, introduced as 'a tribe of a Mongolian race', are indigenous nomads inhabiting the eastern part of Siberia and known today under the ethnonym Evenks.

72 'Shestaia chast' mira. Beseda s Dzigoi Vertovym', *Kino* 33 (17 August 1926): 3, translated in Tsivian, *Lines of Resistance*, p. 182.

73 Tsivian, *Lines of Resistance*, pp. 196–202.

74 Izmail Urazov, 'Shestaia chast' mira', translated in Tsivian, *Lines of Resistance*, p. 185.

75 Grigorii Boltianskii, 'Shestaia chast' mira', *Zhizn' iskusstva* 42 (1926); translated in Tsivian, *Lines of Resistance*, p. 199.

76 A. Zorich, 'O shestoi chasti mira', *Gudok* (8 January 1927); translated in Tsivian, *Lines of Resistance*, p. 223.

77 'Rabkory pishut o 'Shestoi chasti mira', *Kino* (29 January 1927): 4; 'Vypolnennaia zadacha', *Kino* (21 September 1926): 1–2; Izmail Urazov, 'Pafos v deistvii', *Kino* (28

September 1926): 1; Detsenko, 'Dziga Vertov stroit sotsializm', *Komsomol'skaia pravda* (5 January 1927), translated in Tsivian, *Lines of Resistance*, pp. 226–28.

78 L. Sosnovskii, 'Shestaia chast' mira', *Rabochaia gazeta* (5 January 1927); translated in Tsivian, *Lines of Resistance*, pp. 220–22.

79 Tsivian, *Lines of Resistance*, pp. 217–18 and 206–7.

80 Al. G., 'Shestaia chast' mira', *Tikhookeanskaia zvezda* (Khabarovsk) (6 February 1927).

81 Mikhail Bleiman, 'Shestaia chast' mira', *Leningradskaia pravda* (3 February 1927); Krasnov, 'Sovetskoe kino', *Uchitel'skaia gazeta* (5 February 1927), translated in Tsivian, *Lines of Resistance*, pp. 207–8.

82 Osip Beskin, 'Shestaia chast' mira', *Sovetskoe kino* 6–7 (1926): 16–17, translated in Tsivian, *Lines of Resistance*, p. 205.

83 Tsivian, *Lines of Resistance*, p. 212.

84 Liliana Mal'kova, *Sovremennost' kak istoriia: realizatsia mifa v dokumental'nom kino* (Moscow, 2002), p. 36.

85 Nikolai Aseev, 'Shestaia chast' vozmozhnostei', *Kino* (26 October 1926): 2; translated in Tsivian, *Lines of Resistance*, pp. 200–201.

86 Tsivian, *Lines of Resistance*, p. 194.

87 'Shestaia chast' mira (Beseda s Dzigoi Vertovym)', *Kino* (17 August 1926): 3, translated in Tsivian, *Lines of Resistance*, p. 184.

88 RGALI 2091/2/403:101; Tsivian, *Lines of Resistance*, pp. 254–256.

89 Alexander Deriabin, 'Iz istorii rozhdeniia cheloveka s kinoapparatom. Novye dokumenty', *Kinovedcheskie zapiski* 49 (2000): 199–205.

90 John MacKay, 'Film Energy: Process and Metanarrative in Dziga Vertov's The Eleventh Year', *October* 121 (2007): 41–78; Oksana Bulgakova, *Sovetskii slukhoglaz: kino i ego organy chuvstv* (Moscow, 2010).

91 Graham Roberts, *Forward, Soviet! History and Non-Fiction Film in the USSR* (London, 1999), pp. 92–107.

92 Hirsch, *Empire of Nations*, pp. 310–311.

3. Arctic Travelogues: Conquering the Soviet Far North

1 Dmitri Nagishkin (ed.), *Chukotka Fairy Tales* (Moscow, 1958), p. 3.

2 As described by Yuri Slezkine, the small peoples of the North consisted of 26 ethnic groups, lumped together by Russian authorities according to 'tradition, political exigencies, and contemporary linguistic and ethnographic data: the Khanty, Mansi, Chukchi, Koriak, Nenets (Samoed), Enets, Eskimo, Aleut, Saami (Lapps), Evenk (Tungus), Yukagir, Selkup, Nganasan, Dolgan, Ket, Even, Chuvan, Itelmnen, Nivkh (Giliaki), Negidal, Nanai, Ulch, Oroch, Orok,

Udege and Tofalar. Larger groups, such as the Yakut (Sakha), Komi, or Buryat, were not considered part of this category; each was granted its own autonomous region. As late as the 1930s, the small peoples were still primarily nomadic and numbered somewhere between 150,000 and 200,000'. Yuri Slezkine, *Arctic Mirrors: Russia and the Small Peoples of the North* (Ithaca, 1994), p. 1; Adam Kuper, *The Invention of Primitive Society: Transformation of an Illusion* (London, 1988), pp. 2–3.

3 Slezkine, *Arctic Mirrors*, p. 79.

4 Bruce Grant, 'Siberia Hot and Cold: Reconstructing the Image of Siberian Indigenous Peoples', in Galya Diment and Yuri Slezkine (eds), *Between Heaven and Hell: The Myth of Siberia in Russian Culture* (New York, 1993), pp. 227–253; Nathaniel Knight, 'Science, Empire, and Nationality: Ethnography in the Russian Geographical Society, 1845–1855', in Jane Burbank and David L. Ransel (eds), *Imperial Russia. New History for the Empire* (Bloomington, 1998), pp. 108–141.

5 E. Rinchenko, 'Inorodcheskii vopros i zadachi sovetskogo stroitel'stva v Sibiri', *Zhizn' natsional'nostei* 42 (31 December 1920): 1–2; E. Rinchenko, 'Inorodcheskii vopros v Sibiri', *Zhizn' natsional'nostei* 6 (4 March 1921): 2–3; D. Ianovich, 'Severnye tuzemtsy', *Zhizn' natsional'nostei* 1 (1923): 251–254, esp. pp. 251–252; Slezkine, *Arctic Mirrors*, pp. 131–183.

6 Grant, 'Siberia Hot and Cold', p. 231.

7 Vladimir Bogoraz-Tan, 'Ob izuchenii i okhrane okrainnykh narodov', *Zhizn' natsional'nostei* 3–4 (1923): 168–177; Vladimir Bogoraz-Tan, 'Predlozheniia k voprosy ob izuchenii i okhrane okrainnykh narodov', *Zhizn' natsional'nostei* 3–4 (1923): 178–180.

8 Skachko, quoted in Slezkine, *Arctic Mirrors*, p. 270.

9 On the ethnographic principle see Nikolai Ssorin-Chaikov, 'Representing "Primitive Communists": Ethnographic and Political Authority in Early Soviet Siberia', in Jane Burbank, Mark von Hagen, and Anatolyi Remnev (eds), *Russian Empire: Space, People, Power, 1700–1930* (Bloomington, 2007), pp. 268–292 (p. 282).

10 Vera Popova (1892–1974) had worked as a film editor at Khanzhonkov's studio since the 1910s; she was also Khanzhonkov's second wife. After 1917, she continued her career as editor. Popova had great knowledge of the material and may have known Bremer personally. The editing most probably took place right after the trial initiated by OGPU against the management and employers of the Goskino and Proletkino studios (including Khanzhonkov and Popova herself). While all the accused were ultimately released, Khanzhonkov was the only person to be deprived of his civil rights and Popova supported the family by working as a film editor at Sovkino and at other film studios; see Oleg Kapchinskii, 'Podsudimyi Khanzhonkov', *Rodina* 9 (2008): 13–15. However, since all the available sources only use the acronym V. Popova,

one cannot exclude the possibility of another editor. The same hypothesis is advanced in Alexander Deriabin (ed.), *Vladimir Alekseevich Erofeev (1898–1940). Materialy k 100–letiiu so dnia rozhdeniia* (Moscow, 1998), p. 6.

11 Erofeev, 'Ob ekspeditsiiakh voobshchee i v chastnosti', *Sovetskii ekran* 25 (1926): 8–9.

12 V. N. Batalin, *Kino-khronika v Rossii, 1896–1916* (Moscow, 2002), pp. 12, 27, 197, 289.

13 Fedor Bremer, 'Opasnyi reis (Zapiski operatora-turista)', *Pegas. Zhurnal iskusstv* 1 (1915): 62–72 (p. 66).

14 Bremer, 'Opasnyi reis', p. 66.

15 Bremer, 'Opasnyi reis', p. 71.

16 Karl Heider, *Ethnographic Film* (Austin, 1976), p. 125.

17 Tom Gunning, 'Landscape and the Fantasy of Moving Pictures: Early Cinema's Phantom Rides', in Graeme Harper and Jonathan Rayner (eds), *Cinema and Landscape* (Bristol and Chicago, 2010), pp. 31–70 (p. 37).

18 Eleanor Hight and Gary D. Sampson (eds), *Colonialist Photography: Imag(in)ing Race and Place* (London, 2002), p. 5.

19 On ethnographic photographic conventions see Elizabeth Edwards, *Raw Histories: Photographs, Anthropology and Museums* (Oxford and New York, 2001); Elizabeth Edwards (ed.), *Anthropology and Photography, 1860–1920* (New Haven, 1992).

20 Gunning, 'Landscape and the Fantasy of Moving Pictures', p. 37.

21 Conley, *Cartographic Cinema*, p. 2.

22 Hirsch, *Empire of Nations*, pp. 194–195.

23 Slezkine, *Arctic Mirrors*, pp. 248–249; F. Bertran, 'Nauka bez ob"ekta? Sovetskaia etnografiia 1920–30kh godov i voprosy etnicheskoi kategorizatsii', *Zhurnal sotsiologii i sotsial'noi antropologii*, 6.3 (2003): 90–104.

24 Matti Bunzl, 'Franz Boas and the Humboldtian Tradition: From *Volksgeist* and *Nationalcharakter* to an Anthropological Concept of Culture', in George W. Stocking Jr. (ed.), *Volksgeist as Method and Ethic: Essays on Boasian Ethnography and the German Anthropological Tradition* (Madison, 1996), pp. 17–78 (p. 62); Sergei Kan, ' "Moi drug v tupike empirizma i skepsisa": Vladimir Bororaz, Frants Boas i politicheskii kontekst sovetskoi etnologii v kontse 1920–nachale 1930kh godov', *Antropologicheskii forum* 7 (2007) available at http://anthropologie.kunstkamera.ru/files/pdf/007/07_05_kahn_k.pdf (accessed 23 April 2013).

25 Waldemar Bogoras, *The Chukchee* (Leiden, 1904).

26 Bruce Grant, 'Nivkhi, Russians and Others: The Politics of Indigenism in Sakhalin Island', in Stephen Kotkin and David Wolff (eds), *Rediscovering Russia in Asia: Siberia and the Russian Far East* (Armonk, 1995), pp. 160–171 (p. 163).

27 Nikolai Lebedev recalls that the film was screened at the Goskino cinema to an audience of film professionals prior to its official purchase; AMK 26/2/3. The permit to screen *Nanook* to all audiences was signed on 4 November 1927. *Repertuarnyi Biulleten'* 1 (1928): 45.

28 Simon Werrett, 'Technology on Display: Instruments and Identities on Russian Voyages of Exploration', *The Russian Review* 70 (2011): 380–396 (p. 396).

29 William Rothman, 'The Film-maker as Hunter: Robert Flaherty's *Nanook of the North*', in Barry Keith Grant and Jeannette Sloniowski (eds), *Documenting the Documentary: Close Readings of Documentary Film and Video* (Detroit, 1998), pp. 23–39.

30 Peter Davidson, *The Idea of North* (London, 2005), p. 9.

31 Scott MacKenzie and Anna Westerståhl Stenport, 'Introduction: What are Arctic Cinemas?', in Scott MacKenzie and Anna Westerståhl Stenport (eds), *Films on Ice: Cinemas of the Arctic* (Edinburgh, 2015), pp. 1–32 (p. 15).

32 Marina Dahlquist, 'Snow-White: The Aesthetic and Narrative Use of Snow in Swedish Silent Film' in John Fullerton and Jan Olsson (eds), *Nordic Explorations: Film before 1930* (London, 1999), pp. 236–248.

33 Dahlquist, 'Snow-White…', p. 238.

34 John McCannon, *Red Arctic: Polar Exploration and the Myth of the North in the Soviet Union, 1932–1939* (Oxford, 1998), p. 84.

35 Jean-Dominique Lajoux, 'Ethnographic Film and History', in Paul Hockings (ed.), *Principles of Visual Anthropology* (Berlin and New York, 2003), pp. 168–169.

36 Mary Louise Pratt, *Imperial Eyes: Travel Writing and Transculturation* (London, 1992), p. 6.

37 AMK 24/3/32: 41.

38 David Zolotarev, quoted in Hirsch, *Empire of Nations*, p. 251.

39 Marfa Semyonovna Kryukova, 'Tale of the Pole', in James von Geldern and Richard Stites (eds), *Mass Culture in Soviet Russia: Tales, Poems, Songs, Movies, Plays, and Folklore, 1917–1953* (Bloomington, 1995), pp. 287–291 (p. 291).

40 McCannon, *Red Arctic*, p. 111.

41 Susanne Frank, 'Teplaia Arktika: k istorii odnogo starogo literaturnogo motiva', *Novoe literaturnoe obozrenie* 108 (2011): 82–97.

42 Vladimir Shneiderov, *Pokhod 'Sibiriakova'* (Moscow, 1933); V. Vize, *Na 'Sibiriakove' v Tikhii okean* (Leningrad, 1934); John McCannon, 'Positive Heroes at the Pole: Celebrity Status, Socialist-Realist Ideals and the Soviet Myth of the Arctic, 1932–39', *The Russian Review* 56.3 (1997): 346–365.

43 Eduard Kol'chinskii (ed.), *Sovetsko-germanskie nauchnye sviazi vremeni Veimarskoi respubliki* (St. Petersburg, 2001), p. 259.

44 Following the expedition in the summer of 1929, Shneiderov directed five films on Yemen, all produced by Mezhrabpomfilm in cooperation with

Prometheus: *El-Yemen, Mokko, Sana, Khodeida, Ka–Iakhud* (all 1930). See Chapter 7 for his Pamir expedition.

45 Quoted in M. Nechaeva, *Vladimir Shneiderov* (Moscow, 1964), p. 50.

46 Boris Gromov, 'Pokhod "Sibiriakova"', *Smena* 1–2 (1933): 19–20, esp. p. 19. See also Paul Josephson, 'Technology and the Conquest of the Soviet Arctic', *The Russian Review* 70 (2011): 419–439.

47 Vladimir Shneiderov, *Moi kinoputeshestviia* (Moscow, 1973), pp. 34–35.

48 Vladimir Shneiderov, *Velikim severnym* (Moscow, 1963).

49 For a cameraman's perspective on making *Two Oceans*, see Mark Troianovskii, *S vekom naravne. Dnevniki. Pis'ma. Zapiski* (Moscow, 2004), pp. 33–34.

50 Frank J. Miller, *Folklore for Stalin: Russian Folklore and Pseudofolklore of the Stalin Era* (Armonk, 1990), pp. 4, 12. The word 'noviny' was allegedly coined by folklore performer Marfa Kriukova (1876–1954) – a folktale-teller from north Russia who made a Soviet career by adapting traditional folk forms to the political purposes of the regime. McCannon, *Red Arctic*, pp. 125–128; van Geldern and Stites, *Mass Culture in Soviet Russia*, p. 287.

51 McCannon, 'Positive Heroes at the Pole', p. 353.

52 Lapin later participated in the notorious Belomor Writers Brigade's edited volume *The History of Construction*, celebrating the OGPU (State Secret Police) and the Solovki labour camp; See Cynthia A. Ruder, 'Boris Lapin: Unlikely Modernist', *Russian Literature* 34.2 (1993): 207–218; Cynthia A. Ruder, *Making History for Stalin: The Story of the Belomor Canal* (Gainesville, 1998), p. 78.

53 Boris Lapin, 'Amerikanskaia granitsa', in Teodor Grits (ed.), *Pereklichka narodov* (Moscow, 1931), pp. 5–49 (p. 6).

54 Lapin, 'Amerikanskaia granitsa', p. 20.

55 Tom Gunning, 'Landscape and the Fantasy of Moving Pictures: Early Cinema's Phantom Rides', pp. 58, 54.

56 For other visual representations of the Cheliuskin campaign see also the photographic album edited by L. Mekhlis, I. Verite, I. Bogovoi, I. Baevskii (eds), *Geroicheskaia epopeia* (Moscow, 1935); and Iu. Shmidt, I. Baevskii, L. Mekhlis (eds), *Pokhod Cheliuskina*, vols. 1–2 (Moscow, 1934).

57 Mikhail Prishvin, *Dnevniki 1932–35* (St. Petersburg, 2009), p. 760.

58 Slezkine, *Arctic Mirrors*, p. 280.

59 Troianovskii, *S vekom naravne*, p. 40.

60 Troianovskii, *S vekom naravne*, pp. 43–46.

61 Arkadii Shafran, 'S kinoapparatom v ledianoi pustyne' in M. D'iakonov, E. Rubinchik (eds), *Dnevniki Cheliuskintsev* (Leningrad, 1935), pp. 547–558.

62 Prishvin, *Dnevniki 1932–35*, p. 425 (my emphasis).

63 Prishvin, *Dnevniki 1932–35*, p. 426.

64 Arkadii Shafran, 'Kak ia snimal', *Kino* 30 (28 June 1934).

65 Roman Katsman, 'Geroi Arktiki', *Kino* 30 (28 June 1934): 1.

66 Quoted in McCannon, *Red Arctic*, p. 138.
67 Leaving Moscow on 22 March 1937, the first pilots landed on a drifting ice floe in the area of the North Pole on 21 May. An official opening of the polar station, including the raising of the flag of the USSR, took place on 6 June.
68 For the evolution of the 'conquering' rhetoric in other arts and literature, see Katerina Clark, 'Socialist Realism with Shores: Conventions for a Positive Hero', in Thomas Lahusen, Evgeny Dobrenko (eds), *Socialist Realism without Shores* (Durham, 1997), pp. 27–50; Régine Robin, *Socialist Realism: an Impossible Aesthetic* (Stanford, 1992), pp. 217–296; Richard Taylor, 'Red Stars, Positive Heroes, and Personality Cults', in Richard Taylor and Derek Spring (eds), *Stalinism and Soviet Cinema* (London, 1993), pp. 69–89.
69 Widdis, *Visions of a New Land*, p. 150.

4. Forest People, Wild and Tamed: Travelogues in the Far East

1 Evgenii Dolmatovskii, 'Edushchim na vostok – naputstvie' (1937), translated and published in Elena Shulman, *Stalinism on the Frontier of Empire: Women and State Formation in the Soviet Far East* (Cambridge, 2008), p. 238.
2 Teodor Grits (ed.), *Pereklichka narodov* (Moscow, 1931).
3 Shulman, *Stalinism on the Frontier of Empire*, p. 4. On the notion of 'complex frontier' see Alfred J. Rieber, 'The Comparative Ecology of Complex Frontiers' in Miller and Rieber (eds), *Imperial Rule* (Budapest, 2005), pp. 177–207.
4 The Far East Region (Dal'nevostochnyi krai) was established within the RSFSR in January 1926; it replaced the Far East Area (Dal'nevostochnaia oblast'). The Region included five former *guberniia*: Amurskaia, Zabaikal'skaia, Kamchatskaia, Primorskaia, and Northern Sakhalin. Khabarovsk became the main administrative centre. In October 1938 the Far East Region was divided into the Khabarovsk and Primorsk Regions (*krai*). The Primorsk Area (*oblast'*) was established as the easternmost division of the Russian Empire in 1856. It included the territory of the modern Primorsk Region, as well as the territories of the modern Khabarovsk Region and Magadan Area, stretching from Vladivostok to the Chukchi Peninsula in the far north. See Alan Wood, *Russia's Frozen Frontier: A History of Siberia and the Russian Far East 1581–1991* (London, 2011).
5 For the early discursive modes of appropriating the Far East see Mark Bassin, *Imperial Visions. Nationalist Imagination and Geographical Expansion in the Russian Far East, 1840–1865* (Cambridge, 1999).
6 Alexander Deriabin, 'Alexander Litvinov und der sowjetische Expeditionsfilm', in Hans-Joachim Schlegel (ed.), *Die überrumpelte Wirklichkeit: Texte zum sowjetischen Dokumentarfilm der 20er und frühen 30er Jahre* (Leipzig, 2003),

pp. 59–62; Alexander Deriabin, 'O fil'makh-puteshestviiakh i Aleksandre Litvinove', *Zelenoe Spasenie* 11 (1999), available at http://www.greensalvation.org/old/Russian/Publish/11_rus/11_02.htm (last accessed 25 March 2013).

7 Alexander Litvinov, *Puteshestviia s kinokameroi* (Moscow, 1982); Maks Polianovskii, *V strane Udekhe* (Moscow and Leningrad, 1929); Michael G. Smith, 'Cinema for the "Soviet East": National Fact and Revolutionary Fiction in Early Azerbaijani Film', *Slavic Review* 56.4 (1997): 645–678 (pp. 652–654).

8 Maks Polianovskii, 'Kraeved v kino. Pamiati Vladimira Klavdievicha Arsen'eva', *Kino i zhizn'* 26 (1930): 19; Maks Polianovskii, 'V Ussuriiskoi taige. Ekspeditsiia Sovkino', *Sovetskii ekran* 33 (1938): 6; Alexander Litvinov, *Po sledam Arsen'eva: zapiski kinorezhissera* (Vladivostok, 1959).

9 For the fullest annotated collection of Arsen'ev's publications, see Vladimir Arsen'ev, *Sobranie sochinenii v 6 tomakh*, vols. 1–3 (Vladivostok, 2007–12).

10 Sergei Tret'iakov, 'Zhivoi "zhivoi" chelovek. O knige Arsen'eva "V debriakh Ussuriiskogo kraia"', *Novyi LEF* 7 (1928): 44–46.

11 Amir Khisamutdinov, *Vladimir Klavdievich Arsen'ev, 1872–1930* (Moscow, 2005), pp. 164–166; Johanna Nichols, 'Stereotyping Interethnic Communication: The Siberian Native in Soviet Literature', in Slezkine and Diment, *Between Heaven and Hell*, pp. 185–214.

12 Arsen'ev, *Sobranie sochinenii: Nauchno-prakticheskie publikatsii, otchety, doklady, 1906–1916*, vol. 3 (Vladivostok, 2012), pp. 323–522.

13 The film used several quotations from Vladimir Arsen'ev, *Lesnye liudi (Udegeitsy)* (Vladivostok, 1926), pp. 20–21, 26–27, 36, 39.

14 James Clifford, *The Predicament of Culture: Twentieth-Century Ethnography, Literature, and Art*. (Cambridge, 1988), p. 44.

15 Rony, *The Third Eye*, pp. 101–102.

16 On the reception of *Nanook* by Soviet critics, see Khrisanf Khersonskii, 'Nanuk', *Sovetskii Ekran* 36 (1928): 8. On the savage paradigm, see Elizabeth Edwards, *Raw Histories: Photographs, Anthropology savage and Museums* (Oxford and New York, 2001).

17 Litvinov, *Po sledam Arsen'eva*, pp. 144–154.

18 Alexander Litvinov, 'U lesnykh liudei', *Kino* 43 (23 October 1928): 3.

19 Ivan Golovnev, 'Velikaia Kamchatskaia kinoekspeditsiia', *Vestnik VGIKa* 15 (2013): 18–28 (p. 19).

20 Rony, *The Third Eye*, p. 68.

21 Slezkine, *Arctic Mirrors*, p. 221.

22 Litvinov, *Po sledam Arsen'eva*, pp. 195–197.

23 Litvinov, *Po sledam Arsen'eva*, p. 197.

24 David MacDougall, *The Corporeal Image: Film, Ethnography, and the Senses* (Princeton, 2006); Paul Henley, *The Adventure of the Real: Jean Rouch and the Craft of Ethnographic Cinema* (Chicago, 2009); Michael Renov, *The Subject of Documentary* (Minneapolis, 2004).

25 Denis Cosgrove, *Geography and Vision: Seeing, Imagining and Representing the World* (London, 2008), p. 168.

26 Ivan Golovnev, 'Pervoe etnokino. Aleksandr Litvinov', *Vestnik Ural'skogo otdelenia RAN* 1 (2012): 156–167.

27 Golovnev, 'Velikaia Kamchatskaia kinoekspeditsiia', p. 20.

28 Golovnev, 'Velikaia Kamchatskaia kinoekspeditsiia', p. 22.

29 Golovnev, 'Velikaia Kamchatskaia kinoekspeditsiia', p. 21.

30 The Lamut is an earlier ethnonym for the present-day Evens, indigenous nomadic pastoralists. The Evens, the Koryak and the Kamchadal (Itel'men) are indigenous peoples of Kamchatka Krai in the Russian Far East. For further information, see James Forsyth, *A History of the Peoples of Siberia: Russia's North Asian Colony, 1581–1990* (Cambrdige, 1992).

31 Slezkine, *Arctic Mirrors*, pp. 56–57, 98.

32 Stepan Krasheninnikov, *Opisanie zemli Kamchatki* vols. 1–2 (St. Petersburg, 1755); translated into English as *The History of Kamtschatka and the Kurilski Islands with the Countries Adjacent* (London, 1764), p. 149.

33 Oksana Sarkisova, 'Across One Sixth of the World: Dziga Vertov, Travel Cinema, and Soviet Patriotism', *October* 121 (2007): 19–40 (pp. 34–36).

34 Slezkine, *Arctic Mirrors*, p. 215.

35 Pratt, *Imperial Eyes*, p. 6.

36 RGALI 2489/1/39: 14.

37 RGALI 2489/1/37: 48–50, 55.

38 A short-lived name of the leading Soviet film studio, previously Soiuzkino, which was renamed Mosfilm in 1935.

39 Ivan Golovnev, 'Chukotskaia ekspeditsiia Litvinova. Final sovetskogo etnokino', *Ural'skii istoricheskii vestnik* 3 (2014): 118–127.

40 A. Macheret (ed.), *Sovetskie khudozhestvennye fil'my. Annotirovannyi katalog* vol. 1 (Moscow, 1961), pp. 487–488, 501.

41 RGALI 1966/1/183.

42 On the evolution of the 'small peoples' imagery in Soviet literature, see Yuri Slezkine, 'Primitive Communism and the Other Way Around' in Lahusen and Dobrenko, *Socialist Realism without Shores*, pp. 310–336.

43 Konstantin Fel'dman, 'V zashchitu puteshestvii. Po povodu kinofil'ma Dzhou', *Vecherniaia Moskva* (13 May 1934); RGALI 1966/1/184: 2–8.

44 Ippolit Sokolov, 'Put' kul'turfil'my', *Kino i zhizn'* 21 (1931): 15–16.

45 Based on N. Lovtsov's novel, working title 'Zundukai'; *Biulleten' Vostokkino o sostoianii proizvodstva*, 15 November 1928; RGALI 2489/1/1: 72–74.

46 Izmail Urazov, 'Chto na ekrane', *Sovetskii ekran* 5 (1928): 13.

47 For Vostokkino, *Igdenbu* was envisaged as one of the high-budget productions for the year 1929/30; its production cost was 98,024 rubles; RGALI 2489/1/13/15: 166; RGALI 2489/1/111.

48 In Germany and Austria the film was released under the title *Igdenbu, der grosse Jäger*. I would like to thank Thomas Ballhausen from the Filmarchiv Austria for making a copy of *Igdenbu* available for viewing.

49 Modest, 'Igdenbu', *Kino i zhizn'* 21 (1930): 6.

50 Ivan Lopatin, 'V. K. Arsen'ev i issledovanie russkogo Dal'nego Vostoka', *Rodnye dali* (Los Angeles) 92 (1961): 17–22.

51 Slezkine, *Arctic Mirrors*, p. 231.

52 Mikhail Prishvin, *Dnevniki 1930-31* (St. Petersburg, 2006), p. 404.

53 The campaign promoted the policy of Jewish agricultural resettlement in the Far East for which the Biro–Bidzhanskii District was designated in 1928. In May 1934, it acquired the status of Autonomous Region; see Robert Weinberg, *Stalin's Forgotten Zion: Birobidzhan and the Making of a Soviet Jewish Homeland* (Berkeley, 1998), pp. 22–23.

54 'Na prosmotrakh kinokhroniki', *Kino* 51-52 (11 November 1934): 2.

55 Glider was also one of the contributors to a thematic issue on the Far East for the journal *SSSR na stroike* 3-4 (1935). The photographs were made during the same expedition and reflect the conversion of filmic and photographic representational styles.

56 Slezkine, *Arctic Mirrors*, p. 222–224.

57 Evgenii Margolit, 'Pasynki imperii', *Kinovedcheskie zapiski* 100–101 (2012): 543–565; Katerina Clark, *Petersburg: Crucible of Cultural Revolution* (Cambridge, 1995).

58 Jeffrey Brooks, *Thank You, Comrade Stalin! Soviet Public Culture from Revolution to Cold War* (Princeton, 1999).

59 For the political use of folklore, see Miller, *Folklore for Stalin* (Armonk, 1990).

60 Elena Osokina, *Za fasadom "stalinskogo izobiliia": Raspredelenie i rynok v snabzhenii naseleniia v gody industrializatsii, 1927-1941* (Moscow, 1998); Jukka Gronow, *Caviar with Champagne: Common Luxury and the Ideals of the Good Life in Stalin's Russia* (Oxford, 2003).

61 Galina Orlova, ' "Voochiiu vidim": fotografiia i sovetskii proekt v epokhu ikh tekhnicheskoi vosproizvodimosti', in Hans Günther and Sabine Hänsgen (eds), *Sovetskaia vlast' i media* (St. Petersburg, 2006), pp. 188–203; Slutskii's filmography includes *To Live Wealthy* [*Zhit' zazhitochno*, 1933], *1 May 1934* [*Pervoe maia 1934*, 1934], *Happy New Year!* [*S novym godom!*, 1936], *Hello, New Year!* [*Zdravstvui, novyi god!*, 1937], *Song of Youth* [*Pesnia molodosti*, 1938]; *Youth Parade* [*Parad molodosti*, 1939].

62 The decision on the establishment of Jewish settlements in the Far East had been under discussion since 1928, and by 1934 the territory was assigned the status of Jewish Autonomous Region (J.A.R.).

63 Miron Chernenko, *Krasnaia zvezda, zheltaia zvezda. Kinematograficheskaia istoriia evreistva v Rossii, 1919-1999*, Moscow, 2006.

64 Weinberg, *Stalin's Forgotten Zion*, p. 13.

65 Alexander Ivanov, 'La participation de l'OZET à la production du film documentaire "Birobidjan" (1937)', in Valerie Pozner, Natacha Laurent (eds), *Kinojudaica: Les représentation des Juifs dans le cinéma de Russie et d'Union soviétique des années 1910 aux années 1980* (Toulouse, 2009), pp. 197–219.

66 Viktor Shklovskii, 'S tochki zreniia vetra', *Sovetskii ekran* 39 (1926): 6.

67 Yiddish was promoted among Soviet Jewry as the language of the 'toiling masses,' as opposed to Hebrew, which was stigmatized as the language of the 'the bourgeoisie, Zionists, and clerics'. See Zvi Gitelman, 'Introduction' in Weinberg, *Stalin's Forgotten Zion*, pp. 1–12 (p. 6).

68 Evgenii Margolit, 'Fenomen agitpropfil'ma i prikhod zvuka v sovetskoe kino', *Kinovedcheskie zapiski* 84 (2007): 255–266.

69 Weinberg, *Stalin's Forgotten Zion*, p. 31.

70 The issue *SSSR na stroike* 3–4 (1935) was devoted to the Far East.

71 Perets Markish, 'Vozrozhdennyi narod', *Izvestiia* (26 October 1936): 3; Perets Markish, 'Iskateli schast'ia', *Izvestiia* (10 October 1936); available at http://www.jewish.ru/history/press/2011/09/news994299925.php (accessed 15 May 2015).

72 Nora Levin, *The Jews in the Soviet Union: Paradox of Survival*, vol. 1 (New York, 1988), p. 131.

73 By 1935, only 25 per cent (4,404 out of 17,695) of the total Jewish population in the territory lived in the countryside, and not all Jews were engaged in agricultural pursuits. In 1939, Jews were approximately 18,000 of the 109,000 residents of Jewish Autonomous Region (JAR) (of which 75 per cent lived in towns) – 'the number of Jews in the region at the end of the 1930s was far smaller than the number of Russians, Ukrainians, Belorussians, Koreans, Cossacks, and indigenous peoples living there prior to 1928. The dropout rate was 50 per cent. Weinberg, *Stalin's Forgotten Zion*, pp. 32–43.

74 Sergei Tret'iakov, 'Proizvodstvennyi stsenarii', *Novyi LEF* 2 (1928): 29–34.

75 On Prishvin, see Robert Maguire, *Red Virgin Soil: Soviet Literature in the 1920s* (Princeton, 1968), p. 250; Edward Brown, *Russian Literature since the Revolution* (Cambridge, 1982), p. 16.

76 Prishvin, *Dnevniki 1930–31*, p. 618.

77 Mikhail Prishvin, *Zhen-shen' – koren' zhizni* (Moscow, 1934).

78 Prishvin, *Dnevniki 1932–35*, pp. 356, 377.

79 Prishvin, *Dnevniki 1932–35*, p. 415; Vladimir Erofeev, 'O Change', *Sovetskii ekran* 17 (1929): 4. Paramount-produced *Chang: A Drama of the Wilderness* (1927) was the second production of Ernst Shoedsack and Merion C. Cooper made on the heels of the success of an earlier ethnographic adventure film, *Grass* (1925). It was an early example of appealing docu-drama. Filmed in Northern Siam among the Lao tribe, it shows a nuclear family standing up to the beasts of the wild jungle. Hamid Nacify, 'Lured by the East: Ethnographic

and Expedition Films about Nomadic Tribes – The Case of *Grass* (1925)', in Ruoff (ed.), *Virtual Voyages*, pp. 117–138 (pp. 128–129).

80 Prishvin, *Dnevniki 1932–35*, pp. 369–370.
81 Prishvin, *Dnevniki 1932–35*, pp. 372–373.
82 Prishvin, *Dnevniki 1932–35*, p. 179.
83 Vladimir Arsen'ev, *Amba. Li-Tsun-Bin. Rasskazy iz puteshestvii po Ussuriiskomu kraiu* (Nikol'sk-Ussuriiskii, 1920); Prishvin, *Dnevniki 1932–35*, p. 361.
84 Prishvin, *Dnevniki 1932–35*, p. 239.
85 RGALI 1966/1/184: 9–12.
86 V. Tarov, 'V glukhoi ussuriiskoi taige', *Vecherniaia Moskva* (21 October 1934); in RGALI 1966/1/184: 10–11.
87 Prishvin, *Dnevniki 1932–35*, pp. 452–453.
88 Terry Martin, 'The Origins of Soviet Ethnic Cleansing', *The Journal of Modern History* 70 (1998): 813–861; John McCannon, 'The Commissariat of Ice: The Main Administration of the Northern Sea Route (GUSMP) and Stalinist Exploitation of the Arctic, 1932–1939', *The Journal of Slavic Military Studies* 20 (2007): 393–419 (p. 414); 'Martirolog rasstreliannykh', Sakharov Centre, available at http://www.sakharov-center.ru/asfcd/martirolog (accessed 24 March 2014).
89 Slezkine, *Arctic Mirrors*, p. 295.
90 Oksana Sarkisova, 'Taming the Frontier: Aleksandr Litvinov's Expedition Films and Representations of Indigenous Minorities in the Far East', *Studies in Russian and Soviet Cinema* 9.1 (2015): 2–23.
91 RGALI 1966/1/184: 1.
92 RGALI 1966/1/183: 14.
93 Shulman, *Stalinism on the Frontier of Empire*.
94 Hans Günther, 'Der Feind in der totalitären Kultur', in Gabriele Gorzka (ed.), *Kultur im Stalinismus: Sowjetische Kultur und Kunst der 1930er bis 1950er Jahre* (Bremen, 1994), pp. 89–100; Oksana Sarkisova, 'Grenzeprojektionen: Bilder von Grenzgebieten im sowjetischen Film', in Karl Kaser, Dagmar Gramshammer-Hohl and Robert Pichler (eds), *Die Wieser Enzyklopädie des europäischen Ostens*, vol. 11 (Klagenfurt, 2003), pp. 439–467.
95 The concept was originally developed in connection with the French colonial cinema by Barbara Creed and Jeanette Hoorn, 'Memory and History: Early Film, Colonialism and the French Civilising Mission in Indochina', *French History and Civilization* 4 (2011): 223–236.
96 Martin, 'The Origins of Soviet Ethnic Cleansing', pp. 813–861.
97 Alexander Dovzhenko 'Kak my rabotali', *Kino* 51–52 (11 November 1934): 4.
98 Bassin, *Imperial Visions*, p. 186.
99 Grieveson and MacCabe (eds), *Empire and Film*.

5. Diagnosing the Nations: Nationalizing Dirt and Disease on the Screen

1 Kornei Chukovskii, *Moidodyr* (1923), translated by Balázs Trencsényi, 2015.

2 'Zhizn', kak ona est'', *Sovetskoe kino* 4–5 (1926): 30.

3 Galina Orlova, 'Organizm pod nadzorom: Telo v sovetskom diskurse o sotsial'noi gigiene (1920-e gody)', *Teoriia mody* 3 (2007): 251–270.

4 Orlova, 'Organizm pod nadzorom...', p. 252.

5 Tricia Starks, *The Body Soviet: Propaganda, Hygiene, and the Revolutionary State* (Madison, 2008); Dmitry Mikhel, 'Fighting Plague in Southeast European Russia,' in Frances L. Bernstein, Christopher Burton, Dan Healey (eds), *Soviet Medicine: Culture, Practice, and Science* (DeKalb, 2010), pp. 49–70; Michael Worboys, 'Tuberculosis and Race in Britain and its Empire, 1900–50,' in Waltraud Ernst and Bernard Harris (eds), *Race, Science and Medicine, 1700–1960* (London, 1999), pp. 144–166.

6 Susan Gross Solomon, 'Social Hygiene and Soviet Public Health, 1921–1930' in Susan Gross Solomon and John F. Hutchinson (eds), *Health and Society in Revolutionary Russia* (Bloomington, 1990), pp. 175–199 (p. 175).

7 Compare, for example, with colonial practices discussed in James Burns, 'American Philanthropy and Colonial Film-making: The Rockefeller Foundation, the Carnegie Corporation and the Birth of Colonial Cinema', in Grieveson and MacCabe (eds), *Empire and Film*, pp. 55–69.

8 Valerie Traub, 'Mapping the Global Body,' in Peter Erickson and Clark Hulse (eds), *Early Modern Visual Culture: Representation, Race, and Empire in Renaissance England* (Philadelphia, 2000), pp. 44–97 (p. 49).

9 David Woodward, quoted in Traub, 'Mapping the Global Body', p. 49.

10 Sander L. Gilman, *Picturing Health and Illness: Images of Identity and Difference* (Baltimore, 1995), p. 54.

11 Vejas Gabriel Liulevicius, *The German Myth of the East: 1800 to the Present* (Oxford, 2009), pp. 1–2.

12 Liulevicius, *The German Myth*, p. 5; see also Paul Weindling, *Health, Race, and German Politics between National Unification and Nazism, 1870–1945* (Cambridge, 1989).

13 Liulevicius, *The German Myth*, p. 47.

14 Linda Hogle, *Recovering the Nation's Body: Cultural Memory, Medicine, and the Politics of Redemption* (New Brunswick, 1999).

15 Hogle, *Recovering the Nation's Body*, p. 47.

16 Robert Grant, *Representations of British Emigration, Colonisation and Settlement. Imagining Empire, 1800–1860* (London, 2005), p. 177; see also Elisabeth Collingham, *Imperial Bodies: the Physical Experience of the Raj, c. 1800–1947* (Cambridge, 2001).

17 Grant, *Representations of British Emigration*, p. 177.

18 Bruce Grant, 'Siberia Hot and Cold: Reconstructing the Image of Siberian Indigenous Peoples,' in Slezkine and Diment (eds), *Between Heaven and Hell*, pp. 227–253, esp. p. 249.

19 Macheret, *Sovetskie khudozhestvennye fil'my*, vol. 1, p. 326.

20 Rony, *The Third Eye*, pp. 26–27.

21 Rony, *The Third Eye*, p. 36.

22 Mary Douglas, *Purity and Danger: An Analysis of the Concepts of Pollution and Taboo* (London, 1996), p. 36.

23 Starks, *The Body Soviet*, pp. 207–208.

24 See David Thomas Murphy '"First among Savages": The German Romance of the Eskimo from the Enlightenment to National Socialism', *German Studies Review* 25.3 (2002): 533–550.

25 Rony, *The Third Eye*, p. 28.

26 The Buryat-Mongol Autonomous Soviet Socialist Republic was established in May 1923, incorporating part of the territories of the Buryat-Mongol state after its dissolution in 1921. In 1958, the name 'Mongol' was removed from the name of the Republic. In September 1937, the territory of the Autonomous Republic was split into three administrative units: one autonomous republic and two national districts amid the Russian-speaking regions. In 1992, the Buryat ASSR adopted the name Republic of Buryatia and is currently an autonomous republic within the Russian Federation. The Buryat-Mongol Autonomous Republic was seen as one of the potential 'engines' for further expansion of the Soviet Union. I. Arkhincheev, 'Buriat-Mongol'skaia Avtonomnaia Oblast'', *Zhizn' natsional'nostei* 1 (1923): 129–134, esp. p. 134. Similar claims were made in Semen Dimanshtein, 'Sovetskaia vlast' i melkie natsional'nosti', *Zhizn' natsional'nostei* 46 (7 December 1919): 2–3; Melissa Chakars, *The Socialist Way of Life in Siberia: Transformation in Buryatia* (Budapest, 2014); Vsevolod Bashkuev, 'Silencing the Shame: Forgetting of the 1920s Syphilis Epidemic in Buryat-Mongolia as a Strategy of Post-Soviet Identity Construction', *Jefferson Journal of Science and Culture* 3 (2013): 110–132, esp. pp. 110–111.

27 Susan Gross Solomon, 'Foreign Expertise on Russian Terrain – Max Kuczynski on the Kirghiz Steppe, 1923–24', in Bernstein, Burton, Healey, *Soviet Medicine*, pp. 71–91; Dmitrii Alexander, Iudif' Kopelevich, Alexander Dmitriev, *Sovetsko-nemetskie nauchnye sviazi vremeni Veimarskoi respubliki* (St. Petersburg, 2001).

28 Gilman, *Picturing Health and Illness*, p. 54.

29 Laura Engelstein, *Keys to Happiness: Sex and the Search for Modernity in Fin-de-Siècle Russia* (Ithaca, 1992), p. 167.

30 Susan Gross Solomon, 'The Soviet-German Syphilis Expedition to Buriat-Mongolia, 1928: Scientific Research on National Minorities', *Slavic*

Review 52.2 (1993): 204–32. For the Soviet context of the expedition see also Bashkuev, 'Silencing the Shame', pp. 115–121.

31 Pratt, *Imperial Eyes*, p. 23.

32 G. Bazarova, 'Nauchnaia intelligentsiia i kul'turno-natsional'noe stroitel'stvo v respublike v 1920–30e gg.', in Iu. Randalov et al. (eds), *Problemy istorii i kul'turno-natsional'nogo stroitel'stva v respublike Buriatiia* (Ulan-Ude, 1998), pp. 118–122, esp. p. 121.

33 D. Stonov, 'Povesti ob Altae', in Grits, *Pereklichka narodov*, pp. 103–142 (p. 105).

34 Douglas, *Purity and Danger*, p. 11.

35 George Rosen, *A History of Public Health* (Baltimore, 1993), p. 29.

36 Gilman, *Picturing Health and Illness*, p. 81.

37 Solomon, 'The Soviet-German Syphilis Expedition', pp. 204–232.

38 Starks, *The Body Soviet*, p. 191.

39 GARF 8326/2/7: 48; RGALI 2489/1/13: 15.

40 The Oirot Autonomous Republic was established in June 1922. It was later transformed into the Oirot Autonomous Region, which existed until 1948. It was then renamed Gorno-Altai Autonomous Oblast' and its inhabitants were referred to as 'gorno-altaitsy'.

41 For a similar anti-nomadic take in view of the future of the Altai people, see A. Koptelov, 'Oiratia' in Grits, *Pereklichka narodov*, pp. 143–160.

42 Other nationalities, like the Tuvins from the Saian Mountains, were not included in the statistics. According to other data, the Buryat population comprised 56.3 per cent, while Russian were 43.7 per cent. Pavel Varnavskii, 'Granitsy Sovetskoi Buriatskoi Natsii', *Ab Imperio* 1 (2003): 149–176 (p. 154). The quoted statistics excluded other national minorities from their calculations.

43 Michael Hau, *The Cult of Health and Beauty in Germany: a Social History, 1890–1930* (Chicago, 2003).

44 Starks, *The Body Soviet*, p. 167.

45 Vertov, *Iz naslediia*, vol 1, pp. 85–86.

46 Ernst van Alphen, *Staging the Archive* (London, 2014), pp. 97–98.

47 Iurii Murashov, 'Slepye geroi – slepye zriteli: o statuse zreniia i slova v sovetskom kino' in Marina Balina, Evgenii Dobrenko, Iurii Murashov (eds), *Sovetskoe bogatstvo: stat'i o kul'ture, literature i kino* (St. Petersburg, 2002), pp. 412–426.

48 Chuvashkino had previously produced *Volga Rebels* [*Volzhskie buntari*] and *Sar-Pige*. The studio was later incorporated into Vostokfilm; GARF 8326/2/7: 48verso; RGALI 2494/1/102:12.

49 Vlad[islav] Korolevich, 'Strana Chuvashskaia,' *Sovetskoe Kino* 7 (1927): 20–22, esp. p. 20.

50 Korolevich, 'Strana Chuvashskaia', p. 21.

51 Boltianskii's speech at the public screening at ODSK: RGALI 2494/1/102: 10. Other participants approached the film as an ethnographic work; see RGALI 2494/1/102: 12–16.

52 RGALI 2494/1/102: 10.

53 The ODSK screening took place on 29 October 1927, and the ARRK screening on 8 December 1927.

54 RGALI 2494/1/102: 30.

55 RGALI 2494/1/102: 33–34.

56 RGALI 2494/1/102: 31.

57 Sergei Tret'iakov, 'Strana Chuvashskaia', *Novyi LEF* 10 (1927); republished in Sergei Tret'iakov, *Kinematograficheskoe nasledie: Stat'i, ocherki, stenogrammy vystuplenii, doklady, stsenarii* (St. Petersburg, 2010), p. 105.

58 Vlad. Korolevich, 'Smotrite v apparat!', *Sovetskii ekran* 42 (1927): 6.

59 Korolevich, 'Smotrite v apparat!'.

60 Korolevich, 'Smotrite v apparat!'.

61 George Rosen, *A History of Public Health*.

62 Vladislav Korolevich, 'Iomzia', *Sovetskoe kino* 37 (1927): 13.

63 Michelson (ed.), *Kino-Eye*, pp. 5–9 (p. 8).

64 Alexander Lemberg, 'Druzhba, ispytannaia desiatiletiami', in Elizaveta Vertova-Svilova, Anna Vinogradova (eds), *Dziga Vertov v vospominaniiakh sovremennikov* (Moscow, 1976), pp. 79–86.

65 Diane Koenker, *Club Red: Vacation Travel and the Soviet Dream* (Ithaca, 2013); Christian Noack, 'Building Tourism in One Country?: The Sovietization of Vacationing, 1917–1941', in Eric G. Zuelow (ed.), *Touring Beyond the Nation: A Transnational Approach to European Tourism History* (Farnham, 2011), pp. 171–195.

66 Tatiana Dashkova, *Telesnost' – Ideologiia – Kinematograf: Vizual'nyi kanon i sovetskaia povsednevnost'* (Moscow, 2013).

67 Grigorii Usykin, *Ocherki istorii rossiiskogo turizma* (Moscow and St. Petersburg, 2000), available at http://nkosterev.narod.ru/met/ysuskin.html (accessed 15 May 2014); Anne E. Gorsuch and Diane Koenker (eds), *Turizm: The Russian and East European Tourist under Capitalism and Socialism* (Ithaca, 2006).

68 Sandomirskaia, 'Novaia zhizn' na marshe'.

69 Originally published in the periodical *Na sushe i na more* in 1929, quoted in Sandomirskaia, 'Novaia zhizn' na marshe'.

70 Widdis, *Visions of a New Land*, pp. 135–141.

71 On the emergence and evolution of the concept and the representations of tourism and tourists, see Chris Rojek and John Urry, *Touring Cultures: Transformations of Travel and Theory* (London, 1997); John Urry, *The Tourist Gaze: Leisure and Travel in Contemporary Societies* (London, 1990).

72 Christopher Ely, *This Meager Nature: Landscape and National Identity in Imperial Russia* (DeKalb, 2002), p. 224.
73 Widdis, *Visions of a New Land*, p. 141.
74 On *kraevedenie*, see Marina Loskutova, 'A Motherland with a Radius of 300 Miles: Regional Identity in Russian Secondary and Post-Elementary Education from the Early Nineteenth Century to the War and Revolution', *European Review of History* 9.1 (2002): 7–22.

6. Touring the Caucasus

1 Alexander Pushkin, 'Kavkaz' (1829), translated by Martha Gilbert Dickinson Bianchi.
2 Bruce Grant, 'The Good Russian Prisoner: Naturalizing Violence in the Caucasus Mountains', *Cultural Anthropology* 20.1 (2005): 39–67 (p. 40).
3 Sergei Soplenkov, *Doroga v Arzrum: rossiiskaia obshestvennaia mysl' o Vostoke* (Moscow, 2000). Susan Layton, 'The Creation of an Imaginative Caucasian Geography', *Slavic Review* 45.3 (1986): 470–485; Katya Hokanson, 'Literary Imperialism, *Narodnost'*, and Pushkin's Invention of the Caucasus', *The Russian Review* 53 (1994): 336–352.
4 Neia Zorkaia, *Fol'klor, lubok, ekran* (Moscow, 1994), pp. 56–71. On the notion 'abrek' see Vladimir Bobrovnikov, *Musul'mane Severnogo Kavkaza: obychai, pravo, nasilie* (Moscow, 2002), pp. 27–30.
5 Ausin Jersild, 'Faith, Custom, and Ritual in the Borderlands: Orthodoxy, Island, and the "Small Peopls" of the Middle Volga and the North Caucasus', *The Russian Review* 59 (2000): 512–529.
6 Alex Marshall, *The Caucasus under Soviet Rule* (London, 2010), pp. 58–67; Jeronim Perović, 'Uneasy Alliances: Bolshevik Co-optation Policy and the Case of Chechen Sheikh Ali Mitaev', *Kritika* 15.4 (2014): 729–65.
7 Eva Maurer, 'Al'pinizm as Mass Sport and Elite Recreation: Soviet Mountaineering Camps under Stalin' in Gorsuch and Koenker, *Turizm*, pp. 141–162 (p. 142).
8 Zinaida Rikhter, *Kavkaz nashikh dnei, 1923–24* (Moscow, 1924), p. 5.
9 Rikhter, *Kavkaz nashikh dnei*, pp. 4, 87.
10 Historian of photography Alina Akoeff puts forward a convincing and photographically supported argument that the director of the film (only his last name is mentioned in the credits) is Elmurza Tlatov, Ossetian writer publishing under the pen-name Khokh Tlatov. See her blog entry 'Zaskochil na denek' at http://gradus.pro/zaskochil-na-denek/ (accessed 25 May 2015).
11 Henri Barbusse, *Voici ce qu'on a fait de la Géorgie* (Paris, 1929), p. 17. For more on the Western Leftist sympathizers and their travels to the Soviet Union see Michael David-Fox, *Showcasing the Great Experiment: Cultural Diplomacy and Western Visitors to the Soviet Union, 1921–1941* (Oxford, 2011).

12 Michael G. Smith, 'Cinema for the "Soviet East": National Fact and Revolutionary Fiction in Early Azerbaijani Film', *Slavic Review* 56.4 (1997): 645–678.

13 Anon., 'Kavkazskaia kukhnia', *Sovetskoe kino* 4–5 (1926): 29.

14 Berd Kotiev, 'Kino sredi natsional'nostei', *Revoliutsiia i natsional'nosti* 5 (1931): 68–73; Anon., 'Glaza Andozii', *Sovetskoe kino*, 4–5 (1926): 31.

15 Gurgen Levonian, 'Strana 'razboinikov' ili literaturnaia khaltura?', *Revoliutsiia i gorets* 1 (1929): 52–57; IzA, 'Poddel'nye kartiny', *Sovetskoe kino* 2 (1926): 14–16.

16 L. Semenov, 'Obzor russkoi etnograficheskoi literatury o Kavkaze za 1917–1927 gg.', *Etnografiia* 2 (1928): 124–133; Bobrovnikov, *Musul'mane severnogo Kavkaza*, p. 25.

17 Bobrovnikov, *Musul'mane severnogo Kavkaza*, p. 206.

18 Leo Esakiia, 'Levoe dvizhenie v iskusstve Gruzii', *Novyi LEF* 10 (1927): 42–46.

19 Khevsurs are a branch of Kartvelian (Georgian) people professing a syncretic mixture of Orthodox Christianity and pagan cults.

20 The screening and discussion took place at ARRK on 30 August 1928; RGALI 2494/1/190: 13–14. See also Khris[anf] Kh[ersonskii], 'Eliso', *Sovetskii ekran* 41 (1928): 6–7; Sergei Ermolinskii, 'Eliso', *Pravda* (14 November 1928): 6; N. V., 'Eliso', *Izvestiia* (3 November 1928): 5.

21 RGALI 2494/1/190: 17.

22 S. Khamidov, 'O kartine "Eliso" iz 'chechenskoi zhizni', *Revoliutsiia i gorets* 2 (1928): 90–91.

23 Hélène Carrère d'Encausse, *The Great Challenge: Nationalities and the Bolshevik State 1917–1930* (New York, 1992), p. 180; Evgenii Shilling, *Narody Kavkaza: Malye narody Dagestana* (Moscow, 1993).

24 Enver Kisriev, 'Republic of Dagestan: Nation-Building inside Russia's Womb', in Pål Kolstø and Helge Blakkisrud (eds), *Nation-Building and Common Values in Russia* (Lanham, 2004), pp. 123–157 (p. 135).

25 'Privet dvum novym Respublikam!,' *Zhizn' natsional'nostei* 3 (2 February 1921): 1; L. Gunibskii 'Dagestanskaia Avtonomnaia Respublika', *Zhizn' natsional'nostei* 1 (1923): 101–107; Abdurahman Avtorkhanov, 'The Chechens and the Ingush during the Soviet Period and its Antecedents', in Marie Bennigsen Broxup (ed.), *The North Caucasus Barrier: the Russian Advance Towards the Muslim World* (London, 1992), pp. 146–194; Carrere d'Encausse, *The Great Challenge*, pp. 180–181.

26 For the attempts to instrumentalize the legacy of Shamil, see 'Vozzvanie ko vsem trudiashchimsia gortsam Kavkaza', *Zhizn' natsional'nostei* 6 (23 February 1919): 1; Vladimir Bobrovnikov, I. Babich (eds), *Severnyi Kavkaz v sostave Rossiiskoi imperii* (Moscow, 2007), esp. pp. 132–134; Alexander Deriabin, 'Piat' let i tri goda. Predystoria i istoria kalatozovskogo "Shamilia"', *Kinovedcheskie zapiski* 67 (2004): 114–126; Moshe Gammer, *Muslim Resistance to the*

Tsar: Shamil and the Conquest of Chechnia and Dagestan (London, 1994); Anna Zelkina, *In Quest of God and Freedom: Sufi Responses to the Russian Advance in the North Caucasus* (New York, 2000).

27 Shamil was taken prisoner in 1859 after the siege of the settlement Gunib and since then lived in captivity. In 1869, he was given permission to perform the Hajj (pilgrimage) to Mecca and died in Medina in 1871.

28 Gronow, *Caviar with Champagne*; Randi Cox, 'It All Can Be Yours! Soviet Commercial Advertising and the Soviet Construction of Space, 1928–1956', in Dobrenko and Naiman, *The Landscape of Stalinism*, pp. 125–162.

29 A. Kosterin, 'Gorskaia Avtonomnaia Respublika', *Zhizn' natsional'nostei* 1 (1923): 96–101; Smith, *Bolsheviks and the National Question*, pp. 24–25.

30 In 1927, Lebedev made *kulturfilms Oil [Neft']* (with Alexander Litvinov) in Baku, and *In the Land of Lenin [V strane Lenina]*, which accompanies a group of Western tourists visiting Leningrad, Moscow, Nizhnii Novgorod, Stalingrad, Kharkov, as well as the Caucasus (Grozny, Baku, Tbilisi). This travel might have given Lebedev the idea for the following travelogues in the Caucasus. See Lebedev's autobiography in AMK 26/2/106: 21.

31 GARF 8326/2/7: 48.

32 Oshaev describes the ethnonym 'nakh' as people; Khalid Oshaev, *V serdtse Chechni* (Groznyi, 1928). This also became accepted as an official Soviet, and later post-Soviet, interpretation. See Valerii Tishkov, *Narody Rossii: Entsiklopediia* (Moscow, 1994), p. 399.

33 AMK 26/2/276.

34 Nikolai Lebedev, 'Po tropam Kavkaza,' *Sovetskii ekran* 52 (1928): 12.

35 Bobrovnikov, Babich, *Severnyi Kavkaz*, pp. 24–25, 310.

36 Some examples are discussed in Smith, 'Cinema for the "Soviet East"', pp. 657–658.

37 *Zikr* is a male dance and an ecstatic Islamic worship that was introduced by the Quadiriya Sufi order in the mid-nineteenth century in Dagestan and Chechnya; see Sufian Zhemukhov and Charles King, 'Dancing the Nation in the North Caucasus', *Slavic Review* 72.2 (2013): 287–305 (p. 288); see also Moshe Gammer, *The Lone Wolf and the Bear* (Pittsburgh, 2006), pp. 194–196.

38 Bobrovnikov, *Musul'mane severnogo Kavkaza*. Ritual performances ending blood feuds between communities were repeatedly performed in Chechnya and Dagestan in the 1920s.

39 Such mediations were practiced in the North Caucasus and were the traditionally accepted way to stop the blood feud between clans. On Chechen social organization and clan identities see John B. Dunlop, *Russia Confronts Chechnya: Roots of a Separatist Conflict* (Cambridge, 1998), pp. 20–21.

40 Nikolai Lebedev, 'Po tropam Kavkaza', *Sovetskii ekran* 52 (1928), p. 12.

41 Sergei Tret'iakov, 'Staraia Svanetia', in *Gruziia. Poety i pisateli SSSR* (Tiflis, 1931), pp. 94–108; republished in Tret'iakov, *Stat'i, ocherki...*, pp. 171–177 (p. 173).

42 Rikhter, *Kavkaz nashikh dnei*; Filipp Mikharidze, *Svanetiia* (Tiflis, 1925); Sergei Tret'iakov, *Svanetiia* (Moscow, 1928); Sergei Anisimov, *Svanetiia* (Moscow, 1929).

43 Susan Layton, '19th Century Russian Mythologies of Caucasian Savagery,' in Brower and Lazzerini, *Russia's Orient*, pp. 80–99 (p. 85).

44 Tret'iakov, *Stat'i, ocherki...*, pp. 150–183.

45 Tret'iakov, *Stat'i, ocherki...*, p. 169.

46 On the investments and first income see: RGASPI 538/3/70/17, pp. 160–161; Iu[rii] Zheliabuzhskii, 'Serdtse Kavkaza – Svanetia', *Sovetskii ekran* 44 (1926): 6–7.

47 Abramov, 'Vspomnim o vidovoi'; Alexander Fevral'skii, 'Shest' "vostochnykh" kartin', *Pravda* (21 May 1926): 7.

48 RGALI 2354/1/196.

49 Bobrovnikov, Babich, *Severnyi Kavkaz*, p. 21.

50 The English translation of the title does not reflect the ambiguity of the Russian-language version, which could have been rendered also as 'Salt of Svanetia', emphasizing the 'essential' elements of the filmed region. For the first time the script of *Blind Girl* was published in Tret'iakov, *Stat'i, ocherki...*, pp. 220–242.

51 Viktor Shklovskii, *Ob Eizenshteine*, available at http://lib.rus.ec/b/278374/read (accessed 24 April 2014).

52 Tret'iakov, *Stat'i, ocherki...*, pp. 150–183.

53 Tret'iakov, *Stat'i, ocherki...*, p. 153.

54 Sergei Tret'iakov 'Otkuda i kuda (perspektivy futurizma),' *LEF* 1 (1923): 195.

55 Sergei Tret'iakov, *Strana-perekrestok: dokumental'naia proza* (Moscow, 1991), p. 525.

56 Tret'iakov, 'Otkuda i kuda', p. 201.

57 Tret'iakov, 'V pereulkakh gor', *Molodaia Gvardia* 3 (1930): 95–100; republished in Tret'iakov, *Stat'i, ocherki...*, pp. 165–171, p. 168.

58 Tret'iakov, *Stat'i, ocherki...*, p. 166.

7. Camels and Railways: Reframing Central Asia

1 Il'ia Il'f and Evgenii Petrov, *Zolotoi telenok* (1931); translated by Anne O. Fisher as *The Little Golden Calf* (Montpelier, 2009), pp. 333–334.

2 I chose to use 'Central Asia' as a geographic denomination following the common practice of the 1920–30s, however, the constructed and contested nature of this category should not be overlooked. For an overview of the history of territorial concepts, see Sergei Abashin, Dmitrii Arapov, Nailia Bekmakhanova (eds), *Tsentral'naia Aziia v sostave Rossiiskoi imperii* (Moscow, 2008), pp. 11–15.

3 Cloé Drieu, *Fictions nationales: Cinéma, empire et nation en Ouzbékistan (1919–1937)* (Paris, 2013), pp. 91–98, 103–107.

4 Grigorii Levkoev, 'Kino–ekspeditsiia na Vostok. Zametki uchastnika', *ARK* 6–7 (1925): 28. For the director's statement, see Dmitrii Bassalygo, 'O Vostoke dlia Vostoka', *Sovetskii ekran* 24 (1925): n.p.

5 Kh[risanf] Kh[ersonski], 'Poslednie sovetskie postanovki', *ARK* 9 (1925): 31.

6 Levkoev, 'Kino-ekspeditsia na Vostok', p. 28.

7 Subsequently, the Tajik ASSR was reorganized as SSR (in 1929), the Kirghiz and Kara–Kalpak Oblasts to ASSR (in 1926 and 1932 respectively), and the Kirghiz and Kazakh ASSR into an SSR (in 1936). Present-day English transcription renders Kirghiz az Kyrgyz.

8 Juliette Cadiot, *Le laboratoire Imperial: Russie–URSS 1860–1940* (Paris, 2007); in Russian translated as *Laboratoriia imperii* (Moscow, 2010); Alisher Il'khamov, 'Archeology of Uzbek Identity', *Anthropology and Archeology of Eurasia* 44.4 (2006): 10–36; Adeeb Khalid, 'The Fascination of Revolution: Central Asian Intellectuals, 1917–1927', in Uyama Tomohiko (ed.), *Empire, Islam, and Politics in Central Eurasia* (Sapporo, 2007), pp. 137–152.

9 Paul Bergne, *The Birth of Tajikistan: National Identity and the Origins of the Republic* (London, New York, 2007); Adrienne Lynn Edgar, *Tribal Nation: The Making of Soviet Turkmenistan* (Princeton, 2004); Sergei Abashin, 'Ethnogenesis and Historiography: Historical Narratives for Central Asia in the 1940s and 1950s', in Cvetkovski and Hofmeister, *An Empire of Others*, pp. 145–168.

10 Arne Haugen, *The Establishment of National Republics* (Basingstoke, New York, 2003) p. 33.

11 Hirsch, *Empire of Nations*, p. 182.

12 Peter Hopkirk, *The Great Game: The Struggle for Empire in Central Asia* (New York, 1992).

13 The life of Andreev (1873–1948), born in Tashkent, exemplifies the continuity between the imperial and Soviet ethnography and oriental studies, as well as tight connections between ethnographic research, state reforms, intelligence practices and foreign policies. Andreev taught in Khodzhent in the 1890s. From 1896 he served as secretary to Alexander Polovtsev from the Imperial Ministry of Interior. His career continued under the Soviet regime as Commissar of National Education of the Khodzhent region. He also participated in establishing the Turkestan Oriental Institute in Tashkent. In the early 1920s, Andreev was a member of the Scientific Commission for the Study of Daily Life of the Turkestan Indigenous Population. Ia. Vasil'kov, M. Sorokina, *Liudi i sud'by. Biobibliograficheskii slovar' vostokovedov – zhertv politicheskogo terror v sovetskii period (1917–1991)* (St. Petersburg, 2003). Available at http://memory.pvost.org/pages/andreevms.html (accessed 25 January 2015).

14 Quoted in Marianne Kamp, *The New Woman in Uzbekistan: Islam, Modernity, and Unveiling under Communism* (Seattle, 2006), p. 63.

15 According to the 1926 data, the Tajiks constituted close to 1 million in the Uzbek SSR. Alisher Il'khamov, *Etnicheskii atlas Uzbekistana* (Tashkent, 2002), p. 195.

16 Il'khamov, *Etnicheskii atlas Uzbekistana*, p. 198.

17 Hirsch, *Empire of Nations*, p. 182.

18 Haugen, *Establishment of National Republics*, p. 34.

19 Haugen, *Establishment of National Republics*, pp. 160–161.

20 Although no mention had been made of it in the first delimitation plan in early 1924, the status of the Kyrgyz ethno-national unit underwent a speedy 'up-grading' within the Soviet Central Asian delimitation: on 14 October 1924, the Kara-Kirghiz Oblast' was established; in May 1925 it became Kyrgyz AO; in February 1926 it became an Autonomous Republic; in December 1936 – Union Republic SSR; Haugen, *Establishment of National Republics*, pp. 167, 188–194.

21 Paula Michaels, *Curative Powers: Medicine and Empire in Stalin's Central Asia* (Pittsburgh, 2003).

22 Madeleine Reeves, 'Roads of Hope and Dislocation: Infrastructure and the Remaking of Territory at a Central Asian Border,' *Ab Imperio* 2 (2014): 235–257.

23 Sven Hedin, *Through Asia*, vol. 1 (London, 1898), p. 192.

24 Hedin, *Through Asia*, p. 192.

25 Tsivian, *Lines of Resistance*, note 6, p. 122. [original emphasis]

26 Vladimir Erofeev, 'Iz dnevnika Pamirskoi ekspeditsii', *Kino* 1 (3 January 1928): 4; Vladimir Erofeev, *Po 'Kryshe mira' s kinoapparatom (Puteshestvie na Pamir)* (Moscow, 1929).

27 Vladimir Erofeev, 'S kino-apparatom po Pamiru', *Kino* 28 (12 July 1927): 3.

28 Erofeev, 'S kino-apparatom po Pamiru'.

29 Marcus Banks and Howard Morphy (eds), *Rethinking Visual Anthropology* (New Haven, 1999), pp. 13–15.

30 Peter Loizos, 'First exits from observational realism: narrative experiments in re-cent ethnographic films', in Banks and Morphy, *Rethinking Visual Anthropology*, pp. 81–104.

31 Vladimir Erofeev, 'U podnozh'ia Pamira', *Smena* 6 (1928): 12–14 (p. 13).

32 Similar episodes of internal 'othering' are included in Bunuel's *Land without Bread* [*Las Hurdes*, Spain, 1933], which presented the secluded Las Hurdes communities in the mountainous borderland of northern Spain. Maurice Legendre's ethnographic study about Las Hurdes was published in 1927, which points to similar interest in the 'internal others' of the borderlands in Europe.

33 Rony, *The Third Eye*, p. 101.

34 Homi K. Bhabha, *The Location of Culture* (London and New York, 1994), p. 67.

35 Franziska Torma, *Turkestan-Expeditionen. Zur Kulturgeschichte deutscher Forschungsreisen nach Mittelasien (1890–1930)* (Bielefeld, 2011), p. 184.

36 Tolchan and Shneiderov also made a series of shorts including: *Kara-Kul' Lake* [ozero Kara-Kul]; *Fedchenko Glacier* [Lednik Fedchenko]; *Tanymas;*

Experimental Artificial Insemination [Opyty iskusstvennogo oplodotvorenia].
M. Nechaeva, *Vladimir Shneiderov*, Moscow, 1964, p. 31.

37 Willi Rickmer Rickmers, *Alai! Alai! Arbeiten und Erlebnisse der Deutsch-Russischen Alai-Pamir-Expedition*, Leipzig, 1930.

38 Franziska Torma, 'Auf dem Dach der Welt. Die Mittelasien-Expeditionen des Ehepaars Rickmers (1890–1928),' *Alpenvereinsjahrbuch* (Innsbruck, 2010), pp. 204–211.

39 A. Parkhomenko, 'Akademik N. P. Gorbunov: vzlet i tragediia. Shtrikhi k biografii nepremennogo sekretaria Akademii Nauk SSSR', in *Repressirovannaia nauka* (Leningrad, 1991), pp. 408–423.

40 By the end of the expedition the Soviet participants totalled 'a hundred permanent members and fifty temporarily hired Tajik equipment bearers'; Dmitrii Shcherbakov, 'Pamirskaia vysokogornaia sovetsko-germanskaia ekspeditsiia Akademii Nauk' in Krylenko, *Po neissledovannomu Pamiru* (Moscow, 1929), p. 20.

41 Torma, *Turkestan-Expeditionen*, p. 185.

42 Shcherbakov, 'Pamirskaia vysokogornaia,' p. 36; Efim Rossel's, *Banda bat'ki Gorbunova. Pervaia pamirskaia ekspeditsiia 1928* (Moscow, 2013), p. 137, first published 1930; Krylenko, *Po neissledovannomu Pamiru*; Nikolai Krylenko, Dmitrii Shcherbakov, *5 let po Pamiru (itogi Pamirskikh ekspeditsii 1928, 1929, 1931, 1932, 1933)* (Moscow and Leningrad, 1935), pp. 7–24.

43 Rossel's, *Banda Bat'ki Gorbunova*, pp. 65, 71, 83.

44 Krylenko, *Po neissledovannomu Pamiru*, p. 39.

45 Torma, *Turkestan-Expeditionen*, p. 189.

46 Rossel's, *Banda bat'ki Gorbunova*, p. 12.

47 Rossel's, *Banda bat'ki Gorbunova*, pp. 33–34.

48 Rossel's, *Banda bat'ki Gorbunova*, p. 77.

49 Torma, *Turkestan-Expeditionen*, p. 188.

50 Shneiderov, 'Panoramoi po Pamiru', *Kino* 44 (30 October 1928): 5.

51 Shneiderov, *Moi kinoputeshestviia*, p. 23.

52 Shneiderov 'Uroki pamirskoi ekspeditsii', *Kino i kul'tura* 2 (1929): 51–54.

53 Shneiderov, *Moi kinoputeshestviia*, p. 24; Krylenko, *Po neissledovannomu Pamiru*, p. 55; Rossel's, *Banda bat'ki Gorbunova*, pp. 23, 32, 66–68.

54 Shneiderov, *Moi kinoputeshestviia*, p. 24.

55 Krylenko, *Po neissledovannomu Pamiru*, pp. 30, 35.

56 Iurii Murashov, 'Vostok. Radio. Dzhambul', in Konstantin Bogdanov, Rikkardo Nikolozi, Iurii Murashov (eds), *Dzhambul Dzhabaev: Prikliucheniia kazakhskogo akyna v sovetskoi strane* (Moscow, 2013), pp. 138–170; see also David Trotter, 'Representing Connection: A Multimedia Approach to Colonial Film, 1918–39', in Greiveson and MacCabe, *Empire and Film*, pp. 151–165.

57 The ascent was undertaken on 27 September 1928 by the German-Austrian team of Karl Wien, Eugen Allwein and Erwin Schneider. Mezhrabpomfil'm did

not include this episode in the Soviet version of the film, but mentioned the ascent among other joint 'achievements'.

58 As a result of the subsequent trips, many remaining 'blank spots' of the Pamir were studied, and the highest peak of the Pamir range was identified and named after Stalin (from 1962 known as 'Pik Kommunizma', and since 1998 as Ismoil Somoni Peak).

59 I. B-k, 'Podnozhie smerti', *Krasnaia zvezda* 481 (1929), in GFF 6/1/164, n.p.

60 Nechaeva, *Vladimir Shneiderov*, p. 32.

61 For a detailed history of the construction of the Turksib see Matthew Payne, *Stalin's Railroad: Turksib and the Building of Socialism* (Pittsburgh, 2001).

62 *Tainy natsional'noi politiki TsK RKP. Chetvertoe soveshchanie TsK RKP s otvetst-vennymi rabotnikami natsional'nykh respublik i oblastei v g. Moskve 9–12 iiunia 1923 g.*, (Moscow, 1992), p. 261.

63 Benjamin Loring, ' "Colonizers with Party Cards" Soviet Internal Colonialism in Central Asia, 1917–39', *Kritika: Explorations in Russian and Eurasian History* 15.1 (2014): 77–102 (pp. 85–101).

64 Paolo Sartori, 'What Went Wrong? The Failure of Soviet Policy on Sharīa Courts in Turkestan, 1917–1923', *Die Welt des Islams* 50 (2010): 397–434, (p. 498).

65 Choi Han-Woo, Woo Duck-Chan, Jung Keun-Sik, 'Social Change and National Problem in Central Asia', *International Journal of Central Asian Studies* 3 (1998): 78–113. Available at http://www.iacd.or.kr/pdf/journal/03/3–04.pdf (accessed 10 February 2015); Payne, *Stalin's Railroad*, p. 25.

66 Jay Leyda, *Kino: A History of the Russian and Soviet Film* (London, 1960), p. 154; A. Kachura, 'Viktor Turin', in Galina Prozhiko, D. Firsova (eds), *Letopistsy nashego vremeni* (Moscow, 1987), pp. 82–99.

67 GFF 6/1/19/28: 30.

68 RGALI 2489/1/3: 1.

69 GFF 6/1/19/28.

70 GFF 6/1/19/26, original emphasis.

71 GFF 6/1/19/27.

72 GFF 6/1/19/25.

73 RGALI 2489/1/6: 1–4 and 2489/1/13: 103.

74 RGALI 2489/1/1: 72–74.

75 GFF 6/1/19/24.

76 Bill Nichols, 'Documentary Film and the Modernist Avant-Garde', *Critical Inquiry* 27.4 (2001): 580–610 (p. 590).

77 Milan Hauner, *What is Asia to Us? Russia's Asian Heartland Yesterday and To-day* (London, 1992), p. 98; Frithjof Benjamin Schenk, 'Travel, Railroads, and Identity Formation in the Russian Empire', in Eric Weitz and Omer Bartov (eds), *Shatterzone of Empires. Coexistence and Violence in the German, Habsburg, Russian, and Ottoman Borderlands* (Bloomington, 2013), pp. 136–151.

78 Ia. Smolianskii, 'Epopeia stal'nogo puti na ekrane (O Turksibe)', *Izvestiia* (21 September 1930): 3; V. E., 'Eshe o Turksibe', *Kino* 5 (25 January 1930): 4; Ippolit Sokolov, 'Fil'ma, poniatnaia millionam', *Kino* 41 (15 October 1929): 3; Viktor Geiman, 'Ne smeites' nad puzatym parovozom', *Kino* 33 (20 August 1929): 2; 'Rabkory o Turksibe', *Kino* 44 (5 November 1929): 6; 'Turksib pobezhdaet', *Kino–front* 37 (4 August 1930): 1; Leyda, *Kino*, p. 261.

79 Valentin Turkin, 'Uroki Turksiba', *Sovetskii ekran* 23 (1929): 4.

80 Alexander Katsigras, 'Stal'noi put' (Turksib) – politprosvetfil'ma – poema v 5 chastiakh', *Repertuarnyi biulleten' Glaviskusstva RSFSR* 10 (1929): 22–23; S. Balbekov, N. Starosel'tseva, *Turksib. Metodicheskie ukazaniia k fil'me* (Moscow, 1933); Ippolit Sokolov, 'Turksib i ego avtor Turin', *Kino i zhizn'* 9 (1930): 7–8; A. Urenin, 'Khlopok, khleb, les: O Turksibe', *Kino* 40 (1929): 63.

81 W. H. M. ' "Turksib": A Russian Masterpiece. Passed by the British Censor', *The Bioscope*, 12 March 1930. See also Paul Rotha, *Film till Now: A Survey of World Cinema* (New York, 1960), p. 250.

82 The British Film Institute (BFI) has released a DVD with a restored English-language copy (1,666 metres, ca. 78 minutes), with intertitles prepared by Grierson, which do not directly correspond to the Russian-language intertitles of the original release. The version in RGAKFD is 1,538 metres; the Russian television broadcast version of *Turksib* is 52 minutes long.

83 Matthew Payne, 'Victor Turin's *Turksib* (1929) and Soviet Orientalism', *Historical Journal of Film, Radio, and Television* 21.1 (2001): 37–62 (pp. 47–48); Berd Kotiev, 'Biurokratizm ili vreditel'stvo? (O prokate Turksiba)', *Kino* 4 (21 January 1930): 3.

84 Svetlana Gorshenina, 'Zakaspiiskaia zheleznaia doroga: standartizatsiia istoriko-literaturnykh i ikonograficheskh reprezantatsii russkogo Turkestana' in Shahin Mustafaev, Michel Espagne, Svetlana Gorshenina et al. (eds), *Kul'turnyi transfer na perekrestakh Tsentral'noi Azii: Do, vo vremia i posle shelkovogo puti* (Paris and Samarkand, 2013), pp. 258–273 (p. 271).

85 GFF 6/1/19. All the intertitles had to be approved, and no further changes were allowed without consent of Glavrepertkom.

86 Payne, 'Victor Turin's *Turksib*', p. 53.

87 The categories Kazakh and Kyrgyz were not obvious even to the alleged bearers of these identities. In the Russian empire, the Kazakhs were referred to as Kazakh-Kyrgyz, and the Kyrgyz as Kara–Kyrgyz. In 1930, the Kazakh authorities worried that 'Russians are accustomed to thinking of Kazakhs as Kirghiz' and also that many of the Kazakhs would not 'properly' identify themselves in the upcoming census. Hirsch, *Empire of Nations*, p. 281.

88 Adeeb Khalid, *The Politics of Muslim Cultural Reform: Jadidism in Central Asia* (Berkeley, 1999).

89 Art Khalatov, *O Turkestano-Sibirskoi (Semirechenskoi) zheleznoi doroge* (Leningrad, 1927); Zinovii Ostrovskii, *Velikaia magistral'* (Moscow, 1930); M. Shekhter, *Turksib* (Kharkiv, 1931); Alexander Briskin, *Na Iuzhturksibe* (Alma-Ata, 1930); Viktor Shklovskii, *Turksib* (Moscow and Leningrad, 1930); Semen Volk, *Turksib* (Moscow, 1930); A. Sol'kin, *Turksib* (Alma-Ata, 1930); Nikolai Grig, *Na Turksibe* (Leningrad, 1929); B. Lunin, *Turksib* (Moscow and Leningrad, 1931); Demian Bednyi, *Shaitan-Arba* (Moscow, Leningrad, 1930); *Turksib. Sbornik statei uchastnikov stroitel'stva Turksetano-sibirskoi zheleznoi dorogi* (Moscow, 1930); E. Babuskin, *Turksib budet molodezhnym* (Moscow, 1930); *Turksib: zur Eröffnung der Turkestanisch-Sibirischen Eisenbahn am 1. Mai 1930* (Moscow, 1930); Hermann Remmele, *Turksib: 1442 Kilometer für den Fünfjahrplan* (Berlin, 1930); Maximilian Shteinberg, Symphony 4, op. 24 'Turksib' (1933).

90 Turar Ryskulov, *Turksib* (Moscow and Leningrad, 1930).

91 Holly Myer, 'Il'f and Petrov's *Zolotoi telenok*: Russian at the Periphery, Asian at the Core', *Studies in Slavic Cultures* 9 (2010): 43–65.

92 Alexander Feduta, 'Pisatel' Ostap Ibragimovich … Shklovskii?' in Feduta, *Siuzhety i kommentarii* (Vilnuis, 2013), pp. 145–163.

93 Shklovskii, *Turksib*, p. 14.

94 Hirsch, *Empire of Nations*, p. 170.

95 RGALI 2489/1/111.

96 Payne, *Stalin's Railroad*, pp. 237–238.

97 Michael Rouland, 'An Historical Introduction' in Rouland, Abikeyeva, Beumers, *Cinema in Central Asia*, pp. 33–44 (p. 7).

98 N. L., '"Zemlia zhazhdet". Zvukovoi fil'm', *Vecherniaia Moskva* (28 May 1931): 3; Konstantin Fel'dman, '"Zemlia zhazhdet (Vostokkino)', *Vecherniaia Moskva* (12 June 1930): 3; Iv. Astrov, 'Zemlia zhazhdet', *Kino* 34 (15 June 1930): 3; Alexander Katsigrass, 'Zemlia zhazhet', *Repertuarno-instruktivnye pis'ma sektora iskusstv Narkomprosa* (Moscow, 1931), pp. 26–27; Ippolit Sokolov, 'Zemlia zhazhdet', *Sovetskoe iskusstvo* (28 May 1931): 4.

99 Edgar, *Tribal Nation*, pp. 206–212.

100 Aleksei Konsovskii was arrested in 1934 during the shooting of Abram Room's *A Strict Youth* [*Strogii iunosha*]. Kira Andronikashvili, sister of another famous film actress, Nata Vachnadze, and wife of repressed writer Boris Pil'niak, was arrested in 1937; Sergei Ermolinskii was arrested in 1940.

101 Vertov, *Iz naslediia*, vol. 2, p. 215.

102 Gabrielle Chomentowski, 'Vostokkino and the Foundations of Central Asian Cinema in Rouland, Abikeyeva and Beumers, *Cinema in Central Asia*, pp. 33–44 (p. 43).

103 RGALI 2091/2/244: 50–51.

104 Detsenko, 'Dziga Vertov stroit sotsializm', in Tsivian, *Lines of Resistance*, pp. 226–28.

105 The woman in the episode cast off her 'chavchon', or horsehair veil, which was typically worn over the face together with the veiling cloaks called paranjas, which in this case stayed on her body, opening up only the face.

106 The Russian *zavety* can also be translated as a plural form of 'testament'. The Russian slogan was 'v nashi riady pod nashi znamena vse, komu dorogi zavety Il'icha'.

107 Douglas Northrop, *Veiled Empire: Gender and Power in Stalinist Central Asia* (Ithaca, 2004), p. 12; Marianne Kamp, 'Pilgrimage and Performance: Uzbek Women and the Imagining of Uzbekistan in the 1920s', *International Journal of Middle East Studies* 34 (2002): 263–278 (p. 264); The *hujum* coincided with an all-out attack on Islam which included abolishing confessional schools and Islamic courts in 1926–27 and a campaign against mosques and shrines; Adeeb Khalid, 'Between Empire and Revolution: New Work on Soviet Central Asia', *Kritika* 7.4 (2006): 865–884 (p. 880).

108 Numerous Soviet *kulturfilms* and newsreels demonstrated a performative unveiling of women, including Vertov's *Kino-Pravda 21*; Yulia Gradskova, 'Speaking for Those "Backward": Gender and Ethnic Minorities in Soviet Silent Films', *Region: Regional Studies of Russia, Eastern Europe, and Central Asia* 2.2 (2013): 201–220 (pp. 207–208).

109 Elizabeth Waters, 'The Female Form in Soviet Political Iconography, 1917–32', in Barbara Evans Clements, Barbara Alpern Engel, Christine D. Worobec (eds), *Russia's Women: Accommodation, Resistance, Transformation* (Berkeley, 1991), pp. 223–242 (p. 232). On the concept of women in the Soviet East as a 'surrogate proletariat' see Gregory Massell, *The Surrogate Proletariat: Moslem Women and Revolutionary Strategies in Soviet Central Asia, 1919–1929* (Princeton, 1974).

110 See, for example, transformation of the Mari heroine in *Song of Happiness* [*Pesn' o schast'e*, 1934]; Oksana Sarkisova, 'Folk Songs in Soviet Orchestration: Vostokfil'm's *Song of Happiness* and the forging of the New Soviet Musician', *Studies in Russian and Soviet Cinema* 4.3 (2010): 261–281.

111 Reina Lewis, *Gendering Orientalism: Race, Femininity and Representation* (London, 1996), p 116; Ali Behdad, 'The Orientalist Photograph' in Ali Behdad, Luke Garrtlan (eds), *Photography's Orientalism: New Essays on Colonial Representation* (Los Angeles, 2013), pp. 11–32 (pp. 27–28).

112 Inge Boer, *Uncertain Territories: Boundaries in Cultural Analysis* (Amsterdam, 2006), p. 101; Lewis, *Gendering Orientalism*, pp. 154–155.

113 Timothy Nunan, 'Soviet Nationalities Policy, *USSR in Construction* and Soviet Documentary Photography in Comparative Context, 1931–37', *Ab Imperio* 2 (2010): 47–92.

114 John MacKay, 'Allegory and Accommodation: Vertov's *Three Songs of Lenin* (1934) as a Stalinist Film', *Film History* 18.4 (2006): 376–391 (p. 383).

115 Miller, *Folklore for Stalin*, pp. 4–7, 21–22; Ursula Iustus [Justus], 'Vozvrashchenie v rai: sotsrealizm i fol'klor', in Evgenii Dobrenko, Khans Giunter [Hans Günther] (eds), *Sotsrealisticheskii kanon* (St. Petersburg, 2000), pp. 70–86; Bogdanov, Nikkolozi, and Murashov, *Dzhambul Dzhabaev*; Konstantin Bogdanov, *Vox Populi: Fol'klornye zhanry sovetskoi kul'tury* (Moscow, 2009), pp. 102–110.

116 Justus, 'Vozvrashchenie v rai', pp. 74–75.

117 Richard M. Dorson, *Folklore and Fakelore: Essays Toward a Discipline of Folk Studies* (Cambridge, 1976).

118 Bogdanov, *Vox Populi*, pp. 15–16, 21.

119 Oksana Bulgakova, 'Spatial Figures in Soviet Cinema of the 1930s', in Dobrenko and Naiman, *The Landscape of Stalinism*, pp. 51–77.

120 Northrop, *Veiled Empire*, pp. 27, 52; Zeev Levin, 'The *Khujum* Campaign in Uzbekistan and the Bukharan Jewish Women', in Christa Hämmerle, Nikola Langreiter, Margareth Lanzinger, Edith Saurer (eds), *Gender Politics in Central Asia. Historical Perspectives and Current Living Conditions of Women* (Cologne, 2008), pp. 95–111.

121 Il'ia Il'f, for example, titled his 1925 essay describing a trip to Uzbekistan 'Asia without the veil'. See Il'ia Il'f, 'Aziia bez pokryvala' in his *Zapiski provintsiala* (Moscow, 2015), pp. 140–148.

122 The reconstruction was made by Elizaveta Svilova, Il'ia Kopalin and Semiramida Pumpianskaia, and excluded references to Stalin; see MacKay, 'Allegory and Accommodation', p. 376.

123 The silent version differed significantly from the sound version. For a comparison, see the DVD release of Austrian Filmmuseum and the accompanying essay by Adelheid Heftberger, '"The Same Thing from Different Angles": On the Multiple Versions of Dziga Vertov's *Tri pesni o Lenine* (*Three Songs of Lenin*)', brochure of the DVD Edition Filmmuseum 86 (2015), unpaginated.

124 Vertov, *Iz naslediia*, vol. 1, p. 144.

125 Vertov, *Iz naslediia*, vol. 1, p. 171; for full version of the script see pp. 170–176.

126 Khans Giunter [Hans Günther], 'Totalitarnaia narodnost' i ee istoki', in Günther and Dobrenko, *Sotsrealisticheskii kanon*, pp. 377–389; Bogdanov, *Vox Populi*, p. 112, 166.

127 Bulgakova, *Sovetskii slukhoglaz*, pp. 80–97; John MacKay, 'Disorganized Noise: *Enthusiasm* and the Ear of the Collective', *KinoKultura* 7 (2005), available at www.kinokultura.com/articles/jan05–mackay.html (accessed 20 March 2015); Lilya Kaganovsky, 'Electric Speech: Dziga Vertov and the Technologies of Sound' in Oksana Bulgakova (ed.), *Resonanz-Räume: die Stimme und die Medien* (Berlin, 2012), pp. 41–54; Mariano Prunes, 'Dziga Vertov's *Three*

Songs about Lenin (1934): A Visual Tour through the History of the Soviet Avant-Garde in the Interwar Years', *Criticism* 45.2 (2003): 251–78.

128 MacKay, 'Allegory and Accommodation', p. 382.

129 Elizaveta Svilova-Vertova, V. Furtichev, *Tri pesni o Lenine* (Moscow, 1972), pp. 180–181.

130 Oksana Bulgakova, 'Sovetskoe kino v poiskakh obschei modeli', in Günther and Dobrenko, *Sotsrealisticheskii kanon*, pp. 146–165 (p. 158).

131 Mikhail Yampolsky, 'Reality at Second Hand', *Historical Journal of Film, Radio, and Television* 11.2 (1991): 161–171.

132 Andrei Shcherbenok, '"Vzgliani na Lenina i pechal' tvoia razoidetsia, kak voda": estetika travmy u Dzigi Vertova', in Sergei Ushakin [Oushakine], Elena Trubina (eds), *Travma: Punkty* (Moscow, 2009), pp. 704–722.

133 Vertov's argument resonates with the story of an Azeri female weaver making a carpet with Stalin's portrait without ever seeing him. Her claim of having Stalin's image 'always in front of my eyes, [and] in my heart', demonstrates an internalized 'adequate' Soviet vision, which cements a new communicative unity; quoted in Bogdanov, *Vox Populi*, p. 78.

134 Ernest Renan, 'What is a Nation?' in Geoff Eley and Ronald Grigor Suny (eds), *Becoming National: A Reader* (New York and Oxford, 1996), pp. 41–55 (pp. 52–54).

135 Benedict Anderson, *Imagined Communities* (London, 2006), p. 26.

136 Vertov, *Iz naslediia*, vol. 1, p. 493.

137 Bogdanov, *Vox Populi*, pp. 195–217.

138 Alexei Yurchak, 'Bodies of Lenin: The Hidden Science of Communist Sovereignty', *Representations* 129 (2015): 116–57.

139 Eric Hobsbawm, 'Introduction: Inventing Traditions', in Eric Hobsbawm and Terence Ranger (eds), *The Invention of Tradition* (Cambridge, 1983), pp. 1–14.

140 Al. Borisov, 'Dokumentalisty v zvukovom kino', *Proletarskoe kino* 5–6 (1931): 32–35 (p. 33).

141 Madeleine Dobie, *Foreign Bodies: Gender, Language, and Culture in French Orientalism* (Stanford, 2001), p. 27.

142 Dobie, *Foreign Bodies*, p. 28.

143 Jeremy Hicks has pointed out that veiling 'presents a way of seeing that is resistant to the camera's gaze, its panopticon'; Hicks, *Dziga Vertov*, p. 93.

144 RGALI 2091/2/244: 25verso.

145 Quoted in Sven Spieker, *The Big Archive: Art from Bureaucracy* (Cambridge, 2008), p. 22.

146 On Soviet multilingualism in early sound cinema see Evgenii Margolit, 'Problema mnogoiazychiia v rannem sovetskom zvukovom kino (1930–1935)' in Günther and Hänsgen (eds), *Sovetskaia vlast' i media*, pp. 378–386.

147 Widdis, *Visions of a New Land*, p. 164.

148 Widdis, *Visions of a New Land*, p. 162.

149 RGALI 2091/2/244: 25–48.

150 Anon., 'V. Bullit i Sidney Webb o fil'me "Tri pesni o Lenine"', *Pravda* (16 September 1934): 6.

151 Anon., 'Na prosmotre fil'my "Tri Pesni o Lenine"' *Kino* 49 (28 October 1934): 1.

152 Kirill Anderson, Leonid Maksimenkov et al. (eds), *Kremlevskii kinoteatr, 1928–1953. Dokumenty* (Moscow, 2005), pp. 961–962.

153 Heftberger, '"The Same Thing from Different Angles"'.

154 This model was further extended in Vertov's *Lullaby* [*Kolybel'naia*, 1937], which integrated 'Eastern' women on a par with the citizen-mothers across the Soviet Union into a community adoring the leader, and emphasized a distance from the centre by the painstaking travels from the outskirts to Moscow.

155 Anon., 'Ekspeditsii pod control"!', *Kino* 30 (28 June 1934): 1, (original emphasis).

156 Alexander Prokhorov, 'Children's Films', in Birgit Beumers (ed.), *Directory of World Cinema: Russia* (Bristol, 2011), pp. 243–245 (p. 244).

157 Quoted in Payne, *Turin's Turksib*, p. 45.

Epilogue: Day of a New World

1 Sergei Tret'iakov, 'Grazhdane 1940 goda', *Sovetskoe kino* 6–7 (1926): 4–5.

2 The same year, Karmen's co-director Mikhail Slutskii received a second-degree Stalin Award for the film *Our Moscow* [*Nasha Moskva*, 1941].

3 Mikhail Kol'tsov, 'Den' Mira', *Pravda* (3 October 1935): 2; Maksim Gorkii, Mikhail Kol'tsov (eds), *Den' Mira* (Moscow, 1937).

4 Maksim Gorkii, 'Literatura i kino', *Pravda* (14 April 1935): 2.

5 Vertov, *Iz naslediia*, vol. 1, pp. 236–238 (p. 236).

6 Aamir Mufti, quoted in Priya Jaikumar, *Cinema at the End of Empire: A Politics of Transition in Britain and India* (Durham, 2006), pp. 35–36; see also Suny, 'The Contradictions of Identity: Being Soviet and National in the USSR and after', pp. 17–18.

7 Following the Molotov-Ribbentrop Pact, Estonia, and later Latvia and Lithuania were forced to accept so-called "Pacts of Defense and Mutual Assistance" with the USSR in September-October 1939, which allowed Soviet military and naval presence in the countries. In June 1940, the Soviet leadership accused Lithuanian, Latvian and Estonian governments of breaking their pacts and issued ultimatums demanding additional Soviet military and naval units, forcing the countries to yield to Soviet demands. With the formation of transitional governments a

forceful Soviet-orchestrated '"constitutional" metamorphosis of the Baltic states into constituent republics of the USSR' began. Following manipulated elections, all three People's Assemblies convened on 21 July 1940 and formulated 'an application for membership of the USSR'. The requests were 'granted' by the Supreme Soviet in the first days of August 1940. Romuald Misiunas and Rein Taagepera, *The Baltic States: Years of Dependence, 1940–80* (London, 1983), pp. 20–29.

8 Zdravstvui, Rodina bol'shaia / Nenagliadnaia moia – / Trudovaia, boevaia / Neob"iatnaia sem'ia.
9 Dziga Vertov, *Stat'i, dnevniki, zamysly* (Moscow, 1966), p. 69.
10 Vsevolod Pudovkin, 'K edinoi tseli', *20 let sovetskoi kinematografii* (Moscow, 1940), pp. 35–39, esp. 37–38 (original emphasis).
11 Brian Winston, *Claiming the Real: The Griersonian Documentary and Its Legitimations* (London, 1995).
12 Tom Gunning, *D. W. Griffith and the Origins of American Narrative Film: The Early Years at Biograph* (Urbana and Chicago, 1991), p. 17.
13 Vertov, *Stat'i. Dnevniki. Zamysly*, p. 73.
14 Dobrenko and Naiman, *The Landscape of Stalinism*, p. xii.
15 Sandomirskaia, 'One Sixth of the World...'.
16 Daniel Martin Varisco, *Rereading Orientalism: Said and the Unsaid* (Seattle and London, 2007), p. xi.
17 Bill Nichols, *Introduction to Documentary* (Bloomington, 2001), pp. 132–134; Renov, *The Subject of Documentary*.
18 Some of these issues are discussed in Margaret Dikovitskaia, 'Does Russia Qualify for Postcolonial Discourse?', *Ab Imperio* 2 (2002): 551–557.
19 Yuri Slezkine, 'The USSR as a Communal Apartment, or How a Socialist State Promoted Ethnic Particularism', *Slavic Review* 53.2 (1994): 414–452.
20 Nechaeva, *Vladimir Shneiderov*, p. 110.
21 The programme was later led by Iurii Senkevich, who remained its permanent anchor until 2003.
22 Nikolai Lebedev, *Ocherk istorii kino SSSR. Nemoe kino*, vol. 1 (Moscow, 1947).
23 Hirsch, *Empire of Nations*, pp. 313–314.
24 Hirsch, *Empire of Nations*, p. 318.
25 See, for example, Nikolai Pluzhnikov's *The Last Shaman* [*Poslednii shaman*, 2002], Edgar Bartenev's *Yaptik-Hasse* [2006], Ivan Golovnev's *Old Man Peter* [*Starik Petr*, 2008], Alexei Vakhrushev's *The Tundra Book* [*Kniga Tundry*, 2011], or Efim Reznikov's *Great Arctic. The Worship of Fire Spirit* [*Arktika velikaia. Pochitanie dukha ognia*, 2014].
26 Rony, *The Third Eye*, p. 195.
27 See for example, Georgii Gabelia's *Caucasian Face* [*Litso kavkazskoi natsional'nosti*, 2000], Mairam Yusupova's *Gastarbeiter* [*Mardikor*, 2002]).

28 See for example Igor' Voloshin's *Bitch* [*Suka*, 2001], Sergei Bosenko's *Chechen Gambit* [*Chechenskii gambit*, 2001], Alexander Rastorguev's *Clean Thursday* [*Chistyi chetverg*, 2003].

29 See for example Aleksei Popogrebskii's *How I Ended this Summer* [*Kak ia provel etim letom*, 2010], Natalia Meshchaninova's *Hope Factory* [*Kombinat Nadezhda*, 2014], Andrei Zviagintsev's *Leviathan* [*Leviafan*, 2014]).

30 For more on recent productions of regional studios see Caroline Damiens, 'Cinema in Sakha (Yakutia) Republic: Renegotiating Film History', in *KinoKultura* 48 (2015), available at http://www.kinokultura.com/2015/48-damiens.shtml and Sergey Dobrynin, 'New Buryat Cinema: Developments So Far and Challenges for the Future', in *KinoKultura* 48 (2015), available at http://www.kinokultura.com/2015/48-dobrynin.shtml (both accessed 20 August 2015).

31 Ernest Gellner, *Nations and Nationalism* (Oxford, 1983).

32 Quoted in Tsivian, *Lines of Resistance*, p. 170.

Filmography

The information on *kulturfilms* is fragmented, particularly concerning authorship and dates. Certain discrepancies in dating are due to the time gap between the film's completion and release. Unless stated otherwise, all films are produced in Russia (before 1917 and after 1991) and in the Soviet Union (between 1917–1991). D indicates director; S – scriptwriter, C – cameraman; Moskovskaia fabrika Sovkino/Soiuzkino is abbreviated as Sovkino/Soiuzkino M; Leningradskaia fabrika Sovkino as Sovkino L. The film title is followed by the Russian title and/or the title in the original language, the film studio and year of production (when available).

1812 [Khanzhonkov and Pathé Frères, 1913], D: Vasilii Goncharov, Kai Hansen, Alexander Ural'skii; C: Georges Meyer, Alexander Levitskii, Louis Forestier, Alexander Ryllo, Fedor Bremer

235,000,000 [235 millionov, Riga Film Studio, 1967], D: Uldis Brauns, Biruta Veldre, Laima Zurgina; S: Herz Frank; C: Rihards Piks, Valdis Krogis, Ralfs Krumins

4,500 Metres High [Na vysote 4500 metrov, Mezhrabpomfil'm, 1931], D: Vladimir Shneiderov, C: Mstislav Kotel'nikov

Abortion [Abort, Goskino/Kul'tkino, 1924], D: Grigorii Lemberg, Nikolai Baklin; S: Noi Galkin, Ivan Leonov; C: Grigorii Lemberg

Abrek Zaur [Goskino, 1926], D: Boris Mikhin; S: I. Bei-Abai; C: Konstantin Kuznetsov

Across Buryat-Mongolia [Po Buriato-Mongolii, Sovkino, 1929], C: Vasilii Beliaev; Editor: Lidiia Stepanova

Across Dagestan [Po Dagestanu, Mezhrabpomfil'm, 1934], D&C: Georgii Bobrov

Across Europe (Germany, Italy). Travel Notes [Po Evrope (Germaniia, Italiia). Putevye zametki, Kul'tkino-Goskino, 1925], D&S: Nikolai Lebedev

Across Kamchatka and Sakhalin [Po Kamchatke i Sakhalinu, Fabrika kul'turfil'mov Sovkino, 1930], D: Leonid Vul'fov; C: Mikhail Leont'ev

Across Mountains and Glaciers of the Caucasus [Po goram i lednikam Kavkaza, Mezhrabpom-Rus', 1926], D: Iurii Zheliabuzhskii, C: Arkadii Ialovoi

Aerograd [Ukrainfilm/Mosfilm, 1935], D&S: Alexander Dovzhenko; C: Eduard Tissé, Mikhail Gindin, Nikolai Smirnov

Alamas Gorge, The [Ushchel'e Alamasov, Soiuzdetfil'm, 1937], D: Vladimir Shneiderov; S: Mikhail Rozenfel'd; C: Alexander Shelenkov

Alone [Odna, Soiuzkino L., 1931], D&S: Grigorii Kozintsev, Leonid Trauberg; C: Andrei Moskvin

Filmography

Altai-Kizhi [aka *Altaitsy*, Sovkino M., 1929] D&C: Vladimir Stepanov

Arctic Troy [Arkticheskaia Troia, 2003] D&S: Aleksei Vakhrushev; C: Nikita Khokhlov, Viacheslav Makar'ev

At the Foothills of Death [Podnozh'e smerti, Mezhrabpomfil'm, 1928], D&S: Vladimir Shneiderov; C: Il'ia Tolchan

At the North Pole [Na severnom poliuse, Moskovskaia studiia kinokhroniki, 1937], D: Irina Venzher, Mark Troianovskii; C: Mark Troianovskii

Batumi and the Caucasian Seashore [Batum i Kavkazskoe poberezh'e. Sektsiia gigieny, vospitaniia, i obrazovaniia pri Nizhegorodskom otdele obshchestva okhrany narodnogo zdorov'ia, 1911], C: Alexander Digmelov

Beginning [Nachalo, 1967], D: Artavazd Peleshian

Beyond the Arctic Circle [Za poliarnym krugom, Sovkino L., 1927], D: Vladimir Erofeev, Vera Popova; C: Fedor Bremer

Beyond the Arctic Circle [Za poliarnym krugom, Soiuzkino M., 1931], D: Ol'ga Podgoretskaia; C: Grigorii Donets, Boris Chechulin, Iurii Stilianudis

Birobidzhan. Far-Eastern Region. [Birobidzhan. Dal'ne-Vostochnyi krai, Moskovskaia fabrika Soiuzkinokhroniki, 1934], D: Mikhail Slutskii, C: Mikhail Glider

Bukhara [Sovkino M., 1927], C: Iakov Tolchan; Editor: Elizaveta Svilova

Caucasian Vistas. Customs of Indigenous Population [Vidy Kavkaza. Nravy i oby-chai tuzemtsev, Khanzhonkov Studio, 1909], C: V. Svirsen (?)

Chuvash Land, The [Strana Chuvashskaia, Chuvashkino, 1927], D: Vlad[islav] Korolevich; C: Igor' Gelein, Dmitrii Il'in

City of Youth [Gorod iunosti, Moskovskaia fabrika Soiuzkinokhroniki, 1934], D: Mikhail Slutskii; C: Mikhail Glider

Country of Lion and the Sun (Persia) [Strana l'va i solntsa (Persiia), Vostokfilm, 1935], D: Vladimir Erofeev, Co-director: Anatolii Golovnia; C: Anatolii Golovnia, Iurii Fogel'man

Dagestan (aka *Republic of Youth*) [Dagestan. Respublika iunosti, Rostovskaia fabrika Soiuzkinokhroniki, 1938], D: Iakov Avdeenko

Dagestan [Rostov and Severo-Kavkazskaia kinokhronika, 1946], D: Genrietta Satarova; C: Nikolai Golubev, Nikolai Podgornyi, Viktor Petrov, Alexander Sukhov

Dagestan [Sovkino, 1927], C: Petr Zotov, Iakov Tolchan

Dina-Dza-Dzu [Mezhrabpom-Rus', 1926], D: Iurii Zheliabuzhskii; C: Arkadii Ialovoi

Don Cossacks, The [Donskie Kazaki, Khanzhonkov Studio, 1908], C: Georges Meyer

Dzhou [Moskinokombinat, 1934], D: Alexander Litvinov; C: Aleksei Solodkov

Dzhul'bars [Mezhrabpomfil'm, 1936], D: Vladimir Shneiderov; S: Vladimir Shneiderov, Gabriel' Registan; C. Alexander Shelenkov

Earth Thirsts, The [Zemlia zhazhdet, Vostokkino, 1930], D: Iulii Raizman; S: Sergei Ermolinskii; C: Leonid Kosmatov

Filmography

Eleventh Year, The [Odinnadtsatyi, VUFKU, 1928], D: Dziga Vertov; C: Mikhail Kaufman

Eliso [Goskinprom Gruzii, 1928], D: Nikoloz Shengelaia; S: Sergei Tret'iakov, Nikoloz Shengelaia; C: Vladimir Kereselidze

El'-Yemen [Mezhrabpomfil'm, 1930], D: Vladimir Shneiderov; C: Il'ia Tolchan

Emigrants from the Flourishing Country [Emigranty iz tsvetuschei strany, Soiuzkino M., 1932], D&S: Alexander Litvinov; C: Pavel Mershin

Enthusiasm. Symphony of the Donbass [Entuziazm. Simfoniia Donbassa, VUFKU, 1930], D: Dziga Vertov; C: Boris Tseitlin; Editor: Elizaveta Svilova

Eye for Eye, Gas for Gas [Oko za oko, gaz za gaz, AFKU, 1924], D: Alexander Litvinov; S: Pavel Vel'skii, Alexander Litvinov, Sergei Troitskii; C: Vladimir Lemke

Eyes of Andozia [Glaza Andozii, Proletkino, 1926], D&S: Dmitrii Bassalygo; C: Vladimir Dobrzhanskii

Fall of the Romanov Dynasty, The [Padenie dinastii Romanovykh, Sovkino M., 1927], D: Esfir' Shub; S: Mark Tseitlin and Esfir' Shub

Far in Asia [Daleko v Azii, Vostokfil'm, 1933], D: Vladimir Erofeev, C: Roman Karmen, Georgii Blium

Feat in the Ice [Podvig vo l'dakh, Sovkino L., 1928], D: Sergei Vasil'ev, Georgii Vasil'ev, C: Vil'gel'm Bluvshtein, Ignatii Valentei, Evgenii Bogorov

Foreign Tourists in the Soviet Land [Inostrannye turisty v strane Sovetov, Sovkino M., 1930], D: M. Gromov

Forest People [Lesnye liudi, Sovkino M., 1928], D: Alexander Litvinov; C: Pavel Mershin

Four in a Boat. From Nizhnii Novgorod to Astrakhan [Chetvero v lodke. Ot Nizhnego do Astrakhani, Vostokkino, 1930], D: Nikolai Prozorovskii; C: Leonid Sazonov

From the Darkness of Centuries [Iz t'my vekov, Vostokkino, 1931], D: Alexander Lemberg

Gaichi [Soiuzdetfil'm, 1938], D: Vladimir Shneiderov; C: Nikolai Prozorovskii

Gate of the Caucasus, The [Vorota Kavkaza, Moskovskaia fabrika Sovkino-Vostokkino, 1929], D: Nikolai Lebedev; C: Ivan Beliakov

General Line, The [General'naia liniia; aka *The Old and the New* (Staroe i novoe), Sovkino M., 1929], D: Sergei Eisenstein, Grigorii Aleksandrov; C: Eduard Tissé

Girl from Kamchatka, The [Devushka s Kamchatki, Mosfil'm, 1936], S: Mikhail Dubson, D: Alexander Litvinov; C: V. Serebrianikov

Girl with Character, The [Devushka s kharakterom, Mosfil'm, 1939], D: Konstantin Iudin; S: Gennadii Fish, Iosif Skliut; C: Timofei Lebeshev

Golden Lake [Zolotoe ozero, Mezhrabpomfil'm, 1934], D: Vladimir Shneiderov; S: Alexander Pereguda, Vladimir Shneiderov

Great Flight, The [Velikii perelet, Sovkino M., 1925], D: Vladimir Shneiderov; C: Georgii Blium

Great Road, The [Velikii put', Moskovskaia fabrika Sovkino, 1927], D: Esfir' Shub

Heart of Asia, The (Afghanistan) [Serdtse Azii (Afganistan), Sovkino, L., 1929], D: Vladimir Erofeev; C: Vasilii Beliaev

Heart of the Mountains. Svanetia [Serdtse Gor. Svanetia, Mezhrabpom-Rus', 1926], D: Iurii Zheliabuzhskii; C: Arkadii Ialovoi

Heroes of the Arctic [Geroi Arktiki. Cheliuskin, Moskovskaia fabrika Souizkinokhroniki, 1934], D: Iakov Posel'skii; C: Arkadii Shafran, Mark Troianovskii

Hunting and Reindeer Practices in the Komi Region, The [Okhota i olenevodstvo v oblasti Komi, Sovkino M., 1927] C: Samuil Benderskii, Nikolai Iudin; Editor: Sergei Liamin

I Want to Live [Khochu zhit', Moskinokombinat, 1934], D: Alexander Litvinov; S: Georgii Pavliuchenko, Alexander Litvinov, Iurii Smirnitskii; C: Alexei Solodkov

Igdenbu [Vostokkino, 1930], D: Amo Bek-Nazarov; S: Sergei Vitkin; C: Georgii Blium

In the Far East [Na Dal'nem Vostoke, Mosfil'm, 1937], D: David Marian, Efim Aron; S: Pavel Pavlenko, Stanislav Radzinskii; C: Valentin Pavlov

In the Mountains of the Caucasus [V gorakh Kavkaza, 1927], D: E[lmurza] Tlatov

Jews on the Land [Evrei na zemle, OZET–Sovkino M., 1927], D: Abram Room; S: Viktor Shklovskii, Vladimir Maiakovskii; C: Al'bert Kiun

Kaan-Kerede [Sovkino L., 1929], D&S: Vladimir Feinberg; C: Fedor Verigo-Darovskii, Vasilii Kamenskii

Kamchatka [Sovkino M.], C&D: Nikolai Konstantinov

Khabarda [Goskinprom Gruzii, 1931], D: Mikhail Chiaureli; S: Sergei Tret'iakov, Mikhail Chiaureli; C: Anton Polikevich

Khabu [Sovkino L., 1928], D: Viacheslav Viskovskii; S: Iurii Tarich, Viacheslav Viskovskii; C: Feliks Shtertser

Khas-Push [Armenkino, 1927], D: Amo Bek-Nazarov; S: Grigorii Braginskii, Avrorii Ter-Ovanian, Amo Bek-Nazarov; C: Nikolai Anoshchenko

Kino-Eye: Life Caught Unawares [Kinoglaz: Zhizn' vrasplokh, Goskino, 1924], D: Dziga Vertov; C: Mikhail Kaufman

Komsomol'sk [Lenfil'm, 1938], D: Sergei Gerasimov; S: Zinovia Markina, Mikhail Vitukhnovskii; C: Alexander Gintsburg

Lake Baikal [Baikal, Sovkino M., 1928], D: Nikolai Kudriavtsev, C: Vasilii Beliaev

Land of the Golds, The [Strana Gol'dov, Vostokkino, 1930], D: Amo Bek–Nazarov; C: Georgii Blium

Land of the Nakhcho, The [Strana Nakhcho, Sovkino & Vostokkino, 1929], D: Nikolai Lebedev; C: Ivan Beliakov

Law of the Steppes, The [Zakon stepei, Vostokfil'm, 1933], D: Alexander Slobodnik; S: Steppes Kananykin; C: Alexander Zil'bernik

269

Filmography

Life As It Is [Zhizn', kak ona est', Kul'tkino, 1926] D: Alexander Dubrovskii

Liu–Fu [Moskovskaia fabrika Soiuzkinokhroniki, 1934], D: Mikhail Slutskii, C: Mikhail Glider

Lullaby [Kolybel'naia, Moskovskaia studia Soiuzkinokhroniki, 1937], D: Dziga Vertov; C: Sergei Semenov, Ivan Beliakov, Grigorii Griber, Semen Somov, Dmitrii Surenskii et al.

Man with a Movie Camera [Chelovek s kinoapparatom, VUFKU, 1929], D: Dziga Vertov, C: Mikhail Kaufman

Mari People, The [Mariitsy, Vostokkino, 1929], D: Nikolai Prim, C: Viktor Pate-Ipa.

Mechanics of the Brain [Mekhanika golovnogo mozga, Mezhrabpom-Rus', 1926], D: Vsevolod Pudovkin, C: Anatolii Golovnia

Minaret of Death [Minaret smerti, Sevzapkino and Bukhkino, 1925], D: Viacheslav Viskovskii; S: Alexander Balagin, Viacheslav Viskovskii; C: Fedor Verigo-Darovskii

Nanai from the Tunguska River, A [O nanaitse s reki Tunguski, Moskovskaia fabrika Soiuzkinokhroniki, 1934], D: Mikhail Slutskii, C: Mikhail Glider

Natella [Goskinprom Gruzii, 1926], D: Amo Bek-Nazarov; S: Sh. Shishmarev, Amo Bek-Nazarov; C: Sergei Zabozlaev

Oil Workers from the Caucasus on Holidays in Sanatorium [Gorniak-neftianik na otdykhe i lechenii, AFKU, Baku, 1924], D: Alexander Litvinov; S: Pavel Vel'skii, Alexander Litvinov; C: Vladimir Lemke

Oirotia [Zapadno-Sibirskii otdel Soiuzkinokhroniki, 1932], D: Georgii Grebenkin; C: Samuil Davidson

Old Luven's Hut [Khizhina starogo Luvena, Mosfil'm, 1935], D: Alexander Litvinov; S: Mikhail Prishvin; C: Pavel Mershin

On Kamchatka [Na Kamchatke, Moskovskaia fabrika Soiuzkinokhroniki, 1936], D: Lidiia Stepanova, C: Viktor Glass

On the Asian Border [Na granitse Azii, Vostokkino, 1930], D: Nikolai Anoshchenko

On the Far Eastern Roads [Po dorogam Primor'ia, Sverdlovskaia kinostudia nauchno-populiarnykh i khronikal'nykh fil'mov, 1957], D: Alexander Litvinov, C: Konstantin Duplenskii, Fedor Shlykov

On the Merry Hills [Na veselykh gorakh, 1929]

On the Shores of the Chukotka Sea [U beregov Chukotskogo moria, Moskinokombinat, 1934], D: Iurii Smirnitskii, under supervision of Alexander Litvinov; C: Arkadii Levitan

Over the White Sea [Po belomu moriu, Sector of Hygiene, Upbringing, and Education within the Department of National Health Preservation in Nizhnii Novgorod, 1913], C: P. Kobtsov, N. Efremov

Papanin's Team [Papanintsy, Moskovskaia studiia Soiuzkinokhroniki, 1938], D: Iakov Posel'skii, Irina Venzher; C: Mark Troianovskii, Georgii Simonov, Iakov Slavin

Peasant Riches of South Russia, The [Krest'ianskie bogatstva iuga Rossii, Museum of Agriculture and State Property, 1912], C: V. Vishnevskii, D. Sakhnenko et al.

Filmography

Road to the Future [Doroga v budushchee, Moskovskaia studiia kinokhroniki, 1940], D: Rafail Gikov, Lidiia Stepanova; C: Vladimir Solov'ev, S. Semenov

Roof of the World, The (Pamir) [Krysha mira (Pamir), Sovkino, 1927], D: Vladimir
Erofeev; C: Vasilii Beliaev

Russian Types [Rossiiskie Tipy, Pathé Frères, 1908], C: Georges Mayer

Salt for Svanetia [Sol' Svanetii, Goskinprom Gruzii, 1930], D&C: Mikhail Kalatozov;
S: Sergei Tret'iakov, Mikhail Kalatozov

Scourge of Time (aka *The Heritage of the Past*) [Bich vremeni (Nasledie proshlogo),
Vostokkino, 1931], D: Vladimir Iurenev, C: Evgenii Burdon

Seasons of the Year [Vremena goda, aka Tarva Yeghanakner, 1975], D&S: Artavazd
Peleshian

Sectarians [Sektanty, Fabrika kul'turfil'mov Sovkino, 1930], D: Vladislav Korolevich;
C: Gleb Troianskii, Nikolai Vikhirev

Seekers of Happiness, The [Iskateli schast'ia, Belgoskino, 1936], S: Iogann Zeltser,
Grigorii Kobets; D: Vladimir Korsh-Sablin; C: Boris Riabov

Shame to Admit, A [Stydno skazat', Soiuzkino M., 1930] D: Pavel Armand;
C: Mikhail Gindin

Shanghai Document, The [Shankhaiskii dokument, Sovkino M., 1928], D: Iakov
Bliokh; C: Vladimir Stepanov

Sixth Part of the World, A [Shestaia chast' mira, Sovkino, 1926], D: Dziga Vertov;
C: Ivan Beliakov, Samuil Benderskii, Nikolai Konstantinov, Alexander Lemberg,
Nikolai Strukov, Iakov Tolchan, Petr Zotov

Spring [Vesnoi, Kievskaia fabrika VUFKU, 1929], D&C: Mikhail Kaufman

Stalin's Breed [Stalinskoe plemia, Moskovskaia studiia Soiuzkinokhroniki, 1937],
D: Vladimir Erofeev, Iosif Posel'skii, Irina Setkina

Storming and Capture of Erzurum, The [Shturm i vziatie Erzeruma, Skobelev Committee, 1916], C: I. Doreda, P. Ermolov; S: S. Esadze

Stride, Soviet! [Shagai, Sovet!, Sovkino, M. 1926], D: Dziga Vertov, C: Mikhail
Kaufman

Terra Incognita (Kamchatka) [Nevedomaia zemlia (Kamchatka), Sovkino, 1931],
D: Alexander Litvinov; S: Nadezhda Vendelin, Alexander Litvinov; C: Pavel
Mershin

Three Songs of Lenin [Tri pesni o Lenine, Mezhrabpomfil'm, 1934/38], D: Dziga
Vertov, C: Dmitrii Surenskii, Mark Magidson, Bentsion Monastyrskii

Through Samarkand [Po Samarkandu, Fabrika kul'turfil'mov Sovkino, 1930],
D: Konstantin Gavriushin, C: Oleg Skachko

Through the Ussuri Area [Po debriam Ussuriiskogo kraia, Sovkino M., 1928], D:
Alexander Litvinov; C: Pavel Mershin

To Live Wealthy [Zhit' zazhitochno, Moskovskaia fabrika Soiuzkinokhroniki, 1933],
D: Mikhail Slutskii, C: Boris Makaseev, Mikhail Glider

Today [Segodnia, 1930], D: Esfir' Shub; S: Mark Tseitlin and Esfir' Shub

Filmography

Towards a Safe Haven [K schastlivoi gavani, Fabrika kul'turfil'm Sovkino and Derussa, 1930], D: Vladimir Erofeev; C: Iurii Stilianudis

Towards the Shores of the Pacific Ocean [K beregam Tikhogo Okeana, Sovkino, M. 1927], D: Nikolai Konstantinov

Travel across Kamchatka [Puteshestvie na Kamchatke, Museum of Anthropology and Ethnography of the Academy of Sciences, 1911], C: G. Kramarenko

Triumphant over the Ice [Pobeditel' l'dov, Mezhrabpomfil'm, 1934], D: Lev Bronshtein; C: Grigorii Kabalov

Tungus, The [Tungusy, Sovkino M., 1927], D: Petr Zotov; Editor: Elizaveta Svilova

Turksib [Vostokkino, 1929], D: Viktor Turin; C: Evgenii Slavinskii, Boris Frantsisson

Two Oceans [Dva okeana, Mezhrabpomfil'm, 1933], D: Vladimir Shneiderov; C: Mark Troianovskii

Udege [Novosibirskaia studiia uchebnykh fil'mov, 1947], D&S: Alexander Litvinov; C: Boris Zhilin

Under the Burden of Adat [Pod vlast'iu adata, Goskino-Leningrad, 1926], D: Vladimir Kas'ianov; S: Izmail Abai; C: Nikolai Kozlovskii

Valley of Tears, The [Dolina slez, Goskino, 1924], D&C: Alexander Razumnyi; S: Valentin Turkin, Boris Martov

Way is Open, The [Put' otkryt, Moskovskaia studiia kinokhroniki, 1937] D: Vladimir Erofeev, C: Vladimir Solov'ev

We [My/Menk, 1969], D&S: Artavazd Peleshian

We Conquered the North Pole! [Severnyi polius zavoevan nami!, Moskovskaia studiia kinokhroniki, 1937], D: Sergei Gurov, Vladimir Boikov, C: Mark Troianovskii, Sergei Fomin, Konstantin Pisanko, Viktor Dobronitskii, Ottiliia Reizman

Zare [Armenkino, 1926], D&S: Amo Bek-Nazarov, C: Arkadii Ialovoi

Bibliography

Archival Sources

Moscow Film Museum Archive [Arkhiv Muzeiia Kino, AMK]
  Fond 26, Opis' 2: Lebedev, Nikolai Alekseevich (1897–1978)
State Archive of the Russian Federation [Gosudarstvennyi Arkhiv Rossiiskoi Federatsii, GARF]
  Fond 4085, Opis' 12: Narodnyi komissariat raboche-krest'ianskoi inspektsii RSFSR [People's Commissariat of the Worker-Peasant Inspection of the RSFSR]
  Fond 7816, Opis' 1: Kinokomitet pri SNK SSSR 1928–1930 gg. [Committee for Cinema under the Council of People's Commissars, 1928–1930]
  Fond 8326, Opis' 2: Vserossiiskoe fotokinematograficheskoe aktsionernoe obshchestvo 'Sovkino', 1922–1930 gg. [All-Russian Photo-Film Joint Stock Company 'Sovkino', 1922–1930]
  Fond R-8326, Opis' 1: Aktsionernoe obshchestvo 'Proletarskoe kino' (1923–1926 gg.) [Joint Stock Company 'Proletarian Cinema', 1923–1926]
Gosfil'mofond Archive [GFF]: Fond 6, Opis' 1 Opis' dokumental'nogo fonda 1919–1930
Russian State Archive of Literature and Art [Rossiiskii Gosudarstvennyi Arkhiv Literatury i Iskusstva, RGALI]
  Fond 1966, Opis' 1: Kollektsiia Sedykh, Fedora Sergeevicha, sluzhashchego ARRK [Collection of Fedor Sergeevich Sedykh, member of ARRK]
  Fond 2091, Opis' 1 and 2: Vertov, Dziga (Kaufman, Denis Arkad'evich, 1896–1954)
  Fond 2354, Opis' 1: Zheliabuzhskii, Iurii Andreevich (1888–1955)
  Fond 2489, Opis' 1: Gosudarstvennyi trest khudozhestvennykh fil'mov 'Vostokfil'm' (Moskva, 1930–1935) [State Trust for Feature Films Vostokfilm, Moscow, 1930–1935]
  Fond 2494, Opis' 1: Assotsiatsiia rabotnikov revoliutsionnoi kinematografii (ARRK) (Moskva, 1924–1934) [Association of Workers of Revolutionary Cinema ARRK, Moscow 1924–1934]
  Fond 2495, Opis' 1: Obshchestvo druzei sovetskoi kinematografii (ODSK) (Moskva, 1925–1934). [Society of the Friends of Soviet Cinema, Moscow 1925–1934]
  Fond 2496, Opis' 2: Vserossiiskoe fotokinematograficheskoe aktsionernoe obshchestvo 'Sovkino' (Moskva, 1924–1930) [All-Russian Photo and Film Joint Stock Company 'Sovkino', Moscow 1924–1930]

Fond 645, Opis' 1: Glavnoe upravlenie po delam khudozhestvennoi literatury i iskusstva (Glaviskusstvo) Narkomprosa RSFSR (Moskva, 1928–1933) [Main Administration for Literature and Art under the People's Commissariat for Enlightenment, Moscow, 1928–1933]

Russian State Archive of Socio-Political History [Rossiiskii Gosudarstvennyi Arkhiv Sotsial'no-Politicheskoi Istorii, RGASPI]

Fond 17, Opis' 60: Otdel agitatsii i propagandy TsK VKP(b) [Department of Agitation and Propaganda under the Central Committee of the VKP(b)]

Fond 17, Opis' 120: Otdely TsK RKP(b) i TsK VKP(b) [Departments of RKP(b) and VKP(b)]

Fond 538, Opis' 3: Rossiiskoe otdelenie TsK Mezhrabpoma, Aktsionernoe torgovo-promyshlennoe obshchestvo Aufbau, Predstavitel'stvo TsK Mezhrabpoma v SSSR [Russian Section of Mezhrabpom, Joint Stock Trading and Production Company Aufbau, Representation of Mezhrabpom in the USSR]

Primary Sources

Listed here are books and major publications on *kulturfilms* and primary texts by the filmmakers or their crew. Additional literature and reviews in film journals such as *Kino, Kino-Fot, Kino i zhizn', Novyi zritel', Novyi LEF, ARK, Sovetskoe kino, Sovetskii ekran, Zhizn' natsional'nostei* from the 1920s and 1930s are fully referenced in the endnotes.

Abramov, Alexander. 'Vspomnim o vidovoi', *Sovetskoe kino* 4–5 (1926): 10–11.

Anderson, Kirill, and Leonid Maksimenkov, L. Kosheleva, L. Rogovaia (eds). *Kremlevskii kinoteatr, 1928–1953. Dokumenty*. Moscow, 2005.

Anisimov, Sergei. *Svanetia*. Moscow, 1929.

Arsen'ev, Vladimir. *Amba. Li-Tsun-Bin. Rasskazy iz puteshestvii po Ussuriiskomu kraiu*. Nikol'sk-Ussuriiskii, 1920.

_____ *Lesnye liudi (Udegeitsy)*. Vladivostok, 1926.

_____ *Skvoz' taigu. Putevoi dnevnik ekspeditsii po marshrutu ot Sovetskoi gavani k gorodu Khabarovsk*. Moscow-Leningrad, 1930.

_____ *Sobranie sochinenii*, vols. 1–3. Vladivostok, 2007–2012.

Artizov, Andrei, and Oleg Naumov (eds). *Vlast' i khudozhestvennaia intelligentsiia. Dokumenty TsK RKP(b)-VKP(b), VChK-OGPU-NKVD o kul'turnoi politike. 1917–1953*. Moscow, 2002.

Aseev, Nikolai. 'V poiskakh kul'turnoi filmy', *Sovetskii ekran* 2 (1926): 4.

Balbekov S. and N. Starosel'tseva, *Turksib. Metodicheskie ukazaniia k fil'me*. Moscow, 1933.

Balliuzek, Vladimir. 'Kino na Vostoke', *Kino-Nedelia* 6 (3 February 1925): 9.

Bassalygo, Dmitrii. 'O Vostoke dlia Vostoka', *Sovetskii ekran* 24 (1925): n.p.

Bratoliubov, Sergei. *Na zare sovetskoi kinematografii*. Leningrad, 1976.

Bremer, Fedor. 'Opasnyi Reis (Zapiski operatora-turista)', *Pegas. Zhurnal iskusstv* 1 (1915).

Briskin, Alexander. *Na Iuzhturksibe*. Alma-Ata, 1930.

Chuzhak, Nikolai. 'K zadacham dnia', *LEF* 2 (1923): 145–146.

_____ (ed.), *Literatura fakta*. Moscow, 1929.

Dovzhenko, Alexander. 'Kak my rabotali', *Kino* 51–52 (11 November 1934): 4.

Dubrovskii, Aleksei. 'Atel'e i natura', *Sovetskii ekran* 27 (1926): 4–5.

Efremov, Mikhail. 'O prokatnoi deiatel'nosti Sovkino', *Sovetskoe kino* 4–5 (1925): 42–45.

Erofeev, Vladimir. 'Chemu uchit nas Germaniia', *Sovetskii ekran* 23 (1925): n.p.

_____ 'Iz dnevnika Pamirskoi ekspeditsii', *Kino* 1 (3 January 1928): 4.

_____ 'O Change', *Sovetskii ekran* 17 (1929): 4.

_____ 'O fil'makh "vtorogo sorta"', *Sovetskii ekran* 29 (1926): 4.

_____ 'Ob ekspeditsiiakh voobshche i v chastnosti', *Sovetskii ekran* 25 (1926): 8–9.

_____ 'Ot kustarshchiny k fabrike', *Kino i zhizn'* 20 (1930): 10.

_____ 'S kino-apparatom po Pamiru', *Kino* 28 (12 July 1927): 3.

_____ 'Tekhnicheskoe novatorstvo dokumental'noi fil'my', *Proletarskoe kino* 2–3 (1931): 4–13.

_____ 'U podnozh'ia Pamira', *Smena* 6 (1928): 12–14.

_____ *Kinoindustriia Germanii*. Moscow, 1926.

_____ *Po 'Kryshe mira' s kinoapparatom (Puteshestvie na Pamir)*. Moscow, 1929.

Fefer, Vladimir. 'Operator khroniki. Smelost'. Smert'', *Sovetskoe kino* 6–7 (1926): 14–15.

Fel'dman, Konstantin. 'Itogi goda Mezhrabpomfil'm', *Sovetskii ekran* 42 (1928): 6.

Gor'kii, Maksim. 'Literatura i kino', *Pravda* (14 April 1935): 2.

Gor'kii, Maksim, and Mikhail Kol'tsov (eds). *Den' Mira*. Moscow, 1937.

Grig, Nikolai. *Na Turksibe*. Leningrad, 1929.

Grits, Teodor (ed.), *Pereklichka narodov*. Moscow, 1931.

Il'f, Il'ia. *Zapiski provintsiala*. Moscow, 2015.

Katsigras, Alexander. 'Kul'turfil'ma', *Kino i kul'tura* 4 (1929): 10–23.

Khalatov, Art. *O Turkestano-sibirskoi (Semirechenskoi) zheleznoi doroge*. Leningrad, 1927.

Kh[ersonskii], Kh[risanf]. 'Eliso', *Sovetskii ekran* 41 (1928): 6–7.

_____ 'Poslednie sovetskie postanovki', *ARK* 9 (1925): 31.

_____ 'Put' na Vostok: "Velikii Perelet"', *ARK* 2 (1926): 22.

Kol'tsov, Mikhail. 'Den' Mira', *Pravda* (3 October 1935): 2.

Korobkov, N. 'Kinoatlas SSSR', *Sovetskoe kraevedenie* 2 (April 1933): 15–21.

Korolevich Vlad[imir]. 'Iomzia', *Sovetskoe kino* 37 (1927): 13.

_____ 'Smotrite v apparat!', *Sovetskii ekran* 42 (1927): 6.

_____ 'Strana Chuvashskaia', *Sovetskoe kino* 7 (1927): 20–22

Bibliography

Kotiev, Berd. 'Biurokratizm ili vreditel'stvo? (O prokate Turksiba)', *Kino* 4 (21 January 1930): 3.

_____ 'Kino sredi natsional'nostei', *Revoliutsiia i natsional'nosti* 5 (1931): 68–73.

Kristol', M. (ed.), *Nauchnoe kino*. Moscow, 1927.

Krylenko, Nikolai. *Po neissledovannomu Pamiru*. Moscow, 1929.

Krylenko, Nikolai and Dmitrii Shcherbakov. *5 let po Pamiru (itogi Pamirskih ekspeditsii 1928, 1929, 1931, 1932, 1933)*. Moscow–Leningrad, 1935.

Lebedev, Nikolai. 'Po tropam Kavkaza', *Sovetskii ekran* 52 (1928): 12.

_____ 'Tipy kul'turfil'ma', *Kino-Front* 1 (1927): 4 and *Kino-Front* 2 (1927): 5–7.

_____ 'Za proletarskuiu kinopublitsistiku', *Proletarskoe kino* 12 (1931): 20–29.

_____ 'Dva "dokumenta"', *Proletarskoe kino* 5 (1932): 24–29.

_____ *Po germanskoi kinematografii*. Moscow, 1924.

_____ *Ocherk istorii kino SSSR*. Vol. 1. Moscow, 1947.

Levin, D. and I. Maizel'. 'Kinokomitet pri Sovnarkome SSSR', *Kino i kul'tura* 4 (1929): 64–67.

Levkoev, Grigorii. 'Kino–ekspeditsiia na vostok. Zametki uchastnika', *ARK* 6–7 (1925): 28.

Levman, Boris. *Rabochii zritel' i kino: itogi pervoi rabochei kino-konferentsii*. Moscow, 1930.

Litvinov, Alexander. *Po sledam Arsen'eva: zapiski kinorezhissera*. Vladivostok, 1959.

_____ *Puteshestviia s kinokameroi*. Moscow, 1982.

_____ 'U lesnykh liudei', *Kino* 43 (23 October 1928): 3.

Mikharidze, Filipp. *Svanetia*. Tiflis, 1925.

Mosiagin, Petr. 'Za vidovuiu', *Sovetksii ekran* 50 (1926): 3.

Oganezov, Konstantin. 'Kino i etnografiia', *Sovetskii ekran* 19 (July 1925): n.p.

Ostrovskii, Zinovii. *Velikaia magistral'*. Moscow, 1930.

Polianovskii, Maks. 'Kraeved v kino. Pamiati Vladimira Klavdievicha Arsen'eva', *Kino i zhizn'* 26 (1930): 19.

_____ 'Protiv boga', *Sovetskii ekran* 40 (1928): 15.

_____ 'V Ussuriiskoi taige. Ekspeditsiia Sovkino', *Sovetskii ekran* 33 (1938): 6.

_____ *V strane Udekhe*. Moscow–Leningrad, 1929.

Prishvin, Mikhail. *Dnevniki 1930–31*. St. Petersburg, 2006.

_____ *Dnevniki 1932–35*. St. Petersburg, 2009.

Pudovkin, Vsevolod. 'K edinoi tseli', *20 let sovetskoi kinematografii*, Moscow, 1940.

Rikhter, Zinaida. *Kavkaz nashikh dnei 1923–24*. Moscow, 1924.

Ross, Colin. *Fahrten- und Abenteuerbuch*. Leipzig, 1925.

_____ *Der Weg nach Osten: Reise durch Russland, Ukraine, Transkaukasien, Persien, Buchara und Turkestan*. Leipzig, 1924.

Rossel's, Efim. *Banda bat'ki Gorbunova. Pervaia pamirskaia ekspeditsia 1928*. Moscow, 2013.

Ryskulov, Turar. *Turksib*. Moscow–Leningrad, 1930.

Shapovalenko, N. 'Ekonomicheskii analiz kino-seansa', *Sovetskoe kino* 2–3 (1925): 73–74.

Shklovskii, Viktor. 'Kolumbam – kartu i marshrut', *Sovetskii ekran* 15 (1926): 4.

_____ 'S tochki zreniia vetra', *Sovetskii ekran* 39 (1926): 6.

_____ *Abram Room: zhizn' i rabota*. Moscow, 1927.

_____ *Turksib*. Moscow–Leningrad, 1930.

Shneiderov, Vladimir. 'Panoramoi po Pamiru', *Kino* 44 (30 October 1928): 5.

_____ 'Uroki pamirskoi ekspeditsii', *Kino i kul'tura* 2 (1929): 51–54.

_____ *Pokhod 'Sibiriakova'*. Moscow, 1933.

_____ *Velikim Severnym*. Moscow, 1963.

_____ *Moi kinoputeshestviia*. Moscow, 1973.

Shub, Esfir', 'Neigrovaia fil'ma', *Kino i kul'tura* 5–6 (1929): 6–11.

Shumiatskii, Boris. *Kinematografia millionov*. Moscow, 1935.

Shutko, Kirill (ed.). *Kul'turfil'ma. Politiko-prosvetitel'naia fil'ma*. Leningrad, 1929.

_____ 'Kul'turnaia fil'ma k desiatiletiiu', *Sovetskii ekran* 45 (1927): 12–13.

Skachko, Anatolii. 'Organizatsiia vostochnogo kino', *Sovetskoe kino* 2–3 (1925): 16–18.

_____ 'Vostochnaia kino-fil'ma', *Sovetskoe kino* 6 (1925): 24–27.

_____ 'Vostochnoe kino', *Sovetskoe kino* 2–3 (1925): 85.

Sokolov, Ippolit. 'Fil'ma, poniatnaia millionam', *Kino* 41 (15 October 1929): 3.

_____ 'Put' Kul'turfil'my', *Kino i zhizn'* 21 (1931): 15–16.

_____ 'Zemlia zhazhdet', *Sovetskoe iskusstvo* (28 May 1931): 4.

_____ 'Turksib i ego avtor Turin', *Kino i zhizn'* 9 (1930): 7–8.

Solev, Vladimir. 'Govorit kinozritel'', *Sovetskii ekran* 21 (1929): 10–12.

Stepanov, Vladimir. 'Kul't-kino', *ARK* 1 (1925): 38–39.

Sukharebskii, Lazar'. *Nauchnoe kino*. Moscow, 1926.

Sytin, V., 'Kino-atlas', *Kino i kul'tura* 4 (1929): 71.

*Tainy natsional'noi politiki TsK RKP. Chetvertoe soveshchanie TsK RKP s otvetstven-
nymi rabotnikami natsional'nykh respublik i oblastei v g. Moskve 9–12 iiunia
1923 g.*, Moscow, 1992.

Terskoi, Anatolii. *Etnograficheskaia fil'ma*. Lenignrad–Moscow, 1930.

Trainin, Il'ia. 'Na puti k vozrozhdeniiu', *Sovetskoe kino* 1 (1925): 8–14.

_____ *Iskusstvo v kul'turnom pokhode na vostoke SSSR*. Moscow, 1930.

_____ 'Sovetskaia fil'ma i zritel'', *Sovetskoe kino* 6 (1925): 16–23.

Tret'iakov, Sergei. 'Chem zhivo kino', *Novyi LEF* 5 (1928): 28.

_____ 'Dorozhe – deshevle ili deshevle – dorozhe', *Sovetskii ekran* 39 (1926): 3.

_____ 'Otkuda i kuda (perspektivy futurizma)', *LEF* 1 (1923): 195.

_____ 'Zhivoi "zhivoi" chelovek. O knige Arsen'eva "V debriakh Ussuriiskogo
kraia"', *Novyi LEF* 7 (1928): 44–46.

_____ 'Grazhdane 1940 goda', *Sovetskoe kino* 6–7 (1926): 4–5.

_____ *Kinematograficheskoe nasledie: Stat'i, ocherki, stenogrammy vystuplenii, doklady, stsenarii*. St. Petersburg, 2010.

_____ *Strana–perekrestok: dokumental'naia proza*. Moscow, 1991.

_____ *Svanetiia*. Moscow, 1928.

Troianovskii, Mark. *S vekom naravne. Dnevniki. Pis'ma. Zapiski*. Moscow, 2004.

Vertov, Dziga. 'My. Variant manifesta', *Kino-Fot* 1 (1922): 11–12.

_____ 'Kinoki. Perevorot', *LEF* 3 (1923): 135–143.

_____ *Stat'i, dnevniki, zamysly*. Moscow, 1966.

_____ *Iz naslediia. Dramaturgicheskie opyty*, vol. 1. Moscow, 2004.

_____ *Iz naslediia. Stat'i i vystupleniia*, vol. 2. Moscow, 2008.

Za fil'my rekonstruktivnogo perioda. Moskovskaia Assotsiatsiia Rabotnikov Revoliutsionnoi Kinematografii. Moscow, 1931.

Zheliabuzhskii, Iurii. 'Serdtse Kavkaza – Svanetia', *Sovetskii ekran* 44 (1926): 6–7.

Select Secondary Sources

Abashin, Sergei, Dmitrii Arapov and Nailia Bekmakhanova (eds). *Tsentral'naia Aziia v sostave Rossiiskoi imperii*. Moscow, 2008.

Agde, Günther and Alexander Schwarz (eds). *Die rote Traumfabrik. Meschrabpom-Film und Prometheus 1921–1936*. Berlin, 2012.

Alphen, Ernst van. *Staging the Archive*. London, 2014.

Amad, Paula. *Counter-Archive: Film, the Everyday, and Albert Kahn's Archives de la Planète*. New York, 2010.

Anderson, Benedict. *Imagined Communities*. London, 2006.

Ballantyne, Tony, *Orientalism and Race: Aryanism in the British Empire*. Houndmills, 2007.

Bassin, Mark, and Catriona Kelly (eds). *Soviet and Post-Soviet Identities*. Cambridge, 2012.

Bassin, Mark. *Imperial Visions. Nationalist Imagination and Geographical Expansion in the Russian Far East, 1840–1865*. Cambridge, 1999.

Behdad, Ali and Luke Garrtlan (eds). *Photography's Orientalism: New Essays on Colonial Representation*. Los Angeles, 2013.

Ben-Ghiat, Ruth. *Italian Fascism's Empire Cinema*. Bloomington, 2015.

Bergne, Paul. *The Birth of Tajikistan: National Identity and the Origins of the Republic*. London, 2007.

Bernstein, Frances L. and Christopher Burton, Dan Healey (eds). *Soviet Medicine: Culture, Practice, and Science*. DeKalb, 2010.

Bertran, F. [Frédéric Bertrand]. 'Nauka bez ob''ekta? Sovetskaia etnografiia 1920–30kh godov i voprosy etnicheskoi kategorizatsii', *Zhurnal sotsiologii i sotsial'noi antropologii*, 6.3 (2003): 90–104.

Bobrovnikov, Vladimir. *Musul'mane severnogo Kavkaza: obychai, pravo, nasilie.* Moscow, 2002.

Bobrovnikov, Vladimir and Irina Babich (eds). *Severnyi Kavkaz v sostave Rossiiskoi imperii.* Moscow, 2007.

Boer, Inge. *Uncertain Territories: Boundaries in Cultural Analysis.* Amsterdam, 2006.

Bogdanov, Konstantin. *Vox Populi: Fol'klornye zhanry sovetskoi kul'tury.* Moscow, 2009.

Bogdanov, Konstantin and Rikkardo Nikolozi, Iurii Murashov (eds), *Dzhambul Dzhabaev: Prikliucheniia kazakhskogo akyna v sovetskoi strane.* Moscow, 2013.

Bonnell, Victoria. *Iconography of Power: Soviet Political Posters under Lenin and Stalin.* Berkeley, 1997.

Boon, Timothy. *Films of Fact: A History of Science in Documentary Films and Television.* London, 2008.

Brandenberger, David. *National Bolshevism: Stalinist Mass Culture and the Formation of Modern Russian National Identity.* Cambridge, 2002.

Brooks, Jeffrey. *Thank You, Comrade Stalin! Soviet Public Culture from Revolution to Cold War.* Princeton, 1999.

Brower, Daniel, and Edward J Lazzerini (eds). *Russia's Orient: Imperial Borderlands and Peoples, 1700–1917.* Bloomington, 1997.

Buchloh, Benjamin. 'From Faktura to Factography', *October* 30 (1984): 82–119.

Bulgakova, Oksana. *Sovetskii slukhoglaz: kino i ego organy chuvstv.* Moscow, 2010.

_____. 'Der Fall Meshrabpom', in Bulgakowa (ed.), *Die ungewöhnlichen Abenteuer des Dr. Mabuse im Lande der Bolschewiki,* Berlin, 1995, pp. 185–193.

_____ (ed.). *Resonanz-Räume: Die Stimme und die Medien.* Berlin, 2012.

Burbank, Jane, Mark von Hagen and Anatolyi Remnev (eds). *Russian Empire: Space, People, Power, 1700–1930.* Bloomington, 2007.

Cadiot, Juliette. 'Searching for Nationality: Statistics and National Categories at the End of the Russian Empire (1897–1917)', *The Russian Review* 64.3 (2005): 440–55.

_____ *Le laboratoire Impérial: Russie–URSS 1860–1940.* Paris, 2007.

Carrère d'Encausse, Hélène. *The Great Challenge: Nationalities and the Bolshevik State 1917–1930.* New York, 1992.

Cavendish, Philip. *The Men with the Movie Camera: The Poetics of Visual Style in Soviet Avant-Garde Cinema of the 1920s.* New York, 2013.

Chafer Tony and Amanda Sackur (eds). *Promoting the Colonial Idea. Propaganda and Visions of Empire in France.* London, 2002.

Chernenko, Miron. *Krasnaia zvezda, zheltaia zvezda. Kinematograficheskaia istoriia evreistva v Rossii, 1919–1999.* Moscow, 2006.

Clark, Katerina. *Petersburg: Crucible of Cultural Revolution.* Cambridge, 1995.

Clifford, James. *The Predicament of Culture: Twentieth-Century Ethnography, Literature, and Art.* Cambridge, 1988.

279

Condee, Nancy. *The Imperial Trace: Recent Russian Cinema*. Oxford, 2009.

Conley, Tom. *Cartographic Cinema*. Minneapolis, 2007.

Cosgrove, Denis. *Geography and Vision: Seeing, Imagining and Representing the World*. London, 2008.

Crary, Jonathan. *Techniques of the Observer: On Vision and Modernity in the Nineteenth Century*. Cambridge, 1992.

Creed, Barbara, and Jeanette Hoorn. 'Memory and History: Early Film, Colonialism and the French Civilising Mission in Indochina', *French History and Civilization* 4 (2011): 223–236.

Cvetkovski, Roland and Alexis Hofmeister (eds). *Empire of Others: Creating Ethnographic Knowledge in Imperial Russia and the USSR*. Budapest, 2014.

David-Fox, Michael, and Peter Holquist, Alexander Martin (eds). *Orientalism and Empire in Russia*. Bloomington, 2006.

Davidson, Peter. *The Idea of North*. London, 2005.

Deeken, Annette. *Reisefilme: Aesthetic und Geschichte*. Remscheid, 2004.

Deriabin, Alexander. 'Alexandr Litvinov und der sowjetische Expeditionsfilm', in Hans-Joachim Schlegel (ed.), *Die überrumpelte Wirklichkeit: Texte zum sowjetischen Dokumentarfilm der 20er und frühen 30er Jahre*, Leipzig, 2003, pp. 59–62.

_____ 'Iz istorii rozhdeniia cheloveka s kinoapparatom. Novye dokumenty', *Kinovedcheskie zapiski* 49 (2000): 199–205.

_____ (ed.), *Letopis' rossiiskogo kino 1863–1929*. Moscow, 2004.

_____ (ed.), *Letopis' rossiiskogo kino, 1930–1945*. Moscow, 2007.

_____ 'O fil'makh-puteshestviiakh i Aleksandre Litvinove', *Zelenoe spasenie* 11 (1999), available at http://www.greensalvation.org/old/Russian/Publish/11_rus/11_02.htm (last accessed 25 March 2015).

_____ 'Piat' let i tri goda. Predystoriia i istoriia Kalatozovskogo "Shamilia"', *Kinovedcheskie zapiski* 67 (2004): 114–126.

_____ ' "Tam ia uvidel neobychainye veshchi." Sovetskie kinomatografisty o svoikh poezdkakh v Germaniiu', *Kinovedcheskie zapiski*, 58 (2002): 239–285.

_____ (ed.). *Vladimir Alekseevich Erofeev (1898–1940). Materialy k 100–letiiu so dnia rozhdeniia*. Moscow, 1998.

Diment, Galya, and Yuri Slezkine (eds). *Between Heaven and Hell: The Myth of Siberia in Russian Culture*. New York, 1993.

Dobie, Madeleine. *Foreign Bodies: Gender, Language, and Culture in French Orientalism*. Stanford, 2001.

Dobrenko, Evgenii and Khans Giunter [Hans Günther] (eds). *Sotsrealisticheskii kanon*. St. Petersburg, 2000.

Dobrenko, Evgeny and Eric Naiman (eds). *The Landscape of Stalinism: The Art and Ideology of Soviet Space*. Seattle, 2003.

Dorson, Richard. *Folklore and Fakelore: Essays Toward a Discipline of Folk Studies*. Cambridge, 1976.

Douglas, Mary. *Purity and Danger: An Analysis of the Concepts of Pollution and Taboo*. London, 1996.

Drieu, Cloé. *Fictions nationales: Cinéma, empire et nation en Ouzbékistan (1919-1937)*. Paris, 2013.

Edgar, Adrienne Lynn. *Tribal Nation: The Making of Soviet Turkmenistan*. Princeton, 2004.

Edney, Matthew. 'The Irony of Imperial Mapping' in James R. Akerman (ed.), *The Imperial Map: Cartography and the Mastery of Empire*, Chicago, 2009, pp. 11-45.

Edwards, Elizabeth (ed.). *Anthropology and Photography, 1860-1920*. New Haven, 1992.

Ely, Christopher. *This Meager Nature: Landscape and National Identity in Imperial Russia*. DeKalb, 2002.

Engelstein, Laura. *Keys to Happiness: Sex and the Search for Modernity in Fin-de-Siècle Russia*. Ithaca, 1992.

Etkind, Alexander. *Internal Colonization: Russia's Imperial Experience*. Cambridge, 2011.

Filatova, Irina. 'Interpretations of the Dogma: Soviet Concepts of Nation and Ethnicity', *Theoria: A Journal of Social and Political Theory* 90 (1997): 93-120.

Fitzpatrick, Sheila. *The Commissariat of Enlightenment: Soviet Organization of Education and the Arts Under Lunacharsky, October 1917-1921*. Cambridge, 1970.

Fore, Devin. 'The Operative Word in Soviet Factography', *October* 118 (2006): 95-131.

Forsyth, James. *History of the Peoples of Siberia: Russia's North Asian Colony, 1581-1990*. Cambridge, 1992.

Foucault, Michel. *Archaeology of Knowledge and Discourse on Language*. New York, 1972.

Frank, Susanne. 'Teplaia Arktika: k istorii odnogo starogo literaturnogo motiva', *Novoe literaturnoe obozrenie* 108 (2011): 82-97.

Fulks, Barry Alan. *Film Culture and Kulturfilm: Walter Ruttmann, the Avant-garde Film, and the Kulturfilm in Weimar Germany and the Third Reich*, PhD Dissertation, University, of Wisconsin-Madison, 1982.

Fullerton, John and Jan Olsson (eds). *Nordic Explorations: Film before 1930*. London, 1999.

Gammer, Moshe. *Muslim Resistance to the Tsar: Shamil and the Conquest of Chechnia and Dagestan*. London, 1994.

Geldern, James von. *Bolshevik Festivals, 1917-1920*. Berkeley, 1993.

Geldern, James von and Richard Stites (eds). *Mass Culture in Soviet Russia: Tales, Poems, Songs, Movies, Plays, and Folklore, 1917-1953*. Bloomington, 1995.

Bibliography

Gerasimov, Ilya, Jan Kusber and Alexander Semyonov (eds). *Empire Speaks Out: Languages of Rationalization and Self-Description in the Russian Empire.* Leiden, 2009.

Gellner, Ernest. *Nations and Nationalism.* Oxford, 1983.

Getty, John Arch and Oleg Naumov. *The Road to Terror: Stalin and the Self-Destruction of the Bolsheviks, 1932-1939.* New Haven, 1999.

Gilman, Sander. *Picturing Health and Illness: Images of Identity and Difference.* Baltimore, 1995.

Giunter, Khans [Günther, Hans] and Sabina Khensgen [Sabine Hänsgen] (eds). *Sovetskaia vlast' i media.* St. Petersburg, 2006.

Golovnev, Ivan. 'Chukotskaia ekspeditsiia Litvinova. Final sovetskogo etnokino', *Ural'skii istoricheskii vestnik* 3 (2014): 118-127.

_____ 'Pervoe etnokino. Aleksandr Litvinov', *Vestnik Ural'skogo otdeleniia RAN* 1 (2012): 156-167.

_____ 'Velikaia Kamchatskaia kinoekspeditsiia', *Vestnik VGIKa* 15 (2013): 18-28.

Gorsuch, Anne and Diane Koenker (eds). *Turizm: The Russian and East European Tourist under Capitalism and Socialism.* Ithaca, 2006.

Gradskova, Yulia. 'Speaking for Those "Backward": Gender and Ethnic Minorities in Soviet Silent Films', *Region: Regional Studies of Russia, Eastern Europe, and Central Asia* 2.2 (2013): 201-220.

Grant, Bruce. 'Nivkhi, Russians and Others: The Politics of Indigenism in Sakhalin Island' in Stephen Kotkin and David Wolff (eds), *Rediscovering Russia in Asia: Siberia and the Russian Far East*, Armonk, 1995, pp. 160-171.

_____ 'The Good Russian Prisoner: Naturalizing Violence in the Caucasus Mountains', *Cultural Anthropology* 20.1 (2005): 39-67.

Grant, Robert. *Representations of British Emigration, Colonisation and Settlement: Imagining Empire, 1800-1860.* London, 2005.

Grieveson, Lee and Colin MacCabe (eds). *Empire and Film.* London, 2011.

_____ *Film and the End of Empire.* London, 2011.

Griffiths, Alison. *Wondrous Difference: Cinema, Anthropology, and Turn-of-the-Century Visual Culture.* New York, 2002.

Gross Solomon, Susan. 'The Soviet-German Syphilis Expedition to Buriat-Mongolia, 1928: Scientific Research on National Minorities', *Slavic Review* 52.2 (1993): 204-32.

Gross Solomon, Susan and John F. Hutchinson (eds). *Health and Society in Revolutionary Russia.* Bloomington, 1990.

Gunning, Tom. 'Before Documentary: Early Nonfiction Films and the "View" Aesthetic', in Daan Hertogs and Nico de Klerk (eds). *Uncharted Territory: Essays on Early Nonfiction Film*, Amsterdam, 1997, pp. 9-24.

Harper, Graeme and Jonathan Rayner (eds). *Cinema and Landscape.* Bristol, 2010.

Harvey, Brian. 'Maps, Knowledge, and Power', in Denis Cosgrove and Stephen Daniels (eds), *The Iconography of Landscape: Essays on the Symbolic Representation, Design, and Use of Past Environments*, Cambridge, 1988, pp. 277–312.

Hau, Michael. *The Cult of Health and Beauty in Germany: a Social History, 1890–1930*. Chicago, 2003.

Heftberger, Adelheid. ' "The Same Thing from Different Angles": On the Mutliple Versions of Dziga Vertov's *Tri pesni o Lenine* (*Three Songs about Lenin*)', brochure of the DVD Edition Filmmuseum 86, 2015, unpaginated.

Hicks, Jeremy. *Dziga Vertov. Defining Documentary Film*. London, 2007.

Hight, Eleanor and Gary D. Sampson (eds). *Colonialist Photography: Imag(in)ing Race and Place*. London, 2002.

Hirsch, Francine. *Empire of Nations: Ethnographic Knowledge and the Making of the Soviet Union*. Ithaca, 2005.

Hobsbawm, Eric and Terence Ranger (eds). *The Invention of Tradition*. Cambridge, 1983.

Hogle, Linda. *Recovering the Nation's Body: Cultural Memory, Medicine, and the Politics of Redemption*. New Brunswick, 1999.

Huhndorf, Shari M. 'Nanook and His Contemporaries: Imagining Eskimos in American Culture, 1897–1922', *Critical Inquiry* 27.1 (2000): 122–148.

Jaikumar, Priya. *Cinema at the End of Empire: A Politics of Transition in Britain and India*. Durham, 2006.

Jay, Martin. 'Scopic regimes of modernity' in Hal Foster (ed.), *Vision and Visuality*, Seattle, 1988, pp. 3–23.

Jay, Martin and Sumathi Ramaswamy (eds). *Empires of Vision*. Durham, 2014.

Josephson, Paul. 'Technology and the Conquest of the Soviet Arctic', *The Russian Review* 70 (2011): 419–439.

Kachura, A. 'Viktor Turin', in Galina Prozhiko, D. Firsova (eds), *Letopistsy nashego vremeni*, Moscow, 1987, pp. 82–99.

Kamp, Marianne. 'Pilgrimage and Performance: Uzbek Women and the Imagining of Uzbekistan in the 1920s', *International Journal of Middle East Studies* 34 (2002): 263–278.

‗‗‗‗‗‗ *The New Woman in Uzbekistan: Islam, Modernity, and Unveiling under Communism*. Seattle, 2006.

Kapchinskii, Oleg. 'Podsudimyi Khanzhonkov', *Rodina* 9 (2008): 13–15.

Kappeler, Andreas. *The Russian Empire: A Multiethnic History*. Harlow, 2001.

Kelly, Catriona and Vadim Volkov. 'Directed Desires: *Kul'turnost'* and Consumption', in Catriona Kelly and David Shepherd (eds), *Constructing Russian Culture in the Age of Revolution: 1881–1940*, New York, 1998, pp. 291–313.

Kenez, Peter. *Cinema and Soviet Society, 1917–1953*. New York, 1992.

Kepley, Vance Jr. 'Federal cinema: the Soviet Film Industry, 1924–32', *Film History* 8 (1996): 344–356.

Bibliography

_____ 'Soviet Cinema and State Control: Lenin's Nationalization Degree Reconsidered', *Journal of Film and Video* 42.2 (1990): 3–14.

Khalid, Adeeb. 'Between Empire and Revolution: New Work on Soviet Central Asia', *Kritika* 7.4 (2006): 865–884.

_____ 'Russian History and the Debate over Orientalism', *Kritika* 1.4 (2000): 691–699.

_____ *The Politics of Muslim Cultural Reform: Jadidism in Central Asia*. Berkeley, 1999.

Khisamutdinov, Amir. *Vladimir Klavdievich Arsen'ev, 1872–1930*. Moscow, 2005.

Kisriev, Enver. 'Republic of Dagestan: Nation–Building inside Russia's Womb' in Pål Kolstø and Helge Blakkisrud (eds), *Nation-Building and Common Values in Russia*, Lanham, 2004, pp. 123–157.

Kissel', Vol'fgang Stefan [Kissel, Wolfgang Stephan] and Galina Time (eds). *Beglye vzgliady. Novoe prochtenie russkikh travelogov pervoi treti XX veka*. Moscow, 2000.

Kivelson, Valerie. *Cartographies of Tsardom: The Land and its Meanings in Seventeenth-Century Russia*. Ithaca, 2006.

Kivelson, Valerie and Joan Neuberger (eds). *Picturing Russia: Explorations in Visual Culture*. New Haven, 2008.

Koenker, Diane. *Club Red: Vacation Travel and the Soviet Dream*. Ithaca, 2013.

Kolchinskii, Eduard (ed.). *Sovetsko-germanskie nauchnye sviazi vremeni Veimarskoi respubliki*. St. Petersburg, 2001.

Kunichika, Michael. 'The Ecstasy of Breadth: The Odic and Whitmanesque in Vertov's "One Sixth of the World"', *Studies in Russian and Soviet Cinema* 6.1 (2012): 53–74.

Kuper, Adam. *The Invention of Primitive Society: Transformation of an Illusion*. London, 1988.

Lahusen, Thomas and Evgeny Dobrenko (eds). *Socialist Realism without Shores*. Durham NC, 1997.

Lajoux, Jean-Dominique. 'Rhythmic Montage in the Films of Dziga Vertov: A Poetic Use of the Language of Cinema', *Pacific Coast Philology* 13 (1978): 44–50.

Lawton, Anna. *The Red Screen: Politics, Society, Art in Soviet Cinema*. London, 1992.

Layton, Susan. 'The Creation of an Imaginative Caucasian Geography,' *Slavic Review* 45.3 (1986): 470–485.

Levin, Nora. *The Jews in the Soviet Union: Paradox of Survival*, Vol. 1. New York, 1988.

Levin, Zeev. 'The *Khujum* Campaign in Uzbekistan and the Bukharan Jewish Women', in Christa Hämmerle, Nikola Langreiter, Margareth Lanzinger, and Edith Saurer (eds), *Gender Politics in Central Asia. Historical Perspectives and Current Living Conditions of Women*, Cologne, 2008, pp. 95–111.

Lewis, Reina. *Gendering Orientalism: Race, Femininity and Representation*. London, 1996.

Bibliography

Listov, Viktor. *Rossiia, Revoliutsiia, Kinematograf.* Moscow, 1995.

Liulevicius, Vejas Gabriel. *The German Myth of the East: 1800 to the Present.* Oxford, 2009.

Loizos, Peter. 'First exits from observational realism: narrative experiments in recent ethnographic films', in Marcus Banks and Howard Morphy (eds), *Rethinking Visual Anthropology*, New Haven, 1999, pp. 81–104.

Loring, Benjamin. '"Colonizers with Party Cards" Soviet Internal Colonialism in Central Asia, 1917–39', *Kritika* 15.1 (2014): 77–102.

McCannon, John. 'Positive Heroes at the Pole: Celebrity Status, Socialist-Realist Ideals and the Soviet Myth of the Arctic, 1932–39', *The Russian Review* 56.3 (1997): 346–365.

_____ *Red Arctic: Polar Exploration and the Myth of the North in the Soviet Union, 1932–1939.* Oxford, 1998.

MacDougall, David. *The Corporeal Image: Film, Ethnography, and the Senses.* Princeton, 2006.

MacKay, John. 'Allegory and Accommodation: Vertov's *Three Songs of Lenin* (1934) as a Stalinist Film', *Film History* 18.4 (2006): 376–391.

_____ 'Disorganized Noise: *Enthusiasm* and the Ear of the Collective', *KinoKultura* 7 (2005), available at http://www.kinokultura.com/articles/jan05–mackay.html (accessed 20 March 2015).

_____ 'Film Energy: Process and Metanarrative in Dziga Vertov's *The Eleventh Year*', *October* 121 (2007): 41–78.

MacKenzie, Scott, and Anna Westerståhl Stenport (eds). *Films on Ice: Cinemas of the Arctic.* Edinburgh, 2015.

Malitsky, Joshua. *Post-Revolution Non-Fiction Film: Building the Soviet and Cuban Nations.* Bloomington, 2013.

Margolit, Evgenii. 'Fenomen agitpropfil'ma i prikhod zvuka v sovetskoe kino', *Kinovedcheskie zapiski* 84 (2007): 255–266.

Marshall, Alex. *The Caucasus under Soviet Rule.* London, 2010.

Martin, Terry. *The Affirmative Action Empire: Nations and Nationalism in the Soviet Union, 1923–1939.* Ithaca, 2001.

Massell, Gregory. *The Surrogate Proletariat: Moslem Women and Revolutionary Strategies in Soviet Central Asia, 1919–1929.* Princeton, 1974.

Michaels, Paula. *Curative Powers: Medicine and Empire in Stalin's Central Asia.* Pittsburgh, 2003.

Michelson, Annette (ed.). *Kino-Eye: The Writings of Dziga Vertov.* Berkeley, 1984.

Mikhailov, Vladimir. 'Stalinskaia model' upravleniia kinematografom', in Lidiia Mamatova (ed.), *Kino: Politika i liudi*, Moscow, 1995, pp. 9–25.

Miller, Frank J. *Folklore for Stalin: Russian Folklore and Pseudofolklore of the Stalin Era.* Armonk, 1990.

Mitchell, W. J. T. (ed.). *Landscape and Power.* Chicago, 2002.

Bibliography

_____ 'Showing Seeing: A Critique of Visual Culture', in Michael Ann Holly and Keith Moxey (eds), *Art History, Aesthetics, Visual Studies*, London and New Haven, 2002, pp. 231–250.

Murashov, Iurii. 'Slepye geroi – slepye zriteli: o statuse zreniia i slova v sovetskom kino', in Marina Balina, Evgenii Dobrenko, Iurii Murashov (eds), *Sovetskoe bogatstvo: stat'i o kul'ture, literature i kino*, St. Petersburg, 2002, pp. 412–426.

Myers, Holly. 'Il'f and Petrov's *Zolotoi telenok*: Russian at the Periphery, Asian at the Core', *Studies in Slavic Cultures* 9 (2010): 43–65.

Nechaeva, Margarita. *Vladimir Shneiderov*. Moscow, 1964.

Nichols, Bill. 'Documentary Film and the Modernist Avant-Garde', *Critical Inquiry* 27.4 (2001): 580–610.

_____ *Introduction to Documentary*. Bloomington, 2001.

Northrop, Douglas. *Veiled Empire: Gender and Power in Stalinist Central Asia*. Ithaca, 2004.

Nunan, Timothy. 'Soviet Nationalities Policy, *USSR in Construction* and Soviet Documentary Photography in Comparative Context, 1931–37', *Ab Imperio* 2 (2010): 47–92.

O'Brien, Charles. 'The "Cinéma Colonial" of the 1930s France: Film Narration as Social Practice', in Matthew Bernstein and Gaylyn Studlar (eds), *Visions of the East: Orientalism in Film*, New Brunswick, 1997, pp. 207–23.

Oksiloff, Assenka. *Picturing the Primitive: Visual Culture, Ethnography, and Early German Cinema*. London, 2001.

Orlova, Galina. 'Organizm pod nadzorom: Telo v sovetskom diskurse o sotsial'noi gigiene (1920-e gody)', *Teoriia mody* 3 (2007): 251–270.

Osborne, Peter D. *Travelling Light: Photography, Travel, and Visual Culture*. Manchester, 2000.

Palmer, Scott. *Dictatorship of the Air: Aviation Culture and the Fate of Modern Russia*. Cambridge, 2006.

Papazian, Elizabeth. *Manufacturing Truth: the Documentary Moment in Early Soviet Culture*. DeKalb, 2009.

Payne, Matthew. 'Victor Turin's *Turksib* (1929) and Soviet Orientalism', *Historical Journal of Film, Radio, and Television* 21.1 (2001): 37–62.

_____ *Stalin's Railroad: Turksib and the Building of Socialism*. Pittsburgh, 2001.

Petric, Vlada. 'Dziga Vertov as Theorist', *Cinema Journal* 18.1 (1978): 22–44.

Polian, Pavel. *Ne po svoei vole...: Istoriia i geografiia prinuditel'nykh migratsii v SSSR*. Moscow, 2001.

Pratt, Mary Louise. *Imperial Eyes: Travel Writing and Transculturation*. London, 1992.

Prunes, Mariano. 'Dziga Vertov's *Three Songs about Lenin* (1934): A Visual Tour through the History of the Soviet Avant-Garde in the Interwar Years', *Criticism* 45.2 (2003): 251–78.

Razumnyi, Alexander. *U istokov*. Moscow, 1975.

Renov, Michael. *The Subject of Documentary*. Minneapolis, 2004.

Riabchikova, Natal'ia. '"Glaz kino sledoval glazu letchika". *Velikii perelet* Vladimira Shneiderova i Georgiia Bliuma', *Kinovedcheskie zapiski* 98 (2011): 257–290.

_____ '"Proletkino": ot "Goskino" do "Sovkino"', *Kinovedcheskie zapiski* 94 (2010): 90–108.

Roberts, Graham. *Forward, Soviet! History and Non-Fiction Film in the USSR*. London, 1999.

Robin, Régine. *Socialist Realism: an Impossible Aesthetic*. Stanford, 1992.

Rojek, Chris and John Urry. *Touring Cultures: Transformations of Travel and Theory*. London, 1997.

Rony, Fatimah Tobing. *The Third Eye: Race, Cinema, and Ethnographic Spectacle*. Durham NC, 1996.

Rouland, Michael, Gulnara Abikeyeva and Birgit Beumers (eds). *Cinema in Central Asia: Rewriting Cultural Histories*. London, 2013.

Ruder, Cynthia. 'Boris Lapin: Unlikely Modernist', *Russian Literature* 34.2 (1993): 207–218.

_____ *Making History for Stalin: The Story of the Belomor Canal*. Gainesville, 1998.

Ruoff, Jeffrey (ed.). *Virtual Voyages: Cinema and Travel*. Durham NC, 2006.

Sandomirskaia, Irina. 'One Sixth of the World: Avant-garde Film, the Revolution of Vision, and the Colonization of the USSR Periphery during the 1920s', in Kerstin Olofsson (ed.), *From Orientalism to Postcoloniality*, Huddinge, 2008, pp. 8–31.

_____ *Kniga o rodine: opyt analiza diskursivnykh praktik*. Vienna, 2001.

_____ 'Novaia zhizn' na marshe. Stalinskii turizm kak "praktika puti"', *Obshchestvennye nauki i sovremennost'* 4 (1996): 163–172.

Sandomirskaia, Irina and Elena Kolikova (eds). 'Eurasia as a Filmic Assemblage', *Studies in Russian and Soviet Cinema* 4.3 (2010): 321–344.

Sarkisova, Oksana. 'Grenzprojektionen: Bilder von Grenzgebieten im sowjetischen Film', in Karl Kaser, Dagmar Gramshammer-Hohl and Robert Pichler (eds), *Die Wieser Enzyklopädie des europäischen Ostens*, Vol. 11, Klagenfurt, 2003, pp. 439–467.

_____ 'Across One Sixth of the World: Dziga Vertov, Travel Cinema, and Soviet Patriotism', *October* 121 (2007): 19–40.

_____ 'Folk Songs in Soviet Orchestration: Vostokfil'm's *Song of Happiness* and the forging of the New Soviet Musician', *Studies in Russian and Soviet Cinema* 4.3 (2010): 261–281.

_____ 'Taming the Frontier: Aleksandr Litvinov's Expedition Films and Representations of Indigenous Minorities in the Far East', *Studies in Russian and Soviet Cinema* 9.1 (2015): 2–23.

Schenk, Frithjof Benjamin. 'Travel, Railroads, and Identity Formation in the Russian Empire', in Eric Weitz and Omer Bartov (eds), *Shatterzone of Empires*.

Bibliography

Coexistence and Violence in the German, Habsburg, Russian, and Ottoman Borderlands, Bloomington, 2013, pp. 136–151.

Schimmelpenninck van der Oye, David. *Russian Orientalism: Asia in the Russian Mind from Peter the Great to the Emigration*. New Haven, 2010.

Schlegel, Hans-Joachim. 'Nemetskie impul'sy dlia sovetskikh kul'turfil'mov 1920kh godov', *Kinovedcheskie zapiski* 58 (2002): 368–379.

Semenov, Igor. 'Statistical Surveys of the Kanin Peninsula and the Samoed Question' in David Anderson (ed.), *The 1926/27 Soviet Polar Census Expeditions*, New York, 2011, pp. 133–154.

Shcherbenok, Andrei. '"Vzgliani na Lenina i pechal' tvoia razoidetsia, kak voda": estetika travmy u Dzigi Vertova', in Sergei Ushakin [Oushakine] and Elena Trubina (eds), *Travma: Punkty*, Moscow, 2009, pp. 704–722.

Shulman, Elena. *Stalinism on the Frontier of Empire: Women and State Formation in the Soviet Far East*. Cambridge, 2008.

Slavin, Davide Henry. *Colonial Cinema and Imperial France, 1919–1930: White Blind Spots, Male Fantasies, Settler Myths*. Baltimore, 2001.

Slezkin, Iurii. 'Sovetskaia etnografiia v nokdaune, 1928–38', *Etnograficheskoe oboz-renie* 2 (1993): 113–125.

Slezkine, Yuri. 'The USSR as a Communal Apartment, or How a Socialist State Promoted Ethnic Particularism', *Slavic Review* 53.2 (1994): 414–452.

_____ *Arctic Mirrors: Russia and the Small Peoples of the North*. Ithaca, 1994.

Smith, Jeremy (ed.). *Beyond the Limits: The Concept of Space in Russian History and Culture*. Helsinki, 1999.

_____ *Red Nations: The Nationalities Experience in and after the USSR*. Cambridge, 2013.

Smith, Michael. 'Cinema for the "Soviet East": National Fact and Revolutionary Fiction in Early Azerbaijani Film', *Slavic Review* 56.4 (1997): 645–678.

Spieker, Sven. *The Big Archive: Art from Bureaucracy*. Cambridge, 2008.

Spurr, David. *The Rhetoric of Empire: Colonial Discourse in Journalism, Travel Writing, and Imperial Administration*. Durham, 1993.

Starks, Tricia. *The Body Soviet: Propaganda, Hygiene, and the Revolutionary State*. Madison, 2008.

Stockdale, Melissa. 'What is a Fatherland? Changing Notions of Duty, Rights, and Belonging in Russia', in Mark Bassin, Christopher Ely, and Melissa Stockdale (eds), *Space, Place, and Power in Modern Russia*, DeKalb, 2010, pp. 23–48.

Stollery, Martin. *Alternative Empires: European Modernist Cinemas and Cultures of Imperialism*. Exeter, 2000.

Suny, Ronald Grigor. *The Revenge of the Past: Nationalism, Revolution, and the Collapse of the Soviet Union*. Stanford, 1993.

Suny, Ronald Grigor and Terry Martin (eds). *A State of Nations: Empire and Nation-making in the Age of Lenin and Stalin*. New York, 2002.

Bibliography

Svilova-Vertova, Elizaveta and V. Furtichev. *Tri pesni o Lenine*. Moscow, 1972.

Taylor, Richard. 'Agitation, Propaganda and the Cinema: The Search for New Solutions, 1917–1921', in Nils Åke Nillsson (ed.), *Art, Society, Revolution: Russian, 1917–1921*, Stockholm, 1979, pp. 237–263.

—————— *Politics of the Soviet Cinema, 1917–1929*. Cambridge, 1979.

Taylor, Richard and Ian Christie (eds). *Inside the Film Factory: New Approaches to Russian and Soviet Cinema*. London, 1991.

Tolz, Vera. 'Imperial Scholars and Minority Nationalisms in Late Imperial and Early Soviet Russia', *Kritika* 10.2 (2009): 261–290.

—————— *'Russia's Own Orient'. The Politics of Identity and Oriental Studies in the Late Imperial and Early Soviet Periods*. Oxford, 2011.

Torma, Franziska. 'Auf dem Dach der Welt. Die Mittelasien-Expeditionen des Ehepaars Rickmers (1890–1928),' *Alpenvereinsjahrbuch*, Innsbruck, 2010, pp. 204–211.

—————— *Turkestan-Expeditionen. Zur Kulturgeschichte deutscher Forschungsreisen nach Mittelasien (1890–1930)*. Bielefeld, 2011.

Traub, Valerie. 'Mapping the Global Body,' in Peter Erickson and Clark Hulse (eds), *Early Modern Visual Culture: Representation, Race, and Empire in Renaissance England*, Philadelphia, 2000, pp. 44–97.

Tsivian, Yuri (ed.). *Lines of Resistance: Dziga Vertov and the Twenties*. Pordenone, 2004.

Uricchio, William. 'The Kulturfilm: A Brief History of an Early Discursive Practice', in Paolo Chechi Usai and Lorenzo Codelli (eds), *Before Caligari: German Cinema, 1895–1920*, Pordenone, 1990, pp. 356–378.

Urry, John. *The Tourist Gaze: Leisure and Travel in Contemporary Societies*. London, 1990.

Varisco, Daniel Martin. *Rereading Orientalism: Said and the Unsaid*. Seattle and London, 2007.

Vatulescu, Cristina. *Police Aesthetics: Literature, Film, and the Secret Police in Soviet Times*. Stanford, 2010.

Virilio, Paul. *War and Cinema: The Logistics of Perception*. London, 1989.

Vishlenkova, Elena. *Vizual'noe narodovedenie imperii, ili "uvidet' russkogo dano ne kazhdomy"*. Moscow, 2011.

Vishnevskii, Veniamin. *Dokumental'nye fil'my dorevoliutsionnoi Rossii, 1907–1916*. Moscow, 1996.

Vishnevskii, Veniamin and Pavel Fionov. *Sovetskoe kino v datakh i faktakh 1917–1969*. Moscow, 1974.

Weinberg, Robert. *Stalin's Forgotten Zion: Birobidzhan and the Making of a Soviet Jewish Homeland*. Berkeley, 1998.

Weinberger, Eliot. 'The Camera People', in Lucien Taylor (ed.), *Visualizing Theory. Selected Essays from V.A.R. 1990–1994*, New York, 1994, pp. 3–26.

Weindling, Paul. *Health, Race, and German Politics between National Unification and Nazism, 1870–1945*. Cambridge, 1989.

Werrett, Simon. 'Technology on Display: Instruments and Identities on Russian Voyages of Exploration', *The Russian Review* 70 (2011): 380–396.

Werth, Paul W. 'From Resistance to Subversion: Imperial Power, Indigenous Opposition, and Their Entanglement', *Kritika* 1.1 (2000): 21–43.

Widdis, Emma. *Visions of a New Land: Soviet Film from the Revolution to the Second World War*. New Haven, 2003.

Winston, Brian. *Claiming the Real: The Griersonian Documentary and Its Legitimations*. London, 1995.

Wood, Alan. *Russia's Frozen Frontier: A History of Siberia and the Russian Far East 1581–1991*. London, 2011

Yampolsky, Mikhail. 'Reality at Second Hand', *Historical Journal of Film, Radio, and Television* 11.2 (1991): 161–171.

Youngblood, Denise J. *Russian War Films: On the Cinema Front, 1914–2005*. Lawrence, 2006.

_____ *Movies for the Masses, Popular cinema and Soviet society in the 1920s*. Cambridge, 1992.

_____ *Soviet Cinema in the Silent Era, 1918–1935*. Austin, 1991.

Yurchak, Alexei. 'Bodies of Lenin: The Hidden Science of Communist Sovereignty', *Representations* 129 (2015): 116–57.

Zalesskii, Konstantin. *Imperiia Stalina. Biograficheskii entsiklopedicheskii slovar'*. Moscow, 2000.

Zorkaia, Neia. *Fol'klor, lubok, ekran*. Moscow, 1994.

Index

Index

Index

www.ingramcontent.com/pod-product-compliance
Lightning Source LLC
Chambersburg PA
CBHW060146280326
41932CB00012B/1660